Strategic Giving

Strategic Giving
The Art and Science of Philanthropy

Peter Frumkin

The University of Chicago Press | Chicago and London

Peter Frumkin is professor of public affairs at the
Lyndon B. Johnson School of Public Affairs and
director of the RGK Center for Philanthropy and
Community Service, both at the University of Texas
at Austin. He is the author of *On Being Nonprofit.*

The University of Chicago Press, Chicago 60637
The University of Chicago Press, Ltd., London
© 2006 by The University of Chicago
All rights reserved. Published 2006
Printed in the United States of America

15 14 13 12 11 10 09 08 07 06   1 2 3 4 5

ISBN-13: 978-0-226-26626-8 (cloth)
ISBN-10: 0-226-26626-5 (cloth)

Library of Congress Cataloging-in-Publication Data

Frumkin, Peter.
  Strategic giving : the art and science of philanthropy /
Peter Frumkin.
    p. cm.
  Includes bibliographical references and index.
  ISBN 0-226-26626-5 (cloth : alk. paper)
1. Nonprofit organizations—United States. 2. Charities—
United States. 3. Philanthropists—Charitable
contributions—United States. I. Title.
  HD2769.2.U6F78 2006
  361.7—dc22
                                        2005033927

♾ The paper used in this publication meets the minimum
requirements of the American National Standard for
Information Sciences—Permanence of Paper for Printed
Library Materials, ANSI Z39.48-1992.

For Elizabeth, Charles, and Nicholas

Contents

Preface

Philanthropy can be both a potent vehicle through which public needs are met and an instrument for the expression of private beliefs and commitments. Finding a way to maximize both the public benefits of giving and the private fulfillment of donors is critical not just to securing the continued flow of funds into philanthropy, but also to ensuring that private giving in all its many idiosyncratic forms continues to play a vital role in supporting pluralism in society. Based on years of listening to individual and institutional funders talk about the challenges of giving money away sensibly, I set out in writing this book to explore how donors can think strategically about their giving and maximize the public and private benefits of philanthropy.

While this is a complex topic and while my argument is detailed and long, it may be useful to think of the book as containing two main parts. The first part of *Strategic Giving* (introduction through chapter 3) presents an argument about the central problems in modern philanthropy. Tracing the evolution of giving over the past century, the book suggests that lingering questions remain about the ultimate effectiveness of the field and the accountability of donors. Over time, as a large amount of philanthropic capital has been directed by donors to the establishment of perpetual private foundations, the growing class of philanthropic professionals has struggled to address the challenges of effectiveness, accountability, and legitimacy. I argue that the underlying trend toward professional management of philanthropy through foundations has three significant weaknesses. First, questions about effectiveness have been weakly transformed into conversations about the performance of grantee organizations rather than focused on the more central issue of achievement of the donor's philanthropic mission and objective. Second, demands for greater accountability have led professional grantmakers only to increase the flow of public information about foundations, and not to redress the fundamental power imbalance between institutional donors and recipient organizations that makes real accountability difficult. Third, nagging concerns about the fundamental legitimacy of private action on behalf of the public have never been fully resolved.

The challenges facing contemporary philanthropy force a major rethinking of its underlying logic. The second part of the book offers a way of reconstructing practice based on a new theory of philanthropic strategy. Chapters 4 through 9 point to five essential questions that donors must confront as they chart their philanthropic plans: What is valuable to my community and me? What kinds of nonprofit programs will work best? What philanthropic vehicle can best be used to accomplish my goals? When should my giving take place? What level of engagement and visibility do I want for my giving? The challenges of defining a value proposition, a logic model, a vehicle, a style, and a time frame are taken up one after the other in the middle chapters of the book. When each question is posed in isolation from the others, the book notes that there are no universally appropriate answers to any one of these five challenges. There are, however, sets of responses that coalesce more or less well together and that achieve more or less consistency. This points to the following basic claim: Strategic giving should be understood as the achievement of fit and alignment of the five core philanthropic dimensions. Moving toward greater fit and alignment is taken to be the central task of the strategic donor, one that could provide a new basis for understanding and assessing philanthropic effectiveness, create the foundation for a more meaningful accountability system between donors and the organizations they support, and give philanthropy the legitimacy that has at times eluded it.

The book closes with a look at the ways in which knowledge is built in philanthropy and at the obstacles to measuring impact accurately. The conclusion returns to the key strategic framework, revisits the main arguments of the book, and shows how the art of philanthropy allows donors to express their private values and convictions while the science of philanthropy pushes the field toward greater levels of instrumental effectiveness. Because it is aimed at both the researcher and the practitioner, readers should know that the book is neither a pure critique of contemporary philanthropy nor an instruction manual for donors. Instead, I have tried to present both analysis and prescription based on a theory of the essential duality of philanthropy that makes it at once a very public form of action on behalf of others and a private form of expression, an activity that also demands that those seeking to practice giving well be skilled in both its art and its science.

Writing a book is never easy, and this book was no exception to that rule. I have brought together ideas and arguments that for years I have been exploring and developing in my research, testing out in classes and conference presentations, and applying and revising in work with foundations and individual donors. From the start, my goal has been to develop a compelling framing of the problems and challenges in philanthropy today and a model of what strategic giving might entail. This difficult job was made easier, however, by my friends and colleagues who have been a great source of encouragement and wise counsel from the time I began to plan this book to when I neared the end. I have accumulated debts at four institutions, which each played a role in helping me bring this book to completion, and it is a pleasure to finally acknowledge and give thanks here.

At the Harvard University's Hauser Center for Nonprofit Organizations, I owe special thanks to Christine W. Letts, who cotaught with me a course on philanthropy for five years and helped me refine and organize many of the most central ideas in this book. Mark Moore and Derek Bok read the manuscript and provided important guidance throughout. The Hauser Center also gave me a crucial grant that allowed me to take time away from my university obligations and focus on my research. I spent this time enjoying the warm hospitality of Wellesley College, where Jonathan Imber generously provided a place for me to work during this leave. A substantial part of this book was actually written while I was a senior fellow of the New America Foundation in Washington, D.C. There, I am indebted to Ted Halstead, who believed in this project and gave me the time I needed to concentrate on elaborating my argument, and to Simone Frank, who helped me manage the project. Finally, my colleagues at the Lyndon B. Johnson School of Public Affairs at the University of Texas welcomed and supported me as I concluded the project.

Outside the academy, I owe much to the many donors I met while writing this book who shared with me their ideas and concerns about the difficult challenge of translating their personal commitments into public action. I am grateful to Patricia Brown at the Burton G. Bettingen Corporation, Claude Rosenberg at NewTithing, and William Schambra at the Bradley Center for Philanthropy and Civic Renewal, who each provided support to the project at various critical points. John Tryneski at the University of Chicago Press saw potential in the idea of a book about philanthropy, patiently waited for the delivery of a manuscript, and then steadily guided the book through revisions, editing, and publication.

Ideas and resources are necessary to completing a book like this, but they are not ultimately sufficient. I could not have written this book without the support and understanding of my family over time. This book is dedicated to my wife Elizabeth and my sons Charles and Nicholas.

Introduction

Philanthropy allows individuals to express their values, to single out particular issues or causes as being worthy of attention, and, through gifts of money, to support activities that benefit the public.

Philanthropy occupies a complex and conflicted position in American society.

On the surface, there appears to be little explanation for how two such contradictory claims could both be true. After all, why should the act of giving engender controversy? The decision by an individual to use their wealth for public purposes should, in principle, be welcomed for what it appears to be, namely a voluntary effort to satisfy public needs outside of government. Philanthropy allows private actors to act in public ways, and it is this very fact that lies at the heart of much of the tension. The controversy—and even conflict—within and around philanthropy over the past century can be traced to its unresolved relationship to the dominant and more recognizable system of satisfying public needs, namely the fulfillment of needs through government's many institutions and programs. Philanthropy has some of the features of government but it lacks anything closely resembling democratic controls. All of which creates challenges for donors while also opening up some unique opportunities.

Philanthropy is a complex phenomenon precisely because it tends to be individualistic in nature yet it operates in the public sphere. Donors use their wealth, which sometimes can be modest and sometimes immense, to project their values, commitments, and beliefs into the public sphere. This process may be moderated through the collective deliberation of a board of trustees if an institutional vehicle is used. In many cases, however, the link between impulse and action is very personal and individualistic in character. This puts giving in stark contrast to the more recognizable form of deliberation and action about public needs: Liberal society is grounded in the idea of a collectivity deciding together—through democratic processes—what will happen in the public sphere. When donors act as seemingly miniature, undemocratic, and personal governments, tensions may surface around issues of class, race, and politics because the deliberative and consultative aspects of democracy have been bypassed. Uncomfortable as this may be at times, it is the unchecked executive power of donors that often makes philanthropy a valuable and distinctive form of public action. Donors may ruffle feathers when their ideas immediately find full expression in society by virtue of philanthropic fiat, especially when giving is directed at controversial initiatives such as school vouchers or abortion services. However, the freedom and power that donors possess and their ability to act without consultation or real accountability allow them to act quicker and take greater risks than government. Because they do not need to satisfy the majority of either voters or shareholders, donors can sometimes appear to be self-absorbed, outrageous, and wasteful, while at other times they may seem profoundly insightful, innovative, and prescient.

The tension between the private character of giving and its inherent public dimension is only likely to increase over the coming decades as a massive multitrillion dollar intergenerational transfer of wealth is expected to transform the landscape of giving. This anticipated tidal wave of private resources is so large that some predict that the profile of philanthropy in American society will increase substantially as more and more important public needs are met through private acts of generosity. In addition to the wealth that will likely be applied to philanthropic purposes as demographic shifts develop, a rising group of self-made philanthropists with substantial personal resources have already begun to take center stage. Many of these wealthy individuals have expressed an interest in taking a more active role in dispersing their wealth, a hands-on approach that is in keeping with the energy and engagement these entrepreneurs bring to their businesses.

Whether their wealth is inherited or earned, all donors need to take seriously the responsibilities that wealth brings with it. Giving away money effectively requires reflection and work. A critical step in discharging these responsibilities effectively is to develop a deeper understanding of philanthropy. This book offers an interpretation of the main challenges facing the field, an argument about the nature of philanthropic strategy, and some reflections on the place of philanthropy in democratic society.

Philanthropy in its many forms has emerged as a central and distinctive feature not only of the American social and political scene, but also of societies around the world. Giving has been part of societies from the Greeks to the present, although its form and significance have evolved considerably. In the United States, early notions about charity during the colonial era were displaced by ambitious charitable ideas about helping following the Civil War.[1] These concepts in turn were usurped by theories about dispersing "surplus wealth" scientifically following the industrial revolution, only now to be challenged by theories of strategic giving. As insights and ideas about philanthropy have percolated up over time, they have continuously transformed the uneasy juxtaposition of private interests on public needs that lies at the core of philanthropy. Today, as small donors contribute sensible portions of their income to causes they deem important and as wealthy donors plan multimillion—and even multibillion—dollar gifts, philanthropic interventions routinely delight, amuse, and outrage those outside the relationship between giver and recipient.

A few disclaimers are in order given the size and complexity of this topic. Although philanthropy is a worldwide phenomenon,[2] much of the discussion in this book is focused on the American experience with giving, including cases of Americans giving at home and abroad. Painting an accurate description of the empirical dimensions of giving in America is a valuable and important task, but one that I have largely left for others.[3] My focus here is broader, more theoretical, and ultimately more normative. I diagnose the core problems in the world of giving today, offer a framework for reconstructing practice in a way applicable to these problems, and explore how to promote a more vital philanthropic sector.

Still, a few broad descriptive brushstrokes of American philanthropy are useful for setting the context.[4] First, the scale of giving in the United States, which now surpasses $200 billion a year, is far greater than in any other nation. Giving has grown modestly and consistently over time, shaped in part by the state of the economy, the performance of the market, and other economic factors.[5] Second, almost half of all American philanthropy goes to religious organizations and supports both the religious and community service activities of congregations.[6] Religious giving is typically small in size and carried out by individuals on a weekly basis, which is significant because it indicates that a major part of giving is still operating on a personal as opposed to an institutional level. This leads to the third defining characteristic of giving in the United States. Contrary to the perceived importance and publicity garnered by the giving of large foundations and corporations, individuals constitute the majority of all giving. Much of the giving in the United States is local and focuses on organizations providing needed services and to which contributors have some connection.[7] Fourth, though growing annually, giving from all sources now represents a diminishing share of total nonprofit revenues, due in large part to substantial increases in earned income and the heavy funding of human services by government. This does not mean that philanthropy is less important to nonprofit organizations today than in the past, only that there is growing competition for charitable dollars as the nonprofit sector expands quickly. Grants and contributions are still often fought over because they represent critical sources of seed capital for nonprofit organizations, allowing those organizations to get off the ground and begin to develop other revenue streams.

Finally, and most directly pertinent to this study, there is growing interest, particularly among larger donors, in creative and effective ways to use charitable dollars. Philanthropy is a field that is still emerging, still seeking a clear identity, and still trying to figure out its core assumptions and aspirations. Because it is a field in flux where very little received wisdom and settled doctrine are present, it is a particularly tempting target for analysis and study—one that appears ripe for systematic thinking and reconceptualization.[8]

Charity and Philanthropy

Throughout this book, several words are used to describe the act of giving. Sometimes I simply use the word "giving" to refer to acts of generosity that transfer resources voluntarily from one party, the donor, to another party, the recipient. There are times, however, when two other words will be employed to describe or refer to the act of giving. Each has a special meaning grounded in the evolution of giving in the United States.[9] While some have tried to simplify the connection between these two words by positing them to be incompatible or by imposing a historical ordering to them, the reality is that both charity and philanthropy have long operated in parallel.[10] There has never been a precise moment when charity was displaced by philanthropy. Instead charity and philanthropy have come to occupy somewhat different niches over time and persist independently to this day.[11]

What is charity? It can best be understood as the uncomplicated and unconditional transfer of money or assistance to those in need with the intent of helping. It may include gifts of time in the form of volunteering,[12] though I will focus here on gifts of money. Of course, charity has a long history, one that is deeply intertwined with many of the world's religions. Within Christianity, faith and charity have long gone hand in hand.[13] In other faiths, charity has also been a central principle, a way of demonstrating caring and commitment. Charity is based on the presumption that no human being should live in misery and suffering and that those with the ability to help have an obligation to do so.[14] Focusing only on modern times, charity has certainly had its critics, from the progressives at the turn of the century to libertarians more recently. One of the most powerful arguments against charity is that it debases and humiliates the poor. By offering money to others, givers place the poor in the unfortunate position of taking money they have not earned in order to survive. Giving and the resulting taking may undermine the self-esteem of the poor and make them feel hopeless and powerless. The receipt of funds, especially when it is transparent and administered through agencies, reinforces hierarchy and renders the poor mere wards of the wealthy. While the idea of charity as humiliating may be hard to understand today, especially with the rise of large numbers of public transfer programs aimed at giving the poor housing, health care, food, and cash, charity was not always seen in a positive light historically, and its moral effects have been questioned.[15]

A second concern as charity grew in size and scope was that it would not get to the root causes of problems. Charity focuses on the temporary alleviation of the symptoms felt by the poor, rather than toward the construction of lasting solutions to the problems and obstacles that made the poor needy in the first place. Without demanding change and self-help from the poor, charity has long been criticized as superficial and not adequately curative. By providing a hand out rather than a hand up, charity leaves the social order unchanged. Without breaking through to address the reasons behind poverty and suffering, charity is condemned to providing a never-ending series of mild balms and bandages to society's worst sores. Still, the urge to help those in desperate straits is strong, and the fact that this help may not get to the root of all social problems hardly means that aid should not be rendered to those in need. Nevertheless, this weakness has dogged charity: Because it is not systemic and because it does not demand much in return, charity has been seen as more of a manifestation of the donor's need to express caring and compassion than as a potent tool for social change.

A third early worry is that charity lacks professionalism. With settlement houses springing up and with almsgiving expanding,[16] early progressives worried that the fate of the poor was being placed increasingly in the hands of untrained persons. Charity workers may well have been motivated by the highest of ideals and possessed of great caring and compassion, but they were hardly professionals like doctors. It would take decades for the profession of social work to grow and for charities to earn the respect and trust of the public. Today, critics still worry about the training and capacity of charity workers to fashion informed and sophisticated responses to human suffering.

Yet another criticism of charity was that it inadvertently lets government off the hook by carrying its load and doing work that government itself should do. By taking up collections and by attempting to help the poor right their lives, charity workers were creating conditions and expectations for further private action that would make the case for government action less compelling.[17] This concern about charity's potential crowding out of government has become more acute as the size of charitable commitments has risen over time. That charity may be local and have special advantages associated with a close connection between giver and recipient makes it hard for it to achieve broad systematic interventions. In addition, charity may also lessen the government's felt responsibility to act on behalf of the poor, rendering the achievement of greater levels of equality more elusive.

What could be done to remedy some of these real and perceived flaws of charity? A new vision of helping and giving was conjured, one in which charity would be transformed into philanthropy. While charity and the informal and heartfelt desire to help those in need would continue to flourish, the philanthropic tradition would, over time, challenge the tradition of charity. At the very center of the philanthropic alternative to charity are the principles of self-help and opportunity creation. In fact, these two principles were originally thought to differentiate philanthropy from old-fashioned charity so significantly that many still believe the elaboration of this distinction was *the* critical juncture in the evolution of giving.

Rather than just give the poor small alms on an ongoing basis, philanthropy aspires to do something more lasting and radical. A key principle is the enactment of the old teaching: If you give a man a fish you will have fed him for today, but if you teach a man to fish he will feed himself for the rest of his life. By providing help to those willing to help themselves, many of the early donors believed they were improving upon the model of charity by getting to the root causes of poverty and despair. This idea of self-help has been found in American culture for centuries. Benjamin Franklin was a great proponent of philanthropy and argued against perpetual charity. His most famous dictum centered on a razor, which he argued could be given to those in need as a tool for self-care, one that would teach them the joys of self-help, free them from the dull and rusted razors of barbers, and give them a sense of satisfaction stemming from the money they could save by learning to take care of their grooming needs.[18] More contemporary efforts to revive and expand this idea of intervention aimed at solving a problem rather than relieving its symptoms can be found in a range of social programs funded by the largest foundations. Many efforts, particularly those in the human services and education, have focused intensively on locating the most at-risk populations early on and addressing their needs through enrichment and outreach programs of all sorts. Again, the core idea is simple: by spending now on those most in need and by ensuring that they begin life with more opportunities, it will be possible to have a real impact on others and save considerable amounts of money down the road.

At the turn of the twentieth century, two wealthy industrialists entered the philanthropic scene and brought with them new ideas about giving. Both showed inclinations toward philanthropy early in life. The first, Andrew Carnegie, expressed early in his career a desire to devote his fortune to charity. Reflecting on his upbringing, Carnegie noted that from the beginning he was trained to work, to save, and to give. Carnegie bestowed many small gifts as a teenager, and by his twenties, he was giving away thousands of dollars. In 1889, Carnegie published two articles on wealth that set forth his views on philanthropy.[19] Carnegie's "gospel of wealth" suggested that it was the duty of the wealthy to set an example for modest living. Furthermore, after providing for the needs of his family, the man of means should consider the surplus wealth that comes into his hands as trust funds to be administered in a way most beneficial to society. Carnegie argued that surplus wealth should not be allowed to accumulate during a man's life only to be disposed of after his death. Instead, it was the duty of the man who earned the funds to disburse them while still alive.[20] There was no honor in giving away wealth at death when it can no longer be used anymore by the person who earned it. Therefore, Carnegie's claim was: "The man who dies thus rich dies disgraced."[21] On its surface, Carnegie's gospel placed enormous burdens on the individual philanthropist. After all, surplus wealth had to be discharged during life, and it was the duty of the wealthy to accomplish this task in a timely fashion. Though private foundations were rare when Carnegie formulated his dictum, foundations became an appealing way for wealthy individuals to discharge surplus wealth during a donor's life as well as to provide for a lasting philanthropic legacy. It would be many years, however, before Carnegie himself would create a philanthropic foundation to fulfill his broad charitable interests.

Carnegie believed philanthropy could be a powerful force in society. He saw it as a way to return the wealth of a few to a large number of the poor. But philanthropy, he believed, should never degenerate into mere almsgiving. Instead, serious giving should stimulate people to help themselves and should be limited to a narrow range of objects to that end. Carnegie summed up his ethos of self-help: "The best means of benefiting the community is to place within its reach the ladders upon which the aspiring can rise."[22] To that end, he singled out the creation of universities and the expansion of existing ones, and the support of libraries, hospitals, medical colleges, parks, public halls, swimming baths, and churches. In 1911, the Carnegie Corporation, his largest philanthropic entity, was formed with an initial endowment of $125 million to carry on this philanthropic work.[23]

The idea of helping others to help themselves was applauded by the other great philanthropist of the early period. John D. Rockefeller recorded his views on giving in his essay "The Difficult Art of Giving," which argued that the time had come for the wealthy to devote more of their time, effort, and thought to improving the public well-being. Just like Carnegie, Rockefeller espoused philanthropy that removed barriers to self-improvement and that empowered the poor. Stressing the importance of self-help, Rockefeller noted: "If the people can be educated to help themselves, we strike at the root of many evils of the world . . . The only thing that is of lasting benefit to a man is that which he does for himself."[24] Like Carnegie, Rockefeller suggested that the goal of philanthropy should be to identify the underlying causes of poverty, rather than to address only poverty's symptoms: "The best philanthropy . . . is not what is usually called charity. It is, in my judgment, the investment of effort or time or money . . . to expand and develop the resources at hand, and to give opportunity for progress and healthful labor where it did not exist before."[25]

The approach to philanthropy outlined by Carnegie and Rockefeller, stressing self-help and the search for the underlying causes of poverty, became known around the turn of the century as "scientific philanthropy," which contrasted rather sharply with the approach to charity practiced by settlement houses and local charities.[26] These agencies sought to help the poor by meeting their immediate medical, financial, and social needs through direct service programs located in areas of high poverty. Rockefeller and Carnegie's scientific philanthropy eschewed this kind of almsgiving, or "poor aid," and embraced the more difficult goal of removing the underlying forces that made social welfare agencies necessary. In many ways, this radical rejection of mainstream charity represented the central contribution of philanthropy's two founding fathers. Given the strong ideas underlying Carnegie and Rockefeller's philanthropic agendas, it was not surprising that they saw philanthropy as the personal embodiment of the donor's own vision and social philosophy.

While the great industrialists enjoyed most of the philanthropic spotlight, they were not the only actors in the process of reimagining giving. Madam C. J. Walker built a cosmetics business from scratch and adopted innovative ways of using her wealth to effect social change around the same time as Carnegie and Rockefeller were laying out their philanthropic manifestos and disbursing their fortunes. Walker sold scalp and hair treatments for African American women. She lost both of her parents at an early age but drew solace from St. Paul's African Methodist Episcopal Church in St. Louis, Missouri. The church asked its parishioners to make donations and encouraged a culture of giving. After working as a washerwoman for many years, Walker invented a new line of products for African American women. Walker herself traveled the country to sell and promote her products. After her business had taken root across the country, Walker developed a cadre of saleswomen with the agents divided into "Walker Clubs." These clubs provided the best employment opportunities for many African American women at the time and fostered the entrepreneurial spirit in its members. Madam Walker also opened a school, Lelia College, to train sales agents. The Walker Clubs were more than just a clever way of marketing cosmetic products. Madam Walker built a network of agents who sold her products but were also committed to community service. She regularly held conventions of the Madam C. J. Walker Hair Culturists Union of America to spread her vision. At the 1917 convention in Philadelphia, Walker gave a speech in which she urged her agents not to let their love of country cause them to retreat in their protest against wrong and injustice.[27] Walker was committed to ending racial injustices, such as lynching, and building community centers in African American communities where young men and women could meet and learn.

In her lifetime, Walker gave major gifts to a wide variety of organizations including the Tuskegee Institute, the YMCA, and the NAACP. She gave gifts that would generate publicity and change the perception of African American giving in the general public and in her own community. African American giving had focused strongly on the local church before she adopted a more strategic approach to philanthropy. When she was denied an audience with President Wilson to discuss the issue of lynching, she made a large pledge to the NAACP's antilynching fund. During World War I, she mobilized her agents to buy Liberty Bonds and Victory Bonds. When she gave $1,000 to the Indianapolis YMCA, the news made newspaper headlines, which heralded it as the largest gift ever from an African American woman. After her death, the estate of Madam Walker dwindled and her company was eventually dissolved in 1985. But her giving showed that African American women could be involved in philanthropy at the highest levels. She once noted, "My object in life is not simply to make money for myself or to spend it on myself in dressing or running around in an automobile . . . I am endeavoring to provide employment for hundreds of women of my race."[28] Madam Walker provided opportunities for hundreds of women to be self-supporting and accumulate their own wealth, but she also showed her sales agents that once gotten, wealth could also be used to help others. What is most interesting about Madam Walker is that she had many of the same impulses of the more famous industrialists when trying to go beyond charity. She was committed to finding a way of giving that would create financial independence and promote self-help, particularly among African Americans.[29]

Doubtless there are other turn-of-the-century donors who, like Madam Walker, worked to bring lasting change through their giving and to move beyond simple almsgiving. For this reason, starting with the views of Carnegie and Rockefeller about scientific philanthropy is at once a cliché and a necessity. Charity's claim on the minds of Americans was strong and the willingness and imagination of these two wealthy industrialists to challenge this claim was historically important. Even if the idea of getting to the root of problems and creating opportunity, not dependence, seems intuitively obvious, the shift in consciousness that these philanthropic pioneers enabled was significant and lasting. The movement from charity to philanthropy was truly a shift in the paradigm of giving, one in which the underlying assumptions of the field were transformed. Before this shift it would have been hard to use the word "strategic" in connection with charity simply because giving was anything but strategic. The shift away from charity that began at the turn of the century has proceeded apace. Today, bracketing the vast legions of small donors and religiously motivated givers who still collectively contribute the lion's share of gifts, charity is considered somewhat passé, a practice whose time has come and gone. Within some circles, charity has come to symbolize backwardness, lack of imagination, ineffectiveness. But as we shall see, the claims of philanthropy over charity are not as clear-cut as some would have one believe. Indeed, the continued existence and viability of charity today—long after Carnegie and Rockefeller sought to replace it—provides a useful backdrop against which to examine some of the challenges and unresolved issues that remain in the field of contemporary philanthropy. Thus, although the analysis and argument here is more focused on philanthropy than on charity, and while I will generally use the term philanthropy more often than not, many of the issues raised by the distinction between philanthropy and charity remain unsettled and percolate throughout this book.

The Purposes of Giving

If philanthropy is indeed different in its assumptions and ambitions from charity, it is still important to ask the foundational question: What is the purpose of all giving? This question is the natural starting point for a book that proposes to describe the elements of strategic giving. After all, before addressing the practical questions of how donors go about achieving their objectives in philanthropy, it is essential to start by asking what is it that donors are trying to accomplish through philanthropy. It would be useful to begin by acknowledging that there is no single answer to the question of what purpose philanthropy fulfills. Philanthropy is a complex and sprawling concept that has many meanings and whose significance has shifted against the broader political and social backdrop against which it has played itself out. In reality, private giving represents an at times confusing assortment of purposes, each with its own logic and rationale. With some simplification, it is possible to isolate at least five important purposes or functions that have emerged over time as philanthropy has sought to define a distinctive place for itself in public life.[30]

One of the most common arguments about the function of philanthropy focuses on the ability of donors to use private funds to create social and political change. The number of the possible meanings of the term "change" is stunningly large. From community empowerment and organizing aimed at changing patterns of political participation to advocacy efforts to tighten gun laws, the character of social change is truly in the eye of the giver. Still, using private charitable dollars to pursue public purposes is by its very nature an act that implies the status quo must change in some way. As an agent of change, philanthropy brings with it considerable resources and, even more important, a level of freedom from both the public opinion and the bottom line that limit the ability of government and business to play this role. The use of private funds allows philanthropy to pursue a change agenda without having to spend large amounts of time mobilizing other sources of support. Donors can even use their wealth to declare a particular issue or cause worth pursuing with or without achieving consensus among those affected. In this sense, donors can act as both legislatures and executive branches, authorizing themselves to act in the public interest. Of course, this power to deploy money in the name of political and social change makes many worry about the accountability of philanthropy.

Change can occur at many different levels through multiple means or types of interventions. Some donors have attempted to promote change by rearranging power within local communities.[31] Mobilization efforts have at times centered on voter registration drives, such as the Ford Foundation's famous effort in the 1960s to register voters in Cleveland. This effort contributed to the election of Carl Stokes, the first African American mayor of a major American city. Ford's voter registration work, as well as a series of other events, eventually prodded Congress to take an interest in the activities of foundations and eventually led to regulations on their political activities. Still, mobilization efforts aimed at social change have proceeded apace, albeit in different guises. Many funders, such as the Wieboldt Foundation in Chicago, have purposefully defined for themselves missions related primarily to community organizing and empowerment. They have sought out nonprofit organizations whose goal is to invigorate community participation with the ultimate goal of achieving change. Other private funders have interpreted organizing more traditionally and have supported labor organizing efforts in areas that have long been neglected.[32]

Beyond grassroots mobilization strategies, a growing number of donors have been attracted to the idea of achieving change through political advocacy work, ranging from policy research to public information campaigns to ballot initiatives. During the revival of conservatism in the 1980s, individual and institutional funders played an important role in supporting a range of public policy research institutes that shaped policy development in the White House.[33] More recently, individual donors have used their private funds to push ballot initiatives. From financier George Soros's effort to legalize some drugs to high-tech entrepreneur Tim Draper's effort to change public policy to give all California families school vouchers, donors have pursued a change agenda by supporting grassroots initiatives aimed at moving policy and politics. These efforts have had a mixed record of success and have raised difficult questions about the use of philanthropic funds to advance the social change agendas of individuals, which have not always coincided with the broader public agenda. Whether attempting to achieve social and political change through mobilization or policy initiatives, many donors have defined a role for philanthropy that is centered squarely on the idea of reorganizing power and using the political process to achieve desired ends.

A radical critique of philanthropy's political function has emerged over time. Drawing on the Italian "cultural" Marxist Antonio Gramsci's ideas about the use of culture and education by elites to maintain class distinctions,[34] critics of philanthropy have argued that an important purpose of giving is cooptation and social control, not political and social change. Giving is a way of diverting the poor from the central issue of inequality by rendering some assistance, but not by making structural changes in the way the economy, society, and polity are organized. Interestingly, the 1950 *Soviet Concise Dictionary of Foreign Words* contained the following definition of "philanthropy": "A means the bourgeoisie uses to deceive workers and disguise the parasitism and its exploiter's face by rendering hypocritical aid to the poor in order to distract the latter from class struggle." The fifth volume of the second edition of the *Great Soviet Encyclopedia*, also published in 1950, offers a similar interpretation of charity: "Aid hypocritically rendered by representatives of the ruling class in an exploiter society to a part of the poor population in order to deceive workers and divert them from class struggle."[35] The idea here is a simple one. Far from being a force for change, philanthropy masks large social inequities and defuses grassroots opposition and rebellion by offering small amounts of aid. Interestingly, the word "hypocritical" appears in both definitions, which reflects the suspicion that many have of the idea of private resources actually being used to advance public purposes and achieve meaningful changes. The Soviet perspective was that by giving to the needy, the wealthy are only pretending to care about the plight of the poor and tricking them into not rebelling.

Some thirty years later, in a volume entitled *Philanthropy and Cultural Imperialism*, an American academic, Robert Arnove, argued that private philanthropic foundations had a "corrosive influence on democratic society" because they "serve as cooling-out agencies, delaying and preventing more radical, structural change." He concluded that foundations "help maintain an economic and political order, international in scope, which benefits the ruling class interests of philanthropists and philanthropoids—a system which . . . has worked against the interests of minorities, the working class, and Third World peoples."[36] Other American critics of philanthropy have focused on the defensive role that giving plays for wealthy people and the class distinctions it depends on for its very existence. Aileen Ross, for example, has written: "Philanthropy has always been the reflection of a class society because it has depended on a division between rich givers and poor recipients." By alleviating a small part of poverty, the wealthy "have secured their own positions against those who might displace them and thus have avoided revolt."[37] Examples sometimes cited of social movements whose radical element was defused by the power of philanthropy include the women's movement, which was turned from a powerful grassroots movement for power into an institutionalized political effort, and African American colleges and universities, which slowed the broad movement toward greater integration of higher education.

One reason why the political function of philanthropy is controversial is the fact that it appears to extend the boundaries of giving, from the modest enactment of donor's interests to the reshaping of large numbers of people's lives. By stepping across the imposing boundary between individuals and communities, politically motivated and directed giving can be threatening. Not only does it remind us of the power differential between wealthy and average citizens, it conjures up all the negative associations of money's influence on politics. Wealth and power are difficult to separate and this naturally causes suspicion and concern when donors act in very public ways. Philanthropy ultimately allows some individuals to act as their own private governments, whose power can be used to challenge that of the state and force it to reexamine its priorities and policies.

A second and very different purpose of philanthropy is to locate and support important social innovations, which can take the form of research or programmatic breakthroughs. Philanthropic funds have long been viewed as social venture capital designed to be used to promote new thinking and programs.[38] The idea that philanthropy is really about producing innovation is popular among those who question the ability of government to generate new ideas and successful programs, particularly when it comes to addressing enduring social problems.[39] On the surface, at least, philanthropy appears well positioned to be a potent force for innovation in that the freedom donors enjoy opens up endless opportunities. In principle, at least, the absence of strong accountability mechanisms connected to charitable giving should make it possible for donors to strike out in new and unpredictable directions. Many donors like the idea of consciously using their giving to push the frontier of ideas and practice with the goal of generating new ways of conceptualizing problems and responding to them. The search for innovation is a product, in part, of the realization that the actual solution of many important public problems requires large and expensive interventions, which few donors are in a position to underwrite. However, by researching or actually developing innovative new ways of achieving a particular programmatic result, donors can show the way to others.

When it comes to funding innovative research, philanthropy does indeed have a strong track record. Many important medical breakthroughs have been achieved in research labs underwritten with private philanthropic funds. In the 1950s, the Scaife Foundation invested in the lab of Jonas Salk, though few could have predicted at the time that this support would be translated into a vaccine against polio.[40] In other fields, including astronomy and physics, private support to universities, sometimes coupled with federal research support, has allowed science to progress. In the area of programmatic innovations, over the past century donors have helped to develop a number of innovative pilot programs in fields ranging from health to education to social services to the arts. Some of these programs have shown great promise, while others, to be sure, have had more mixed results. Because many funders recognize that their ability to bring projects to scale is limited, many times the search for innovation has been structured in a way to encourage the public sector to pick up and expand the implementation of the initiative.[41] The freedom of donors to experiment and to act quickly gives philanthropy a chance to lead rather than follow public policy. To take full advantage of this freedom and to fulfill its function as social innovator, philanthropy must be willing to assume high levels of risk, evaluate carefully, and communicate widely. Whether funding new projects or recasting existing work in new ways, philanthropy has been understood as a tool of innovation aimed at advancing a diverse array of fields.

One obstacle to the pursuit of the innovation function of philanthropy is related to the contested nature of social innovations.[42] When donors fund new and untested programs, they venture into contested terrain and find themselves pitted against entrenched interests. To overcome this resistance to new ways of handling tasks, donors need to exercise extreme patience and determination, and not give up too quickly should results not be immediately discernable. Breaking through a field's standard mode of operation requires a willingness to take on professionals and their claims to control knowledge. In this sense, philanthropy can play a critical role as a social inquisitor, asking questions about what is possible, what works best, and what design change in programs might lead to improved performance. Achieving an authentic social innovation can change an entire field's self-understanding, which is why so many philanthropic dollars are devoted to finding new ways of providing services.

A third purpose of philanthropy is more traditional and prosaic. It is focused not on ambitious social and political change agendas, nor on the relentless pursuit of innovation. A large number of donors, particularly smaller contributors, use their giving simply to achieve a modest measure of economic equity. By giving money to nonprofit organizations that provide services to needy populations, donors often try to accomplish small-scale redistribution of resources. When focusing on making marginal improvements in the life conditions of disadvantaged populations, philanthropy tends to emphasize programs that entail at least some measure of personal responsibility and commitment. While the impulse to help those in need is great, interest in uncomplicated efforts to alleviate suffering is attractive only in some corners. Thus, even when donors want to use their wealth to help others, it often takes a more complex form than a simple check that can be cashed without any questions. Help is most often embedded in programs and services designed to provide long-term solutions to the problems facing the needy.[43]

Equity or redistributive giving often takes a local form, where caring is expressed for those in the community who are less well off and where the concept of equity is more manageable. The ability of donors—acting either individually or collectively—to execute broad-scale redistribution is limited, given the needs and the level of charitable resources available. Still, by transferring some funds from those with resources to those without, giving can represent a small step toward greater equality and sharing. Equitable redistribution, albeit on a small-scale and within focused geographical boundaries, lies at the heart of many of the oldest and most enduring social service organizations. These service providers are able to sustain themselves over long periods of time precisely because their missions are timeless and appeal to donors who simply want to see some of the present disparities in resources and life chances reduced. The equity-seeking, redistributive function of charitable giving is thus the least controversial of philanthropic functions—one that could see a renaissance in the years ahead. It represents a relatively low-risk approach to philanthropy, though it is not without its own controversy. After all, redistribution raises some complex issues when it is pursued by government through tax policy, and there will always be those who bristle at the transfer of wealth from those who earned the funds to those who have not. When redistribution is carried out through philanthropy rather than through tax policy, many of the objections and concerns about the worthiness of the poor begin to ease.

A fourth rationale for philanthropy is the pure and unapologetic affirmation of pluralism as a civic value.[44] The fact that hundreds of billions of dollars are applied each year to public purposes by disparate groups of individuals and private institutions, rather than by government, holds forth the possibility that pluralism as a value is affirmed. To be sure, without coordination or outside control, philanthropy can be disorganized, unruly, and unpredictable. To some, however, this is not a problem but instead a core rationale for having a philanthropic tradition. Giving allows a multiplicity of ideas and programs to exist in the public domain, rather than a limited number of "preferred" solutions.[45] The argument that philanthropy affirms pluralism strikes some as both inefficient and undemocratic in that private parties are acting in competing fashions rather than through a single, democratically selected course of action. Given the overlay of private interests on public needs that occurs when gifts are made, these shortcomings may not be a problem. After all, with a myriad of competing conceptions of the public good competing in the public square, power within philanthropy is dispersed and stable.

Some worry that the ability of philanthropy to continue to affirm pluralism is threatened to some extent by the creation of a few very large private foundations that control important portions of the philanthropic assets. While it is certainly true that the information technology revolution created a number of multibillionaires, the sheer size of organized philanthropy makes it hard for even the largest donors to assert a dominant position. The concentration of philanthropic funds is an important concern as the Bill and Melinda Gates Foundation grows by leaps and bounds, but a little historical distance is reassuring. When the first perpetual foundations were created at the turn of the twentieth century, some in Congress worried that they would become a threat to the power of the federal government.[46] Today, however, the number of foundations continues to soar, but institutional giving is still dwarfed by the collective resources allocated to charity by individuals each year. Philanthropy's ability to affirm pluralism is far more resilient than many believe. It is a field that is continuously attracting new donors, each coming forward with a distinctive vision and charitable mission that takes its place among many others. The fact that private charitable giving can be seen as an affirmation of pluralism is important because in many fields of activity there is little consensus on what issues, theories, and programs are most worth pursuing. Lacking clear consensus on most important public matters, philanthropy's role in such circumstances has evolved into the promotion of a multiplicity of responses. By letting a thousand flowers bloom, philanthropy can contribute to a vibrant and diverse civil society, one in which multiple and competing conceptions of the public good can coexist. Philanthropy is a counterbalance to the tendency of government toward bureaucratization. By celebrating and promoting pluralism, philanthropy contributes to the decentralization of power in society.

These four identified public functions of philanthropy hardly exhaust the possibilities. An entirely different way of defining the purpose of philanthropy starts not with the public benefits generated by giving, but with the donor's needs and desires. When donors make gifts they act in both public and private ways. The *public* function of philanthropy includes the four broad goals of change, innovation, redistribution, and pluralism. The *private*, consumptive, and expressive function of philanthropy is directed at meeting the psychic and social needs of donors. It constitutes a complex multipart fifth function of giving. The fact that giving very often benefits the giver has been a starting point for some researchers in terms of explaining why people give. My argument in this book is that the private benefits of giving are more than just a means for explaining the practice of giving. Both the private and personal benefits of giving are an important end in their own right and need to be taken very seriously.

In its simplest and most earnest form, philanthropy's fifth core function is to support the self-actualization of donors by helping givers translate their values into action. By giving to specific causes or organizations, donors can and do engage in a kind of speech, one that propels the donor's conception of what is important into public space and into concrete action.[47] While it is tempting to simply define the function of giving in terms of the benefits that this projection might have for the public, this would be a limiting and even dangerous way to construe the act of giving. Make no mistake: Philanthropy can and should be about producing public benefits. However, it can and should also be about presenting the giver with the chance to enjoy the fruits of philanthropy in the form of psychic satisfaction. In many cases, philanthropy performs an essential purpose of allowing individuals to find meaning and purpose in their lives. While work and personal achievement may satisfy some, those who give affirm that helping others can be a potent source for meaning and even happiness. This alternative interpretation of philanthropy's role is one that sees philanthropy as a form of consumption designed to satisfy the donor. On this account, philanthropy is simultaneously about enacting and expressing the values of the donor and achieving public purposes. Although giving may generate benefits that accrue to communities and seeing these benefits may actually be part of the satisfaction realized by a donor, philanthropy has a rationale that is distinctly personal and private: to give the donor some measure of satisfaction and psychic reward.

Giving may appear to be about doing something for others, but the process of getting outside one's own narrow needs is such that it often turns out to be transformative for the person who is giving. Philanthropy exposes donors to new ways of seeing the world and brings givers into contact with people whom they otherwise would never meet. It also allows givers to translate passions and commitments into action and worldly deeds, a process that can be profoundly satisfying. In this sense, it is impossible to talk about the functions or purposes of philanthropy without recognizing that it has an important impact on the giver that must be considered part of the core rationale for philanthropy. Beyond simple self-actualization and fulfillment as part of the process of translating values into action, the forms that these private benefits can take are numerous and not always easy to pin down. Though the effect of giving is not always clear to donors when they decide to give, many donors understand and accept that they would not give in the absence of some "personal return" on their philanthropy. In this sense, this most narrow and least public function of giving is also the one that may be closest to the engine that actually drives giving forward. Philanthropy is about achieving important purposes, but these purposes are necessarily constructed by donors in a way that often creates some meaning and value for them.

To date, this critical fifth function of philanthropy has largely been ignored, and when it had been acknowledged, it has been treated with suspicion and even contempt.[48] After all, some might ask why one should care about the psychic benefits generated by giving when the needs of communities are so desperate. The answer lies in the complex dependence of philanthropy on the goodwill and motivation of donors. Without validating and taking seriously the donor side to philanthropy, the field runs the very real risk of failing to provide a viable long-term explanation for philanthropy's continued growth and its ability to carry out any of its other more public purposes. As soon as one begins to think about the way in which philanthropy contributes to the development of the donor, a more balanced and realistic picture of philanthropy emerges. It is a phenomenon that has important public purposes, but it is also a phenomenon that is profoundly personal in nature. In the best cases, the interaction of these two characteristics leads toward mutual reinforcement.

In all fairness, philanthropy can have less noble functions than the five set forward here. Philanthropy can be driven by less lofty public intentions and it can create less elevating personal transformations. For example, giving can be turned into little more than a tool for forging networks among elites.[49] In certain social situations, philanthropy brings the wealthy into contact with one another, either through board service, through special gala events, or through joint efforts on fund-raising campaigns. Being part of the philanthropic elite network is not only a way of signaling power and influence, but also a critical way to make important social connections that can be useful in business and even in politics. The use of philanthropy as a tool of social status building is one that is confined largely to the major metropolitan areas where philanthropic leadership is a sign of civic power.[50]

Charitable giving can also advance a donor's political career. Media mogul and New York City mayor Michael Bloomberg increased his charitable giving from $26.6 million in 1988 to over $100 million in 2000, the year he decided to run for office. In an effort to allay fears that his charity was a tool of his campaign and that he was secretly using it to advance his political ambitions, Bloomberg released the names of all of the nonprofits that he has supported. Still, the use of philanthropic funds surely allowed the candidate to make new connections and friends. Giving has thus been seen as a form of consumption by the donor that is oriented just as much toward the fulfillment of the donor's private interests as to the public's needs.

Giving can also improve public relations and burnish the image of the donor. Giving is a great cleanser of the character and donors have used philanthropy either to enhance or to repair their public personas. In New York, pet supply tycoon Leonard Stern turned to giving while prosecution was looming. Stern provided $30 million to New York University to have its business school named after him precisely when Hartz Mountain Industries, the firm he chaired, was being investigated for antitrust violations and its executives were being investigated for perjury and obstruction of justice. Other times, the philanthropic impulse appears after a person's reputation has been tarnished. The financier Michael Milken substantially increased his existing philanthropic efforts and profile following his completion of prison time for securities violations and reporting irregularities connected to his work in the area of junk bonds in the 1980s. Corporations are particularly attracted to this rehabilitative function of philanthropy and use contribution programs to rebuild their public image following bad news. One of the most transparent efforts to use philanthropy for public relations purposes is the charitable work of cigarette manufacturer Philip Morris, which spends hundreds of millions of dollars promoting its philanthropy through advertisements. The use of philanthropy for such narrow and self-interested purposes is troublesome, not because it exposes the fact that giving can be about more than just good causes, but because the donor appears to have gone too far at too great a cost to ensure that giving is followed by taking.

In the end, the purpose of giving cannot be limited to achieving a specific positive end result, be it change, innovation, redistribution, pluralism, or personal expression. Nor can it be simply dismissed as a tool of social control, elite reputation enhancement, or network building. In reality, the meaning of philanthropy is negotiated and defined every time donors and recipients are joined through philanthropy. Philanthropy translates the private expressive desires of donors into public action aimed at meeting needs. It has both public and private functions, enabling communities to solve problems and allowing individuals to express and enact their values. What makes philanthropy at once exciting and perplexing is the strange and at times jarring interaction of public needs and private choices that giving promotes. While philanthropy may begin with the individual's impulse to help others, it often ends in a set of relations and arrangements that may or may not achieve this simple end. Often the personal values and motives of the donor are strong enough to leave a clear imprint on the cause or issue that the donor selects. In fact, many donors consciously select causes based on their ability to make a clear connection between what they value and what they believe are public needs. At times this is a very personal process, one borne out of difficult life experiences such as the one faced by Linda and Peter Biehl.[51]

The Amy Biehl Foundation Trust (ABFT) was created by the parents of the foundation's namesake as a response to her murder. On August 25, 1993, Amy Biehl, while completing her Fulbright Scholarship project on the role of women in South Africa and helping support the democratic transition in South Africa, was killed by four South African youths during a political rally in the town where she had spent many months gaining the trust and friendship of the local community. While most parents would respond in bitterness and overwhelming resentment to the murder of their child, Amy's parents, Linda and Peter Biehl, instead traveled to South Africa to learn more about the region and the complex political, economic, and social contexts of the violence. In 1997, with an initial contribution of $100,000 from USAID and the philosophy of Amy's approach to trust building, the Biehls started the Amy Biehl Foundation Trust to support and develop sustainable, holistic solutions to violence in South Africa. They chose to work with new community-based organizations, rather than partnering up with NGOs, which the Biehls found had a tarnished reputation among locals. At first, funding was distributed in an unsystematic manner. Over time, however, the foundation has progressively formalized and structured its project funding selection process. The ABFT has since flourished as an organization that supports community projects such as after-school programs, first aid training (initiated by an ambulance driver who tended to Amy after she was attacked), employment, and vocational training and has attracted endorsements from the likes of Nelson Mandela and Bishop Desmond Tutu.

Despite growth and expansion, the ABFT continues to express many of the feelings of Amy's family. There are rarely any public statements made by Biehl family members without mention of Amy's name. In 1998, two of Amy's murderers were released from prison, after being granted amnesty—endorsed by the Biehls—by the Truth and Reconciliation Commission, and they began to work for the foundation. This gesture of personal reconciliation illustrates that ABFT's principles are still very much rooted in the family's personal healing process. Yet, over time, the foundation has shown signs of taking its personal mission and philanthropic scope to a larger level: the foundation has made powerful social statements via controversial advertisements that caused South Africa's Advertising Standards Authority to call for their removal.

The translation of personal feelings into philanthropic action does not always occur slowly and scientifically. In the case of the Biehls and many other donors, giving springs from raw emotion and the desire to act. While there may be considerable thought and planning driving the action of donors, beneath all the concept papers, theories of action, and scenario building, there is usually a conviction and a desire to translate values and beliefs into something concrete and lasting. When the donor is alive and engaged, this translation can be very direct and powerful. When the donor is no longer living, the work of giving may be carried out by others through a philanthropic institution whose lasting mission is to do some good in the name of the donor. All of which raises the question of just how giving works to bring two parties together through the single element that has variously been termed a gift, grant, or contribution.

Mechanics of Philanthropy

Philanthropy starts in one of three places. First, individual donors may give away financial assets, real assets, or cash during their lifetimes. Second, individuals may opt to conduct their giving by making bequests from their estates. Third, corporations, which are owned by shareholders, may contribute money or products to charities. To complicate matters some, these sources of funds can be mediated through other institutions and entities, such as bank trustees, foundations, combined giving campaigns, or federated fund-raising groups. All these institutional options are reviewed in greater detail later in the book. For now, it is important simply to set up the image of three main starting pools of charitable funds that will work through intermediary organizations on the way to nonprofit organizations, and ultimately to the clients or beneficiaries of these organizations.

Nonprofit organizations of all different types wait for charitable dollars to filter down to them. Tax laws in the United States allow donors, to varying degrees, to claim tax advantages in exchange for donating to public charities. In order to qualify for these tax advantages, the recipient organization must be legally defined as a publicly supported charity under a section of the U.S. tax code. These tax-exempt entities are referred to as "501(c)(3) organizations."[52] Political parties, unions, and advocacy organizations are all tax-exempt, but they cannot offer their contributors a tax deduction for their gifts. Only donations to nonprofits with broad charitable purposes qualify for the added benefit of a tax deduction. Figure I.1[53] shows the structure of the philanthropic field and the flow of funds from donors to recipients.

Some important facts about philanthropy jump out from this picture. First, giving can originate from both living and dead individuals or from business corporations. Second, philanthropy can be transacted directly with recipient organizations or through institutional intermediaries whose purpose may include assisting in the selection of worthy recipients, shielding the donor from the public, or making giving a simpler and more cost-efficient activity for donors. Third, almost all philanthropy ultimately finds its way to tax-exempt organizations, which have registered with some government and have agreed to some oversight. As funds move across this chart, donor and recipient are sometimes brought into direct contact with one another. This encounter can be a challenging one, particularly since the relationship is grounded in an exchange that has both financial and personal dimensions. The character of the relationship is shaped to some

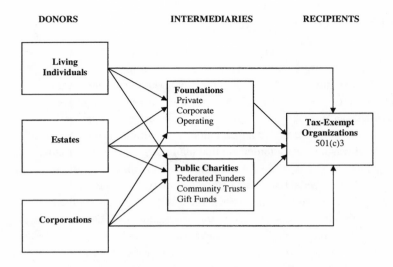

Figure I.1 **The movement of philanthropic funds from donors to recipients.**

extent by the dependence of the nonprofit organization on the donor.[54] In some fields, philanthropic funds still play a major role in enabling nonprofit service provision. It is still possible, for example, for foundations, corporations, and individuals to underwrite the majority of costs associated with artistic exhibitions and productions. In other fields, however, the power of donors has been diminished over the years by greater reliance on earned income and government funding. For donors, the varying degree of influence that private funds have on nonprofit organizations in different fields creates both a challenge and an opportunity. It is a challenge because it is difficult to make high-impact grants to organizations when other sources of agency finance have the attention of the organization and where the impetus for change is weakened as a result. At the same time, it is an opportunity in situations where the organization is willing to work with the donor and where private funds can, as a consequence, drive important programmatic changes.

The tension between a donor's desire for impact and a nonprofit organization's search for autonomy has led both sides of the philanthropic exchange to ponder the fundamental question of whose needs philanthropy is really designed to meet. Two very different points of view have emerged on this question. Among donors, there is a growing sense that it is important for givers to assert their rights and prerogatives because they are being asked to assume risk and forgo other philanthropic opportunities. This often translates into having access to all the information needed to make sound decisions and having a relationship that is built on openness and trust. Fund-raising professionals that work with major donors have promulgated "a donor's bill of rights" designed to protect the interests of givers. This bill asserted that "to assure that philanthropy merits the respect and trust of the general public and that donors and prospective donors can have full confidence in the nonprofit organizations and causes they are asked to support,"[55] it was necessary to declare that all donors have certain rights, which include: "To be informed of the organization's mission, of the way the organization intends to use donated resources, and of its capacity to use donations effectively for their intended purposes; To be informed of the identity of those serving on the organization's governing board, and to expect the board to exercise prudent judgment in its stewardship responsibilities; To be assured that their gifts will be used for the purposes for which they were given; To receive appropriate acknowledgment and recognition; To feel free to ask questions when making a donation and to receive prompt, truthful, and forthright answers."[56]

For nonprofit organizations, the question of rights is not a one-way street. Not to be outdone, a leader concerned about the fate of grassroots organizations crafted a grantee bill of rights around which nonprofits could rally. This document affirmed that nonprofit organizations have rights of their own when it comes to working with funders. These rights include "the right to know a donor's interests, the right just to hear 'no,' the right to a meeting, the right to grants larger than the cost of getting them, the right to general operating support, the right to multi-year support, the right to uniform paperwork and reporting, and the right to respect."[57] In claiming these rights, nonprofits affirm that philanthropy is not simply about enacting the donor's desires. It is a process that demands a thoughtful and respectful collaboration, one in which both sides receive something of value. Given the power that donors have, it is not always easy to achieve this balance or to ensure that the process of seeking grants does not become a procedural nightmare for nonprofits, sapping time and energy away from the fulfillment of mission. By demanding to be treated fairly and respectfully, nonprofits expose the hidden side of philanthropy, the side where hubris and caprice exact a real toll on grantseeking organizations.

These dueling declarations of rights highlight the radically different perspectives that donors and recipients have on charitable giving. From the donors' perspective, those receiving philanthropic funds take on responsibilities and those providing funds have rights. From the recipients' perspective, those supplying the funds have responsibilities and those seeking grants have rights. In some ways, it is possible to sympathize with both points of view. Too often, donors receive little in return for their gifts except a modest tax deduction and some psychic return for having done something for others. Because giving requires donors to forgo discretionary spending on things for themselves, those who contribute funds must be accorded some rights and privileges in recognition of this act of charity. Yet nonprofit organizations counter that without their work there would be no philanthropy at all. Nonprofits see donors as necessary but not sufficient forces in the production of public good. Because it is the service-delivering organizations that are on the front line working with the most needy clients and confronting emerging social problems, these organizations deserve protection and rights that donors must be held responsible for respecting. There is at least one thing that everyone can agree about: Closing the gap between these perspectives would reduce many of the distortions and distractions that prevent donors and donees from achieving their objectives.[58] Narrowing the distance between giver and getter and finding a connection between the private values of donors and the public purposes pursued by nonprofits turns out to be a central element of philanthropic strategy.

Moving Ahead

The field of philanthropy—if indeed it is a field—is fractured and disorganized in more ways than one. While it is hardly surprising that there is little consensus on what causes or issues are worth pursuing, there is little coherence in the field even beyond this most basic issue. Substantial diversity and confusion exist in terms of the philanthropic actors—individuals and institutions—that constitute the field. Philanthropy includes small individual donors who channel gifts to local charities and large individual donors who attempt to use their wealth to leave a profound mark on society. It also includes big foundations that operate nationally and internationally while depending on staff to make grant decisions, smaller family foundations that have close ties to communities, corporate foundations that are at once giving and taking by connecting philanthropy to the core business functions of the firms such as marketing and public relations, community foundations that are attempting simultaneously to execute geographically focused philanthropic agendas and to fulfill the diverse and even conflicting wishes of their many donors, and a small number of operating foundations that use their endowments not for grants to others but to finance their own programmatic interventions. Finally, it is also home to a host of newer vehicles and structures—ranging from informal giving circles to gift funds operated by mutual fund companies that are now challenging the community foundation model.

Amidst all this confusion related to the level of the field's many actors and institutions there are deep divisions over how best to do the work of giving. Across the diverse organizational and individual landscape of giving, funds are disbursed according to stringent standards and tightly written guidelines, given away in haphazard and casual fashion once and then never again, sent in every year with absolute faithful loyalty in return envelopes as part of regular mass mailings, donated to nonprofits only after a close personal connection is established between donor and recipient, contributed after close scrutiny of the financial position of the recipient is completed, and sometimes even given conditionally and with the threat of rescission if performance standards are not met. In short, there are countless different giving practices within philanthropy, each grounded in a set of beliefs and convictions about the best way to give.

As if that were not enough, there is almost no consensus about when to give. Donors have at times done all their giving while alive in order to see what happens, postponed giving until lying on their deathbeds, given away fortunes through their estates to favored institutions, and placed their philanthropic resources into a foundation established in perpetuity so as to spread out their philanthropy potentially over centuries. Moreover, there has been tremendous variation in the profiles assumed by donors, with some donors seeking and getting tremendous amounts of publicity, while others have operated in complete anonymity, and still others have vacillated between these two extremes—starting out in one camp only to migrate into the other.

In all these ways and more, philanthropy is a field of activity that exposes rather than resolves deep-seated differences between individuals in terms of how they believe society should be organized and what public needs should take priority. The introduction of private resources into the public domain that is a central feature of giving cannot help but create confusion and contention. Unlike government, which has elections to set policy directions, and unlike corporations, which have shareholders to whom they must be responsive, philanthropy is able to operate across the boundaries of public and private and to do so with little or no accountability to its many stakeholders. This is what makes philanthropy both an exciting domain in which almost anything is possible and at times an incoherent and controversial field.

In this book, I attempt to bring some order to this landscape through an analysis of how the field has gotten to where it is today and how the practice of giving might be advanced. In building my argument, I have drawn on conversations, interviews, and prolonged interactions with over one hundred donors of all kinds over the course of a five-year period. Thirty of these donors were part of an extended three-year-long conversation designed to engage leading practitioners in philanthropy in an exploration of the future of philanthropy. This process, which was part focus group and part peer-learning network, was convened by Harvard University's Hauser Center for Nonprofit Organizations twice a year for three days of discussion on each occasion, starting in 2000 and concluding in 2003.[59] The goal of these sessions was to sort through some of the major questions of practice facing the field of philanthropy in the years ahead. I learned much from other donors through an annual executive education program for individual philanthropists hosted jointly by the Kennedy School of Government and the Harvard Business School, during which time the donors discussed their philanthropic goals and aspirations. Finally, I interviewed notable donors across the country to learn about the choices they made in their giving and the insights they had about philanthropy. While I have listened carefully to donors and learned greatly from them, I have used their stories not as ends that illustrate "best practices," but as means to highlight pressing issues and problems in philanthropy and to advance my own interpretation of what their experiences tell us about the nature of the elusive concept of strategic giving.

One final caveat is needed. Although this is a large book that covers a great deal of conceptual territory and advances a number of interrelated arguments about strategy in philanthropy, I have purposively avoided focusing on the substantive choices of donors and rendering judgments about their worth or worthiness. I believe almost any philanthropic purpose can be valuable if wisely pursued. Hence my real interest here is on exposing as systematically as possible what good strategy looks like and how to work toward it, while neither applauding nor dismissing any single philanthropic substantive agenda. With this much said, it is now time to begin the journey.

1. Philanthropy and the Public Sphere

Private donors may face complex choices relating to how they go about delivering philanthropic funds, but this work hardly occurs in a vacuum. Because it operates across the public and private domains, because it both enacts and expresses, and because it is so difficult to know for sure which grants and contributions produce meaningful results, government has taken a relatively cautious approach to fashioning public policy and regulation around philanthropy. To be sure, there are plenty of procedural guidelines, rules, and regulations bearing on the administration of philanthropic assets. But on the most important substantive issue of all, namely what kinds of causes are to be supported, government has remained silent. It has left the ultimate choice of philanthropic purposes to donors and resisted rendering judgment about the comparative public value realized when private gifts support a vast range of causes and programs. In the face of many gifts that seem misdirected, wrongheaded, and even foolish, the fundamentally sound and correct nature of this permissive policy position requires some explanation.

Giving and Public Policy

The tax code defines and reinforces some of the most important categories of nonprofit organizations. It alternatively conveys privileges and imposes regulations on organizations based on their legal status and form. While all nonprofit organizations are exempt from taxation, only some—those that serve the public, not just a restricted membership—receive the added benefit of being able to confer on donors an income tax deduction for their support. The simple principle of *tax exemption* can be understood as an acknowledgment of the independence and freedom of private action. It allows nonprofits to operate in a way that is fundamentally different from for-profit entities that owe taxes to the state based on the profits they generate. By contrast, nonprofits are allowed to keep any excess revenues and simply apply them to future charitable purposes. The history of the line between government and nonprofits is long and winding, going back centuries in the United States, but its essential course is clear: Federal and state government in the United States accept the desirability of having independent actors in society working for the common good and shield them from taxation so that they can operate without owing government funds in the form of taxes. Beyond the principle of autonomy that tax exemption conveys (even more so for churches, which do not have to file any reports at all), the tax treatment of nonprofits includes a second feature: namely a public subsidy for charitable activity that serves the public in the form of a *tax deduction* conferred to supporters of nonprofits. This subsidy of nonprofits, given in the form of tax relief to the contributors to nonprofits, is designed to reward those who commit private funds to public purposes.[1] It recognizes that there is a value in private support of charitable work, and it makes giving less expensive than it would be in the absence of a tax deduction for charitable giving. Although there is considerable debate about how efficient this subsidy is and how much giving it actually does encourage, the tax deduction for charitable gifts is still the second critical leg in the public sector's relationship with the nonprofit sector.[2]

One explanation for the tax code's inclination to support giving is that government sees private philanthropy as a necessary partner in the pursuit of public purposes. The difficulty in setting up a policy that encourages privately financed and directed solutions to public problems is that if taken to its logical conclusion, it raises difficult questions about accountability. By moving public services out of government and forgoing tax revenues in order to encourage the private provision of publicly valued services, government risks introducing both greater inefficiency and inequity into the process of public provision. It is important to examine this issue carefully for within it lies the difficult question of what social function philanthropy should emphasize. Government is left, in effect, with the prospect of subsidizing private philanthropic action carried out for the benefit of the public, with government given little say, beyond the vaguest notion of fulfilling a charitable purpose, over the actual causes that will be supported. This might appear to be a disaster waiting to happen or at least a very inefficient way of accomplishing public purposes.

The lack of real substantive accountability around ultimate purposes is astounding.[3] Of course, a few areas are forbidden that cannot be construed as anything other than self-serving action and that fail to fall under even the broadest definition of public benefit. For the most part, the range of charitable purposes permitted is as broad as the human mind can imagine. The loose accountability demands of government to qualify for subsidization in the form as a tax deduction do not even apply to all philanthropy. There is much giving that operates independently of the policy regime and that seeks no recognition from it. Still, among donors seeking a deduction, the accountability demands placed on them are weak, particularly when compared to those government places upon itself. When it comes to accountability, government has several time-tested tools it can fall back on. There are elections designed to hold representatives accountable to their constituents. There are often ample opportunities for interested and affected parties to voice their opinion about legislation or regulation before it is acted upon. There are multiple layers of decision making in government that create internal accountability within the process. There is oversight and review that take place after funds are disbursed. And of course, there are auditing and evaluation processes that can be used to maintain accountability all the way through the implementation process. Throughout all these steps, democratic systems are designed to give stakeholders access and voice. In philanthropy almost none of these conditions exist. Private philanthropic funds are largely disbursed with little or no input from the public, and while there are internal accountability systems between donors and trustees and between trustees and staff, the external world is largely left with its nose pressed up against the glass when it comes to the actual substantive work of philanthropy.

Thus, as one considers the relationship between government and philanthropy, and as the full range of policy approaches comes into focus (ranging from very supportive policies to more neutral or even more negative ones), it is clear that moving responsibility for the provision of public needs from government to philanthropy involves a trade-off of some control in the name of decentralization. Philanthropy simply does not have the controls, safeguards, and accountability devices that government guarantees. By its nature, philanthropy is hard to organize and direct, almost never predictable, subject to the whims of a few, and largely unresponsive to pressures from stakeholders.[4] The one major exception is when government decides to investigate and regulate the administrative side of institutional philanthropy, but, over the past century, such efforts have focused mostly on technical questions related to the management of philanthropic resources and issues related to financial accountability.

The most difficult question to answer about the accountability issue connected with public support of philanthropy is whether the benefits of this devolution of authority create sufficient benefits to outweigh its costs. One way to think about this cost-benefit calculus is to juxtapose once more the instrumental and expressive purposes in philanthropy, the fact that philanthropy is about both the rational and effective application of resources to address human needs and the passionate enactment of the values, commitments, and beliefs of individuals who have defined a public problem as worthy of private attention. Government could surely craft a more restrictive and directive regulatory and policy regime that would push philanthropy toward a far greater emphasis on its instrumental dimension. By the same token, public policy toward giving could be relaxed even more in ways that would enable and encourage a more expansive, expressive function for giving. In many ways, one's view on how this trade-off between public purposes and private values should be handled through public policy will depend heavily on how one defines the core function of philanthropy, whether its chief role is in the area of social innovation, pluralism, and self-expression, or whether its core rationale resides in redistribution and social change. The amount of freedom and the amount of social responsibility that government vests in philanthropy will ultimately constitute an answer to this question. Given ample support through public policy or constrained considerably by tax law and regulation, philanthropy can be positioned more or less advantageously to fulfill any of its core functions.

The stakes are high in this delicate balancing act. The lack of social control over ultimate results of philanthropy, which a loose policy grip on philanthropy entails, will unnerve many citizens and be taken to be an acceptance of the power that wealthy donors possess. By not directing giving in any particular direction, public policy runs the risk of failing to take ample advantage of the opportunity to channel large amounts of private wealth from the hands of a relatively small few to those who need assistance the most. At the same time, efforts to control the direction of philanthropy can be threatening to the idea of a vital and independent civil society. Philanthropy is a central part of the engine that drives the nonprofit sector forward, no matter how earned income and government contracts have changed the funding picture. If government through a tightening of the regulation of charitable giving attempted to steer philanthropy toward more universally accepted and instrumental purposes, something very significant would be lost. To have a vital sector of society working to solve pressing problems outside of government is an important element in an open society; it moves power outward and allows philanthropy to question government priorities and approaches to public problems.[5] Public tolerance of some of the inefficiencies of an open and free civil society has a number of interesting parallels to the quandary government faces when it comes to regulating private enterprise and the operation of markets.

There is a vast and detailed set of theories about why free markets produce beneficial results. From Adam Smith to Milton Friedman, economists have long embraced the view that the freedom to choose and the presence of a way to exchange lead to results that benefit people. At the heart of an economist's appreciation of markets is the belief that competition and consumer sovereignty are great controlling devices that help ensure that the best products at the lowest price reach the market. As producers compete for the attention of consumers, markets move to punish inefficient and low-quality producers, while rewarding those that are able to offer consumers value. The model has been refined and expanded over the centuries but its core assumptions remain fairly constant. The attraction of markets is also enhanced by the prospect that individuals participating in it and acting from self-interest will be led, in Smith's words, by an invisible hand, to decisions and results that benefit society.

One of the deepest and most intriguing questions about philanthropy is whether donors will be led through a new invisible hand to a set of philanthropic decisions and arrangements that truly benefit the public. If this were the case, then there would be little need for government regulation as donors and causes would quietly find one another and maximize social welfare in the process. This optimistic perspective on philanthropy would argue against much government intervention, regulation, or subsidization of particular causes, believing that donors freely pursuing their own philanthropic interests with passion and conviction will lead in aggregate to the funding of projects that reflect both the interests of donors and the needs of the public. On this view, the unfettered pursuit of personal philanthropic interests is the best mechanism for both arriving at broad social results that are optimal and giving that produces the most possible psychic satisfaction for donors. Each part of this kind of claim about the sound functioning of philanthropic markets—the maximization of social welfare and the fulfillment of donors—needs to be examined carefully, because consumption and production in philanthropy are complicated concepts.

The first part of this puzzle is relatively straightforward. It is entirely plausible to hold that donors will be able to maximize their own satisfaction when they have total control over the targets of their generosity. Without regulations favoring one type of giving over another, philanthropic funds will flow to causes that resonate most with donors and that satisfy their philanthropic goals most fully. Donors will select charities and causes that allow them to get meaning and satisfaction. Looking within at their values, beliefs, and personal experiences, donors will direct their giving in ways that make them feel good about supporting the cause that is supported, be it simply because they like what the organizations represent or because they get pleasure from knowing that their giving might make a real difference. Philanthropy is a form of consumption in that it produces, in all its guises, forms, and styles, a sense of satisfaction in having done something for others. To the extent that donor choices are not constrained by outside forces, those who give are able to follow their most basic impulse to help in ways that are meaningful to them.

The other side of the problem—the side associated with public benefits—is far less obvious. After all, there is no clear evidence that the maximization of psychic satisfaction in giving will in turn maximize the public benefits that result from giving. This proposition can be softened a bit and turned into a question: how well does the freedom to give exercised by donors translate into value for society? When the productive side of giving is scrutinized and opposed to its consumptive side, it is ultimately very difficult to sustain the argument that philanthropy has the same characteristics as markets. There is at least one major force missing from philanthropy that might drive donors to maximize public benefits: competition. While there is some pride associated with funding successful and visible programs, donors do not compete in order to stay in the field of philanthropy. Ineffective donors who have chosen to give in areas that no one else believes are significant are never required to change direction. Donors that give to poorly run nonprofit organizations are never forced to relinquish their charitable assets. Donors that give so many small grants that nothing of consequence ever results from their giving are not cited and regulated out of business. Indeed, ineffectiveness is not only excused in philanthropy, it is accepted as an occupational hazard. The institutional structure of the field is geared to ensuring perpetual life regardless of the results that are achieved. There is thus no threat of demise or pressure from other donors that can drive poorly performing donors out of the field. Donors are welcomed with open arms indefinitely. Even if there were competition among donors, it is not clear how winners and losers could be sorted out given the immense obstacles to measuring performance. Thus, while it would be comforting to think that donors are part of a tightly structured market that drives them through invisible pressures to give grants that maximize the utility of others, there are too many real and conceptual obstacles to ever making the free market analogy apply compellingly.

Not only is there no real competition for profit or survival, but there is also no certainty that the private perspectives of donors will actually match the demand for charitable services in the aggregate. There are few clear mechanisms other than overt human suffering to draw philanthropists into areas that have been neglected. And this is a process, especially when dealing with issues such as urban neighborhood decline, that can take long periods of time to work itself out. In this sense, the response of donors to "demand" is not immediate or even assured, given the amount of public need that goes unattended simply because of the inadequacy of philanthropic resources. Beyond the lack of an active and accurate pull from the consumers of philanthropy on the supply of charitable dollars, there are other conceptual problems in the application of a market metaphor to philanthropy. Still, no matter how weak the case is for a philanthropic invisible hand, the arguments for regulation and state intervention in giving are even weaker and less compelling.

The counterargument to a policy that promotes donor choice is one that argues that policy needs to shape the giving of donors to help maximize the public benefits that are produced through the subsidy that the tax deductibility of gifts provides. This is the position that has in effect won out over time and that has been dominant for more than a century in the United States. The tax code treats all public-serving nonprofits alike and awards them all tax exemption and the ability to give contributors a tax deduction for their gift. By remaining neutral about the comparative value of a soup kitchen and a community theater, government has entrusted citizens to decide for themselves which causes they value and want to support.

There have been occasional calls for changes to this system, ones that might give greater public subsidies—in the form of more advantageous tax deductibility or credits—to gifts helping the poor, for example. None of these plans has ever succeeded in garnering much public support, however.

At times, Congress has considered a far more directive approach to the public policy treatment of charities. Wanting once and for all to get past the agnosticism that treats a gift to the symphony the same way that a gift to a homeless shelter is treated, Congress once considered a bill that would have granted donors a $500 tax credit—a one-dollar reduction in taxes due for every dollar given away—with the caveat that the gift must be to a poverty alleviation organization. The intent of the Senate where this bill was advanced came down to a desire to see a more clear commitment in public to recognizing giving that is complementary or even supplementary to government. By singling out the organizations that work with the most difficult and desperate clients for special tax advantages, the intent was to encourage philanthropy to address the most urgent needs that government would likely have to address in the face of philanthropic failure.[6]

The bill was defeated and was ill conceived from many points of view, no matter that its sponsor's intentions were certainly good. The first problem with the idea of public policy rewarding certain philanthropic purposes more than others is that it does real violence to the pluralism function of philanthropy. By nominating certain causes as more worthwhile than others, the approach plays favorites in an arena in which neutrality is needed to preserve diversity and autonomy. The idea that government should be able to rank social causes and drive giving through incentives assumes that public officials are in a better position than donors to define the nature of public needs and what constitutes a significant public benefit. There is no real evidence for such a view, and in fact the history of philanthropy demonstrates that donors can and often have gotten out ahead of the curve and helped government understand how to address social problems in new ways. The second problem with this approach to policy is that it assumes, wrongly I believe, that clear definitional lines can be drawn around concepts and goals such as poverty alleviation, and that policy can be built on distinctions between nonprofit interpretations of these concepts and can clearly identify their impact and client base. This assumption is not supportable in the end since almost any nonprofit can manipulate any categorization system that attempts to define "preferred" missions. Many arts organizations such as theaters and symphonies do make tickets available and run arts education programs for disadvantaged youth. In this sense, the very idea that poverty alleviation can serve as the dividing line between arts organizations and shelters is misplaced. Large numbers of nonprofits, if pressed, could make an argument that at least part of their work deals with poverty. In this sense, the whole idea of making clear distinctions related to the worthiness of a charitable cause, the urgency of an organization's mission, or the comparative need of the clients to be served is impossible to render into clear and enforceable distinctions. Not only would nonprofit organizations attempt to game any system that provided differential tax treatment to nonprofits working in specific fields, but donors would also likely play a role in this process by encouraging nonprofits to qualify themselves so that tax breaks could be passed on.

While the federal government has not had much experience or opportunity to tinker with the choices of donors, some states have developed their own plans to both increase giving and direct it to certain causes through tax policy. One of the most significant such efforts took place in Arizona, where a state law gave residents a tax credit for charitable gifts that were above and beyond their previous level of giving and went to organizations that had been certified for participation in the effort. The effort was a not so subtle attempt to spur and channel philanthropic giving in the state. The results were mixed. The program did boost giving somewhat, but the main beneficiaries were larger and more well-established charities that were able to get through the process of being qualified for participation in the program. The questions emerging from this experiment were focused on the trade-off between the amount of contributions and the diversity of causes and organizations supported. The difficulty in sorting through the results of this and other efforts to shape giving through tax policy is that the only element that is typically measured is aggregate giving levels, when what really needs to be known is the effectiveness of the giving and the impact it had on those who took part in the program. Thus, while tax credits may well spur some additional giving, their effort to certify certain nonprofits as qualifying as recipients of tax-privileged giving may have the effect of driving philanthropy toward greater levels of convergence, which tends to benefit the larger, more well-established organizations.[7]

Doing nothing more than just providing a mild and universal tax deduction for charitable gifts remains the dominant public policy posture toward giving. It promotes charitable giving, but it does not put too much faith in it as a substitute for government spending. The looseness of the public policy frame places a fair amount of weight on the shoulders of donors to ensure that philanthropy does indeed legitimately produce public benefits.

With caps on the amount that can be deducted and close to blind agnosticism in terms of causes that can be supported, federal policy has struck a compromise position—one that allows the expressive dimension to flourish and that mildly encourages giving that will, when all is said and done, lead to the delivery of programs that contribute to the public good, broadly construed.

Philanthropy and Speech

In thinking about the relationship between government and philanthropy, it is hard to ignore some of the parallels between giving and political speech. Protected by the First Amendment and viewed as central to democracy and a free society, political speech is afforded tremendous protection. In a few critical dimensions, philanthropy shares some of the features of political speech. Giving is in many ways a statement about what is important and what matters. It is translated into grants and gifts, but at its heart are a declaration about the significance of certain public purposes and a set of assertions about how best to pursue these purposes. Giving can be controversial or it can be absolutely safe and innocuous. In all cases, however, philanthropy pushes the private values of individuals into the public and connects them to causes that create some benefit for others. Just as a central part of politics is the formulation of claims about what is in the public interest and how best to strive toward common goals, so too in philanthropy is declaring one vision for a better society part of the process. Because lines of race and class are often crossed in philanthropy as these visions of the common good are enacted, tensions can arise as donors make their statements. At its core, philanthropy consists of more than just the satisfaction of accepted public needs and involves the acting out by donors of beliefs and values about what really deserves collective attention. Moreover, behind every philanthropic act is a charitable intention. Some of these intentions may be innocuous and seemingly inconsequential. Others shock, offend, and delight the public. Seeing in philanthropy a kind of political speech will strike many in the nonprofit service sector as odd, given the charitable nature of most endeavors. To be sure, there are large parts of the philanthropic landscape that are nonpartisan. At the same time, it is almost certainly the case that much of philanthropy involves the expression by donors—or the institutional actors they have left behind—of views about the nature of public needs and the public interest. This expressive content in giving thus embodies elements of political speech.

The voice of donors can be heard across a whole range of fields and in many different pitches. Philanthropy can be considered a form of speech in that a large part of philanthropy is about the intentions and aspirations of donors, not their worldly achievement of results. While the whole move to apply business concepts and frameworks to philanthropy has focused attention on the results of giving, there is something significant and valuable in the very attempt to help that the act of giving represents. Just as speech does not always lead to action but still has value in a democratic society, so too does philanthropy have value even if it falls short of its goals. In many ways, the intent of donors when they make their gifts represents their claim about what is important. Gifts and grants may or may not succeed in affirming these claims, but it remains significant that the intent was translated into a recognizable commitment and caring.

As the amount of money dedicated to philanthropy has risen steadily in recent decades and as discretionary funds in government have tightened amid growing commitments to entitlement programs, debt payments, and national defense needs, public tolerance—and even understanding—of the expressive value of philanthropy as speech has progressively been challenged. Most observers outside the field and many of the activists within the nonprofit sector see the hundreds of billion dollars given away each year and held by foundations for future use as the source of potential solutions to urgent problems that government has failed to redress. In this sense, the natural impulse of clients, concerned community members, and workers who deliver critical services is to view philanthropic funds in terms of what concrete good they can achieve. This perspective can be relatively short term, especially if a community is in trouble or if the human needs are urgent. While these concerns are real and have an authentic claim to the attention of donors, philanthropy places an added burden on those who are in a position to give generously. This obligation is to think strategically about giving and to locate opportunities in which the distinctive voice of donors can best be heard. The public interest is ultimately best served when donors do not simply capitulate to the call for short-term needs— which are, in principle, limitless—but instead look for ways to connect their personal values and commitments to the call of the community. This requires balancing the expressive and instrumental functions of giving so that philanthropy can not only promote equity and social change, but also drive social innovation and support a pluralistic society.

Defending the importance of philanthropic "speech" is not a popular calling, but one that is necessary both for the promotion of a sound strategy and a philanthropy that contributes substantially to the public good. There are a number of ways that the expressive content of giving could be supported more fully, including rethinking the distinction between political participation in the legislative and electoral process and charitable activity. One of the most significant aspects of the current policy toward giving is that it treats contributions supporting activities as narrow and specialized as university-based research on Byzantine iconography more favorably and generously than gifts to a political party. Indeed, a gift for research on iconography qualifies a donor for a tax deduction or allows the donor to support the cause with foundation funds. However, a gift in support of a political campaign or to a political action committee or to a political party is not given the same treatment and is denied a tax deduction. On the surface, the line between charitable causes and political causes seems sensible enough. Politics are partisan, while charitable giving is about producing broad public benefits. Restricting the tax deductibility of gifts to purposes that are nonpartisan is a way—in theory at least—of extending the benefits of philanthropy broadly and shielding the political process from the infusion of even larger blocks of money than currently enter the system without a subsidy. The line in the sand also represents an acknowledgment that money in politics may involve not only elements of speech but also issues of equality and access. For this reason, there are limits on contributions to political candidates along with other efforts to recognize that too much voice located in a select and privileged group of people can be just as undemocratic as actual limits on speech.

However, there are elements of this distinction that do not hold up very well when subject to careful scrutiny of the underlying organizational reality. A large number of charitable organizations that qualify for tax-deductible gifts and that have earned the status of a 501(c)3 organization are deeply political in their work and actively influence and support political agendas, no matter their protestations and denials. Of course, the distinction between support of broad political agendas on the one hand and support of parties, candidates, and political action committees on the other is real, at least in terms of formal roles in political life. Still, the reluctance of public policy to treat political action as just as publicly valuable as traditional charitable activities has become harder to sustain as nonprofits have pushed the boundaries around acceptable political behavior and lobbying. While there are set limits on lobbying for charitable organizations, these boundaries are, at times, crossed through the establishment of independent political and advocacy subsidiaries. Clever nonprofit managers are able to use their organizations' tax-exempt status to qualify for grants while also engaging in cost shifting and cost sharing with political counterparts across formal organizational boundaries. It is virtually impossible, given the current chaotic and inadequate reporting system used by the IRS, to really track and render concrete the scope of this cross-subsidization. To make matters worse, the definition of permissible political work by nonprofit organizations is the subject of much confusion, since by law they are allowed to devote a limited amount of their time to lobbying. This has led to a tremendous amount of uncertainty within organizations about how to document their work in order to demonstrate compliance with these limits.[8]

Another issue is larger than that of enforcement, however. Even if government could actually direct tax subsidies to charitable work and deny them to more partisan political work, the question arises as to why it would want to do so. Political action is by its nature action on behalf of others in the name of public interest. There might be a substantial difference in perspective on what the public interest is and how to pursue it, but almost all mainstream forms of political participation are public spirited in nature. A major thrust of public policy has been to seek to minimize the role of money in elections within the bounds of the First Amendment. While there are profoundly good reasons behind this impulse, namely controlling the power of special interest groups and preserving a semblance of access and equality in the political sphere, there is some conflict between this policy inclination and the current tax treatment of charitable giving. This is particularly so as donors have turned to a range of intermediary organizations to transmit messages to the public relating to candidates and campaigns, where their gifts are not deductible, while also supporting think tanks and policy organizations that are less directly involved in elective and legislative matters but that still produce research and proposals that shape the national political agenda.[9]

While philanthropic institutions such as private foundations and gift funds can be used to make grants to organizations that qualify for tax-deductible contributions, donors have to make nondeductible, political gifts out of their own personal or business pockets. The distinction between the charitable nonprofits and political nonprofits ultimately only determines the origin of contributed funds, while doing little about the actual flow of funds. The lines between all the different organizations that engage in various ways in political life are thus hopelessly blurred, even though public policy draws black lines between what constitutes a tax-deductible gift and what does not. It is this false sense of clarity that requires serious rethinking.

Philanthropy is in some ways lucky. The entire struggle over boundaries and limits takes place within the context of classifying nonprofit organizations. Individual donors can simply give however they see fit as long as they understand that some gifts will be deemed charitable and others political. For institutional donors, the situation is a bit more complex. Private foundations usually focus on the support of 501(c)3 organizations. All of the emphasis on proper classification of recipient organizations and the tailoring of the tax treatment of gifts based on this classification represents an imperfect but likely necessary effort to encourage the expressive dimension of giving, while also tempering blind affirmation with a concern about access, equality, and fairness. Philanthropy has a significant speech component that deserves protection, but it also has a fair amount of capricious power that demands containment. With all its flaws and imprecision, the current policy regime is designed to come as close as possible to striking this balance.

Philanthropy without Borders

In recent decades, American donors have increasingly attempted to craft a relationship to the public sphere not just within but across national boundaries. As they have carried out their work, donors have tried to overcome their comparatively modest resources by experimenting with a wide array of tools and techniques aimed at improving the impact of their grantmaking.[10] Changes in the nature, size, and location of human problems over time have made this quest for impact crucial. Never has this been more the case than in recent years. One of the most important challenges that American donors have faced recently is the transformation of the playing field on which their grantmaking unfolds. For years, most donors have concentrated on discrete geographical areas, often the cities or regions around them, with the intention of using philanthropic dollars in a concentrated way. Yet as the nature, scope, and source of many human problems have changed, so too has the direction of the gaze of donors.[11]

As many issues have taken on simultaneously local, regional, national, and global dimensions, a few donors have come to recognize that their grantmaking must be integrated into broader social systems, directed at problems that have porous borders, and related to trends that are playing out in countries around the world.[12] Given the technical and logistic challenges that international giving presents, the majority of this special kind of philanthropy has been carried out by large foundations. In theory, there is little that prevents an individual donor from reaching out beyond the borders of the United States. In practice, however, international giving requires a substantial amount of resources and oversight to carry out effectively and to overcome the inherent difficulties of supporting an organization or cause that may be on the other side of the globe.[13]

The decision to focus giving on public problems outside the United States raises a number of interesting challenges for donors. While some narrow aspects of the philanthropic transaction look the same when carried out domestically and internationally, other elements change in significant ways.[14] Some of the more standard models of generating impact may prove difficult to implement in cultures that are substantially different from the United States, where the local nonprofit field is less developed, and where the tolerance of foreign government institutions for philanthropic interventions is lower. American donors, seeking to work overseas, must be sensitive to these differences and begin to craft a new approach to grantmaking that takes into consideration the powerful changes wrought by globalization.

International grantmaking includes both direct overseas funding and support of U.S.-based agencies with international activities. Historically, the majority of international grants have been made to U.S.-based agencies. Only a few large American foundations with broad overseas networks have been able to allocate a substantial portion of their international grants directly to foreign organizations. With the explosion of civil society worldwide in the 1980s and 1990s,[15] many donors worked to develop partnerships with local NGOs, cultivated relationships with intermediary organizations, and brought in new staff to increase their share of grants directly made to overseas organizations. These trends aside, deeper questions about ultimate ends lurk: What special challenges do international donors face as they attempt to shape public problem solving around the world? The answer depends on which of the core functions of giving presented in the previous chapter—change, innovation, equity, pluralism, or expression— is being pursued. But each poses special challenges when projected across national boundaries.

Many large American foundations are attracted to the idea of using their funds to intervene in political issues abroad, especially when these issues have global implications. Funding political change, be it through advocacy or grassroots mobilization, appears to be a relatively high-leverage proposition in that small amounts of money can purchase substantial amounts of influence and impact. When transposed to international giving, however, this political approach to philanthropy has a number of problems. Attempting to foment social and political change overseas can easily expose American donors to criticism of inappropriate meddling or even, in some circumstances, to charges of philanthropic imperialism.[16] Since many countries have weak civil societies and governments that grant only limited freedom to nonprofit organizations, inserting foreign philanthropic funds in the middle of pitched political battles can create a backlash against local civil society actors. For this reason, American philanthropy abroad must be especially sensitive to the unintended effects of their desire to see wholesale social and political change.

There is another consideration for American donors to consider before they attempt to shape policy or political arrangements overseas: Focusing on political action may overlook the local desire for more direct forms of assistance. Since civil society can be weak in developing countries where traditions of independent action do not exist, focusing giving on generating social and political change may assume a capacity for activities and interventions not present in local organizations. After all, effectuating complex advocacy, lobbying, and public information campaigns may often prove more challenging than providing direct services. In countries where civil societies are just forming, asking them to play a political role may be premature and assume a level of capacity and a breadth of contacts that simply is not present. International grantmakers must also guard against putting local nonprofits in untenable situations simply because American donors find the prospect of leverage associated with policy change attractive. Ultimately, work on social and political change must be grounded in local concerns and supported by organizations that have the capacity and expertise to carry out this kind of work. For all these reasons and others, donors need to be careful when applying this first classic model of philanthropic action outside the American context.

International philanthropy's adaptation of the role of program innovator has proven more complex than one might have thought. While American donors have regularly scoured the world for the best ideas and the most significant social innovations, donors have had less than complete success replicating and translating these innovations across borders. Perhaps the most publicized such effort involves microfinance, a movement to give small loans to poor people in order to help them create small businesses and improve their lives. While there is little doubt that the idea of microfinance has been promoted and replicated in countries around the world with significant foundation support, it remains unclear whether this replication proceeded before the underlying approaches and methodologies were fully understood and perfected. In seeking to fund innovations abroad, American foundations need to be careful not to engage in premature replication of programs based on early experiments, especially when the innovation is deeply embedded in local cultural contexts. Some of the most promising manifestations of civil society abroad may come in forms of action that are unfamiliar to outsiders and profoundly driven by local conditions and needs. Thus, as they make grants outside the United States, American foundations must not only seek out the best and most promising social innovations, but also remind themselves that what works in India may simply not be appropriate in Chile.

Redistributive giving often takes a local form, in which caring is expressed for those in the community who are less well off. The ability of foundations to execute a universal redistribution effort is limited, however, given the breadth of needs and the level of philanthropic resources available. This mismatch between needs and capacity becomes particularly imposing when the scope of giving spans national borders. Still, by transferring some funds from those with resources to those without, foundations can take a small step toward greater equality and sharing. Redistribution, albeit on a small scale, is at the heart of many of the oldest and most broadly supported social service organizations. These service providers are able to sustain themselves over long periods of time precisely because their missions are timeless and of broad appeal. Not surprisingly, the redistributive function of foundation giving is the least controversial of philanthropy functions.

In the context of international grantmaking, redistributive giving aimed at greater equity can take at least two major forms. The first is one that works with civil society in foreign lands to spread resources among local people. When redistribution is a local concept, the sphere of distributive justice is manageable.[17] The introduction of American dollars into other countries not only can make a difference, but the leverage these funds can generate overseas can be considerable. After all, the value of a charitable dollar—how far it will go and how much redistribution it will purchase— is far greater in Africa, for example, than in the United States. For this reason, American foundations have ample opportunity to use their funds overseas in ways that maximize impact for poor populations. However, when the concept of redistribution takes on a second, more expansive and global form, the prospects for a meaningful role for American philanthropy are diminished greatly, simply due to the resource limitations facing the field. If the goal of redistribution is to achieve global equity, foundations will have to confront the fact there is not enough money in American foundations to begin to tackle some of the gross inequities that beset the planet. Of course, foundations can and do try to make small and symbolic efforts at promoting global equity, funding labor movements and efforts aimed at influencing companies to pay better wages, but these efforts have had only very limited effect.[18]

As American foundations venture overseas, they have a unique opportunity to promote pluralism. In many societies where democratic norms and civic engagement are weak, working to expand the range and breadth of civil society actors is crucially important. Above and beyond accomplishing programmatic goals, American foundations need to have stable, diverse, and capable civil society organizations with which to work. Supporting pluralism is often tantamount to supporting capacity building and institution building. For American foundations, this sort of embracing and inclusive agenda, directed at building the number and quality of civil society actors, represents a central challenge that in many ways is a prerequisite to all of the other grand rationales for philanthropy. Without a capable and diverse universe of civil society organizations, the prospects of political change, innovation, and redistribution are very hard to achieve.

The last function of philanthropy in the international domain is the most contested, and the one that raises the toughest ethical dilemmas. International giving can be about the expressive needs of the donors, but there are sensitive questions attached to this function when the psychic satisfaction of the donor is purchased at the expense of poor and disenfranchised people who are safely separated from the donor. As the distances and cultural divides widen through international giving, the power asymmetry in philanthropy tends to become more acute. For this reason, the idea that international giving can be a potent source of satisfaction and contentment for donors is difficult for many to accept. After all, affirming this role is tantamount to endorsing philanthropic tourism. Donors may glean real pleasure from their cross-border philanthropic adventures, particularly when such experiences allow them to connect to new issues and people. However, the ability of donors to enact their values and commitments becomes troublesome when those on the receiving end of this projection often have little option but to accept the giving, no matter the consequences, simply because resources are scarce and conditions are desperate. One way in which the satisfaction of the donor can be achieved is through the support of organizations or regions with which the donor is familiar. International giving often proceeds with the assumption that those in positions of authority know best, when in reality this is a contested proposition.

Each of the five functions of philanthropy can be and to a greater or lesser extent has been pursued across national borders. Yet the application of American philanthropic funds around the world raises special challenges related to each of these functions. Within the context of globalization, the ability of foundations to promote social change, to pursue programmatic innovation, to redistribute wealth, to affirm pluralism, and to meet the needs of donors is contingent on a number of new factors, many of which lie well outside the control of the foundations. In this sense, globalization raises a set of new challenges for American donors, especially when it comes to applying any existing rationales for philanthropy to the work of international giving.

Changing giving from something done in the comfort and security of one's own backyard to something that spans national boundaries will happen only if the benefits of international giving outweigh the costs. International giving does have a strong appeal because of its own inherent financial leverage: dollars spent overseas buy more than dollars spent at home. While no philanthropic price index exists that would compare the cost of creating a new clinic in San Francisco with one in Ethiopia, it is fair to say that operating in developing nations is less expensive than in industrialized nations, even if one were to factor in the additional oversight and management challenges that would be involved. This is in large part due to a huge difference in wages among nations, a critical element in the overall cost of delivering nonprofit services because so many are labor intensive. Beyond labor cost savings, there are also large differences in the cost of acquiring land and buildings, which make the establishment of more permanent programs easier overseas than in the United States. The cost savings, however, are not enough in themselves to justify transnational giving.

A better argument is that international grantmaking can be a potent tool for the construction of bridging social capital, which manifests itself in linkages of trust that transcend traditional boundaries and comfort zones. By getting away from the communities and contexts that are familiar, donors who do venture overseas are putting themselves in a position to learn and grow philanthropically. It is very easy for donors to become comfortable with the status quo and the grantmaking patterns they have established. New friendships that cross boundaries of class, race, and nationality can emerge through grantmaking with a more global perspective. Donors can escape some of the constraints and patterns of action that often are embedded in local communities with well-established philanthropic traditions. In the process, they can experiment with new forms of helping and caring that are not bound by expectations of others based on prior experience. By looking across large distances for philanthropic opportunities, donors can not only meet new people and build new friendships and alliances, but also take steps toward reinventing themselves.

To enjoy the privilege of doing more than just reinforcing existing local bonds, donors may have to sacrifice in the short run. After all, there will be a decrease in invitations to special galas, openings, and plaque exchanging ceremonies, which follow from the simple disbursal of grants within a defined community. It is hard to break out of the strong bonds that often connect a donor to the local community, but the rewards can be significant. Working in communities abroad can open the eyes of donors and constitute a crash course on the cultures of other countries. International giving exposes a donor to a different set of problems and issues than usual, and in the process forces the donor to rethink many assumptions. Some of the insights and fresh perspectives gained by learning about a new society can later on be useful in revisiting the assumptions guiding a donor's domestic giving. While few donors would want to think of their giving as a classroom in which they are the main student, the learning that philanthropy promotes will be more intensive depending on how far it pushes the donor's horizon and core assumptions.

There are several challenges that must be overcome for international grantmaking to truly become a major part of American giving. The first is that new tools and information are needed to overcome the information gap that often lies at the heart of the resistance to this kind of giving. Some refer to this gap as a "contract failure" that makes it hard for the donors supporting the delivery of charitable services to be certain that needy users receive quality assistance. As the distance between the financer of a charitable activity and the end user of the funded programs becomes great, there is a need to overcome this contract failure. One way to resolve this issue under the American system is for nonprofit organizations to adhere to the nondistribution constraint, which prohibits the diversion of surplus revenues to insiders and requires that these revenues be applied to mission-related purposes. In the international context, the strength of local nonprofit regulatory and oversight regimes is weak enough to make it hard for American donors to have much confidence that others will protect their investments. For this reason, donors will find it useful to have some personal knowledge and experience with the country where they chose to work.

As the relevance of national boundaries has decreased and as important human problems increasingly span these boundaries, American philanthropy is facing a wake-up call to broaden its outlook. New intermediaries that connect American donors to carefully screened projects abroad are emerging in greater numbers. These institutions are helping to overcome some of the potential contract failure that might occur without the presence of some local knowledge. These institutions are lowering the barriers to entry to international grantmaking and allowing donors with relatively modest resources to connect to causes and projects in faraway locations. The future of American philanthropy lies not only at home but abroad. With boundaries fading and problems becoming more universal, American philanthropy will find an ever stronger imperative to think and act transnationally.

Government and Philanthropy: Four Relationships

At home, American philanthropy is shaped by government through regulation and the application of subsidies. Still, donors are to some extent in a position to set the terms of their relationship with government.[19] There are four main ways in which this relationship between philanthropy and government can be fashioned. Each has its advantages and disadvantages, and each has consequences for the nature of the actual philanthropic work that is to be done by donors.[20]

The first option is to see giving as being in a supplementary relationship to government. If government at the federal, state, or local level happens to be working in the same programmatic area of a particular donor, the supplementary model would suggest that philanthropy track what the public sector is doing and look for opportunities to add funds where needed in order to strengthen the public sector's ability to meet needs. In this conception of the relationship, government is driving the process and has primary responsibility for choosing causes and issues. Philanthropy's role is to dutifully add to this agenda by working in fields and in places where government, for one reason or another, is in need of help. Seeing philanthropy as supplementary eases some of the burdens on donors because it does not ask that philanthropy break new ground or solve long-standing problems;

instead it focuses on resources and works toward supporting and extending government's agenda. Whether philanthropic resources are adequate to this task is difficult to know since accounts vary greatly, both in terms of which government programs need to be privately supplemented and in terms of how large philanthropic resources are likely to be over time. Lingering doubts about this supplementary conception have been explored through empirical examinations of whether government funding actually crowds out private giving. Far from inviting giving into areas where government is working, the crowding-out hypothesis suggests that public funding will drive away donors and work against a supplementary relationship. Evidence suggests that even though this effect may exist, its magnitude is relatively small.[21]

Regardless of its feasibility or significance, the idea of philanthropy mirroring government is problematic at least in terms of the consequences it would have for the expressive and instrumental content of giving. Even the most ardent advocate for greater equity and efficiency in philanthropy would blanch at the idea that philanthropy's unfettered resources should be principally devoted to doing what government could do through greater levels of taxation. The argument against a supplementary role for philanthropy in social provision is that it would push giving too far away from its expressive, personalistic side and in the process shut down a major motive behind giving: the desire to enact one's values through charitable action. While there might be plenty of overlap between public priorities and private charitable interests, this coincidence in purposes takes on a different form depending on whether it is the happy result of circumstances or the product of directive public policy designed to achieve it through new subsidies or regulation.

Philanthropy can assume a second posture in relation to government by defining for itself a complementary role. Instead of simply tracking government priorities and supplementing public expenditures where needed, philanthropy can seek to define a relationship whose central feature is the sensible and productive division of labor between sectors. As government does its work, it inevitably leaves many public needs unattended, not only because funds are limited for discretionary programs, but also because some groups have more ability to press their case for support than others. Organization in the form of lobbying and advocacy can shape the allocation of public funds in ways that may not be entirely equitable. For philanthropy, this problem can be an opportunity. Locating significant gaps in funding and helping groups that have been left outside the political process voice their concerns and needs can be a potent and valuable role for philanthropy. When donors seek out and fill gaps that are left by government, they can correct "government failure" and also bring into public view the needs of citizens which may have been obscured for long periods of time. If successful in crafting a complementary role to government, philanthropy can thus serve both as a funder of last resort and as a social spotlight, shining attention on issues and problems that have not been seen or heard enough.

There is at least one significant problem with the idea of philanthropy complementing government and filling the funding gaps that it creates. Philanthropy cannot really be effective if its agenda and focus are driven by forces outside the field and if its primary mode of operation is reactive. There is some danger that if donors spend their time seeking to isolate significant gaps in public funding and then providing philanthropic resources needed to close these gaps, an important element in creative philanthropy will be lost: the capacity of donors to shape agendas in ways that others inside and outside of government may never have even considered. In this sense, the challenge for funders who adopt a complementary role in relation to government is to hold on to the power of initiative that allows donors to move ahead with ideas and projects even when evidence and support for their work is just emerging or not even present. Philanthropy should be thinking thoughts, drawing up plans, and supporting the execution of programs that government has not even thought of supporting. It is very hard for donors to be in the vanguard if they are simply looking for gaps to fill in the current programmatic landscape.

To counter the constraining character of complementary relations, donors can take a third approach to structuring their relations with government. Donors can strike up and maintain an adversarial relationship with government, one in which philanthropy actively challenges the assumptions of the public sector and works to counter its influence. Thus, rather than look either to supplement or complement, donors can pursue philanthropic agendas that are actively geared toward counterbalancing and reversing wrong directions and bad choices made by government. As an adversary, philanthropy may have to rely to some extent on government to set the direction, albeit in a contrarian sort of way. As an adversary, philanthropy needs to know what government's priorities and programs are in order to work in the opposite direction, be it by delivering services differently or supporting policies that run counter to the dominant paradigm. There is a relatively small component of organized philanthropy that has adopted an adversarial position with regard to government. With a heavy emphasis on radical politics, community empowerment, and progressive policies, some funders of social change have declared that there is already plenty of money supporting mainstream approaches to political and social problems and that the real opportunities lie in supporting causes that stand in stark opposition to the status quo.

The problem with an adversarial stance is that it assumes disagreement about policy as a starting point and then builds an agenda based on this assumption. Not only is it limiting for philanthropy to focus on what government does, it also makes little sense to constrain giving simply to challenging and reversing in often small and symbolic ways the broader policy direction of the country. Rather than start with the question "What do I oppose?" donors are probably much better off, all things considered, starting with the more basic question of "What do I believe and stand for?" Only by starting with the more affirmative question will donors have the opportunity to convert their most deeply held convictions into charitable activity rather than simply pursuing the more alienating and impersonal work of mounting a political opposition. While being a force of opposition might engage and satisfy a donor with a penchant for taking unpopular positions, it is unlikely that remaining in an adversarial role indefinitely will produce the kind of psychic feedback that is needed to generate long-lasting enthusiasm for giving. Just as supplementary and complementary roles are too limiting for donors, so too is an adversarial approach. Given the tremendous freedom of philanthropy, it would be a shame to give over large amounts of this freedom to the narrow cause of opposition.

Thankfully, a fourth main option is open to donors. Philanthropy can define for itself an autonomous relationship from government, one in which the direction of giving is sheltered from policy directives emanating from government. Absolute autonomy is hard to achieve. By its very nature, philanthropy is active in the public sphere and will frequently collide, overlap, and interact with government programs and policies. However, there is a meaningful difference between having these points of intersection as the result of mission pursuit grounded in independent consideration of philanthropic interests and opportunities and having them as the product of a careful calculus resulting in a decision grounded in the decisions taken by public sector agencies. Still, in defining a posture in relation to government, both individual and institutional donors can consciously craft for themselves a relationship in which plenty of distance is maintained between the sides and in which philanthropy is able to act in a proactive way to address the social problems that emerge. To do so requires more work than taking any of the other three postures toward government, in which a more reactive mode of operation is possible. To act autonomously, philanthropy needs the guidance not only of efficient administrators and processors of applications but also of visionary leaders who are capable of analyzing community needs creatively and then developing innovative responses.

There are several good arguments for encouraging philanthropy to doggedly guard its autonomy. The first is that any of the first three options for philanthropy's interaction with government essentially put giving at something of a disadvantage: Public policy is seen as the trigger and benchmark that drives private giving in one direction or another. Looking too closely at what other actors are doing, even when it is an actor as significant as government, can be a significant mistake akin to looking for a key under the lamppost simply because that is where the light is located. Donors can reserve for themselves the right to work in areas that government has not yet even identified as worthy of public sector attention or that are too controversial for policy to address. To preserve the capacity of the field to innovate—not only at the level of the design of intervention but also at the level of the conceptualization of public needs—donors need at least some space between their work and that of government.

How can donors sensibly navigate this difficult terrain and establish a relationship between their giving and existing public priorities? The answer lies in the difficult work of finding causes that connect to their values and passions and that intervene effectively in the world to produce significant public benefits. This is nothing other than the core challenge of philanthropy, one that pushes donors to make difficult choices about all the elements involved in giving, including the value to be produced, the logic model to be pursued, the vehicles to be deployed, the style to be adopted, and the time frame that will guide the effort. While there are many ways in which government and philanthropy can and do interact productively through partnerships, the probability that alignment and fit will be achieved will be higher if donors claim—at least during the early stages of the philanthropic work—a fair amount of autonomy. Freedom from external constraints and expectations is ultimately critical to donors being able to deliver on the promise of more strategic forms of giving.

Elaborating the relationship of philanthropy to government is an important exercise because private giving and public policy have one important thing in common: a desire to improve the well-being of others. In this shared endeavor, private philanthropy need not track, imitate, or supplement government, however. Indeed, one of the central claims in this book is that the special interaction of private values and public purposes in philanthropy is what gives giving its distinctive identity and the opportunity to make a significant contribution to the public sphere. With all the freedom enjoyed by philanthropy come some self-imposed constraints, however. Donors worry about the effectiveness of their giving (even if government is not watching closely or rewarding donors who perform well through incentives), the accountability of their philanthropic efforts (even if the reporting requirements are minimal), and their own fundamental legitimacy as private actors working on behalf of the public. With a forgiving policy framework around it, American philanthropy depends heavily on the donors themselves to address these challenges.

2. Central Problems in Philanthropy: Effectiveness, Accountability, and Legitimacy

The very idea that something called "central problems in philanthropy" might exist could strike some as odd. After all, philanthropy is a field in which donors give freely to others, and it is hard to imagine why there would be any problems at all associated with the simple exercise of generosity. The philanthropic exchange linking donor and recipient can take innumerable forms, but the basic structure of the relationship remains fairly straightforward. Donors and recipients are joined in an act of giving and getting.[1] Even though this voluntary transfer of resources seems simple, it can and does create a number of complex challenges for both sides, particularly when the amounts of money changing hands is significant and when the public needs to be addressed are substantial. Today, there can be little doubt that important problems lurk within both individual and institutional giving, and that leaders within the field have expended large amounts of effort and resources searching for solutions. At the core of the angst within philanthropy are three complex and intertwined issues that have long confronted donors of all kinds: effectiveness, accountability, and legitimacy.

It is hard to imagine a donor faced with the choice of "being effective" or "being ineffective" who would consciously opt for ineffectiveness. People engage in giving because they want to accomplish something, either for someone else or for themselves, or for both. In all three cases, if being effective means achieving one's stated objectives, effectiveness is as close to a universal aspiration in the balkanized field of philanthropy as one is likely to encounter. The problem is that this consensus is thin and has little practical meaning. Donors do not agree on how to define philanthropic objectives, how to assess whether they have been realized, and, perhaps most important of all, how to use knowledge and experience to improve their work over time.[2]

The second major problem in the field today is accountability. One of the nagging issues in philanthropy today is whether donors are ever held adequately accountable for their giving. The accountability issue arises in part from the tax deduction that donors receive for their giving, but it also is connected to the power donors have to use resources to enact agendas. Interestingly, the accountability issue is more pressing in some parts of the field than in others. For individual donors who operate quietly or who give only modest amounts of money, there are rarely groups complaining about access, transparency, and fairness. For large institutional donors, including private, corporate, and community foundations, the accountability issue is far more pressing. These donors face several organized and mobilized watchdog groups that do nothing but monitor and critique foundation practices. At the center of the accountability issue is the concern that philanthropy's fundamental power asymmetry between donor and recipient makes it very hard to create accountability systems appropriate for a field that now delivers hundreds of billions of dollars a year.

Lurking within all of this is the bigger question of philanthropic legitimacy, an issue that rarely gets explored and debated. Legitimacy is a touchy issue in philanthropy. Fueled by private wealth but directed at producing public benefits, philanthropy has a built-in tension. On the one hand, one is tempted to ask who has the right to say anything about how individuals and institutions carry out their philanthropic work. These are private funds that supplement public programs and they should simply be welcomed as a voluntary contribution to the improvement of society. On the other hand, one wonders who exactly these wealthy actors are to take it unto themselves to interpret public needs and to act as miniature and undemocratic regimes. There is a part of philanthropy, the speaking for others without their consent or consultation, that seems to require a fair amount of hubris and is off-putting to some. Given this tension, one can reasonably ask when and why the exercise of philanthropic power is just and rightful. It is this line of thought that leads directly to the question of what makes philanthropy legitimate.

Naturally, the issues of effectiveness, accountability, and legitimacy intersect and interact frequently. In the absence of good measurement of goal achievement and effectiveness, many donors turn to measures of the quality of their grantmaking process and emphasize their transparency, clarity of purpose, and accountability. Similarly, when charges are leveled that donors have not acted responsibly in the way they have disbursed funds, the indictment often comes in the form of complaints about missed opportunities, lack of impact, and generally ineffective grantmaking. Effectiveness and accountability are thus joined at the hip. Unaccountable donors are seen as ineffective and ineffective donors are portrayed as unaccountable. Above effectiveness and accountability hovers the larger and less well understood concept of legitimacy: Effectiveness and accountability are necessary but not sufficient elements of philanthropic legitimacy. Are there other important problems facing the field of philanthropy? Of course there are. However, during my three-year-long conversation with leading individual donors and foundation executives, effectiveness, accountability, and—in a more implicit way—legitimacy were the challenges that came up time and time again as infuriatingly nagging and ultimately unresolved.

Effectiveness

When thinking about philanthropic effectiveness, one of the first and most perplexing questions is whose effectiveness is at issue. One popular option is to define effectiveness in terms of the work done by those who receive philanthropic support. Under such a conception of effectiveness, a donor would monitor and track the work of grant recipients and do whatever is possible to increase the likelihood that these nonprofits succeed. Effectiveness is thus something that is constructed in the world through the hard work of those who receive grants. Accordingly, for donors, doing well means picking good organizations to support and claiming some credit for the public benefits that arise from others' work. This conception of effectiveness can be called "program effectiveness" because it focuses attention on the programmatic work of recipient organizations. This is not the only way to think of philanthropic effectiveness. There is a second way to define the concept, which instead of looking outward and assessing the performance of recipient organizations, looks inside at the quality of the grant-making that is being done by the donor, writ large. This second conception of effectiveness can be termed "mission effectiveness" because it points our attention to how well donors are doing at achieving their stated goals or missions. Mission effectiveness is not simply the sum of the programmatic effects achieved by nonprofits, but instead is related to the quality of strategy and level of execution achieved by the donor. This is an extremely complex conception of effectiveness that raises a whole host of problems when it comes to measurement.

It is hardly surprising therefore that the field of philanthropy today is very much focused on the first definition of effectiveness, and many donors have invested heavily in evaluation in order to report on what has happened to their funds once they have been spent. One reason program effectiveness is so much more appealing than mission effectiveness is that it casts the spotlight of evaluation outward and provides donors not just with a buffer against criticism (both internal and external), but also with a set of well-established protocols, procedures, and tools that can be used to carry out assessments. Armies of consultants and technical assistance providers await the call of major donors to go out and measure the performance of grant recipients. Moreover, many donors simply think of their ultimate impact in terms of what recipients do and do not even raise the question of mission effectiveness. As one foundation leader noted: "Because we have kind of a nonspecific program goal, we operate our foundations under an operating plan rather than a formal business plan. We're trying to work with the grantees' mission and business plan rather than our own mission and business plan. And our performance measures are linked to the mission and objectives of the grantees."

Program effectiveness data is viewed as more valuable and usable than mission effectiveness data. It can be used to justify continuation or termination of support to nonprofit organizations. It can be used, in principle at least, to ensure some measure of rationality to the disbursement of funds within the recipient population, with more effective organizations receiving more support than organizations that are less successful at achieving social objectives, be it counseling AIDS sufferers so that they can receive proper treatment or helping the homeless to lead fuller lives. Armed with good data on which organizations are more effective compared to their peers, donors could both use their philanthropic resources more effectively and guard against criticism that philanthropic decisions were based on something other than merit.

The problem with using program effectiveness as a tool to bring reason and fairness to philanthropy lies in the primitive and imprecise nature of almost all forms of performance measurement in the nonprofit sector. Even in those areas where performance data are present and usable (for example, test scores for students in schools, job placement statistics for job training and employment service providers, and relapse rates for drug treatment centers), significant obstacles are still present. In very few cases do nonprofits attempt to control other factors that might influence the program outcomes (parents' education level and involvement with students, the state of the economy for the prospects of unemployed persons, and the number of prior attempts at rehabilitation for drug users). In short, the performance data that are used in the nonprofit sector are often incomplete, unreliable, and incommensurable. Measures of program effectiveness are almost never taken using formal experimental techniques (control and treatment groups) and almost always have a number of assumptions embedded within them that, depending on how these assumptions are addressed or not addressed, can and do often materially affect the conclusions of the evaluation. Regardless of these technical limitations, the concept of program effectiveness has largely triumphed over the concept of mission effectiveness.

Still, there are profound obstacles to reaching a broader, more meaningful understanding of effectiveness that transcends the calculus about whether individual programs "worked" or not. When discussing these issues, leaders in philanthropy expressed a broad concern that an aggregation problem was blocking the way to a more encompassing definition of mission effectiveness: "My guess is if every nonprofit organization pursued effectiveness a little more aggressively, performance would increase. But that's at an organizational level. When we extrapolate from that organizational level, I do not understand what that is." The difficulty in summing up nonprofit results is so great that one donor worries about losing track of the entire topic of effectiveness unless it is grounded in small and petty measures or short-term results in discrete programmatic areas: "Whenever we aggregate, whenever we go up to 30,000 feet, I get lost in the clouds, because we are comparing apples and oranges. It is awfully hard. It's a real struggle to even figure out effectiveness at an organizational level, because so much of the ultimate results can't be measured. If you can't do it at the organizational level, I'm really struggling with how to think about aggregating. How would you even think about that?"

Further complicating the measurement problems related to program effectiveness is the issue of the relative size, timing, and conditions under which a philanthropic contribution is delivered. Consider the following two scenarios. In the first scenario, a donor is lucky enough to receive over the transom a proposal from a promising organization that is looking to expand its operations. After careful consideration, a site visit, and persistent questioning about the proposed budget, a small grant is made in support of the organization at the urging of other funders. The grant represents only 5 percent of the total needed by the organization to execute its growth strategy and it arrives late in the process. Eventually, the nonprofit draws national attention for its innovative and effective programs. The donor demands a detailed financial and narrative report, then places links to the news stories of the organization's success on the donor's Web site, trumpeting its partnership with the organization. Was the donor effective?

Consider a second scenario. A donor in the course of actively scanning the local nonprofit community for promising new developments hears about an exciting but underfunded organization. The donor reaches out to the organization, listens and learns about the nonprofit's desire to grow, helps meet the technical assistance and planning needs of the organization, provides a large proportion of the funds need for the expansion, and encourages other funders, including the donor in the first scenario, to provide the remaining pieces of support that are needed. When the recognition and publicity arrives, the donor points the media to the organization's leaders and works to make sure that other nonprofits working in the same field learn about the programmatic breakthroughs achieved by the organization.

The purpose of these two very different giving scenarios is simply to highlight that the issue of program effectiveness in philanthropy cannot be separated from the issue of the relative philanthropic contribution provided by a donor. Effectiveness—even the narrow concept of program effectiveness—requires that there be a meaningful causal link between the giving and the results. Effectiveness requires a certain proximity to the reality of nonprofit organizations, not distance. Giving a meaningful amount of money is but one way to meet this test of causal proximity. Other ways include being first among funders to make the philanthropic leap, providing support over time not just episodically, giving sound advice when needed, and helping recipients access other resources. No matter how a donor chooses to do more than provide a small check, the question will be whether the programmatic achievements of those who received support were in any meaningful way attributable to the donor's giving. Establishing a causal connection—or even a plausible attribution—is never easy. Still, the more the donor does to make a gift meaningful, the greater the chance that claims of effectiveness will be supportable in the future.

The issue of mission effectiveness takes on very different meanings depending on whether one is talking about individual or institutional donors. For individuals, being effective has several possible meanings owing to the fact that individual donors often seek both to do good work in the world and to feel good about themselves. There are both instrumental and expressive purposes behind individual giving. The instrumental purposes, focused on accomplishing a set of defined social objectives, are those that are most clearly connected with the issue of effectiveness; being effective comes down to being technically proficient at achieving the philanthropic goals one has defined. There are, however, more expressive goals connected to giving that have little to do with concerns over the achievement of social outcomes and more to do with the feelings and experiences of the donor. The expressive purposes in philanthropy are often neglected or even condemned as self-serving and insignificant. For many individuals that give, the notion of effectiveness involves, to a greater or lesser extent, some psychic satisfaction from the act of giving, experienced either in the form of the simple pleasure of expressing caring or in the feelings of solidarity donors enjoy when translating their wealth into some measure of greater happiness for others. The greater the extent an individual donor is focused on the expressive aspect of giving, the more trivial some of the persistent questions about effectiveness appear. For one expressive donor, what counts is the feeling of satisfaction and reward that philanthropy brings, above and beyond the actual worldly effects it might produce: "I take the position that [giving] is highly personal and that this notion of homogenizing the field in some way is not a very productive one . . . I'm literally trying to find what God's will is for my money and life, which is not to say that I'm always clear about what that is, but I'm at least working at it." The fact that many individual donors believe being effective comes down to using philanthropy to enact their personal and spiritual beliefs highlights the gulf that often exists between individual and institutional givers. Some foundations with living donors have to straddle this line: "There's a big difference between the institutional and the individual donor. I'm right in the middle. My donor's values are in the organization, and we'll probably try to keep them for as many generations as the business is involved in the philanthropy . . . Yet, we're using the business's tools to try to accomplish the family's values." Depending on the role of the donor in the philanthropic process, the expressive dimension to giving can pose a real challenge to nailing down in tight instrumental terms the full meaning of effectiveness.

When giving moves from individuals to professionally managed institutions no longer controlled by the founder or family, the stakes connected to effectiveness increase notably. While most individual donors are moved by some mix of expressive and instrumental purposes, institutions like foundations—particularly those managed by staff who have no connection to or knowledge of the founding donor—are rarely animated by anything other than a desire to use funds efficiently and effectively. The introduction of agency brings a clinical rigor and discipline to grantmaking and changes the whole nature of the question of effectiveness. Because philanthropic agents are unable to convey to a donor absent from the scene any psychic benefits from giving, boards and staff tend to concentrate on maximizing the public benefits generated through philanthropy. The professionalization of large segments of institutional philanthropy in recent decades has been an important development because it has moved the target of philanthropy and the focus of the concept of effectiveness away from the satisfaction of the donor and toward the production of public and community benefits.

When companies give, the agnosticism and impersonalism of philanthropy grow even greater, and the effectiveness questions become starker. Most companies want to assist the communities in which the company operates and reach directly or indirectly the customers that rely on their products. Effective corporate giving thus comes down to finding ways to act philanthropically that produce tangible benefits not just for others, but for the company as well. Corporate philanthropy truly does involve both "give and take." While there are a small number of companies that are animated purely by strongly held social purposes, most corporate donors want their giving to contribute to the company's bottom line, either by enhancing marketing efforts, improving government relations, or creating good public relations.[3] Effectiveness is not so much linked to the outcomes that are produced by grants, but rather by the impact philanthropy has on the company's overall competitive position. This is a meaningful difference compared to other forms of philanthropy in which the interests of the donor are far more hidden and subordinated to the public purposes being pursued.

While it may be hard to pin down the meaning of effectiveness across individual and institutional auspices, in listening to leaders of the largest American foundations and major individual donors discuss for three years the central challenges in their field, I have heard a number of different traits of effective donors offered as an alternative to any universal definition of philanthropic effectiveness. Four signal traits emerged, which taken together begin to outline what an effective donor might look like, even if the precise nature of philanthropic effectiveness remains difficult to define and measure: a willingness to act decisively and opportunistically, a capacity to collaborate and leverage resources, a willingness to fight in order to win the battle of the day, and an orientation that allows room for dynamic learning over time.

Given all the questions and doubts that almost all large requests for funding raise, it is surprising that any money is ever given away. The uncertainty and doubts that can plague even the most confident donor make it hard to reach philanthropic decisions. Nevertheless, philanthropic leaders seem to agree that decisiveness is very important in philanthropy. Timing is important; this means that many giving decisions must be reached swiftly so that the funds in question can be put to use when they are most useful. Connected to the issue of decisiveness is the need for opportunism. Instead of planning and strategizing about how to use resources to maximize a set of social outcomes selected by the donor, one approach described started with a question about where the best grantmaking opportunities were to be found and constructed a set of expectations about effectiveness based on situational variables. Rather than saying that a funder is effective if it finds a way to achieve its objective, one could say that a funder is effective if it uses its resources to help organizations accomplish their missions. This idea of effectiveness as opportunistic giving thus starts with the environment within which the donor operates and seeks to use nonprofit capacity to its fullest—no matter if it might lead the donor to go off in directions that seem new and untested.

Because philanthropic resources are limited, even within the largest foundations, there is a sense in which effectiveness must be linked to collaboration. Without leveraging resources from other funders, few donors can hope to achieve a real and lasting impact on large and complex problems.[5] "The real uncharted territory is how effectiveness translates into the field as a whole. And by that I mean our ability to work collectively in groupings, how foundations and philanthropic organizations can consolidate their information and their knowledge into one base of information, how we can work together in networks . . . to do things collectively and how interventions taken in the philanthropic sector can relate to those taken in other sectors." The underlying assumption here is that donors need to collaborate in fighting major social problems in order to stand a chance of being effective. This is a notion that is in some tension with the idea of opportunistic giving, in which impact is a function of the selection of the appropriate nonprofit partner rather than a search for agreement among donors on what to do. While not incompatible, it demands a different focus and approach.

Another key to effectiveness in philanthropy may come down to the instinct to win and prevail over opponents. Philanthropy was characterized by one large individual donor as a kind of war, pitting soldiers armed with money on different sides of issues against one another: "Philanthropy is like war. We're continuously fighting with somebody else who thinks that their sense of good is better than our sense of good." This construction of effectiveness does not emphasize a rational search for ways to collaborate and cooperate. Instead, it looks at who wins and assigns a judgment about effectiveness based on the nasty, brutish, and unattractive reality of which donor is able to emerge victorious from the battle for impact. By switching the focus from the process of giving to the results of the programs that donors fund, the war metaphor draws our attention to the fact that for every philanthropic action there is, more often than not, an equal reaction. Being effective means countering the forces aligned against one's agenda and getting movement in a particular direction. There are at least three types of funding situations, only one of which is conflict free: "One of them is that kind of philanthropy where there is broad agreement on the goal as well as on the methods [e.g., arts]. The second one is where there is broad agreement on the goal but not on the methodologies [e.g., education]. The third one is where there's absolutely no agreement on the goal [e.g., gay rights]." Being effective and measuring is particularly difficult in the second and third situations, because there is underlying disagreement about ends and/or means. Still, effectiveness can be seen as being related directly to winning in conflict-ridden situations.

Even if donors can achieve the results they want, it is certainly not clear that the world will remain the same over time and that what works once will work again. Unfortunately, it is equally uncertain that donors who fail to achieve their objective take full advantage of the learning that can follow failure. Another trait of effective donors is thus the ability to learn from experience, to adjust on the go, and to move forward using information and data gathered through practice. As one foundation leader explained: "One of the things that has been most striking for me [in philanthropy] is the lack of feedback loops. Organizations have feedback loops. Children learn because there's feedback, you touch the hot thing and you get burned. Your parents say do this, don't do that. In philanthropy, the quality and amount of feedback is limited and this limits the ability of donors to become more effective over time." To be effective, donors must be willing to study what works but also be flexible enough to realize that what worked in the past may not work in the future. Only a continuous series of assessments and reassessments of decisions will do, as a large institutional funder explained: "In business, performance changes over time and must be studied dynamically over time. This means checking and rechecking information that comes back and using it to make an endless series of adjustments all aimed at improving performance. In philanthropy, a similar dynamic learning is needed to be effective." On this account, effectiveness turns out to be something that emerges from an interactive process of experimentation and learning or what one donor called "a relentless self-examination" leading to continuous learning.

The multiple meanings of effectiveness are complicated by the split between institutional and individual donors. The definition of effectiveness and the urgency of its call vary considerably across these two groups. Institutional donors tend to possess a strong desire to see concrete evidence that their philanthropy is making a difference and are willing to spend a great deal of time and money trying to wrestle with their effectiveness and then to link it to institutional accountability. Getting results is a mandate that starts with the foundation board, is conveyed to the CEO, and then is passed on to the staff that do the bulk of the grantmaking work. Throughout this chain of command, there is usually an earnest drive to act as a reliable steward of the charitable funds that have been left behind by the donor. For individual donors who are alive and in charge of their giving, the calling of effectiveness may be just as strong, though it may be tempered by other considerations. The desire to achieve results can be a function of the more general tendency toward success and achievement that allowed the donor to accumulate wealth in the first place. However, there is one significant difference. This impulse is not complicated by the same issues of agency and stewardship that are present in foundations. The issue of effectiveness for individuals may also be tempered by the desire to enact commitments and values by supporting causes, even if it is difficult to know what the ultimate results may be. In this sense, individual donors have both an instrumental interest in philanthropy and expressive needs, the latter of which is not as strongly manifest among institutional donors.

Philanthropic Failure: Between Effectiveness and Accountability

Because the idea of philanthropic effectiveness raises a host of difficult definitional and conceptual issues, it is helpful to look at the other side of the question by examining what ineffectiveness actually looks like in philanthropy. Donors have many ideas of what effective grantmaking might entail and enjoy talking about the topic, but few want to spend much time defining and clarifying the nature and causes of ineffective and unsuccessful grantmaking—especially if the examples hit too close to home. Still, if one is to take seriously the idea of dynamic learning as a central trait of effective donors, then examining and understanding the meaning of failure becomes important. Understanding the varieties of failures that occur in philanthropy is also a useful entry point to the second major issue in the field today, namely accountability.

On the surface, there appears to be little reason for donors to be reticent about accepting and discussing both success and failure. No matter how philanthropic decisions turn out, the huge endowments of foundations and the wealth of individual donors provide a powerful shield that allows these privileged institutions and powerful individuals to roll along quietly and securely. For most donors, the mailbag is always full of new proposals, and a long line of grant applicants are delighted to accept their largesse, regardless of how well or poorly a donor has performed in the past. Unlike government, which must worry about public opinion, and unlike business firms, which must respond to shareholders, donors do not face a demanding constituency or a rigorous market test. Ultimately, there is no hostile audience in the nonprofit sector to which philanthropic failures must be reported, nor any profound repercussion from admitting that some grants go awry or fail. Yet donors remain strangely skittish about communicating evaluation results and discussing their failures.[6]

Though not a popular subject, failure in philanthropy is important because it cuts across a range of stakeholders and issues. It touches both donors, whose decisions are implicated, and nonprofit managers, whose performance is scrutinized. In addition, talking about program outcomes also raises a number of important issues about what functions the nonprofit sector can and cannot realistically be expected to perform in society. An open discussion of grant outcomes may be a first step in bringing some reality and frankness to the distorted communication between foundations and their grant recipients. It may also represent a first step toward giving the concept of effectiveness some real meaning.

What exactly is a failed grant? In philanthropy, a failed grant is not simply one that underwrites an ineffective program or an unsuccessful intervention. In this sense, it is wrong to equate failure in nonprofit program management with failure in philanthropy. Failure in philanthropy is a far more complex and variegated phenomenon, which is defined less by the actual program outcome and more on the knowledge—or lack thereof—generated by the funded initiative. It is ultimately necessary to distinguish two fundamental forms of failure: one constructive and the other unconstructive. The difference between the two kinds of failure comes down to knowledge creation. While all failed grants start with ineffective programs, constructive failures create value by helping us understand what went wrong and adding to the reservoir of understanding across the field. By contrast, unconstructive failures produce no new knowledge to inform future practice. The challenge for foundations in the future is to gain a greater understanding of constructive failures and to begin appreciating them as central to the diagnostic function of foundations. A pair of recent examples highlight the difference between these two kinds of failures in philanthropy.

From 1982 to 1988, the Rockefeller Foundation provided grants to four community-based organizations in cities around the country to operate employment training programs for minority single mothers. The goal of the Minority Female Single Parent (MFSP) demonstration was to determine whether comprehensive employment training and counseling services could reduce welfare dependency and enhance self-sufficiency. The four projects were conducted by capable organizations: the Atlanta Urban League in Atlanta, Georgia; the Opportunities Industrialization Center in Providence, Rhode Island; the Center for Employment Training in San Jose, California; and Wider Opportunities for Women in Washington, D.C. The programs enrolled a total of 3,965 women in the demonstration projects. Services offered at the four sites included basic skills and job-skills assessments, counseling, remedial education, job-skill training, job-placement assistance, and child care assistance. Following the kind of rigorous experimental design used in scientific studies to isolate the impact of an intervention, applicants in each of the four cities were assigned randomly to either a treatment group that was offered services or to a control group that was not eligible to receive services at the funded agencies but could seek services elsewhere.

The evaluators tracked the progress of both those who were enrolled in the programs and those who were excluded from them at each of the four sites and measured the net impact of the interventions. After two and a half years of treatment and study, the evaluation produced some notable results: (1) none of the four programs had a significant long-term impact on psychological well-being; (2) two of three programs offering high-school equivalency courses had no impact on GED attainment; (3) none of the programs had long-term impacts on the types of child care used; and (4) most important of all, three of the four programs had no significant impact on earnings or welfare dependency.[7]

These outcomes—and the care with which they were documented—make Rockefeller's MFSP demonstration one of philanthropy's most constructive and important failures in recent times. Though three of the four sites failed to achieve significant results, it would be wrong to conclude that philanthropic funds were wasted on this large-scale experiment. In fact, a good argument can be made for the opposite conclusion. By fully and openly documenting the program's failure at three sites, the project as a whole created significant public value and information. The outside evaluators of the MFSP demonstration scrupulously studied the reasons for the disappointing results and catalogued their findings. In addition to measuring and explaining failure, the evaluation also studied in depth why one of the four sites managed to achieve more encouraging outcomes.[8]

As a consequence of the detailed evaluation, other foundations or government agencies interested in welfare-to-work programs can gain a tremendous amount of knowledge from this experiment—not just from the small part of the MFSP demonstration that worked, but from the much larger part that failed. Rockefeller's MFSP demonstration is thus a valuable and constructive failure because it was coupled with an independent evaluation that created value in spite of disappointing program design and implementation at the site level. The multivolume longitudinal study, which draws on both quantitative and qualitative data, represents one of the very best evaluations of a foundation program conducted to date.[9] Though they did not receive much attention from the press at the time of their release, these reports should now be required reading for all foundations and state agencies working to move families from welfare to work. Such a constructive failure occurs when a foundation grant is used to carry out a program exactly as proposed and when a good evaluation reveals that the program had no significant impact. In this sense, constructive failures are best thought of as failed experiments, cases in which funds are invested, hypotheses are tested, and results are obtained. Constructive failures may not be appreciated by many in the foundation field, but they have potentially tremendous value. They can inform future practices, lay the groundwork for more successful programs, and represent a fulfillment of key accountability responsibilities.[10] Unfortunately, constructive failures in contemporary philanthropy remain all too rare.

The second kind of failure is vastly more common today. An unconstructive failure in philanthropy produces no knowledge because the funder either chooses not to communicate openly the results of the evaluation or does not conduct any evaluation at all. Unconstructive failures are discussed very discreetly among close philanthropic friends or glossed over entirely. Since foundation grantmaking can benefit from increased knowledge about both what works and what does not, this lack of open communication poses an obstacle to more effective philanthropy in the long run. Thus, the trouble with unconstructive failures is not that they produce disappointing programmatic outcomes, but rather that they produce no new usable knowledge when it is clearly needed.

Perhaps the most spectacular and wholly unconstructive failure in philanthropy occurred in Chicago in 1994. That September, talk show host Oprah Winfrey made the surprising announcement that she was funding a new program designed to move one hundred families out of public housing, off welfare, and toward independence.[11] Jane Addams Hull House Association, one of Chicago's most prominent social service agencies, was promised $3 million and given total freedom in designing and implementing the program. Soon after the announcement of the program, which was named Families for a Better Life, over 30,000 persons from around the city responded and requested assistance.[12] In the end, only 4,000 of these respondents met the program's requirement of living in public housing and, from this group, 1,600 families formally applied to the program. Amid all the early excitement about the program, Winfrey was chosen as one of seven Chicagoans of the year for her charitable work in the city. There were even rumors and questions about whether Winfrey would seek public office after her foray into social policy.

By 1996, however, the program had spent $1.3 million and had managed to serve only seven families. Of the five families who completed the program (two families dropped out), three succeeded in moving out of public housing. The employment gains were equally disappointing: two parents found full-time work, two worked part-time, and one parent was enrolled in a training program. Of course, these modest outcomes do not justify the program costs, which amounted to over $250,000 for each of the five families. What exactly went wrong? It is difficult to say for certain, although one news report noted that the program spent too much time screening potential participants and then lost time by retooling the comprehensive counseling and training program in midcourse.[13]

The program was soon officially closed and Jane Addams Hull House Association has never made plans to resuscitate the program. The problem with Families for a Better Life was not that it failed, but that it was a wholly unconstructive failure that produced no systematic knowledge about the transition from welfare to work. No public narrative report on the program was ever written and no systematic outside evaluation was ever made available to other funders and interested parties. It was particularly disappointing that this experimental project proved so unconstructive, given the sizable resources that were invested and the fact that information on what works in the area of welfare-to-work and what does not continues to be urgently needed.

Failures in philanthropy occur more often than one might think. In fact, a high failure rate is actually a sign that donors are aiming high and trying to address difficult problems. If there were no failures, one might conclude that philanthropy as a whole had failed to take full advantage of its special status as a provider of risk capital in society. The Rockefeller and Winfrey experiences starkly highlight how failure in philanthropy can, however, mean two very different things. While there should be no stigma attached to constructive failures that build knowledge the way the Rockefeller Foundation's program did, heavily funded initiatives that end in unconstructive failures like Winfrey's deserve all the criticism they presently receive, and more. This is due in part to the fact that while it may be tolerable to be ineffective and accountable, there is no excuse for being both ineffective and unaccountable. Accountability is a great curative force in philanthropy that can counter some of the pressures and distortions that plague the field. If donors take seriously their responsibility to evaluate their work openly and rigorously and build and disseminate knowledge within the broader field, frightening as this might seem at times, and if donors learn from their experiences and adjust as they move forward, they can free themselves from some of the constraints that being effective in all their work imposes. High levels of accountability do expose ineffective philanthropy, but in the process they also empower donors to take full advantage of all the freedom that philanthropy allows.

Accountability

In many conversations over the years, the group of leading donors I listened to repeated the basic proposition that philanthropy, as it is structured today, does not have adequate accountability mechanisms. Without any real way to hold donors accountable, many leaders in the field worry that philanthropy will never have the impetus to improve its performance and become more effective. Yet strangely, until philanthropy becomes more confident about its work and the results that are produced by giving, it is hard to see the field opening itself up to much scrutiny and rigorous analysis. Accountability and effectiveness are thus locked in a strange mutual dependence in which progress on one dimension will likely lead to progress on the other. Conversely, lack of progress on one dimension will almost certainly stall progress on the other.

Setting aside the matter of the connection of accountability to effectiveness, it is important to step back and ask why the field of philanthropy should worry at all in principle about being accountable. After all, no one is held accountable for how they spend their private wealth when it comes to the consumption of real estate, automobiles, food, clothing, entertainment, or any other good or service. Some might ask, Why should the expenditure of philanthropic funds raise any issues related to accountability since the decision to give is a private and voluntary one about how to expend wealth? The answer lies in the fact that philanthropy has several features that distinguish it from ordinary private consumption decisions.

The first is that giving often is accompanied by a tax break, which can take the form of a deduction on personal income taxes or lower estate taxes if gifts are made upon death. When money passes from private hands into the charitable world, government rewards donors and bestows on them privileges and benefits that other citizens do not enjoy. Along with this subsidy, one might argue, comes a responsibility to use philanthropic funds wisely and effectively, since at least part of the cost of philanthropy is borne by government in the form of forgone tax revenue. Accepting subsidies creates responsibilities in the minds of some. Thus, the first argument for accountability stems from the fact that giving, unlike most forms of private consumption, is accompanied by a public subsidy.

This first argument is reasonable enough until it is examined more closely. It is not entirely clear that the charitable deduction is a subsidy. The deduction can be viewed as an incentive put in place by government to ensure that voluntary acts of helping continue to address public needs and that solutions to community problems emanate not only from government but also from the private sector. Even if the charitable deduction is construed as a public subsidy, one might reasonably argue that the receipt of a subsidy does not create any special responsibilities or additional accountability requirements. After all, large numbers of Americans receive a very generous deduction for the interest on their home mortgages, and few people would hold that this creates special public responsibilities for home owners or that this gives renters any special accountability claims in specific relation to those who benefit from this subsidy. Thus, while the charitable deduction may appear to be the element of philanthropy that creates an obligation for donors to be accountable for their actions, the case is shaky, to say the least.

The second feature of giving that makes philanthropy quite different from other forms of private consumption stems from the effect it has on others. While the purchase and use of private goods in the market rarely has as its goal generating direct consequence for others, philanthropy by its very nature works in communities and neighborhoods and affects others. Sometimes these effects are very direct, such as when human services are being offered, other times the effects are more indirectly felt, such as when a public policy change is being researched and advocated. The very fact, however, that philanthropy is public in its intentions and seeks to enact a private vision of the common good raises accountability issues precisely because the act of giving projects private values and commitments into the public sphere. The individuals and communities on which these values are projected can and do make accountability demands on donors.

This is a stronger argument, but it too is somewhat flawed. There is no denying that philanthropy involves the projection of private interests and commitments into the public sphere. But the same could just as easily be said of nonprofit organizations. Most grant recipients are in a more proximate relationship with their community and play a more direct role in defining what local public needs are, and what the response will look like. Nonprofits, not donors, make most operational decisions, though some donors seek to have a say in how services are delivered. Still, it is hard to claim that donors have special responsibilities by virtue of their decision to work in the public sphere, especially since they are not in direct contact with vulnerable populations or on the front line of service delivery.

All of which points to the third common argument for philanthropic accountability. Even if nonprofits are delivering services and connecting with the public, there are unavoidable power asymmetries that result when one person or institution gives money to another person or institution. Although many donors work hard to break down some of the boundaries of class and power that philanthropy raises, these cleavages are real and cause many to worry about the intentions and methods of donors. Few grant applicants feel at ease with donors, and they sometimes feel as though they must work hard to put their best foot forward. While it would be useful if donors and recipients could openly discuss projects, the reality is that the wealth and power differential makes this kind of conversation difficult. In light of these cleavages and the fundamentally unequal position that givers and recipients occupy in the philanthropic exchange, accountability concerns naturally arise—although they may have to be raised by third parties who have some distance from the particular philanthropic transaction in question.

This may be the best of the three cases for accountability. Power can corrupt, and donors enjoy considerable but not absolute power. Still, the fact that donors control the flow of substantial resources into the nonprofit sector does raise difficult questions about what controls are being placed on donors to ensure that they are acting sensibly and fairly. There are few avenues of appeal for nonprofit organizations that are either denied funding or that receive funding but are dissatisfied with the donors' conduct. The fact that philanthropy requires that two parties be locked into a relationship in which there are no real avenues of redress for the weaker side lays the groundwork for a fairly compelling argument that some kind of account-ability system is needed. The presence of a power differential may not mean that anyone is entitled to accountability, though it certainly suggests that some form of accountability would help the system work more effectively and equitably.

Given these three more or less compelling arguments and the amount of money now involved in philanthropy, nonprofit organizations, local com-munities, government agencies, and increasingly certain segments of the general public have taken the stance that donors should be made more accountable for their use of charitable funds. One reason for the growing interest in the actual workings of philanthropy is related to the political and budgetary shifts that have occurred in recent decades. As large entitle-ment programs such as Social Security and Medicare consume greater and greater proportions of the national budget, the amount of money available for discretionary social spending has declined proportionally. This has made it harder for the federal government to support the creation of major new domestic programs and has pushed some of its responsibilities to state and local government, and even to charities. In many fields of nonprofit activity, the importance of receiving charitable dollars has increased substantially. Private grants represent one of the key ways that nonprofits launch new program initiatives, which only later attempt to achieve sustainability through the charging of program fees or through other forms of long-term financing.

The budgetary squeeze of entitlement programs has increased philanthropy's market share of domestic discretionary spending. Philanthropy simply constitutes a greater share of the pie of discretionary social spending than it has in the past. An interesting debate has taken place over just how big a piece of the social spending universe philanthropy actually represents, but few argue with the fact that giving is now a very critical part of the overall social program funding picture, especially when it comes to new projects and initiatives. Within the context of philanthropy's growing market share of the risk capital for social innovation, it is hardly surprising that calls for greater accountability have been heard. In these calls, however, the meaning of accountability is not clear. It is a term that is used in many different ways by many different stakeholders in philanthropy. In some ways, accountability is a concept that is just as confused and conflicted as effectiveness. Part of the problem stems from the fact that two of the three dominant conceptions of accountability do not apply well to the world of giving.[14]

One conception of accountability is rooted in democratic theory. It holds that accountability becomes a reality when the tether of the vote is established between representatives and constituents. In politics, for example, citizens can exercise the right to vote, allowing them both to select those who will represent them and to hold these persons accountable for the decisions they take in government. The right to vote breathes meaning into the idea of accountability because it expresses consent and creates a sanctioning mechanism that can be used if the behavior of the representative is not faithful to the interest of the constituency. Of course, democratic accountability assumes that citizens actually go out and vote and keep abreast of political debates and issues, something that does not always occur. Still, the vote gives citizens a tool for keeping their representatives responsive.

Attractive as it might be, democratic accountability is not an option in the field of philanthropy, or at least it is not an option for the vast universe of donors and institutions that populate the field. Philanthropy is profoundly undemocratic in that donors do not give their grant recipients or the communities in which they operate the ability to recall them or reverse their behavior. In fact, philanthropy is almost always profoundly undemocratic in that the wealthy elite use their resources to enact their own vision of the public good. Some donors may convene people and listen to the opinions of others before making major commitments, but by and large philanthropic decision making is a private affair. The board meetings of private foundations are not open to the public, board members do not stand for election, either political or corporate, and foundations operate largely as they (or the founder or family) see fit.

Mutual accountability is substantially different from democratic accountability. One way to establish accountability is to have a commitment that each party to an agreement or collective effort will hold the other side accountable. In the nonprofit world, systems of mutual accountability have been established in a wide array of fields, ranging from community development to welfare to work services. One of the clearest examples of how mutual accountability works can be found in the emerging field of microfinance. At least one of the more prominent nonprofits making small loans for business development around the world relies on a unique form of mutual accountability in many of its programs in Latin America. Instead of lending to one person, money is lent to groups of five persons. Not only are the members of these "solidarity circles" responsible individually for the loans they have taken out, but each is responsible for the others' loans; if one person defaults, the others are responsible for the debt. This system of mutual accountability and shared responsibility has allowed microfinance organizations to achieve low default rates. Mutual accountability builds solidarity and trust among the parties to the agreements. It also is a way to cultivate commitment and enforce rules.

Unfortunately, grants do not commit donors to anything,[15] and mainstream philanthropy largely operates as a one-way street. The idea of implementing a system of mutual accountability runs counter to the basic precept that funders provide capital and nonprofit organizations are responsible for implementation. There is little room in most philanthropy for mutual accountability, either among a group of nonprofits or between donors and recipients. Nonprofits generally guard their independence fiercely and would not want to cast their lot with that of other organizations, and givers and getters generally do not view themselves as part of a common enterprise. On the first account, mutual accountability would demand that nonprofits take responsibility for the performance of other organizations, not just their own. Given the huge pressures and harried conditions within which many nonprofits operate, it is hard to imagine this ever happening. On the second account, mutual accountability would mean that funders would have responsibilities to nonprofits after a grant is issued. And while donors do sometimes make multiyear commitments, funding is often limited to a few years, and donors rarely deny themselves the freedom to cut off a nonprofit should it initially perform poorly or should the interests and focus of the donor simply shift.

There is another possible way to construe the concept of mutual accountability in the world of philanthropy, one that connects donors to other donors. The idea of mutual accountability might have some traction within two different contexts. The first is the tightly bound geographical communities of donors. In some cities like Minneapolis, Chicago, and San Francisco, foundations are part of tight professional networks organized around regional associations of grantmakers. Within these local groupings, institutional donors might reasonably feel some sense of peer accountability and could develop learning networks around frank peer assessments. A second context in which donors might respond to mutual accountability claims involves issue areas in which groups of donors are concentrated, such as health and the arts, where large affinity groups of donors are organized. Again, within such groups, donors might be willing to engage one another in a system of mutual accountability aimed at fostering dynamic learning.

During one stage in the long-term discussion with leaders from the field, an idea regarding mutual accountability emerged. It involved the creation of a peer review process in the world of philanthropy that would focus on the quality and clarity of philanthropic endeavors. Using planning documents and program statements, the review entailed rendering a judgment not about outcomes but about how well the donor defined objectives, specified an approach to achieving these objectives, and set forward a compelling set of metrics for knowing whether these objectives were met. As one donor noted: "If we could just be clear about our objectives, that would be a huge step forward." Others noted that philanthropists are by their nature competitive and that introducing some peer pressure would push the field toward better decision making: "If we know that others are going to be looking at our work and rendering judgments, we're going to be a lot more motivated to get it right." Although centered on the intent and plans of donors, not on their actual actions or impact, the idea was to focus on that part of giving that is actually free from some of the measurement problems plaguing the field. In the end, however, when the idea of peer review was modeled as a small-group activity among these donors, there was a distinct lack of interest when it came to criticizing the work of others, even though large differences in quality were apparent in the strategic plans discussed. Still, if mutual accountability is ever to be applied in the world of philanthropy, it will likely have to involve, at least to some extent, donors being held accountable by other donors. The chasm between givers and recipients is also too great for real systems of mutual accountability to take hold in any meaningful form.

In recent decades, there have been a few isolated cases of donors who have tried to overcome the lack of either democratic or mutual accountability by changing the fundamental rules of the game. The work of the "alternative funds" is the most obvious example. Unhappy with the hierarchy and detachment of conventional private and community foundations, in the 1960s a movement was started to transform institutional philanthropy from the ground up.[16] Groups of wealthy individuals with progressive political outlooks started alternative funds to disburse philanthropic money in a new way. Rather than have donors sit on the board of these new funds and control the use of the money that was collected, the alternative funds brought in community members, organizers, and representatives from the nonprofit community to serve on the grants committees, in which funding decisions would be made. By turning the tables in philanthropy and by giving power to the grassroots, these progressive philanthropists believed they had broken through the accountability trap in which conventional philanthropy had long been mired.[17] These funds created both democratic and mutual accountability among community leaders and funders. Not surprisingly, the alternative funds movement reached its apex in the 1970s at the height of progressivism and has been on the decline since, never constituting more than a minuscule fraction of the philanthropic universe. Contributions to alternative funds have dwindled, and today they operate on a small level on the very fringes of the field. Mainstream individual and institutional philanthropy, having taken note of this utopian vision of shared governance, decided that this vision is just not that attractive and taken a pass. For the vast majority of donors, the loss of power and control in the approach taken by alternative funds has proven too extreme and final.

If the models of democratic and mutual accountability do not apply well to the broader field of philanthropy, there is a reason. The most common form of accountability practiced in the world of philanthropy actually involves a third model: a principal agent model grounded in a more corporate approach to accountability. This form of accountability works to control the power of staff members by tethering them to boards. It also anchors boards to the intent of donors and sets limits on their ability to deviate radically from the mission set in place by the donor. If staff members are agents of boards and boards are agents of donors, the only flaw in this accountability model is that it does not readily explain how accountability works outside the world of institutional giving, nor how accountability is achieved to the multiple stakeholders of philanthropic funds.

To make some progress on how this model of accountability works in philanthropy, it may be helpful to examine three simple clarifying questions: Who is being held accountable? For what? And to whom? The accountability problem in philanthropy starts with the issue of who is to be held accountable. This is also where the confusion runs deep and where the contention begins. It turns out this is not such an easy question because philanthropy has evolved many different organizational forms and has surrounded the donor with many possible scapegoats. In its most basic form, philanthropic accountability starts with the donor. In cases where the donor is alive and acting alone, it is the donor who is held primarily accountable. Thus, for example, when a wealthy donor decides to give to a particular cause or organization, proceeds to write a check, and thereby establishes a funding relationship with the organization, the accountability question is fairly straightforward: to the extent that there are accountability claims made, they will be made to the donor. Things get more complicated when the donor creates a foundation, appoints a board, and hires staff to carry out the philanthropy. In such cases, the focus of accountability demands may change, depending on the issue at hand. When it comes to the character of the investments held by a foundation, including the environmental and social performance of the companies whose stock it holds, the foundation board is usually the first target of accountability claims. When it comes to the actual decisions made about which organizations get funded and which do not, the staff and chief executive officer may be the main objects of scrutiny, and nonprofits have the option of registering any complaints about the grantmaking process with the board. This is a risky proposition for most nonprofits since it risks permanently alienating the foundation's staff, whose support is critical to any prospects of receiving funding. As a result, accountability demands are only rarely made to either the board or the staff, and the foundation staff end up acting with a fair measure of impunity.

The real problem with answering the question of who is to be held accountable in philanthropy is that many donors think it is the grant recipient who has the most to be accountable for since it is taking money with a promise to do certain things in return. Donors are primarily distributing funds, not taking on obligations to perform. In this way, grants can look like contracts and services for hire, especially when the letter that accompanies the check specifies a series of conditions attached to the receipt of the funds, to which the recipient organizations must signal acceptance by signing the grant letter or contract. Under such circumstances, it is indeed plausible to say the real accountability burden in the world of philanthropy lies not directly with the donors, but with the organizations that propose to carry out certain activities in order to receive philanthropic support. Donors may be responsible for selecting nonprofits, but they are only indirectly responsible for what happens to the funds they distribute since the nonprofits are far closer than the donor to the actual activities being carried out. Thus, even though this first question of who is to be held accountable might seem simple and straightforward enough, it is very much under dispute and subject to interpretation, depending on whom one asks—the donors or the recipients.

The line between donor and recipient breaks down, however, in the case of operating foundations, which are endowed philanthropic institutions that use their resources not to make grants but instead to carry out programs of the foundation's own design. Operating foundations tend to work in areas where there are economies of scale to be captured and where donors want to exert greater control over the implementation of their philanthropic intents. When donors choose an operating foundation, they put the accountability onus squarely on their own shoulders because there are no nonprofits involved; accountability claims can be directed only at the foundation itself. The line between operating foundations and other philanthropic forms has been blurred over time as other donors have taken on roles that go well beyond distributing funds. In a number of large private foundations, the primary activity may still be grantmaking, but many other activities are being undertaken by staff. The creation of new nonprofit organizations by foundations, sometimes directly affiliated with the originating foundation and sometimes more or less autonomous, has changed the accountability equation significantly in that a broader group of donors have taken greater responsibility for the actual use of the funds they distribute. In this way, the question of who is to be held accountable in philanthropy is far from clear and is in fact quite murky.

Assuming that donors are at least central subjects of accountability demands, the second piece of the philanthropic accountability puzzle relates to the substance of accountability claims and can be reduced to the question: For what are donors to be held accountable? If the answer is effectiveness, then we already know that this is a very contested definition of the subject matter of accountability. Still, at the core of the substantive question is the issue of performance, one that connects again to both the actions of the giver and the receiver. One way to sidestep the issue of effectiveness is to switch the focus of accountability from the social outcomes that are produced to something much easier to observe and track, namely process. Philanthropy involves a long series of procedural issues related to the handling and processing of grant applications. Given the perceived difficulty in arguing about the comparative effectiveness of donors and recipients, the few accountability demands that are ever made in the world of philanthropy tend to focus on process, not substance. Thus, donors are much more likely to get away with making foolish grants that amount to nothing than with being aloof, dismissive, or unwilling to listen. Donors are expected to follow the same procedures with all nonprofits, to show little favoritism, and to allow all organizations an equal opportunity to make their case. Of course, all this emphasis on process and ritual misses the fact that many philanthropic decisions are made not on a careful calculation of an organization's past performance and likely future results or even on the quality of the plans spelled out in the proposal, but rather on visceral judgments about the quality, intelligence, and competence of a nonprofit organization's leadership.

In more legal terms, the question of what donors are to be held responsible for takes on greater clarity, though not greater depth. Here too the focus is on process, not performance. When donors create foundations and entrust others to carry out their philanthropic intentions, there are several important duties that trustees must fulfill and for which they are held accountable by state regulators. The most basic is the duty of loyalty. Trustees must put their own interests squarely behind those of the public. They must respect their fiduciary duties, and doing so means avoiding any action that compromises their role as an agent for another.[18] Another fundamental duty is that of care. Trustees must take reasonable steps to protect the interests of the institution by acting with prudence and discretion at all times, particularly when it comes to management of investment assets. Trustees also have a duty of obedience. They must remain loyal to the donor's intent and purpose, pursue it doggedly, and govern the institution accordingly. These basic legal concepts, about which much has been written, are useful only to a limited degree because very rarely, and only under extraordinary circumstances in which abuses are beyond the pale, do state regulators attempt to take action against trustees or institutions on the grounds that they have failed to meet these legal obligations.

Still, over the years, there have been a few cases where donors and foundation trustees have engaged in unethical and illegal behavior, including using philanthropic funds to pay their trustees exorbitant fees, to purchase lavish office appointments, and to generally divert charitable dollars toward expenses that do not benefit the public. Interestingly, on the singularly important issue of the management of foundation endowments, many institutions have performed poorly, sometimes losing large amounts of money in the market, with little or no consequences. The ability of state attorneys general to supervise, investigate, and prosecute within the world of philanthropy is very limited due to a general lack of staff and resources.

The last question embedded in the issue of philanthropic accountability is "To whom are donors to be held accountable?" Individual and institutional donors are in some ways accountable first and foremost to themselves. No one engaging in philanthropy wants to waste money and support undeserving projects. In fact, some donors put a fair amount of pressure on themselves—often alluding to their stewardship responsibilities—to use their charitable resources wisely. There is also a sense that donors are accountable to one another, particularly within geographical communities in which there is a lot of contact and collaboration among local donors. In some specialty fields of giving, such as health and the arts, donors feel some sense of peer pressure. But this nascent form of peer accountability needs to be cultivated and formalized substantially before it has much effect on the actual behavior of donors.

The federal government, through the IRS, can and does regulate giving behavior. There are minimal reporting requirements that individual donors must adhere to when giving funds away. The requirements only come into play if the donor seeks to receive a tax deduction for the gift. For foundations, the legal constraints are more complex and more significant. In exchange for the privilege of operating in perpetuity,[19] private foundations are required to pay out from their endowment a minimum of 5 percent of the average monthly balance of their endowments the previous year. This payout requirement was designed to ensure that foundations use their resources in productive ways and that communities receive some benefit from the tax incentives given to donors. At the state level, nonprofits are subject to oversight from attorneys general, though this is limited by resource and staffing constraints.

Finally, there is some sense that donors have an obligation to the communities in which they operate. Philanthropy can be a force for change, but sometimes this change is not positive. For this reason, it is important that donors listen to representatives of the communities in which they give in order to understand their perspective on how philanthropy might be used to improve local conditions. Because the concept of community is fairly diffuse and broad, establishing the precise interests of a community and who within a community is entitled to speak for others can be difficult. And without precision in terms of boundaries and representation, the communities affected by philanthropy have a hard time finding a way to play an active role in keeping donors accountable for their actions.

Instead of taking the fateful step of actually building robust accountability structures, the vast majority of donors have simply learned to live with the accountability problems that dominate the field today. Less radical steps have been taken by the largest donors, the most significant of which has been the movement to offer up increased transparency in place of accountability. If accountability involves a noisy and contentious dialogue between the world of philanthropy and its many stakeholders, transparency can be pursued by donors as a long and uninterrupted monologue. It involves pushing out toward the world information and details about philanthropy, and it makes no real commitment to listen or to respond. Transparency is far less threatening to donors than accountability, and as a consequence it has emerged as an attractive alternative. A substantial increase in the transparency of philanthropy has been achieved in recent decades, particularly within the world of private foundations, which have taken a host of information-sharing steps aimed at ensuring that questions about philanthropy are readily answerable for anyone seeking answers. This transparency work has produced greater understanding of the field of philanthropy among the general public and allowed nonprofit organizations to research and direct their funding proposals more efficiently.

Although moving information out into the open is laudable, it is neither the functional nor moral equivalent of creating an accountability mechanism. As traffic on this one-way street of information has increased, there remain strikingly few meaningful feedback loops bringing information back to donors. To be sure, a few large foundations have experimented with surveys of their grant recipients.[20] These data collection efforts have ended up looking like customer satisfaction surveys. Even with a grant of anonymity to respondents, however, it has been a struggle to get honest comments. These efforts thus represent only a modest step toward making donors ac-

countable for the procedural side of their work. These surveys may
some insight into how nonprofits are treated by foundation staff, b
provide no information on the substantive issue of whether wise p
thropic choices and effective grants are being made. Other funders
ularly those with a flair for theatrics, have experimented with open houses
and town hall events, in which nonprofits are invited to pose any questions
they wish to the foundation's leadership, who typically sit on stage. Like
shareholder meetings of large companies, these events can have a staged
and surreal quality to them. But unlike shareholder meetings, which can be
contentious, foundation open houses are quiet affairs, since few nonprofits
are ever able to really express themselves candidly in such a situation, even
if they have major complaints and concerns.

The most common transparency move involves the simple release of
information. Institutional donors have set up elaborate and informative Web
pages, published annual reports in ever greater numbers, issued concise
grantmaking guidelines explaining what the donor intends to fund, and
released concept papers laying out assumptions and preferred approaches
to particular problems. While this information flow has certainly made it
easier to understand what givers are thinking and what they are seeking to
support, it can be a very broad but shallow form of disclosure. Releasing
information can and does make the grantmaking process appear less mysterious, but it is still a weak proxy for real accountability systems. It allows
donors to appear open without requiring that they listen or respond to the
expressed needs or concerns of the communities in which they work.

Legitimacy

The most significant problem with all the talk about accountability in philanthropy is not its subsequent feeble translation into transparency measures. It is that accountability has often obscured a larger and more important question: that of legitimacy. The question of legitimacy is hard to avoid
when thinking about philanthropy. After all, giving asserts the power and
resources of a few people and allows private parties to act on the behalf of
the public. It is therefore reasonable enough to ask whether and why philanthropy is legitimate. By "legitimate," I mean at first simply being perceived as legitimate by stakeholders—not actually acting in a way that renders these perceptions of the fair and just exercise of power meaningful and
credible. The answer to the legitimacy question in philanthropy requires
that one plumb the multiple sources of support and acceptance on which

philanthropy can potentially draw and from which legitimacy can flow. It also demands that the distinction between individual givers and institutional funders be examined. The issue of legitimacy arises sharply once funds are domiciled in institutions that enjoy tax exemption and operate for public purposes.[21] While individual givers may feel some pressure to act in ways that are perceived to be just as legitimate as those of some of the large foundations, they in fact often are able to give with relative impunity and remain well under the radar screen. Principals are also protected to some extent by the fact that philanthropic funds are really "their money" to be deployed as the person who earned the funds sees fit. When professional staff take on the responsibility of disbursing the funds of donors, legitimacy challenges surface and tough questions emerge about the choices that are made in the name of someone else.

Philanthropy can seek legitimacy from government. By sacrificing some of its precious autonomy, by collaborating with public agencies, by even funding government programs, or by simply staying out of the regulatory spotlight, philanthropy can draw legitimacy from government. Many donors who create foundations start with the impulse to seek the benefit of either a major tax deduction, a reduction of estate taxes, or simply the ability to operate as a tax-exempt organization. In so doing, they point to one aspect of foundation creation that appears to confer some legitimacy on institutional philanthropy, namely that government supports this activity indirectly. For those who want to question the right of donors to make decisions that ultimately may mean survival or collapse of charitable organizations and that might have important human consequences for those who depend on programs funded with philanthropic dollars, the presence of government policy—affirming the idea of private action in the public good—creates some political cover and supports legitimacy for foundations. If philanthropy were not legitimate, government would not endorse it and support it through public policy. Of course, there are some problems with this argument, namely that many goals supported by policy may not ultimately be legitimate. However, to the extent that philanthropy works on problems that are part of the mainstream consensus about public needs (e.g., reduction in poverty, improving health care, strengthening education) it will likely find acceptance. By sacrificing a fair amount of its precious independence and focusing on issues that government itself deems priorities, private philanthropy can achieve a weak and temporary kind of legitimacy.

Philanthropy can draw legitimacy from the organizations that it supports. Nonprofit organizations are in a unique position to see donors do their work. The grantseeking process may humiliate and infuriate non-profit managers if too many hoops must be jumped through or if the process appears capricious or stacked in favor of certain organizations. However, donors can handle the difficult challenge of sifting through requests and choosing among them in ways that create greater levels of trust and ultimately greater levels of legitimacy. Attending to procedural issues, including the returning of phone calls, the prompt acknowledgment of proposals, and the issuance of credible letters explaining the decision reached by the board, is part and parcel of what it takes to make a donor appear to be rightly and justly exercising control over philanthropic resources. While it would be difficult for donors if the legitimacy of their work boiled down to the frequency with which they selected the most qualified and highest-impact organizations for funding, in practice, the most significant thing that donors can do is garner the acceptance and respect of the organizations that work most closely with them. By funding nonprofits and treating grantees fairly, some measure of support and legitimacy from the broader sector can be built.

The legitimacy of philanthropy can also be bolstered by peer consultation, by collaboration with entities that already possess legitimacy, and by securing the approbation of leaders in the philanthropy field itself. Given the profound power imbalance between givers and receivers, few channels of redress are open to nonprofit organizations that may have been denied support or have a grievance. To create the semblance of an open system in which donors are able to receive and act on information about their grant-making processes and policies not only from the nonprofits that have gotten grants but from a more neutral group of observers, donors can create together networks of collaboration and consultation through which they can build at least the appearance that donors are legitimately exercising philanthropic power.

Finally, enterprising and aggressive donors can attempt to legitimate themselves. That is, through their own actions, particularly by giving grants to organizations that contribute to the public interest in significant and visible ways, donors can bask in the reflected light of the good work done by grant recipients. This form of self-legitimization through strategic grant-making is appealing since it depends largely on the insightful philanthropic processing of requests for funding and the initiation when appropriate of programs that have high potential return. Philanthropy can act and give in ways that build public support and understanding of the field, creating a reservoir of goodwill that can later be tapped should challenges arise.

The main problem with this model of self-legitimization is that it depends to some extent on program effectiveness, or what grantees do with grants, and does not speak to the larger issue of mission effectiveness, or how well donors do at achieving their philanthropic objectives. To be truly effective, donors would need to ground their legitimacy in sound evidence of mission effectiveness.

There is a major flaw with this framing of the legitimacy question in philanthropy, however. It is a problem that raises a whole host of complex issues that many donors likely would find inconvenient: legitimacy in philanthropy must mean more than the narrow *descriptive* claim that donors are legitimate when they are perceived or thought to rightly possess the power and position to enact their commitments through giving. Philanthropic legitimacy, to be meaningful, must also have a *normative* dimension:[22] legitimate philanthropy needs to actually reflect the rightful discharge of philanthropic duties. It must have a substantive dimension that allows those on the outside not only to note that large individual donors and foundations in America legally and legitimately possess great wealth they can deploy however they see fit, but that these individuals and institutions are discharging their responsibilities wisely. The obstacle to defining philanthropic legitimacy in a normative way, so that it sets standards for the just use of philanthropic power and resources, is clear: it inevitably leads to confusion about standards for legitimate philanthropic work. While there are some minimal standards for giving (supporting charitable organizations registered with the public and complying with existing rules and regulations bearing on the administration and governance of philanthropic institutions), these signposts hardly provide much real guidance or assurance that philanthropic resources are being used wisely and effectively.

It is fair to say that the field of philanthropy has made substantial progress in defining the conditions under which descriptive claims about the legitimacy of the field can be supported. There are minimal standards for conduct and reporting that allow most donors to be legally compliant without too much trouble. Moreover, since recipient organizations fear displeasing their funders, few challenges to the legitimacy of donors are ever forthcoming. On the whole, the field has made far less progress in understanding and spelling out the normative framework that could be used to help donors and their institutions achieve a form of legitimacy and support that is normative in character and that illuminates the just and right application of private wealth to public problems. One possible way to define the normative basis of philanthropic legitimacy would be to link to both effectiveness and accountability.[23] However, with little progress on the measurement of the philanthropic effectiveness and difficulty getting past transparency to a fuller affirmation of accountability, a legitimacy crisis still looms over philanthropy.

Perhaps the most visible response of the philanthropic community to the legitimacy challenge has been to hire professional staff to manage the grantmaking process. The staff of foundations acts as a mix of talent scouts, evaluators, and public relations specialists, providing a buffer between the board, which may include the founder and family member, and the general public. Beyond what they do, professionals within philanthropy represent something more significant: a commitment to taking philanthropy seriously. In many ways, the rise of professional grantmakers represents the single most significant development in the field of philanthropy in recent decades. Only with professionalization have the issues of effectiveness, accountability, and legitimacy truly risen to the surface and become amplified. Professionals in philanthropy have worked to create field-wide norms and standards for conduct, training programs to develop grantmaking skills, and a body of expert knowledge to guide practice. All this work has focused on fulfilling the instrumental dimension in philanthropy by ratcheting up the technology around giving, rationalizing practices, building administrative structures, and generally legitimizing the field in the eyes of the nonprofit community and the general public.[24]

When philanthropy is carried out by individual donors who simply enact their values and connect them to public needs, philanthropy is an expressive exercise through which donors project their commitments and beliefs onto the world. While it may aim at achieving clear goals and producing tangible public benefits, the stakes of individual giving tend to be relatively modest, especially when the amounts of money involved are small. Giving is an experience that allows donors to make a connection to an organization or cause that means something to them. When giving is done by professionals on behalf of a donor, the relative mix of expressiveness and instrumentalism shifts in favor of the latter. Few staff, particularly those who come onto the scene long after the donor is gone, see their work as anything other than using philanthropic resources as effectively as possible in support of the mission. Being effective is also a way for professionals to achieve recognition within the field and to advance to positions of greater responsibility. Since they are giving away money that they did not earn themselves, professionals within philanthropy are also naturally concerned about accountability and their own legitimacy. Though solutions to the accountability quagmire remain elusive, the related move to greater levels of transparency has largely been driven by professionals seeking to publicize their own work.

Over time, the field of philanthropy has been embarrassed by revelations of isolated cases of fraud, abuse, and waste. Donors have used philanthropic funds to support family and friends. A few foundations have been shown to pay inflated fees to trustees. Many of the larger foundations have been the subject of exposés and critiques arguing that little has actually come from the millions—or even billions—of dollars that have been spent to date. These attacks on the legitimacy of the field over the past century have led to periodic government investigation of institutional philanthropy. These periods of scrutiny and public debate have occurred at regular intervals, including during the Progressive Era, when foundations were portrayed as dangerous concentrations of wealth; during the McCarthy years, when foundations were thought to be subversive forces; during the late 1960s, when concerns about financial abuses surfaced; and more recently as once again the public responsibilities of foundations have been debated. Often the attention of Congress and state attorneys general have been directed at a small number of highly visible and obvious cases of financial abuse, such as insider transactions benefiting trustees, excessive spending on travel and office space, and a host of other clear-cut instances of improper behavior. Many of these cases have been brought to the attention of regulators, frequently through investigative journalism and independent research. Almost always the public outcry and regulatory impulse have centered on issues of ethics and stewardship. These cases have led to a series of narrow and technical policy debates about the mechanics of institutional giving and focused on regulatory reforms aimed at eliminating the misallocation of charitable funds for purposes that are clearly not in the public interest. Interestingly, almost none of the public debate and criticism of foundations has centered on the actual effectiveness of foundations. Clearly, eliminating obvious cases of financial fraud and abuse is far easier than getting to the knotty question of whether philanthropic funds are being used wisely.

Conversations about effectiveness, accountability, and legitimacy have thus occurred largely behind the scenes in philanthropy and within a relatively small subgroup within the field. With individual donors working in isolated bliss and largely under the radar of public or government scrutiny save a very small number of massive gifts, foundations have been the focus of effectiveness debates, where performance measurement methodologies have been discussed and strategy considerations have been examined. The growing cadre of professional grantmakers, located mostly in the largest independent foundations, have taken this issue to heart and focused a great deal of effort on trying to advance the entire field through experimentation, research, and demonstrations. The problem with this arrangement has been that effectiveness, accountability, and legitimacy issues have not permeated the broader field of individual giving nor have they really informed or guided the policy debates that have taken place in government. More significantly, the question of what makes philanthropy legitimate has been systematically avoided by professional grantmakers.

The overall effect of professionalization in philanthropy has been mixed.[25] On the one hand the field has certainly contributed to the easing of the boundaries between donors and recipients, and it has removed some of the caprice and personalization inherent in donor-controlled giving. My argument here is that this shift has had more subtle effects that have gone largely unexamined. On the other hand, professionalization has also impoverished the field in many ways by robbing it of an important part of what makes philanthropy truly distinctive, namely the convergence—and at times collision—of private values with public purposes.[26] By focusing on maximizing the impact of giving, the pronounced shift toward professional grantmaking that has taken place in recent decades may have ultimately made it harder to achieve the most important form of strategic alignment. Understanding how and why instrumental, technical, and dispassionate giving conducted through institutions came into prominence is the subject of the next chapter. It is a historical excursion that is essential to setting up the larger argument made here about the reconstruction of a strategy around a more even balance between private values and public purposes in philanthropy. My larger aim, which emerges in the second half of the book, is to argue that the best and only source of real lasting legitimacy for philanthropy rests in the development of sound strategy.

3. Donors and Professionals

How did philanthropy arrive at the point where it now finds itself, where effectiveness has become an ill-defined obsession, where accountability concerns remain largely unresolved, and where legitimacy is neither understood nor achieved? The answer lies in the slow changes that have pushed giving from charity to philanthropy over the past century, which has been accompanied by a transfer of philanthropic responsibility from donor to trustees and finally to professionals. One of the most important changes characterizing this transformation has been at the level of the forces animating giving. As philanthropic duties have shifted from principals to agents, the private values of the donors that are critical to philanthropy have slowly been sublimated and overtaken by the public purposes related to the object of giving. This transformation has been gradual, but the effect has been profound. As philanthropy has been rendered more agnostic by its professionalization and rationalization, the problems of effectiveness, accountability, and legitimacy have only gotten more acute, more pressing, and more infuriatingly difficult to disentangle.

Although great freedom exists in philanthropy, constraints and norms have still managed to shape the evolution of the field, particularly in recent decades. The field has quietly undergone profound change and reinvention at the level of its basic practices and fundamental self-understanding. Before describing how and why this important shift took place, it may be useful to start with two snapshots of American philanthropy. In the first snapshot, dating from around the turn of the twentieth century to about 1960, American philanthropy appears to be a relatively simple matter carried out by wealthy donors and their families through uncomplicated institutions with minimal administrative staffs. The early foundations were dominated by the leadership of a small cadre of highly visible and very opinionated donors who set the standards for large-scale philanthropy. Private foundations often operated discreetly, avoided public controversy, and had as their mission the fulfillment of the private philanthropic interests and values of wealthy donors. Nonfamily trustees charged with running the foundation and eventually carrying on the donor's philanthropic mission were mostly Ivy League graduates who enjoyed careers in business, law, government, and higher education.[1] With small or nonexistent administrative staffs and little concern with public accountability, donors used their tremendous resources however they saw fit.

In the second snapshot, dating from the 1970s and beyond, most large-scale giving is conducted through foundations, which have become dramatically transformed. Gone is the simple administrative structure that enabled early foundations to act quickly and decisively in response to directions from the founder. In its place is a complex administrative bureaucracy staffed by a new cadre of foundation professionals, often with multiple approval levels through which grant decisions must travel. More important than staffing changes, however, is a conceptual shift in the understanding of foundations' place in society. Foundations emerge as profoundly public institutions, open and accessible to all, committed to building better relations with grant applicants and the public. Far from shying away from publicity, the new institutional philanthropy actually seeks out opportunities to explain and advertise its work to anyone who will listen.

How and why did philanthropy transform itself from a small set of private donors pursuing private agendas through obedient organizational intermediaries into a large national field in which public institutions are managed by grantmaking professionals? My answer ultimately rests on the slow transfer over the past century of most philanthropic authority from donors to trustees to professionals in the face of growing public awareness and increased regulation of the field. After a long history of quiet giving by donors, the dawn of the twentieth century saw the creation of philanthropic institutions and with them the need for board governance and the consequent appearance of trustees and directors in philanthropy. Later, a series of contentious encounters with Congress, culminating in the passage of regulations on private foundations, propelled the field to increase transparency and professionalize operations. In an effort to defend philanthropy from further government investigation and regulation, foundations strategically recast themselves as public trusts to be governed by public purposes and brought in a new class of foundation professionals to manage external relations. Beyond this historical claim, my argument is that the move toward institutions, toward the reliance of donors on grantmaking agents, and toward an ever greater public conception of philanthropy lies at the heart of the problems of effectiveness, accountability, and legitimacy. With a little historical perspective, some of the pressing issues of practice and strategy facing philanthropy come more into focus. In order to provide a full and fair diagnosis of the situation of contemporary philanthropy, it is thus useful to look back, at least in summary fashion, on the sweep of philanthropic history in the United States, with a special focus on the fateful developments in the 1960s and 1970s.

Donors and Their Trustees

It is difficult to pinpoint the start of American charitable giving. Some historians trace the origins of organized philanthropy in America back to the pilgrims,[2] while others see the real origins in eighteenth-century efforts to establish public and private civic institutions.[3] Part of the problem in pinpointing the origins of organized giving stems from the fact that charitable giving has taken many forms over the years, from volunteering, to cash contributions, to in-kind donations. When charitable giving is defined more narrowly as foundation giving, the problem of where to begin the narrative becomes easier. The history of American philanthropic foundations is relatively brief and its evolution can be tracked through a series of legal and legislative precedents that have made it possible for charitable giving to grow within new institutional forms.

The start of organized, large-scale philanthropy is usually linked to the emergence of independent colleges. From 1800 to 1860, the number of colleges grew from around 20 to over 500, with the total reaching 1,000 by 1900. Many of the colleges started early in the nineteenth century were begun with modest resources. Colleges such as Amherst, Williams, and Oberlin were established with sums of less than $50,000, and these colleges had to work hard to raise funds. Individual giving sustained these institutions and annual pledges—not large endowments—were the norm. With large industrial fortunes increasing during the second half of the century, many wealthy benefactors sought to establish colleges and universities. Cooper Union, Cornell, and Vassar were all started between 1859 and 1869 with gifts of around $500,000. The founding of Johns Hopkins University in 1876 with a gift of $7 million, Stanford University in 1885 with a $20 million bequest, and the University of Chicago in 1891 with Rockefeller gifts totaling $35 million marked the true arrival of organized giving and established a precedent for large-scale philanthropy. In these early gifts to higher education, many historians see a qualitative shift away from isolated acts of charity toward a much more ambitious form of philanthropy that would eventually find institutional support in private foundations.[4]

The earliest philanthropic foundations were actually not conceived with higher education in mind, but rather with the special goal of assisting freemen after the Civil War. In 1867, George Peabody established the Peabody Education Fund with $1 million to be used for the improvement of education in the South. In 1882, a New England textile manufacturer established the John F. Slater Fund with $1 million to help educate freemen in the South. These early foundations, with their narrow purposes dictated by important historical events along with philanthropic support for major institution founding, set the stage for the kind of enduring wide-ranging philanthropy that would emerge over time.

As the first wave of major donors possessing large industrial fortunes arrived on the scene, philanthropy was split between two opposing tendencies. First, Carnegie argued that philanthropy ought to create opportunities and be done during one's lifetime; other donors, like Sears, Roebuck founder Julius Rosenwald, made a strong case against perpetuity.[5] By urging that donors do their own giving during their lifetimes, these industrialists were essentially committing to returning their wealth to society in order to reinforce the social and economic system that made their own success possible. Far from disturbing the social order by interjecting their power and wealth, major donors could play a supportive role by creating libraries and universities, which opened doors of opportunity to all. Second, the close connection of the early donors with their philanthropic works eventually became problematic, when perpetual foundations, not universities, became a central object of philanthropic giving.

The mood in government toward philanthropy changed swiftly and substantially, as proposals surfaced for the creation of private foundations, new institutions that would be endowed in perpetuity and given broad mandates. When Rockefeller made out a deed of trust for $50 million worth of Standard Oil stock to be used to establish the Rockefeller Foundation, he could hardly have foreseen the controversy that this action would provoke. Unlike the General Education Board or the Carnegie Endowment for Teaching, which were focused on clear education-related missions, the Rockefeller Foundation would have a more sweeping goal, namely improving the welfare of humanity. Selected to serve on the foundation's board were Rockefeller's closest friends and family members. The initial board was made up of John D. Rockefeller, John D. Rockefeller, Jr., family associates, and noted educators.[6] Almost all observers at the time viewed this board as family dominated, meaning Rockefeller would be able to exert considerable if not complete control on the foundation. Before the foundation's philanthropic work could begin, administrative details needed to be worked out: Rockefeller instructed the trustees he had selected to seek a federal corporate charter that would grant the new foundation tax exemption in perpetuity.

When Rockefeller's representatives were initially questioned by congressional staff about whether too much discretion was being sought, they objected to any changes in the charter that would limit the scope of work of the foundation, set a limit to the life of the foundation, or require that public officials be included on the board.[7] Hearings were organized and opposition increased. President Taft denounced the proposed legislation as a dangerous scheme to perpetuate private wealth indefinitely. The controversy created by Rockefeller's request for a federal charter for his foundation must have caught Carnegie's attention. In June 1911, Carnegie sought articles of incorporation for his major philanthropic vehicle, the Carnegie Corporation, not from Congress, but rather from the New York state legislature. Carnegie's request for a charter was granted by a unanimous vote. In Washington, however, Rockefeller's quest for a federal charter still languished in committee despite two years of efforts. Finally, after much frustration with attempts to secure a federal charter, Rockefeller received his charter from New York State in 1913. Rockefeller's new general-purpose foundation still had as its mission the promotion of the well-being of mankind throughout the world. Starting with a modest initial endowment, the Rockefeller Foundation received additional endowment gifts during its early years, increasing its assets to $180 million by 1919.[8]

While the Milbank Memorial Fund (1905) and the Russell Sage Foundation (1907) predated the Rockefeller Foundation and may have provided some impetus toward creating a general-purpose foundation, Rockefeller organized his foundation in his own way:

> The Rockefeller Foundation was in one sense the culmination of John D. Rockefeller's application of business and religious models to education. Structurally it was a philanthropic mirror of a business corporation: It had a self-perpetuating board of trustees, a charter virtually without limits (so long as the activity was philanthropic), and a paid-in capital. Like that of many modern corporations, the Rockefeller Foundation's constituency was the entire human race.[9]

The rise of large private foundations made some in Congress uneasy as philanthropic resources threatened government's monopoly over social policy. The fact that foundation money came from America's wealthiest industrialists only intensified Congress's concern over philanthropy's influence and independence. In questioning both John D. Rockefeller and his assistants at the foundation, Congress considered the question of who should have ultimate control over foundation funds to ensure that they would be dedicated to serving the public welfare rather than to advancing the interests of private business.[10]

While major donors experienced some initial difficulties in Washington when they sought to charter the first private foundations, these institutions would eventually earn federal recognition as legitimate tax-exempt organizations. The Revenue Act of 1913, adopted after ratification of the Sixteenth Amendment, exempted institutions organized and operated exclusively for religious, charitable, scientific, or educational purposes. Subsequent acts added the prevention of cruelty to children and animals and the promotion of literary purposes; a 1921 amendment specifically recognized community chests and private foundations. The early evolution of foundations as vehicles for scientific philanthropy was profoundly shaped by Carnegie and Rockefeller, who not only led the way but widely preached their new approach. These industrialists helped define the proper purview and methods of philanthropy and, by virtue of their strength of personality and convictions, set an example that placed control of these new philanthropic institutions squarely in the hands of donors.

A number of large national foundations were started around this time and constituted the first wave of generously endowed general purpose foundations in the Rockefeller and Carnegie mold. However, the most significant development during this period was the creation in 1914 of the Cleveland Foundation, which was the first community foundation.[11] The creation of a new foundation structure, one that pooled resources and placed them under the stewardship of a board of community leaders,[12] was significant for two reasons. First, it represented a broadening of the organizational forms through which organized philanthropy could be conducted. Second, and more important, it signaled a transition in philanthropic management, one that placed trustees in key authoritative roles and displaced the donor as the center of philanthropy. Local contributors would surrender funds either during their lives or upon their death to the Cleveland Foundation and allow its trustees to administer the funds—sometimes with detailed instructions, at other times only with broad guidelines. The appearance of the first community foundation marked the start of a slow but steady shift in philanthropic power away from donors to trustees, a shift that would play itself out over the next four decades.

In the years following Carnegie's death, the question of succession naturally became more than just a legal issue. Donors needed institutions, plans, and people in the event that all surplus wealth had not been given away. New stewards of philanthropy were needed when the first wave of donors passed from the scene. Over the next forty years—a period during which the number of foundations would explode—philanthropic control became vested in the trustees of foundations, whose responsibility it would be to ensure the long-term viability of the foundation and the pursuit of the founding donor's vision.[13]

Carnegie and Rockefeller may have opened the door of American philanthropy, but it was not until World War II and its aftermath that large private foundations were created in great numbers. One explanation of the boom years in foundation creation during the 1940s and 1950s is the intersection of two trends: substantial increases in personal income and higher rates of taxation drove funds into foundations.[14] Not only were income taxes raised during World War II, but estates were subject to heavy taxation. From 1941 to 1971, the top federal estate tax was 77 percent on amounts above $10 million. Under such conditions, charitable giving was quite appealing. Moreover, there was no prohibition against conveying business interests to foundations and thereby maintaining control of large blocks of stock. Foundations became the vehicle of choice of donors seeking to preserve assets for philanthropy after death. The significant growth in the number of private foundations during the 1940s and 1950s was concentrated in the East. There are many possible explanations of this concentration. First, many of the wealthiest families were located in cities such as New York, Boston, and Philadelphia.[15] Second, New York State's early welcoming of the Rockefeller Foundation contributed significantly to the heavy concentration of early philanthropic activity in New York.

As the founding rate of new foundations boomed in the 1940s and 1950s (see figure 3.1), many of the early foundations faced a critical management challenge: finding new leadership after the death of the founding donor. The natural candidates to fill this gap were trustees. Trustees began to assert themselves at major foundations such as Rockefeller and Carnegie during the 1920s and 1930s, and other foundations soon began to see the wisdom of delegating philanthropic responsibilities to trustees. By the 1940s and 1950s, highly visible and charismatic philanthropists became more rare, as foundation control shifted to trustees under a new model of foundation governance. Many foundation trustees were recruited from the founder's circle of friends and business associates. While the original donor was present and involved, foundation trustees could be counted on to offer advice and encouragement. After the donor had left the scene, the responsibilities of foundation trustees inevitably increased as many foundations experienced leadership vacuums. Who then were these new foundation managers charged with carrying on the legacies of departed donors? Writing in 1930, a researcher described the typical foundation trustee as

> [A] man well past middle age; he is more often than not a man of considerable affluence, or one whose economic security ranks high; . . . he is, presumably, respectable and conventional and belongs to the best clubs and churches, and he associates with men of prestige, power and affluence. His training has been largely in the arts and humanities . . . He resides in the Northeast section of the United States and has attended one of the private colleges in that region. His intelligence is ranked high by various institutions of higher learning from whom he has received signal honors. In short he is a member of that successful and conservative class . . . whose status is based primarily upon pecuniary success.[16]

Two early studies reveal that foundation trustees came mostly from business, law, and higher education during philanthropy's growth period.[17] Many of these men—and most were men—knew the donor personally, either as a business partner or as a legal client.

The central characteristic of the trustees who began to assume responsibility for American foundations ultimately had little to do with their demographic characteristics or political views. Trustees were first and foremost a new class of caretakers whose main responsibility would be to see that the

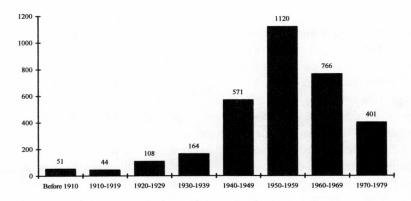

Figure 3.1 **Founding of new foundations holding assets of more than $1 million or making at least $100,000 in annual grants.** *Source:* Odendahl (1987).

interests and values of founding donors were pursued and, when appropriate, expanded:

> In Rockefeller and in Carnegie what had begun as a small group of secretaries, friends, trusted lawyers, and, later, a few acceptable presidents from a few acceptable universities had become, by the end of the 1920s, an administrative system which still included many of the same types, but with a clear sense now of their own independence as a community or group of communities from the intentions of one wealthy man. In both cases, efforts were made to interpret the intentions of "the Founder" in a tone which at times seems somewhat mystical; but those intentions were, quite rapidly, transformed into ideas of preferred policies.[18]

While trustees for the most part sought to preserve the private character of foundations, they were more than caretakers of the donor's philanthropic legacy. Over time, trustees began to assert themselves and make programmatic decisions with little or no guidance from the donor. Many of the early foundations were created with broad charters like that of the Rockefeller Foundation. In such cases, trustees had far more to do than merely preserve the philanthropic intent of the donor; when only a broad charitable intent was present, trustees had to interpret this intent or even substitute their own judgment for that of the phantom donor.

The Rockefeller family's experience with trusteeship is instructive.[19] Ten years after Rockefeller's death, his son, John D. Rockefeller, Jr., learned firsthand of the growing role trustees would play in the management of philanthropic foundations. Rockefeller had put the young JDR, Jr., on the board of the Rockefeller Foundation and some of its related entities. For years, JDR, Jr., was content simply to observe. One of the endowed entities created by Rockefeller was the China Medical Board, an operating foundation with a public health agenda. In 1932, soon after graduating from college, Rockefeller's son assumed a seat on the board of the CMB as secretary. However, when he tried to take an active role in running one of the board meetings, he was rebuffed by one of the CMB outside directors, Roger Greene. After being told off in front of the entire board, JDR, Jr., sought to work out a compromise with Greene, one that would allow the young Rockefeller to play more than a stenographic role in the meetings. JDR, Jr., eventually gave up, however, and bowing to the pressure of the trustees, resigned from the board. This incident foreshadowed how little deference donors could expect from trustees, and it is a useful symbol of the changes that were occurring throughout American foundations as the original donors to the major foundations of the turn of the century passed away. Carnegie's death in 1919, followed by Rockefeller's death in 1937, truly marked the end of an era in which charismatic donors would play a central role in the administration of foundations. Trustees stepped into this void and inserted their private agendas and interests into their philanthropic work.

The early development of the Ford Foundation also presents a good example of growing trustee influence. The Ford Foundation was set up in 1936, but did not begin grantmaking in earnest until 1950, when the estates of Henry and Edsel Ford were settled after their deaths in 1947 and 1943, respectively. The foundation had made small grants totaling about $1 million a year to Michigan charities before its activation in 1950, but this narrow focus was expanded when its assets reached $500 million. In 1948 the trustees appointed an eight-member committee of independent consultants from higher education and public life to chart the future of the institution, which had become the largest foundation in the country.[20] The committee was chaired by H. Rowan Gaither, who later served as president of the foundation (1953–1956) and as chairman of its board (1956–1958). The findings of the committee were published in 1949 and were "adopted by the trustees virtually without change."[21] The trustees then declared their intent to work in five broad areas: to promote world peace and a world of law and justice, freedom and democracy, economic development, educational opportunity, and knowledge building through research. These programmatic objectives were so broad that almost all of the grants the Ford

Foundation trustees would make in the years ahead would fall under their purview. There was also substantial latitude in the kinds of grants trustees could make. During the 1950s, the trustees exerted considerable influence. As a former Ford Foundation executive noted: "In the beginning the trustees alone made most of the choices. They were guided in part by the Gaither study, but their choices also reflected personal experiences and proclivities. Thus, the presence on the board of the dean of a business school surely influenced our decision to support business education, an activity we defined as falling within one of the five original areas of action."[22]

Active governance by trustees was efficient, since few received payment for their work. Even among the largest and most administratively developed foundations, administrative costs remained low in the 1950s. For foundations with significant assets (over $50 million), administrative expenses were between 8 and 9 percent. In 1953, smaller foundations (assets under $25 million) actually spent a larger percentage of their resources on administration (see table 3.1).[23] This fact can probably be attributed to the existence of a number of fixed costs that all foundations encounter, but which represent a greater administrative burden for smaller foundations.

Whatever the legal and financial forces leading Americans to establish foundations in great numbers, these independent institutions were still seen with suspicion by some in government. The status of foundations as independent, privately endowed institutions ultimately had contradictory implications for philanthropy's relationship with government. On the one hand, foundations were above the political fray since they did not require government largesse to pursue their work. On the other hand, this freedom was a source of concern since the large foundation endowments made organized philanthropy appear unaccountable and gave it an aura of unchecked power.

Regulation and the Foundation Response

While the world of philanthropy emerged from several congressional inquiries during the first half of the twentieth century relatively unscathed, everything changed in the early 1960s as private foundations were under siege on a number of fronts. Financial abuses at a few small foundations and highly politicized grants by some of the larger foundations brought increased public and congressional scrutiny. In 1961, Congressman Wright Patman, a populist from Texas, launched what would become an eight-year inquiry into the grantmaking and management practices of founda-

Table 3.1 **Administrative expenditures of seventy-two foundations in 1953.**

Assets	Number of foundations	Total expenditures (in millions of dollars)	Administrative expenditures (in millions of dollars)	Administrative as percentage of expenditures
Over $100 million	6	77.315	6.337	8.2
$50 to $100 million	6	14.834	1.310	8.8
$25 to $50 million	12	17.631	1.271	7.2
Under $25 million	48	45.253	5.391	11.9
Total	72	155.033	14.309	9.2

Source: Andrews (1956).

tions. After extended hearings and negotiations in the House and Senate, Congress settled on a package of regulations designed to bring foundations under greater oversight. Although Congress had considered as punishment a requirement that all foundations expend all their assets in forty years and go out of business, this proposal was ultimately left out of the final bill. The Tax Reform Act 1969 (TRA 1969) set in place the following major regulations on foundations: an annual excise tax on net investment income, prohibitions against self-dealing, an annual payout requirement, a limitation on ownership of shares in any single corporation, and various disclosure requirements. For a world used to operating freely, the regulations were painful and caused much reflection.[24]

Writing in 1970, Carnegie Corporation president Alan Pifer reflected on philanthropy's encounter with government and the imposition of new regulations:

> It was a period during which foundations were kicked in the shins and had their noses bloodied, and consequently we who work for them tend now to harbor an understandable sense of injustice. We resent the unfairness and shortsightedness of some of the features of the legislation and the extra administrative burden these will cause us. We resent the irrational emphasis placed by the Congress on a few uncharacteristic instances of administrative caprice in foundations and the excessive attention given to a few egregious cases of real abuse, while the overall positive record of foundations in American life was ignored. We resent the impression left with the public as a result of the legislation, that foundations were simply indicted, tried, found guilty and punished.[25]

In the months following the passage of TRA 1969, foundations went through a period of extensive self-examination. As a Luce Foundation vice president noted at that time: "Suddenly we realized we were not the conscientious, silent do-gooders we thought we were, but a vast array of extremely diverse organizations—with little or no constituency to come to our collective defense. Even more eye opening was the sudden realization that we needed defense—and needed it badly."[26] What could be done to improve the positions of foundations after the embarrassment of 1969? Foundation leaders ultimately pulled closer together to defend philanthropy from any further outside intrusion. They did so by pushing a two-pronged strategy: first, through an aggressive campaign mounted by their national association, private foundations abandoned any claim to privacy and recast themselves as public institutions that were open and accessible to all; second, they took important steps to professionalize foundation work.

These two fateful steps, taken decades ago, continue to cast a long shadow over the field of philanthropy. The move to define philanthropic institutions as public trusts operated for public purposes put a significant crimp on the ability of donors to engage in idiosyncratic and highly personal forms of large-scale giving. With the move afoot to de-privatize and open up foundations, donors could not very easily maintain that their values, beliefs, and commitments had a central place in organized philanthropy. Similarly, the introduction of large numbers of professional staff made it hard for donors to hold on to the control of their philanthropic institutions and led over time to the progressive diminution of donor influence and control in institutional philanthropy. My claim here is that these two moves, one at the level of ideology and beliefs, the other at the level of practices and procedures, have helped make the field appear more transparent, but have also made effective giving ever more elusive. With the accelerating professionalization of philanthropy, the private values and commitments of donors have been squeezed out of institutional giving and rendered it more neutral, technocratic, and homogeneous. In a field in which one would expect to see profound disagreements about what constitutes an authentic public need and how best to address complex social problems, there has emerged a remarkable level of agreement and complacency. This is hardly a recipe for achieving philanthropic breakthroughs. Thus, while regulations are often thought to have economic implications, in the case of foundations, the most important effects of government intervention turned out to be organizational in nature. Defensiveness and convergence were the ultimate products of this shock to the philanthropic system.

Soon after TRA 1969 was enacted on December 31, 1969, the foundation community was awash in recriminations and dire predictions of the impending decline in charitable giving. In the midst of the general confusion, conferences were hurriedly organized to discuss the implications of the new regulations. One lawyer, who helped explain the new regulations to foundations in 1970, recalled the mood of the time:

> There was an atmosphere of terror. There was great fright and lack of understanding by most of the foundations that had not been closely involved with the legislative process. Most foundations around the country had not stayed close to the process. They'd read about it in the newspapers, and the descriptions there had been very frightening. The whole thrust of the publicity about the bearing of this legislation on foundations was that it's terrible, foundations are at least an endangered species, and they may well be on their way to extinction. The mood was almost one of panic.[27]

What could be done in light of the unfortunate precedent set by TRA 1969? In February 1970, only two months after the passage of TRA 1969, the Council on Foundations, the Foundation Center, and the National Council on Philanthropy moved to set up a special Committee on the Foundation Field. The mission of the committee was to "delineate and examine in light of present circumstances those services that need to be provided to the foundation field, and to recommend an organizational structure for the field most appropriate thereto."[28] Chaired by John Gardner, the former secretary of the U.S. Department of Health, Education, and Welfare, the committee included three foundation officials and a dean from Harvard University. With three existing but weak and ineffectual membership and service organizations vying for control of the field, the committee faced a difficult charge. Nevertheless, the committee was able to see that "the fragile position of foundations" called for action. The committee urged change on seven fronts: (1) increased reporting and information dissemination by foundations; (2) support of independent research and publications on foundations; (3) continuation and extension of library services for the general public; (4) improved government relations; (5) development of voluntary standards of good practice; (6) provision of a central clearinghouse and forum to facilitate the exchange of information and cooperation among foundations; and (7) development of a public relations strategy for the field as a whole.

Most significantly, the Committee on the Foundation Field highlighted the need to eliminate some of the competing voices within the sector. The Council on Foundations eventually moved to Washington, D.C., where it could have more direct access to Congress, the Treasury Department, and the Internal Revenue Service. As the council's visibility and membership grew, the rival National Council on Philanthropy declined. The committee's recommendation that philanthropy organize itself around a single association was realized when the National Council on Philanthropy was merged with the Coalition of National Voluntary Organizations to form the Independent Sector, a new national organization representing the entire nonprofit sector, including both giving and recipient organizations.[29] By January 1980, the Council on Foundations had become the prime spokesman for organized philanthropy by mounting a sustained effort to expand its membership in the years after TRA 1969. The council brought in new members each year by moving its national meeting to different sites around the country, each time attracting nonmember foundations from the host city. Attendance at the national meetings increased between 1970 and 1979 from 550 to 1,200.[30]

In the aftermath of TRA 1969, foundation administrators were confused and frightened and needed help understanding the implications of the legislation. Senior staff at the council traveled extensively around the country in dozens of cities in which foundation administrators met to hear about the new regulations and the measures necessary to bring foundations into compliance. Foundation executives were particularly confused and concerned about "expenditure responsibility" as defined in the legislation, which forced foundations to be more careful in documenting the recipients of their grants. As a result of its outreach efforts during the early 1970s, the council cemented its position as the main spokesman and organizer of the field.

One of the main battles that leaders in the field aimed to fight was against philanthropic timidity. Avoiding capitulation and retreat after TRA 1969 was a recurrent theme in many of the council's meetings with foundation administrators during its national tour. One official at the council observed: "Many tax lawyers and accountants were counseling everybody to do only the most obviously safe things. There was a great tendency on the part of foundations to let their accountants and their tax lawyers make their charitable judgments for them. The Council was saying don't do that. You are the people who are the experts in your field."[31] The effort to keep foundations from becoming too cautious was significant because it necessitated a broader effort to place foundation management in the hands of a budding class of professionals. In the decades ahead, these philanthropic experts would not only make safe grants to private universities and hospitals but would also push the frontiers of charitable giving into new areas corresponding to new social needs.

Throughout the 1970s, the Council on Foundations thus defined for itself two important missions. First, the council sought to define a new understanding of the place of foundations within society, one that defined foundations as public trusts, open and accessible to all and, most important, operated for public purposes. This first mission was vital because Patman's populist antifoundation crusade was founded on the notion that foundations were only tax dodges for the wealthy and a way to pursue their private agendas without accountability. Second, the council sought to reform foundation management and eradicate those practices that had brought the entire field before Congress for scrutiny and criticism.

In the end, the council's two missions, to create a professional culture within organized philanthropy and to reposition foundations as public institutions, fit well together. As foundations slowly embraced their new public responsibilities, they naturally sought to expand their professional staff to improve relations with the public, including, most importantly, the myriad of grantseeking organizations in the broader nonprofit sector. At the same time, the new foundation managers wholeheartedly embraced the new public trust conception of foundations because it coincided with their own understanding of their role and supported the start of careers in grantmaking.

Public Trust Conception of Foundations

Acting strategically, organized philanthropy's principal concern following TRA 1969 was to open up foundations to the public and to instill in foundation workers the belief that foundations were really public trusts to be operated for public purposes. One of the first and most important goals of the field was therefore to increase the visibility and accessibility of foundations through improved reporting. As a foundation executive remarked about the move towards greater openness:

> Foundations have adopted communications programs after hewing to an ethic of privacy for years. They decide to "go public" for a variety of reasons. They may be swayed by the example of other foundations, persuaded by the accountability effort of the Council on Foundations, or impelled by crisis. Many foundations took the step as a result of the Tax Reform Act of 1969, in the realization that each had a vital stake in dispelling mystery and myth about the field as a whole.[32]

For many foundations, the first step in "going public" was the publication of an annual report, a move that the leaders in the field enthusiastically endorsed. Institutional philanthropy was thus going through a transformation at least in terms of its transparency, with self-disclosed reports about foundations being made available in large numbers for the first time.

Improving Foundation Reporting

One area in which almost everyone agreed there was room for improvement was the publication of annual reports. In the years immediately following TRA 1969, numerous articles in *Foundation News* trumpeted increased foundation accountability through greater reporting. Some foundations issued their first annual reports, while others held "town meetings" at which grantseekers could ask questions and express concerns. In a 1974 editorial, the council informed its members that "to paraphrase the New Hampshire state motto, foundations are going to have to learn to 'Communicate Freely, Or Die.' "[33]

Failure to report adequately was a main complaint of the congressional investigators, with one member of the Senate Finance Committee commenting during the hearings that he deplored "the concealment of foundation activities." The Senate staff charged with assembling data on foundations was also frustrated by the lack of reporting, noting that only 140 foundations issued annual reports and that thousands did not even respond to a request for information. Even though in 1970 foundations were beginning to see the need to change their ways, the information flow within philanthropy was uneven. Many of the smaller foundations had yet to follow the urgings of the council's leadership. One foundation worker noted in 1970 that foundations could be divided into four groups: "The first includes the 140 who issue annual reports plus those who unquestionably take the public into their confidence." Not all foundations were so responsible: "The second [group] we can call 'the public be damned' group." These foundations sought to protect their anonymity and to stay as far outside of the limelight as possible. The third group was where the problem lay, for its "members are engaged in a free-wheeling variety of abuses, and they are well aware of it. Not much chance for reporting here, not willingly that is." This left a final category:

> The fourth category is much the largest and is composed of the many foundations, most small, who have never been made to realize the threat they constitute to the entire foundation field by their refusal to adequately

communicate their activities to the public . . . Some say that if they reported they would call attention to themselves and invite requests that they neither want to consider nor have the staff to answer. Their comments have at least a dash of "the public be damned" and are liberally laced with the "it's my foundation, so it's my money."[34]

One idea for addressing the reporting problem discussed at some length in the 1970s involved the creation of a "Foundation Press," which would assist smaller foundations to produce and publish annual reports. If greater public disclosure was needed by all foundations, the argument went, then the philanthropic community as a whole had a responsibility to join together and help the smaller foundations find ways—even with their limited staffs—to be open and accessible. As the head of the Twentieth Century Fund noted, "All of us should endorse and practice the principle of full disclosure. Every form of cronyism and self-dealing should be banned."[35]

Typical of the response to the new call for openness was the Field Foundation's public promulgation of new principles guiding its operation. Chief among these was a pledge to improve public information[36] and accessibility:

[Foundations] should be open to public scrutiny, making public reports at reasonable intervals and constantly sharing information and ideas with other persons and groups, including other foundations, active in the same areas. They should conduct their deliberations and reach their decisions by established and non-arbitrary procedures made known to all who seek their assistance.[37]

Resistance to this trend toward openness was not met kindly. As one foundation executive put it: "Foundations not yet ready to assume their responsibilities [for reporting] should perhaps rethink their role in the foundation picture. It has been said that 'it is easy to dodge our responsibilities, but it is impossible to dodge the consequences of dodging our responsibilities.'"[38] In 1971 the Council on Foundations also began the practice of surveying its members on their reporting. By 1975, 275 members of the council—72 percent of the membership—were issuing annual reports. At the same time, the number of foundations producing a newsletter increased from three in 1969 to over forty in 1984.[39]

Although the campaign to open up foundations through increased reporting started in 1970, it has continued in various forms ever since. For example, the council launched an awards program in the 1980s to recognize the best-produced annual reports by its members. Even in 1979, the first item on the council's "Checklist for Foundations" emphasized the continued need for openness: "We must be open, honest and candid about what we do . . . Disclosure is no longer an option; it is a necessity. Annual reports by foundations are a minimum form of disclosure that far too many foundations still do not use."[40] For many leaders in philanthropy, increased reporting was a first and critical step in building a strong defense for the field.

While there was and continues to be some value in the kind of disclosure practiced by foundations, difficult questions remain about the meaningfulness of this data. After all, being transparent about the grants that are made and the expenses incurred in the process of grantmaking is certainly part of the accountability challenge. But it is—and was in the 1970s—only a piece of the puzzle. Transparency was trumpeted and embraced as an easy answer to calls for accountability. By generating documents describing their work, foundations attempted to break down some of the perceived walls that insulated them from the rest of the nonprofit community. Unfortunately, the concepts of transparency and accountability were confused during the panicked and hurried response of the foundation field in the 1970s, and these two concepts continue to be wrongly conflated to this day.

Joining Givers and Receivers

As part of the effort to open themselves up to the public and appear more engaged, foundations began to rethink their relationship with their grantees. Instead of seeing themselves simply as the purveyors of funds, anonymous check writers supporting worthy causes, foundations began to assert for themselves a more direct relationship with their grantees. A new relationship with, and responsibility to, nonprofit projects was thought to offer the best chance of affecting the recipient organization on a long-term basis. Foundations in the 1970s were urged to be team players, which meant encouraging other funders to join in projects and coordinating the involvement of outside parties. This new role would entail "indemnifying, recruiting, and providing technical assistance to the funded organization"—not just sending a check.[41]

Instead of seeing the nonprofit grantseeker as a burden to be dealt with either by rejecting or approving its grant request, many foundations—particularly those involved in the council's work—reconceived their relationship with grantees in more collaborative terms. The strategic value of the repositioning was obvious. As long as foundations were seen as partners in the nonprofit sector, working side by side with community organizations and social service agencies of all sorts, charges of elitism and detachment would be more difficult to support. One foundation official noted at the time that the passage of TRA 1969 had "prompted foundations to examine themselves and the ways they have traditionally operated." Changed practices were found to have resulted from this self-examination: "Not surprisingly, some consternation is apparent . . . because the extra care with which grants must now be made seems to do violence to some aspects of the prevailing view that philanthropy has come to have of itself during the last century. This is a view of legitimacy and honor."[42]

The regulations, though only "a signal" that a reassessment of foundations was overdue, were leading foundations to rethink their relationship with grantees. The traditional view within philanthropy held that once a grant is made, "the relationship between foundation and grantee should be characterized by mutual trust and a hands-off attitude on the part of the foundation."[43] In place of this detached style, foundations were moving toward a more engaged grantmaking style in which grantees are closely monitored in their work and foundations offer support and resources to those carrying out programs.

One of the most dramatic attempts to make this shift was undertaken by the Cummins Engine Foundation immediately following the enactment of TRA 1969. At a time when urban racial strife was increasing, Cummins announced its intention to focus all of its philanthropic energies on urban problems. Cummins soon announced with some fanfare its hiring of four African American program officers to administer the program. The goal of this reorientation was threefold: first, Cummins hoped to make its grantmaking more socially relevant and direct it to the most needy; second, the program was a step toward opening up grantmaking to disadvantaged populations; and third, the new staff would work hand in hand with community groups in a new way.

Other notable efforts to improve foundation relations with the nonprofit community included a series of open houses held in the 1970s across the country. At these philanthropic town meetings, nonprofit organizations were invited to ask trustees and professional staff of foundations about their operations. One such meeting that attracted national press in 1976 was hosted by the Bush Foundation in Minnesota, which drew over 400 representatives from the local nonprofit community. Because it had encouraged increased reporting, the Council on Foundations supported these public meetings through a series of editorials and reports.

As in other areas, the Council on Foundations played a leadership role by clearly defining proper foundation policy in the area of grantee relations.

Soon after taking over as president of the council, James Joseph focused on the importance of including grant recipients in the operation of foundations. Joseph argued that the grant recipient could be the most effective defender of the charitable sector—when properly cultivated. To ensure that the donee would be a proponent rather than an opponent of foundations, Joseph advocated three measures: (1) treating donees as if they are important to the foundation's mission; (2) allowing donees to provide input on the foundation's priorities; (3) making donees feel that they have a stake in the continued health and well-being of foundations.[44]

The idea of connecting givers and recipients seemed in the 1970s as natural and as necessary as anything else the foundation field could pursue. It did have its costs, however. The removal of the barriers between the two sides of the philanthropic exchange removed some of the critical distance from grantmaking. It also positioned foundations as part of the nonprofit community rather than as standing apart and aloof from it. The most important effect of this move was to shift giving away from the independent pursuit of the donor's vision and passion and closer to the expressed needs of communities. Foundations may have convinced themselves during the post–regulatory reform period that they needed to listen more to those in the recipient community, but they failed to recognize that strategic and effective philanthropy demands more of donors than just being the dutiful respondents to community demands for resources. In the rush to be responsive and to "collaborate" with nonprofits, foundations ultimately failed to take into full account the need for donors to lead public opinion sometimes, rather than follow it.

A Code of Conduct

One of the most visible moments in the emergence of a profession is the propagation of a code of ethics governing the behavior of professionals.[45] In philanthropy, the adoption of a code of ethics represented the final step toward instilling a new ethos of openness. A code of ethics was slow in coming for two reasons: first, the council did not want to impose a code unilaterally too soon after 1969 for fear of alienating its new and growing membership; and second, foundation officials prided themselves on their independence and were generally resistant to outside parties seeking to influence a foundation's policies. However, many foundation officials felt there was a need for some kind of statement from the field as a whole that would outline acceptable foundation practices and demonstrate to the public that foundations were capable of self-governance and self-regulation.

In 1973, leaders within the field made a first effort after TRA 1969 at laying down operating principles for foundations. The council published an early version of what would become its code of conduct for foundations: *Some General Principles and Guidelines for Grantmaking Foundations: A Policy Statement of the Directors of the Council on Foundations.*[46] The principles were nonbinding and generally sought to reinforce the notion that foundations must make a special effort to be open and accessible. Included in the principles was a clear reference to TRA 1969 as a lesson not to be forgotten:

> Despite the "overkill" contained in these provisions—which one must hope will prove open to Congressional adjustment as working experience with the effects of the Tax Reform Act of 1969 become clearer—the act's forceful reminders that foundations exist for the public benefit and must be so directed have to be recognized as necessary and for the good.[47]

The policy pronouncements of 1973 set in place the cornerstone on which a more ambitious effort to develop operating principles for foundations was built six years later.

In 1979, the board of directors of the Council on Foundations took the first step toward creating an ethics code by appointing a special committee. Meeting often over the course of a year, the committee worked through numerous drafts and presented them at meetings of various regional gatherings and at the annual meeting of the council in Dallas. The council was clear about the purpose of the code: it was "to provide practical counsel to new foundations just establishing their operating guidelines and to existing foundations and other donor organizations that may be re-examining their policies and procedures."[48]

The statement, entitled "Recommended Principles and Practices for Effective Grantmaking," also served an important public relations function. In the aftermath of regulation, the council went to considerable lengths to help its members increase their public profile and improve relations with recipient organizations. The code fit well into this plan. The council noted that "it draws heavily on the experience and insights of foundations executives and corporate giving administrators and is couched in terms of what has proved useful in the successful handling of grants and in the maintaining of good relations with the various publics with which grantmakers must be concerned."[49]

The eleven principles and practices amounted to complete endorsement of the view that private foundations have important public responsibilities and must be governed in the public interest. The first three principles urged foundations to establish a set of policies that clearly define fundamental objectives, appoint a board of directors committed to implementing these objectives, and set up processes for receiving, examining, and deciding on grant applications. The fourth through seventh principles focused on transparency and accessibility. The council urged that foundations recognize their public responsibilities to a broad range of constituents, including recipient organizations, state government, and the IRS. Open communication with the public and grantseekers was recommended, including prompt and honest responses to all grant requests and the publication of an annual report. These ideas flowed directly from the experience of foundations during the 1960s, when an inability to communicate the good work of foundations opened the door to congressional attacks. The ninth through eleventh principles supported commonsense measures to improve foundation performance. The council recommended the periodic evaluation of foundation programs, the careful avoidance of any transactions that might appear self-interested, and active participation in the council, regional associations, and organizations representing the entire nonprofit sector.

Ten of the eleven principles were uncontroversial and predictable in that they pushed the council's accountability and openness agenda while seeking to ensure that foundations continue to improve and professionalize grantmaking practices. One of the eleven principles did, however, provoke some consternation. The eighth principle urged foundations to professionalize their staffs and rely on affirmative action in their hiring. This caused some resistance among conservative funders, who left the council in protest when acceptance of the principles became a prerequisite for membership. The alienation of a small number of council members in 1983 was a small price to pay for having a large and influential number of private foundations publicly endorse the council's ethics code. For the council, the passage of a code of conduct was a momentous event. Not only did it signify that foundations were serious about patrolling their own ranks, but it also demonstrated that the council leadership could govern the field and successfully spread its vision of foundations as public institutions.[50] Looking back at the process of creating and propagating the "Principles and Practices," council president James Joseph noted that the attempt to identify and affirm the principles constituted "a marriage of private and public values." For Joseph, the development of a code of conduct was a critical public relations coup and a triumph of the council's public agenda: "This union [of public and private values] preserves the social contract between private philanthropy and American society and protects the legal charter which makes each foundation a trustee of the public good."[51] For Joseph, the passage and acceptance of the "Principles and Practices" represented the most important step in positioning foundations: "It is our 'public purpose' commitment which is the most persuasive in convincing critics and public policy makers that we should be permitted to hold philanthropic resources in trust for perpetuity."[52]

For Joseph and the Council on Foundations, the development and later required acceptance of the "Principles and Practices" in the early 1980s were events of signal importance. Not only did they mark a significant moment in the move to "fix" philanthropy, but they also confirmed the view that foundations were indeed public trusts to be operated for public purposes. With a set of common principles and standards and a strong national association, foundations were moving decisively to cement into place a new normative order, one that began in the early 1970s with the Council on Foundations' proclamation: " 'Not our money, but charity's' should be the key principle guiding each act of foundation donors, trustees, and managers, whether in earning money or giving it away."[53]

The idea that the field of foundation philanthropy required a code of conduct is at once reasonable and dangerous. Reasonable, in that significant amounts of money and power are at issue, and this means that there is a burden to act in a way that is just, appropriate, and respectful. Dangerous, in that philanthropy is at least in part about innovation and pluralism, and the attempt to lay down standards risks normalizing a field that should be anything but normal. There is little doubt that the reformers were well meaning in their efforts to improve the conduct of foundations, but they never appeared to come fully to terms with the major underlying issue, namely whether convergence and agreement on any principles and practices—no matter how procedural and nonsubstantive many may have been—were really in the best long-term interests of the field. With pressure to fix and reform the world of institutional philanthropy still strong in the aftermath of major regulation, the foundation field did largely embrace both a code of conduct and the idea that private philanthropy had significant public responsibilities.

In retrospect, the strategic repositioning of foundations as public trusts was a potent public relations strategy that spoke to some of the central concerns of those who had criticized foundations. By becoming more transparent and by adopting standards, foundations were able to effectively counter the most damaging charges that they had faced, namely that they were elitist organizations, secretive in their work, and out of touch with the communities they were supposed to serve. Of course, by taking steps to reverse negative perceptions, the foundation field had to make some concessions and changes. Yet when the dust fully settled after TRA 1969, few could reasonably argue that institutional philanthropy had not begun to change in significant ways.

Professionalization and New Practices

With the Council on Foundations leading the way, foundations began to change their management structures and hiring practices. Most significantly, the new open and transparent foundations of the 1970s and 1980s discovered that they needed new staff to manage their increasingly complex external relations. It is therefore not surprising that one of the most obvious changes within private foundations in the 1970s occurred on the balance sheet: the new regulations drove up administrative costs. Indeed, looking at the administrative expenses of foundations after TRA 1969, one observer at the time remarked:

> For foundations that attempted to adapt their procedures to the new restrictions, a lengthy review process was required. The day-to-day involvement of legal counsel in the operation of foundations increased dramatically—hardly an unmixed blessing. Many foundations began to ask their lawyers to review each grant they were considering and sought opinion letters on a wide variety of other transactions . . . Legal fees paid by foundations have almost certainly increased since 1969; the paperwork the lawyers recommended has led to higher clerical costs and has in some instances required additional staff.[54]

The implementation costs of the new regulations are evident when one considers changes in foundation administrative expenses between 1966 and 1972. Administrative expenses include all costs related to the operation of a foundation, excluding grant outlays. During this six-year period, administrative expenses as a percent of grant outlays increased from 6.4 percent to 14.9 percent (see figure 3.2). This increase was a significant change from the trend during the previous decade, when administrative costs were dropping.

To some foundation managers, the increasing administrative costs were simply a requirement of the new regulations. Increased administrative costs immediately after TRA 1969 were an early indication of what would be a broader trend in the field toward more staffing.

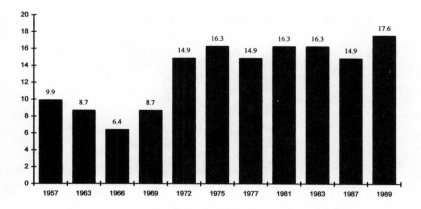

Figure 3.2 **Foundation administrative expenses as a percentage of grant outlays, 1957–1989. Data are from multiple volumes of** *Foundation Directory*, **1960–1991.**

> The foundation of the seventies will be far more professionally staffed than has been the case to date . . . It will no longer be possible to operate a foundation out of a banker's pocket. The new legislation regarding private foundations—the possible stiff penalties, the danger of personal liability for each and every officer and trustee, the more extensive reporting and auditing requirements, expenditure responsibility for particular grants—all lead inevitably to the conclusion that someone had best be on duty full-time, minding the store.[55]

To fill the new openings within private foundations with a cadre of professional grantmakers, foundations began to change their recruiting in the 1970s.

Seeking Philanthropic Expertise

A key element in the emergence of any profession is the recognition of the salience of specialized expertise. Throughout the 1970s and 1980s, foundations began to recognize philanthropic expertise as a qualification for foundation work and to seek it out. No longer interested in generalists from higher education and government who could come to foundation work fresh, many foundations began to look favorably on previous professional experience in philanthropy. To illustrate and document the growing salience of professional expertise and experience, I have collected data on the hiring practices of foundations over the two decades following TRA 1969 (see table 3.2).[56]

Table 3.2 **Previous employment of all foundation professional staff, 1970–1989.**

	Foundation	Nonprofit	University	Government	Other	Total
1970–74	22	26	53	26	12	139
	(15.8)	(18.7)	(38.1)	(18.7)	(8.6)	
1975–79	38	30	53	24	22	167
	(22.8)	(18.0)	(31.7)	(14.4)	(13.2)	
1980–84	39	22	31	31	24	147
	(26.5)	(15.0)	(21.1)	(21.1)	(16.3)	
1985–89	87	44	38	25	15	209
	(41.6)	(21.1)	(18.2)	(12.0)	(7.2)	
Total	186	122	175	106	73	662
	(28.1)	(18.4)	(26.4)	(16.0)	(11.0)	

Note: parenthetical numbers are percentages.
Sources: (1) the hiring announcements in *Foundation News*; and (2) the appointments column in the *Ford Foundation Letter*. In addition, some supplementary data were gathered from the newsletters of regional associations of grantmakers and from books on foundations. The database contains information on the foundation that the individuals joined, the position assumed there, the organization from which the individual came, and the previous position of the individual.

Two significant trends in hiring are apparent. First, there has been a substantial increase in the hiring of foundation staff with previous grant-making experience. This increase confirms that the move to professionalize foundation work was not merely rhetorical and that philanthropic expertise became valued. The second trend is a steady decline in recruitment from higher education over the past two decades, from 38 percent in 1970–1974 to 18 percent in 1985–1989. As foundations began to recruit staff with foundation and nonprofit experience, the number of academics within philanthropy declined. The large number of foundation workers recruited from colleges and universities in the 1970s coincided with a general decline in the academic job market, a decline that pushed many Ph.D. recipients into nonacademic professions. By the 1980s, however, as the philanthropic experience began to trump disciplinary expertise and training, the numbers of foundations workers recruited from outside the field declined steadily.

The growing salience of philanthropic expertise was made most clear in 1996, when the Ford Foundation selected its new president. For the most visible and important position in the entire field, no national search was launched. Instead, without much fanfare and as many observers had predicted, Susan Berresford, a twenty-five-year Ford Foundation veteran who had begun work at the foundation soon after graduation from college, was elevated from vice president to president. The significance of this move was twofold: first, it confirmed once and for all that philanthropic expertise was one of the key qualifications for foundation work; and second, it made it clear that work in philanthropy was indeed a legitimate professional career in and unto itself.

In addition to the move to seek out professional expertise, another trend within the field is manifest: a field-wide move toward increased diversity has led to the steady increase of women and minorities in professional positions within foundations. While women and minorities began to enter philanthropy in significant numbers in the 1970s, only in the 1980s and 1990s did they reach proportions that surpass those in other professions; in 1992, for example, one major survey of foundation demographics revealed that fully 61 percent of all foundation program officers were women and 28 percent were minority group members.[57] These numbers are particularly significant when one considers that in 1993 in the broader American workplace, minorities represented only 14.3 percent of all professionals and only 10.8 percent of all managers, while women constituted 50.2 percent of all professionals and 29.9 of all managers.[58] That foundations managed in a period of only two decades to increase both minority and female employment well beyond national averages is a clear sign of the field's interest in creating an open, inclusive, and legitimizing workplace. The trend toward increased diversity dovetails with the trend toward hiring more program staff from the nonprofit sector, in which many of the health and social service organizations have traditionally employed substantial numbers of women and minorities. By making foundations look more like the broader nonprofit sector, foundations managed simultaneously to improve relations with recipient organizations and defuse charges of elitism.

The events of 1969 made it clear that the costs of professional staffing were minor in comparison to the costs of appearing unresponsive and unaccountable. In the early years, only the larger foundations had full-time grantmaking staff. However, two decades of encouragement by the Council on Foundations changed this situation dramatically. In recent years, the majority of council members have come to accept the need for professional staff. The field today is staffed by an increasingly well-networked group of professionals who take great interest in the long-term prospects of spending a career in grantmaking.

Training Programs
In the early 1970s, foundation administrators had little literature to draw upon in their efforts to improve foundation management. Not only was

there no practitioner's manual on how to operate a foundation, but there was also little understanding of what good foundation management actually entailed. After 1969, standards for proper philanthropic management were all too clearly spelled out in the new regulations, which prohibited various self-interested transactions and certain investments. All that was needed was for the legal requirement to be melded with practical tips into a real operating manual.

In 1972, the Cleveland Foundation convened a group of representatives from eighteen major foundations to discuss the state of the art in foundation administration. A year later, the result was a 250-page administrative manual for the Cleveland Foundation, which included eleven chapters on everything from budgeting, grantmaking, personnel selection, and portfolio management to financial administration. Although this "staff reference manual" was originally intended for internal use only, it soon began to circulate in the foundation world, particularly among small and midsize foundations. The foundation made copies available to any interested foundation; the manual was a point of departure for many foundations to discuss their own administrative policies.[59]

Appreciating the need identified by the Cleveland Foundation, private foundations began searching for literature on the practice of grantmaking to guide their work. Over the past decades, a long list of titles has appeared, aimed at explicating the many procedural challenges of managing a private foundation. The most important of these books was *The Handbook on Private Foundations*,[60] which in addition to focusing on the art of grantmaking in some detail gave step-by-step instructions for setting up a foundation from scratch. The volume was widely used among the growing number of individuals who were setting up foundations. In one place, they could find answers to questions that previously only an attorney could have answered about the rules governing institutional forms of giving.

Efforts at large foundations to build extensive training programs for staff were part of the move to professionalize grantmaking and build credibility for the field. Having well-trained, experienced staff was no longer a luxury to be enjoyed by the largest foundations. As one foundation manager observed, professional staffing was nothing short of survival strategy in the 1970s:

> I believe that the rapid development of a cadre of foundation executives capable of advancing the enlightened interests of foundations is a matter of organizational survival. Foundation executives are yet to be included in any

current listing of the professions. However, they do have a vocation requiring specialized knowledge and substantial academic preparation. One only has to look back at the events leading to the TRA 1969 to see the results of the paucity of leadership and how thinly spread was whatever existed.[61]

By the early 1980s, the Council on Foundations declared that "professional development has become one of the Council's highest priorities."[62] Professionalizing foundation work was critical because it was essential that the judgment of foundation workers have legitimacy and hold up to scrutiny. As James Joseph noted: "Despite an endless list of contributions to the public good—meeting a wide variety of human needs, feeding the hungry and housing the homeless, articulating social values and a sense of civic culture—private foundations are periodically forced to engage in a subtle form of competition for legitimacy."[63] Improving training and professional development programs was thus an obvious direction for philanthropy during turbulent times, and it has remained a central thrust of the field ever since.

The drive to professionalize philanthropy through training programs has increased in recent years, as foundations have begun attempting to work with individual donors before they have even set up a foundation. The regional associations of grantmakers and other foundation service organizations have developed programs aimed at introducing new foundation staff to the challenges of giving away funds effectively.

New Funding Practices

In philanthropy, organizational form did not follow function, but rather the opposite. The organizational transformation of American philanthropy brought new grantmaking practices; with new professional staff appearing within many foundations, trustees could no longer justify simply making decisions based on personal connections. Grantmaking decisions were in large measure handed over to the new staff, as boards gravitated more toward a policy and planning role. As foundations became more heavily staffed, they began to change the way grants were made. No longer content to simply write unrestricted checks based on the overall reputation of a grantseeker, foundations began requiring more convincing and more details before they would agree to a grant. Beginning in the 1970s and continuing during the next two decades, the grants nexus would undergo profound changes. In the 1950s and 1960s, the best way to land a grant was to have a personal connection to a trustee who would secure the requested funds in the time-honored process of logrolling, which allowed all trustees to fund their favored charities. The professionalization of foundations challenged this trustee-centered system and eventually displaced it with a new, more legitimate grantmaking process that placed the detached professional at the center of grantmaking decisions.

Professionalization also brought about a shift from "general operating grants" to what became termed "project grants," restricted to specific purposes defined in advance of the awarding of a grant. Foundation staff, imbued with new responsibilities, needed to find ways to judge grant requests beyond simply relying on the reputation of the grantseeker. In the quest for a more objective and more legitimate basis for evaluating grant requests, many foundations reformulated their grantmaking guidelines to reflect a new focus on project requests. Under the new system, grantseekers would no longer simply submit a letter requesting support, but instead would outline a specific program or project within their organization that needed support. As one grantmaker noted in 1971: "Once a professional staff develops, you can be pretty sure of an even stronger inclination toward project funding and a predominance of foundations which feel it is vital to develop their own program thrust—and locate projects which meet certain defined objectives. This is very different from the foundation of the sixties, which merely served as a conduit for the donor's giving program."[64]

As a consequence of this shift, grant requests to foundations became longer and more detailed throughout the 1970s and 1980s. Proposals began to describe not only charitable missions and programs, but also outcomes and expectations. To meet the requirements of foundation professionals, grantseekers began tailoring requests to individual foundations, offering each a different funding opportunity. What was gained by the shift away from general operating to project and program support? For foundations, the new system brought more detailed proposals through the doors, which in turn allowed foundation staffers to argue that their judgments were based on a set of objective criteria grounded in the content of proposals. The shift also justified the cost and administrative burden brought on by the introduction of professional workers into foundations. Quite simply, for the new foundation decision makers to remain occupied both before and after recommending a grant, proposals needed to become narrower in their scope and more subject to external oversight and tracking.

For nonprofits, the shift meant more fund-raising effort and more postgrant work. After specifying how funds would be expended in great detail, discussing these plans with a foundation staffer, submitting to a site visit, and writing a report on the project, nonprofit organizations found themselves increasingly burdened by the new foundation procedures. The shift also necessitated the recruitment and training of development directors and program staff who would know how to handle foundation professionals and the new rigors of securing and reporting on grants.

Instead of having to make a subjective decision based on the overall quality of a grantseeker—always a difficult and subjective process—foundation staff sought more "objective" and measurable standards. They began to base their decisions on detailed information about how funds would be expended, and they expected a more thorough accounting after the grant period was over.[65] Project giving thus brought with it a heightened ability to judge, oversee, and evaluate grant requests—features that foundation professionals embraced in the name of openness and accountability.

While the move to bring in large numbers of professionals to manage foundations smoothed the interactions between givers and receivers, the unanswered question is whether these changes substantially improved the performance of foundations. It is difficult to measure effectiveness in philanthropy and even harder to attribute it to foundation staff action. Hence, the move to professionalize foundations must be understood first and foremost as a change in the terms of interaction between nonprofits and foundations. Although some foundations clearly believe that staff has improved the quality of grantmaking in foundations and helped answer the effectiveness challenge in the field, the evidence for this claim remains elusive.

Change and Its Aftermath

The decade of the 1970s was a significant point in the development of modern philanthropy. The changes ushered in during this period did have clear precedents, however. Early philanthropic leaders, like the Carnegie Corporation's Frederick Keppel, had urged increased openness in the 1930s. Similarly, the Russell Sage Foundation advocated early on the improvement of foundation administrative practices. However, it took a regulatory shock to the field in the 1970s and the strengthening of the Council on Foundations for philanthropy's two major transformations to take root among a broad range of foundations.

First, foundations embraced a new understanding of their status as public trusts to be operated for public purposes. With the council pushing for increased reporting and better relations with grantees, foundations fundamentally redefined their work. Gone was the tendency toward secrecy and aloofness. In its place was a new sense of the public responsibilities of foundations. The 1970s ushered in a whole new conception of private foundations as public trusts, open and accessible to all. A second major transformation took place in the administrative practices of foundations. New staff entered foundation work to fulfill philanthropy's new public mission. If foundations were to be open, accessible, and responsive, new professionals had to be brought in to meet these new objectives. Although administrative expenses soared at many of the larger foundations, no price was too high to defend philanthropy from further attack and from further government encroachment.

These two transformations—in beliefs and practices—were, of course, mutually reinforcing and overlapping. And it would be a mistake to see the two phenomena as independent. The new conception of foundations as public trusts may have begun to emerge earlier than the move to increase staffing, but both developments unfolded over a period of years and each reinforced the other. After all, newly hired foundation staff had a vested interest in pushing forward the new ethos of openness. Selling the idea that foundations must increase visibility and external relations created the very conditions under which professional staff entered the field of philanthropy in large numbers. As more and more staff entered the field, it was only natural they in turn would embrace and promulgate the principle of openness that made professionalism possible in the first place.

In the end, openness and professionalism hardly guarantee that resources are being used effectively and creatively. The new ethos of openness and the introduction of a new cadre of foundation professionals have, however, successfully lulled many into believing that foundations are now better managed and making a greater contribution to society than ever before. Though processes may be more rigorous, grantmaking more fair, and transparency more common than before, the underlying practical problems of effectiveness and accountability actually have become more acute as a result of this transformation. With openness and professionalism come heightened expectations.

As large-scale American philanthropy moved from something individual donors did during their retirement to something that was carried out by professionals in perpetuity, effectiveness and accountability in particular have become central concerns. It is not hard to understand why professionals would be concerned about both topics. For staff, the issue of effectiveness is central because it speaks directly to their own role within foundations, which is to improve the quality of grants that are made. This amounts to a mandate to maximize the effectiveness of foundation programs, something that staff spends a great deal of time and effort doing. At the same time, accountability is also a central concern of professional grantmakers who, owing to the fact they are giving away money that someone else earned, find it necessary to justify their decisions convincingly. Absent the ability to fall back on the individualistic claim that "it's my money and I can spend it any way I see fit," professional grantmakers must take great pains to defend and inoculate their decisions from any complaints about favoritism, capriciousness, or, worse still, illegitimacy.

The professionalization of philanthropy has had some unfortunate consequences above and beyond the fact that it gave birth to and then accelerated the perceived effectiveness and accountability crises in the field. Most important of all, the move away from donor-driven philanthropy toward more agnostic, professional, and institutional forms of giving has removed from the field some of the passion and unpredictability that are present when individuals take their private wealth and project into public space their vision of the common good. To this day, many of the most interesting and inspiring attempts to use philanthropic dollars creatively have been made by individual donors working independently or through institutions that they are actively managing. Many of the older and most institutionalized foundations, in which the donor is no longer even a meaningful memory, suffer from a lack of grounding in substantive commitments and operate without the passion that is needed for philanthropy to innovate and inspire.

All of this is not to say that all institutional philanthropy is always, or by its very nature, inferior to individual philanthropy. In fact, donors can and do use philanthropic institutions to enhance the quality of their giving. My claim is simply that when the private values of donors and the public needs of a community are not simultaneously represented in philanthropy, something significant is lost. In many professionally managed foundations in which the donor is no longer present, the balance between public and private is skewed toward the former, and giving tends over time toward a safe but bland philanthropic agnosticism. Under such circumstances, procedural issues—often focused on how to measure effectiveness or promote accountability—become central obsessions, which are never truly resolved, only discussed and debated at length. All of which distracts from the task of asking whether philanthropic dollars are being used in the most creative way possible to enact new and compelling visions of the common good. To the extent that the postregulatory environment of the 1970s led a significant part of the field of giving toward a focused and cautious proceduralism, the capacity of philanthropy to tackle the important substantive questions embedded in giving was likely diminished.

The implications for the future of American philanthropy of the dual move toward a more public-oriented foundation field and the creation of a grantmaking profession are significant and worth considering. First, while foundations are only a small part of the American philanthropic landscape, they are a very significant part of the future of the field. The vast majority of very wealthy donors will continue to build the foundation field. In fact, the amount of resources controlled by foundations in relation to the annual overall amount of private giving is increasing noticeably, as hundreds of billions now reside in foundations. What this trend indicates is that the developments in the world of foundation philanthropy are particularly significant because they represent the leading edge of the field and may be an indicator of the future course of philanthropy's evolution. There is a more significant implication to the institutionalization of philanthropy. Because they typically are established in perpetuity and require no new resources to survive, foundations are not well positioned to engage the legitimacy question as it relates either to themselves or to the broader field.

My argument ahead is that consciously considering the many strategic choices open to donors and choosing wisely is a critical way for both individual and institutional donors to answer lingering questions about philanthropy's effectiveness, its accountability, and most significantly, its legitimacy. One of the great shortcomings of the professionalization movement in philanthropy is that it has left many of the most important substantive questions unanswered and substituted instead symbolic procedural reforms and weak concessions. These measures have increased public awareness of philanthropy but hardly solidified the position of private philanthropy in the public sphere. The model of strategic giving that is presented in the rest of this book is designed to provide a roadmap to donors who want to answer the challenges that face the field by grounding their giving in a more strategic approach.

4. The Idea of Strategic Giving

The important changes that have swept across the world of foundation philanthropy have left many unanswered questions in their wake. Chief among these is whether the field made any progress toward solving the effectiveness, accountability, and legitimacy challenges. My answer is largely no. Structures and practices in the highly visible institutional segment of the philanthropy field may have been reformed, but discontent and dysfunction still run deep. Although the amount of money given away each year continues to rise, there are lingering doubts about what the billions of dollars backed by good intentions have ultimately produced. Of course, almost all major donors can point to some grants that have led to impressive results. It remains very difficult, however, to see how the many small and isolated success stories of donors around the country ever amount to anything vaguely resembling a meaningful response to any of the major social problems—be it economic development in the inner city, access to health care, reduction in youth violence, or reform of public schools—that private philanthropy has long targeted. Amid continued doubts in recent years about the impact of philanthropy's diverse and diluted efforts, many ideas have emerged about how the field might be strengthened. The framework and theory presented in this book are designed to speak to some of these lurking issues and doubts.

My starting assumption is that one of the important gaps in philanthropy is in the area of strategy. While business firms have an enormous literature to draw on when it comes to strategy formulation,[1] donors have little theory they can call on to guide their work and few frameworks for clarifying the fundamental challenges in philanthropy.[2] Part of the strategic deficit stems from the broadly held assumption that philanthropy does not have a bottom line and hence there is little need to focus on strategy. Part of this is true. When donors give, it may be hard to measure the exact impact of their gifts. However, the very fact that it is hard to know how well one is doing in philanthropy makes it especially critical that donors focus on logic, process, and decision making. Setting in place a strong strategic basis for philanthropic decisions is a critical element of this process. With a clearer model of what good strategy might look like, some of the doubts about performance measurement might become less painfully nagging. Knowing what good strategy on the front end looks like is not a perfect substitute for back-end measures of effectiveness, but it can be a very useful starting proxy. Being able to defend the strategic soundness of a philanthropic agenda is ultimately the first step both in getting closer to effective philanthropy and in holding philanthropy meaningfully accountable for the sensible use of tax-privileged resources.

As philanthropy has undergone a major transformation over the past century and as new and ever more professionalized forms of giving have taken root, it would be tempting to assume that the strategy challenge embedded in giving is now in capable hands. After all, who could possibly know more about strategy formulation than professionally trained and experienced grantmakers? While there are many functions that these philanthropic agents can do well for their principals, setting in place a compelling strategy that is centered on the alignment of private values and public purposes may not be one of them. For at the core of any strategy are the selection of a public problem, issue, or cause as worthy of attention and the mobilization of a private commitment to deal with it. Professionals may be able to assist in the implementation of good strategy, but donors have the prime responsibility and most essential resource for developing a strategy, namely a sense of what is worth doing. One of the main arguments of this book is that often philanthropy works best and strategy is most compelling when the donor brings its value set and assumptions to bear on the process of setting forth a philanthropic direction. Without this critical differentiating ingredient, giving can never reach its true potential. When individuals draw upon their life experience and their reservoir of commitment and caring, however, philanthropy can take on problems that government and community stakeholders may not yet recognize or prioritize. Getting free of the pull of demand and following the push of philanthropic commitments may be uncomfortable for some, since it looks like a retreat from some of the transformations that occurred in the 1970s. The validation of the fifth function of philanthropy—the expression and satisfaction of the donors' psychic needs—turns out to be, however, one of the most critical requirements if philanthropy is to make good on two of the other functions it performs: supporting social innovations and affirming the value of a pluralistic society.

In this way, it is possible to see the turn of the philanthropic establishment away from private passions and personalism and toward responsiveness and publicness as an important change in the way the field understands its role. By listening to communities, by working more closely with nonprofits, by setting in place a code of conduct, philanthropy turned both outward and downward toward the grassroots. What foundations heard from the communities in which they work was often an inchoate and deafening call for help of all kinds. After all, there is often much disagreement about needs and priorities. Nevertheless, there is little doubt that the external voices of the field did render the foundation field over time far more oriented toward the social change and redistributive functions of philanthropy. As foundations became more open and distanced from the private values of donors, they came to reflect the core values of many nonprofits, which are centered around equity and political change. While it is difficult to generalize about these matters given the absence of good data, it is still likely that the orientation of wealthy donors toward equity and change is generally weaker than that of persons working for mission-focused nonprofit organizations. Still, everyone should be able to agree that institutional philanthropy has shifted an important part of the responsibility for giving away from the donor and toward the public, and that this development cannot help but have implications for the kind of giving that gets done.

In taking seriously the importance of donors' values and the psychic satisfaction from expressing these values, it is not my intention to privilege it (along with the innovation and pluralism functions of giving) over the social change and redistribution functions of giving. Instead, my goal is simply to bring out into the open and consider carefully the long-term implications of the move from individual to institutional giving, which I have sketched in the previous chapter and, I believe, has lasting consequences for the way philanthropy operates and the kinds of missions it pursues. As donors appear and then recede from the scene, leaving professionals to play a central role in the execution of philanthropic work, a case can be made that it may become harder and harder for balance to be achieved across all five of philanthropy's functions. This is particularly the case if professionals efficiently direct perpetual institutions and at times modify the values, worldviews, obsessions, issues, preconceived notions, powerful insights, pet peeves, and core commitments of the donors that lie behind and drive philanthropy.

Having a set of real convictions and values and tethering them to a meaningful public purpose is not enough in philanthropy, however. Although it may not guarantee a greater distribution of giving across philanthropy's five functions because it is agnostic on substantive matters, sound strategy in philanthropy is ultimately a good way to make progress on effectiveness, accountability, and legitimacy. Having a good strategy is a first step that any donor can take toward satisfying both the expressive and instrumental dimensions of giving, which is an essential part of executing what I believe to be the art and science of philanthropy. To introduce the idea of strategic giving, it is helpful to consider two very different philanthropic decisions reached by two very different donors.

A Tale of Two Donors

We begin with Henry and Edith Everett,[3] wealthy New Yorkers who both enjoyed considerable professional success during their careers with investment firms. In the 1950s, they created a small family foundation, the Everett Foundation, that would serve as their vehicle for philanthropy over the coming decades. By the mid-1990s, the foundation had assets of over $10 million, which allowed the Everetts to be modest but serious donors by New York City's lofty standards.[4] Living on the Upper East Side, the Everetts were neighbors of the Central Park Zoo, an institution with a long and successful history of educating adults and children. The Central Park Zoo and the city's four other zoos were all operated by the nonprofit Wildlife Conservation Society (WCS), formerly known as the New York Zoological Society. In 1998 WCS completed an extensive renovation of the Central Park Zoo's main facilities and reopened with a newer, more natural habitat for its collection of bears, gorillas, seals, and other animals.

One long-standing feature at the zoo was its famous Children's Zoo, which featured a motley group of farm animals that children could visit and pet in a colorful and imaginative setting focused on children's fairy tales, including a large Mother Hubbard's Shoe filled with animals, cottages for the Three Little Pigs, and a gingerbread house. The Children's Zoo, however, had fallen into disrepair over time because of heavy use and only occasional maintenance. A major conflict also raged over whether the zoo should restore the fanciful exhibits or whether it should clear the property and create a more naturalistic environment in which to view the animals. After legal wrangling with architectural historians who sought to preserve the imaginative if outmoded structures, the zoo moved forward with a compromise plan that would preserve the interactive petting-zoo idea, while creating a more natural environment. In early 1996, the zoo began to search for donors to support this major capital project.

After reading about the Children's Zoo's struggles in the *New York Times* and listening to friends with young children and grandchildren bemoan the extended period the institution had been closed, the Everetts decided to approach the Wildlife Conservation Society and offer their support for the renovation of the Children's Zoo. The Everetts' interest in helping WCS coincided with the zoo's need to expand its base of support. The WCS had recently completed a $100 million campaign and needed to expand the reach of its fund-raising work to new donors. WCS had a tradition of working quietly with major donors, many of whom were board members. When needs arose, supporters such as Brooke Astor, Laurence S. Rockefeller, and Lila Acheson Wallace would gracefully reach for their checkbooks so that the organization's work could move forward smoothly. After dipping deeply into its pool of longtime supporters to meet its ambitious fund-raising objectives in the 1980s, WCS sought to expand its base of support and find new supporters who might be drawn to a wildlife preservation and education mission. The society realized that these new donors might seek more recognition than old-line donors, and that naming opportunities—naming a building, plaza, or edifice after a donor—might be a key tool for attracting contributors who had earned their fortunes in the technology and finance fields.

The Everetts were the model of the new donors that WCS was eyeing. They had been major contributors to Democratic political candidates and had supported important Jewish philanthropic initiatives in the United States and abroad. The Everett Foundation had made a mark in the arts in New York with gifts for the Harlem Dance Theater's Everett Center for the Performing Arts, a lecture series at the New York Public Library, and an

Everett's Children's Adventure Garden at the New York Botanical Garden, and with support for campaigns to keep children from starting to smoke. While the Everetts avoided the New York social scene, they were active volunteers for many years, serving on numerous boards and devoting the majority of their time to nonprofit, civic, and cultural causes. The Children's Zoo seemed like a natural fit, and the Everetts wasted no time in setting up a meeting with the president of WCS.

At this first meeting, the Everetts surprised Zoo officials with a generous offer of $3 million for the estimated restoration budget of $5.9 million. It was agreed that the completed facility would be known as the Everett Children's Zoo, though exact details would need to be worked out in consultation with the zoo's many constituents and stakeholders. After working on the design and securing support for the renovation plan from all parties except the Landmark Preservation Commission and the Art Commission, WCS and the Everetts signed a contract, and a first installment of $750,000 was paid. As with all their gifts, the Everetts sought and secured wording in the agreement requiring that WCS bar any tobacco company from sponsoring any event or having any association with the Everett Children's Zoo.

Henry Everett, who thought of himself as a hands-on donor, lost no time in working with WCS on the project. Visiting other children's zoos when he traveled, Everett sent in design ideas and suggestions to WCS executives. Soon, however, the relationship began to fray. Delays in getting final approval, a failure to publicly announce the gift, and disagreements about the final design exposed differences between the WCS board and the Everetts. One particularly sensitive issue was how the Everetts' name would be displayed on the zoo's entrance. Something was needed that would both satisfy the Everetts and acknowledge the initial donors. The Children's Zoo's entrance featured three large granite columns supporting a bronze arch with figures of animals. On the center column in large letters was "Children's Zoo" and beneath this was a plaque recognizing former Governor Herbert Lehman and his wife Edith. According to WCS, the Everetts wanted their name carved in the granite above the existing words to create the effect of "Everett Children's Zoo." This would be accompanied by a plaque underneath acknowledging their gift, which would cover the original acknowledgment of the Lehman gift. A new plaque on one of the side columns was to give credit to the Lehmans for the Children's Zoo's creation. The Art Commission reviewed this proposal and rejected it along with a plan for a plaque with four-inch letters for the Everetts. Instead, the commission proposed a smaller plaque with two-inch letters for the Everetts on the center column and smaller plaques on the other outside columns acknowledging the Lehmans—a solution that avoided any new carving of the granite.

Amid all this negotiation and tension, the agreement between donor and recipient fell apart. According to the Everetts, WCS asked them to write a letter stating that they were withdrawing their gift because the contract had been breached, a letter that the zoo could then use with the Art Commission as leverage in resolving the logjam. The Everetts wrote the letter and faxed it to the WCS. However, the Everetts learned that the letter was never shown and the commission approved a new design that the Everetts never saw. For Henry and Edith Everett, this was the straw that broke the donor's back, and they finalized their decision to withdraw their support. Public criticism and bad publicity would soon ensue, as their perceived pettiness was spread across the pages of New York's newspapers.

The final resolution of this entire philanthropic imbroglio involved an ironic twist that no one could have foreseen. On May 15, the day the Everetts' decision to withdraw their gift was first publicized, James Tisch was elected president of the United Jewish Appeal-Federation of Jewish Philanthropies of New York City (UJA-Federation). Tisch was part of a very prominent family who controlled the Loews Corporation, the parent corporation of Lorillard Tobacco, the manufacturer of numerous brands of cigarettes. UJA-Federation board member Henry Everett had mounted a campaign to block Tisch's election to head the philanthropy on the grounds that no one involved in tobacco should head an organization dedicated to doing good work. To make matters worse for the Everetts, five days later, the press announced that new donors had come forward to replace the Everetts' gift to the zoo with an even more generous offer of $4.5 million. The donors were none other than Preston Tisch and his brother Laurence Tisch, father of James. In a letter to the WCS, Henry Everett wrote: "A Tisch Children's Zoo would not only represent a personal vendetta against us and the values we try to espouse but, more importantly, be a cynical rebuke of the children of our town." The Everetts never heard back from the society.

The story of the Everetts' philanthropic debacle leaves many questions unanswered: Were the Everetts acting in an unreasonable manner? Were they punished for violating the WCS tradition of low-key philanthropy? Did WCS double-cross the Everetts by seeking from them a letter withdrawing their gift so that it could negotiate secretly with the Tisches? Is philanthropy really just a contractual agreement without a moral dimension? What is the appropriate form of acknowledgment for major donors? Do an institution's initial donors have perpetual claim to acknowledgment? Were the Tisches using philanthropy to settle a personal grudge? For the purposes of under-standing philanthropic strategy, the most important question that emerges from this cautionary tale is: What could the donors have done to avoid all these problems in the first place? I suggest that the answer is to have a clearer and sounder philanthropic strategy.

Before explaining how the Everetts might have improved their giving strategy, consider by way of contrast the experience of another donor. For much of her life, Irene Diamond's claim to fame stemmed from her career in the 1940s, when she worked as a producer in Hollywood and spotted a rough script called *Rick's Bar*. Though she never received much credit for her work, Diamond helped guide this script through development; what emerged was *Casablanca*. By the time she was in her eighties, Irene Dia-mond's eye for good projects would earn her widespread recognition in the world of philanthropy.[5]

When her husband, Aaron Diamond, a New York real estate developer, died in 1984, Irene Diamond was left with the philanthropic task of giving away $200 million in ten years. While the Diamonds had created a founda-tion through which to conduct their philanthropy, they decided not to give away their funds in small increments in perpetuity.[6] Instead, they agreed that the money should be given away over a decade by whoever survived the other. They would focus on three main areas: medical research, mi-nority education, and cultural programs. One explanation for their deci-sion not to set up a conventional foundation was that both Diamonds had strong dislikes for bureaucracies and did not want their legacy to be a phil-anthropic institution that spent large amounts on overhead rather than on grants. Both also were very impatient and liked to take quick, decisive ac-tion. Still, the task of giving away the funds was not an easy one for Irene Diamond, given the competing claims of various New York charities on charitable dollars. To help her in the task, Diamond engaged an experienced grantmaker and consultant to donors to help her examine her options.

Knowing of her husband's interest in medical research, Irene Diamond became interested in the burgeoning AIDS crisis that was gripping New York City in the 1980s. A meeting in August 1988 between Diamond and the city's health commissioner led to important medical breakthroughs that few could have foreseen. The first meeting between Diamond and the city was disrupted by the AIDS protest group ACT-UP, which demanded the res-ignation of the commissioner. This acrimonious meeting, brokered by the president of Sloan Kettering Cancer Research Center, who had learned of Irene Diamond's interest in doing something about AIDS, was convened to explore ways in which the Diamond Foundation might work with the city to address the AIDS crisis. At the August meeting, the commissioner pressed Diamond to help create an independent AIDS research laboratory. The city would move quickly to supply a facility it owned if Diamond would help fund the research and use her influence in New York to convince other individuals and foundations to contribute to the effort.

Diamond considered doing this, but decided that it would take too long. Instead, she decided to go it alone and provide $8.5 million in private funding to get the laboratory up and running and an additional $21 million for postdoctoral fellowships. The goal would be quite simple: to build the world's premier AIDS research laboratory. The city would provide $3.5 million and lease to the new lab 22,000 square feet in a public health laboratory building in Manhattan at a rate of $1 a year for twenty years. Diamond sought immediate help with legal and licensing issues, began to work on architectural plans for the aging city building, and chose the head of Mt. Sinai Medical School to head the search committee to find a director for the lab. The issue of who would run the lab was, of course, the most important decision that faced Diamond. Eventually, Diamond and her advisers overrode the recommendations of the search committee, which favored more seasoned and experienced researchers, and instead hired David Ho, a young and promising researcher, still in his thirties.

Born in Taiwan, educated at Harvard, and a faculty member at the UCLA School of Medicine, Ho began to make a name for himself as someone who did bold and ambitious research using polymerase chain reaction (PCR), a tool for locating and counting genes in human cells. Ho had also made waves in the AIDS research field by proving that HIV was present in far higher levels in the body than was generally thought. Ho was offered the job, and he jumped at the opportunity to lead a major new lab, hire researchers from all over the country, and do research at the highest level. One of the earliest decisions he made was to focus more on basic research on HIV rather than immediately focus on clinical research. Over time, Ho and his team's work would lead to a number of breakthroughs, from findings that proposed vaccines would not work to findings related to the genetic doorway used by HIV to infect human cells. Ho's most famous discovery was protease inhibitors, which have been shown to be a potent tool for treating persons with HIV. When used in combination with standard antiviral medications—especially during the early stages of infection—these "cocktails" showed great potential for combating the progression of HIV into AIDS. For his work on protease inhibitors, Ho was named *Time* magazine's Man of the Year in 1996, a level of recognition and celebrity signaling to all that Irene Diamond's investment in the lab and her selection of Ho had borne real fruit. Following Ho's amazingly quick and important success, Irene Diamond was recognized by the White House as a philanthropist who made a difference, profiled in magazines, and celebrated by other donors for her contributions to the field.

The Aaron Diamond AIDS Research Center has continued its work in AIDS research and expanded substantially with the infusion of public funds from the National Institutes of Health. It has influenced the way research is conducted at other labs and become the paradigmatic philanthropic intervention in medical research. What made this intervention so successful? Was it just luck? Why did Irene Diamond produce so much public value through her philanthropy while the Everetts' philanthropy led to such a calamitous and embarrassing failure?

It is important to dismiss a number of obvious but erroneous explanations for the different outcomes of the Everett and Diamond gifts. First, it would be tempting to point to the choice of medical research compared to cultural arts, and to assume that success only comes when life and death are at stake. After all, choosing a good target for philanthropy is important and the best grantmaking can amount to nothing unless giving is directed at a timely and important problem. There is certainly a significant difference between going after a disease that kills millions worldwide and working to rehabilitate a cultural facility for children in New York. The scale and ambition of Diamond's giving clearly outstrips that of the Everetts, no matter how hard it is to render clear judgments about the comparative worth of competing public needs. This difference does not explain, however, the different results because it is entirely possible that a children's zoo could turn out to be a major success and that a search for a cure could lead nowhere. Thus, while Diamond did chose a more ambitious project, one with greater potential benefits, this alone does not advance us toward a clearer sense of why the results achieved in the two cases were so divergent.

Second, it would not be fair to attribute the difference to a more leveraged approach to funding basic research in one instance compared to support of bricks and mortar in the other. Diamond decided to use her philanthropy in an attempt to generate new scientific research that could be disseminated around the world as part of a larger search for a cure. Gifts supporting research are risky but potentially very rewarding. If the investigators are successful, creating new knowledge can transform large areas of practice and lead to very significant applications. In the case of medical research, this means the production of medicines capable of treating illnesses around the world. Gifts to capital campaigns, like the one made by the Everetts, are more modest in the potential impact. They are often necessary for nonprofits to carry out their work, but they rarely make breakthroughs. Instead, the construction of new buildings and facilities is best viewed as a necessary but relatively conservative form of philanthropic giving, one that has a relatively high likelihood of leaving a meaningful long-term mark. While Diamond's appears to be higher risk and potentially more leveraged, this alone does not explain the outcomes that were achieved.

Third, it is natural to take a structural perspective on the two cases and argue that the particular philanthropic vehicle or institution used by these two donors determined the ultimate outcomes.[7] However, on closer inspection, the structures deployed by both donors were not that different. While in both cases the donors were alive, in the Everetts' case the couple sought to work together through their evolving and growing foundation to achieve their goals. With Irene Diamond, the situation was different in that she was acting through a foundation named after her late husband, which had a specified term to operate in before it would be spent. The Everetts did most of their work themselves, interacting directly with the recipient and communicating their concerns immediately to the leadership of the zoo. Diamond's foundation had a small staff that worked with her on her giving, although it allowed her to put her imprint on the giving and make many of the most important philanthropic calls. Thus, while it would be convenient to point to either the existence or nonexistence of a particular philanthropic vehicle or institution as the determining factor in the two cases, this simply is not possible. In both cases, donors were working through foundations to achieve their objectives, and neither reaped inordinate benefits from their choice of organizational vehicle for philanthropy.

Fourth, it would be easy to argue that the answer lies in a difference of style, temperament, and personal approach. There is, after all, a great contrast between Irene Diamond's low-key behind-the-scenes approach and the Everetts' more visible, engaged, and demanding philanthropic style. When Henry Everett became more engaged with the zoo, doing some research and looking at plans, he was doing what a lot of donors deep down dream of doing. He was taking part in his gift and managing it actively so as to produce the best possible outcome. Diamond, by virtue of her decision to fund scientific research, was at an immediate disadvantage when it came to cultivating an engaged relationship. Much of her involvement was up front, choosing the best possible person to run the lab and helping to make it a reality. More to the point, there was a difference between the Everetts and Diamond in the area of the amount of recognition sought in return for philanthropic support. The Everetts pursued to a greater or lesser extent—depending on which side of the dispute one listens to—name recognition and public profile. Diamond, on the other hand, was known for her low-key approach, which focused the spotlight on her projects, not herself. Even though significant stylistic differences emerge when these two tales are juxtaposed, the outcomes achieved cannot be explained in terms of personality and profile alone.

Fifth and finally, one might want to point to a major difference in time horizons. It would, however, be a gross simplification to focus on the temporal dimension of philanthropy and to assume that the ten-year time limit for the existence of the Aaron Diamond Foundation pushed Irene Diamond to achieve so much. The time constraints the Diamond Foundation operated under led to the selection of major actionable objectives that had relatively urgent and time-pressured features. The use of a limited-life foundation may have helped Diamond take some chances and produce some important public benefits that she could see, but it does not fully explain the divergent results achieved by these two foundations.

Each of these candidate explanations falls short of the mark. The presence of a strategy behind Diamond's giving and a lack of clear strategy in the case of the Everetts explains these strikingly different stories. One way to think about strategy is to focus on the level of fit and alignment between the five critical elements in giving, each of which was nominated in isolation previously: the underlying value that is to be produced, the logic model that is applied, the philanthropic vehicle or structure that is selected, the style or level of engagement of the donor, and the time frame for giving. These elements lie at the core of the idea of philanthropic strategy. Diamond's commitment to AIDS research, her use of a limited-life foundation, her decision to spend money quickly rather than at a slow dribble, her focus on basic research, and her active role in setting a direction—all contributed to a strategic synergy and fit that bore important public benefits. Strategy is not about finding the right approach to any one particular area; it is about finding answers to the core philanthropic questions consistently and coherently.

A Model of Philanthropic Strategy

To help explain the nature of strategic giving, I advance here a framework for both analyzing and informing philanthropic choices. Because philanthropy allows individuals to enact their private visions of the public good, developing a coherent strategy for giving is a difficult challenge. It is a process that can and does become controversial as the boundaries between the donor's interests and the needs of the community come into contact. Dissipating this tension by normalizing and converging philanthropy around a narrow set of acceptable practices would not be a promising approach. After all, if giving were reduced to a set of precise principles and precepts acceptable and applicable to all, much of the variety and the capacity to innovate would likely be compromised. Most donors do not need or want a set of restrictive rules that tell them what they should support, how they should conduct their giving, or when they should make their philanthropic decisions. Instead, donors can most benefit from a simple, usable framework for thinking about all the complex issues that charitable giving raises, a framework that allows donors to make their own decisions compassionately and intelligently.

The framework presented here, while neutral on substantive issues, points to five essential questions that donors need to confront as they begin to make their plans. First, all donors must declare for themselves the value to be produced through their giving. This means answering the question: What is valuable to my community and me? Second, donors need to define the type and scope of program that will be supported. In so doing, they must answer the question: What kinds of nonprofit activity will work best? Third, donors have to select a vehicle or structure through which they will conduct their giving. They must answer the question: What vehicle can best be used to accomplish my goals? Fourth, donors must find a giving style and profile level that is satisfying and productive. They should reflect on the question: What level of engagement and visibility do I want for my giving? Fifth and finally, donors have to settle on a time frame that will guide their giving. This means thinking about how to respond to the question: When should my giving take place?

Taken in isolation, there are no clear and unequivocally appropriate answers to any one of these five questions. There are, however, sets of answers that demonstrably fit more or less well together. This points to the basic premise that strategic giving can be defined as the clear alignment of the five important philanthropic dimensions. Some donors will start with clear answers to one or more of the five questions. Others will approach this task of building strategy with a more blank slate. In either case, constructing a coherent strategy in philanthropy involves checking and rechecking the alignment and fit of all elements in an effort to find a consistent supporting model for giving in which each element supports the others.

When answers to all five questions are in complete alignment, the possibilities for social impact and donor satisfaction are high. Moving toward alignment is the central task of the strategic donor.

The framework I develop (see figure 4.1) later in the book, "the philanthropic prism,"[8] has three uses, all aimed at moving the field of philanthropy toward a more strategic approach. The first and most obvious pertains to donors. The prism can be a planning tool that guides the direction of a donor's philanthropic work. It can serve as a structured checklist and diagnostic device that donors can hold up to their philanthropy. By revealing points of alignment and fit as well as points of tension and misalignment, the prism can guide donors toward philanthropic choices that are more internally consistent. Under ideal circumstances, this analytic work will be completed before donors have gone very far with their giving. However, recognizing that many people learn best by doing, the prism can also be used by those who have made many philanthropic commitments only to realize that greater order and discipline was called for in their giving. Applying this analysis to quagmires and contentious situations will likely isolate the trouble spots while guiding the donor toward greater levels of coherence and fit.

The second use of the framework is less obvious: it may be useful to recipient organizations—the often overlooked other part of the world of philanthropy. For nonprofit managers and development professionals, the prism can be used as a focusing device to hone and strengthen philanthropic appeals. By thinking through how best to present donors with giving opportunities that connect to their core strategic concerns, nonprofits can improve the quality and sophistication of the grant appeals. At a time when competition for philanthropic funds has become very intense, having a better way of understanding how donors think about their objectives— or ought to think about their objectives—could provide a decisive edge in this competition. The prism can thus be used by grantseekers to make arguments for decisions that might ultimately benefit them. To be sure, some donors might object to the overly assertive and possibly self-interested application of a strategic model. The prism could lurk behind the scenes and simply guide the structuring of fund-raising appeals. In either event, having a working definition of strategic fit and alignment in philanthropy cannot help but increase the coherence and attractiveness of funding requests.[9]

Finally, researchers can use the prism as a tool to assess the strengths and weaknesses of philanthropic initiatives and agendas. Understanding the constitutive elements of philanthropic strategy will allow observers of

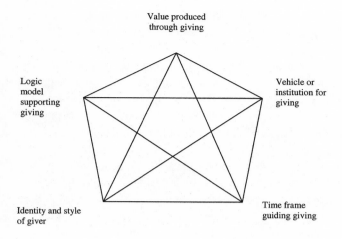

Figure 4.1 **The philanthropic prism.**

the field to begin to compare, contrast, and explicate better the vast range of choices that donors confront. To make this analysis possible, some simplification and reductionism are necessary. The model of strategy has five central elements, each of which represents a core decision-making point in philanthropy. By achieving fit and alignment among these dimensions, all parties committed to improving the field of philanthropy can move reactive charity closer to strategic giving.

Strategic giving must start with the definition of a core value proposition that declares a particular purpose or activity to be worth pursuing. This challenge can be approached from two different directions. Some donors may make a substantive commitment by turning inward, reflecting on their values and interests, and eventually seeking out organizations or causes with which they can identify.[10] Other donors will approach this task by looking outward, researching the most pressing public needs, and locating organizations that can fulfill these needs. Of course, these two approaches are not mutually exclusive. In fact, they define a broad spectrum of rationales for philanthropy, ranging from the very personal to the very public. Most donors seek to situate their giving somewhere between these two pure conceptions of giving. The chapter suggests that the starting point for strategy in philanthropy should be the search for a value proposition that maximizes both the public benefits of giving and the personal satisfaction of the donor.

Donors must take steps to clarify the underlying logic model that will animate their giving. This means making a decision about a theory of change that will determine the kind of programs to be funded and the expected results of these activities. Strategic giving requires that contextually appropriate decisions be made about when to pursue top-down strategies aimed at changing the intellectual grounding of a field of practice and when to seek a bottom-up or grassroots solution aimed at working through local groups. Donors must also confront a set of more operational issues relating to the form of support that will be supplied, be it general operating support, project grants, matching awards, loans, in-kind contributions, or capital funding.[11] These decisions will turn on how leverage can best be gained, given the purpose to be achieved. Finally, donors may want to think through how their giving will achieve meaningful scale, whether through organizational expansion or through some form of program replication. Developing a logic model is important because it defines the causal linkages that start with the making of a grant and end with the achievement of results. While it is likely that many grants will fail to produce each and every one of their intended effects, having a clear and compelling logic model will at least give the donor the opportunity to diagnose where a given philanthropic intervention went right and where it went wrong. In this sense, a logic model that includes a theory of change, leverage, and scale can be a potent tool for both planning and learning.

Few donors work completely independently of any institutional support for their giving. Early on, donors face important choices about the vehicles and structures that will guide and shape their decisions. Over the years, philanthropy has generated a number of distinctive organizational forms that are available to donors.[12] In addition to private independent foundations (that usually exist in perpetuity and simply make grants), donors have three main institutional options: operating foundations (that use endowment interest to fund program activities carried out by foundation staff), community foundations (that solicit endowment funds from residents of the surrounding city or region), and charitable gift funds (that are operated by mutual fund companies and act as charitable checkbooks). Donors can also choose to eschew structure entirely and simply make gifts directly, or they can select a range of planned giving options. Some donors prefer to act collaboratively either through federated funders or through the growing ranks of giving circles. Selecting the appropriate structure through which to give requires a conscious effort aimed at overall alignment. Donors must examine the full menu with regard to the structure through which their giving takes place and understand how philanthropic vehicles can both enable and cripple giving.

In assembling a plan for giving, donors need to think carefully about the question of what their giving style will be and how they want to construct their philanthropic identity. In some cases, donors will seek out the advice and counsel of family members, friends, lawyers, staff, and consultants.[13] A trend toward philanthropic disintermediation has, however, emerged in recent years; many wealthy entrepreneurs have decided to cut out all philanthropic assistants and middlemen and instead look to themselves as the principal agents of their own philanthropy.[14] Forming a clear picture of the identity of the giver is important because it leads directly into the challenge of selecting a giving style. Among donors, styles range from a very hands-off approach, in which a check is simply mailed to a recipient organization, to a more deeply engaged approach, in which the donor and recipient work together on program development and problem solving. At the same time, some donors will seek to act completely anonymously,[15] while others will want recognition and visibility. In deciding upon a grantmaking identity and style, donors need to do more than just assess their private comfort levels. They must ask which form of agency is most aligned with the type of program being funded and the structure through which their giving is taking place. Only when the donor's style and identity are understood in terms of their relationship to other points in the philanthropic prism is it possible to come to an assessment of their effectiveness and appropriateness.

Donors are also confronted with the issue of how much to give out now and how much to give later. This decision involves weighing the question of perpetuity and thinking about the appropriate payout rate for their giving. The question of when to give points to the fact that strategy demands that donors engage in some kind of "philanthropic discounting" in making difficult intertemporal trade-offs. In thinking about the payout rate for their giving, donors must assess the costs of acting sooner rather than later, a calculus that will involve assessing the likely cost escalation in the field, the rate at which the problem will or will not become exacerbated over time, and the cost of deferring benefits over time. The time dimension to giving requires not just thought about the timing of a donation, but also the timing of the use of the gift. Donors need to make a judgment about when and at what pace their philanthropic resources should be consumed by recipient organizations, and whether the funds should be used for endowment purposes or to meet current expenses. Most important of all, the time frame that will guide a donor's giving must fit the projected contour or development of the issue to be addressed. In cases in which the costs of delaying action are great, as is the case with major diseases, famines, and intense social crises, donors may need to consider a time frame that privileges current giving. However, when the issue that the donor chooses to address is likely to be present for decades or centuries, as is the case with many global environment and population problems, a longer time frame may be needed.

The art of philanthropy allows donors to express their private values and convictions, while the science of philanthropy pushes the field toward greater levels of instrumental effectiveness. The long-term advancement of the field rests on both the art and science of philanthropy being affirmed and developed simultaneously. This book argues that philanthropy—particularly large-scale giving—demands some level of strategy and that the essence of strategic philanthropy comes down to the alignment of the five points of the philanthropic prism. That is, giving only moves from being haphazard to strategic through the achievement of fit between the elements of the prism. Drawing on many cases and examples, the chapter concludes that the task of the strategic donor is to work on the *entirety* of the philanthropic prism until each point is defined, polished, and in alignment with the others. Only when donors have achieved this complex and challenging level of fit can they claim that their giving has truly become strategic. This leads to the final conclusion that only when giving becomes strategic will donors have a higher probability of creating value for the public and for themselves.

Are strategy and strategic alignment the be-all and end-all of philanthropy? Hardly. There will always be room and a place for disjointed, emotive, and personalistic giving that operates with no concern about effectiveness or strategy, as well as for narrow and unimaginative giving that simply responds to an urgent need. Thus, it is very important to stress from the outset that my goal here is not to push donors toward an exclusive and narrow vision of strategic philanthropy as the only defensible form of giving. Instead, I want to suggest that, for those donors seeking both to find personal satisfaction from their giving and to maximize the chances of producing significant public benefits, thinking about the quality and character of one philanthropic strategy might well be useful. This is particularly the case if one of two conditions exists, namely that the philanthropic objectives are ambitious or that the resources available are significant.

If a donor has the modest and limited goal of recognizing and thanking the hospital that provided quality and compassionate service to the donor's family, the philanthropic task need not be excessively complicated. A simple gift will do the work at hand. If the donor wants to both recognize the fine work of the hospital and push it to continue to advance the frontier of medicine in a particular field, the task is suddenly more ambitious and complex. Not only is a personal exchange taking place that recognizes and renders thanks, but a very specific decision connected to a defined set of activities is part of the gift. As the philanthropic intentions of donors become broader and as the clarity of their vision of the public good increases, donors begin to demand more than just personal satisfaction from their giving. They see a part of their own psychic return from engaging in philanthropy as deeply connected to the impact their giving has on society. When donors seek public impact and when their intentions are ambitious, strategy comes into play and becomes a central challenge. This model of strategic giving is directed toward donors that possess both private and public agendas.

The other factor that may be behind a demand for higher levels of strategy in giving is related to resources. When a donor has only a small amount of money to spend on philanthropy, two choices are open. The donor may choose to spend these funds without asking too many questions, feeling that small amounts of money cannot really amount to much. On the other hand, sensing that resources are scarce, the donor might feel a tremendous burden to develop and implement a strategy for giving, one that will maximize the impact of the funds at hand. The situation is different when a donor has a large amount of money to give away. These two practical options are no longer equally viable. When personal resources reach the hundreds of millions of dollars or more, the call of strategic giving becomes very strong. While structuring giving in such a way as to meet the personal expressive needs of donors remains critical, it is harder for major donors to retreat from the challenge of identifying important public needs and finding a way through philanthropy to address some of these needs. Scale of resources brings with it a strategic imperative to act wisely and to give in a way that meets both the needs of the donor and those of the community.

In the end, however, it is important to recognize that not all donors do come to their philanthropy with profound problems and challenges that nag them doggedly, nor do all donors need to carefully elaborate a strategic vision for their giving. Strategy is a calling for some donors by virtue of their scope of their vision or the breadth of their resources.

Before proceeding in this exploration of the elements of philanthropic strategy, it is critical to explain the order of the exposition chosen here.

While strategic donors must grapple at one point or another with each of the five big questions in philanthropy, the order in which they do this work will vary considerably. The value proposition in philanthropy is a logical place to start in establishing philanthropic strategy because it is an important decision that can then direct and guide the other four decisions, which can proceed in any number of different orders. While it may be logical to begin with the mission or value proposition, in reality, many donors enter the prism from other starting points. For example, some donors know that they want to create a family foundation more than anything else. They crave the personal ties that this institutional form will create and reinforce among family members, or they see family philanthropy as a tool for conveying values from one generation to another.[16] For these donors, setting in place the right institutional structure is the critical starting point for planning, a decision from which others follow.

This is not the only way to proceed, however. Other donors are very clear that no matter the cause to be pursued, they want to be deeply engaged in the work that they support financially. Early retirement, strong social commitment, or uncontrollable urge to micromanage operations: all can drive donors to demand high levels of engagement. Wanting to work hand in hand with nonprofit organizations may thus be a starting point for some donors, which then begins to establish the possible parameters of the other four elements of strategy. Other donors have a particular theory of change in mind—be it a predilection for advocacy work or a passion for direct service programs—that serves as their starting point. These donors will start with the giving model that resonates with them and look for the best and most promising applications. Commitments of this sort can be based on previous philanthropic experience or represent a translation of political or ideological positions. Finally, it is not uncommon for some donors to start with a clear decision to do all their giving while they are alive or to wait until after they are dead. A decision either to accelerate the pace of giving so as to see the process unfold or a decision to allow others to execute one's philanthropic intent can drive many of the other considerations and be a legitimate starting point. In the end, the choice of point of entry will always be a function of the values and priorities of the donor.

Are donors who proceed in a different order than the one adopted here diminishing their chances of success? Most likely they are not. In thinking about achieving alignment and fit among these many complex dimensions of giving, where one starts is ultimately less important than where one finishes. It may be helpful to focus on the purpose of philanthropy as a starting point, but this may be too daunting a task for some. Starting with a choice of institutional structure or with a giving style may simply be easier or more comfortable for some. Many donors have made decisions about one or more of the five critical questions only to find that the decision must be revisited once their giving had progressed. Thus, it is probably impossible to commit entirely to any single dimension until the broader picture emerges. Although the next five chapters move through each of these elements one after the other, there is no profound rationale for the sequence followed here. Building a philanthropic strategy is ultimately not a linear process that begins at one precise point and ends at another. It is a circular process that involves continuous rethinking and realignment, as the donor's interests shift, as the problems demanding attention change, and as the donor's experience and expertise in bringing these two elements together improves and evolves with practice.

5. Dimensions of Philanthropic Value

The core diagnosis offered thus far is that philanthropy's structure and purpose have shifted in recent decades as large-scale giving has increasingly been relocated into professionally managed institutions, a process that sometimes occurred quickly and at other times evolved more slowly. This shift results from the fact that all individuals face death, while almost all private foundations—the institutions of choice for major donors—enjoy eternal life. The radically asymmetry in life spans means that unless donors possessing substantial wealth elect to give it all away during their lives, they are likely to see their control over their philanthropy diminish as successive waves of boards and staff push institutional giving in new directions. While there are many ways to interpret the incredible increase in the number of private foundations over the past fifty years and the astonishing run-up in the value of foundation endowments, it is clear that the rising profile of institutional giving is leading to fundamental shifts in the field. The most pronounced and visible of these changes can be found in the importance given to public needs, the way these needs are defined, and how philanthropic resources are marshaled to address these needs.

I contend that the rise of private foundations has gently changed the relative mix of public purposes and private values in American philanthropy, and that this shift is likely to continue well into the future. With growing amounts of philanthropic resources located in foundations, governed by boards, and managed by professional staff, the public purposes behind philanthropy have been pursued and promoted actively, while the private values and commitments of donors have been tamed. This move to institutional forms of giving—designed and executed by agents rather than principals—has made it harder for philanthropy to generate the distinctive energy that develops when public purposes and private values are joined together. Finding this balance is critical to philanthropy fulfilling all its functions. Any narrowing of the range of purposes pursued by philanthropy ought to promote competing, and at times unruly, visions of the public good.

The choice of what to support lies at the heart of defining a strategy for giving. The sheer range of possibilities is daunting to many donors. Not only are there countless causes and issues deserving attention, but within broad fields of activity there are many choices that need to be made to narrow the mission or a value proposition to be pursued.[1] Donors cannot say yes to every grantseeker. To do so would inevitably deplete resources quickly and lead to a large disconnected group of grants. While most organizations seeking funds may be deserving, it is impossible to make all philanthropic decisions based exclusively on the expressed needs of every prospective recipient. Philanthropic strategy demands that donors make some effort to bring coherence and order to giving. This process starts with the definition of a mission to be pursued or a value to be produced. Choosing a purpose can be difficult, especially if the expressed needs—and demands—of the community are strong while the commitment of donors to any particular issue is weak. No matter whether the focus comes as a result of listening to appeals from others or soul searching by the donor, focus is needed to concentrate limited resources on problems having some hope of impact.

To be sure, the idea of the donor imposing some order and direction on philanthropy will be resisted in some quarters. Sometimes philanthropy must react quickly to changing circumstances and be allowed to proceed from the interaction of events and donor commitments. However, even allowing for some flexibility and freedom, boundaries need to be placed on the kinds of activities that will be considered. The idea of defining a single philanthropic value may seem constraining, but this need not be the case. The idea of focusing on a particular value proposition should be understood as making a commitment that is part of a portfolio of choices. In fact, most institutional funders choose a diversification strategy of sorts by selecting three or four defined program areas in which to operate. For individuals, particularly newcomers to philanthropy, having a small number of purposes can be helpful, especially if it allows the donors to see how different fields, such as child welfare and education, have unique internal logics yet do interact in complex ways.

Making a choice about what value is to be produced for the public is often the starting point for donors. It seems natural to start with the mission and then to work around it in developing a philanthropic strategy. While clarifying the value proposition of giving can be a useful starting point for many donors, it can also be a minefield that delays and confuses the process of strategic giving. There are reasons for starting elsewhere in the philanthropic prism. It is hard for many donors to forgo options and choices in a field that is all about freedom and limitless possibilities. Moreover, many individuals begin their giving only with a vague sense of what their philanthropic calling might be; they want to discover and define their mission by making grants and practicing their giving across many fields. In the absence of a clear and strong commitment to a particular cause, and with an endless stream of legitimate supplicants waiting just around the corner, starting with the mission can be a daunting and even overwhelming first step. Whether done through study and reflection or achieved slowly through experience and practice, the hard work of making a value commitment must get done, even if the definition of mission, purpose, or value is broad and multidimensional.

Public Needs and Private Values

All philanthropic activity involves a choice about how to join public needs with private commitments in a way that is both beneficial for others and satisfying for the giver. Without both dimensions working closely together, philanthropy can degenerate either into a bland and disconnected exercise in administering transfer payments or into a selfish and shallow indulgence of the leisure class. While it is tempting to view the value proposition in philanthropy—the choice of what goal or mission to pursue—as involving a zero-sum trade-off between public benefits and private satisfaction in which more of one implies less of the other, this would be grossly misleading. The most strategic forms of philanthropy are those that start with a tight and energizing link between the donor's passions and the community's needs that leads to high levels of both public impact and private satisfaction.

Unfortunately, too many donors conceive the public and private dimensions of philanthropy as constituting distinct and irreconcilable starting points that frame a fateful choice. From one extreme perspective, the call of philanthropy demands the conscious abrogation of the self and the pursuit of the most urgent community needs. From this vantage point, philanthropy produces tangible results that meet critical needs left unmet by the market and that government has failed to fulfill adequately. This conception of giving is understandable, given the range of human problems that present themselves to all donors. Faced with issues such as youth violence, drug abuse, failing public schools, and a lack of affordable housing, donors can be led to sublimate their own interests and values and focus instead on the world. Almost all donors begin their search for a cause without an awareness of the massive scope of problems that could legitimately benefit from their attention. With pressure coming from many directions, it is tempting for donors to think of their giving as an agnostic and selfless response mechanism that should be driven by public needs. This perspective is actually rendered far more nuanced by the nature of the concept of public needs.

There are two fundamental dimensions to the concept of public needs. The first relates to who is doing the defining. Here there is an important distinction between definitions of public needs that are arrived at through collective deliberation and those that are set in place by individuals. The struggle to define public needs can often take place in the sphere of politics, although many times in philanthropy the definition of a public need is simply whatever the donor or a foundation's trustees declare is a need. While there is no simple answer to how many people are needed to agree before a problem becomes a legitimate human need, one thing is clear. There is pressure from the many stakeholders in philanthropy to spread responsibility beyond the donor to include others. One challenge in this move is maintaining a semblance of coherence and specificity, because there is an inverse correlation between the number of people engaged in decision making and the ability of parties to reach narrow and precise agreement on terms. Individual donors may be able to set down clear statements about what they believe are public needs, but large groups, even entire communities, may find it considerably more difficult to agree on the precise nature of public needs and their relative priority.

The second dimension is more complex and relates to the character of the definition that is advanced, which can be positive or normative in nature. Some believe that needs are nothing other than facts subject to measurement and specification through research. The social sciences have long aspired to render objective, positivistic assessments of public needs through surveys and field research. Against this perspective, there will always be those who assert that a concept as contested as "public needs" must be defined in normative terms, owing to the subjective nature of the concept. Those engaged in political advocacy make compelling moral arguments about the significance of certain public needs and why they should not be overlooked. This process leads to the construction of normative arguments that are designed to guide decision making. Often donors are hesitant to proceed on anything less than solid positivistic definitions of needs for fear that they lack the facts necessary to sensibly discharge their responsibilities. Ironically, many donors also have serious doubts about the capacity of researchers to provide much guidance in terms of the objective conditions and needs of communities. Thus, donors can and do find themselves caught between the desire for grounding and the sense that such grounding is hard to ever carry out systematically. It is in this context that more overtly normative arguments about public needs often surface and win the day. Without good data, claims from stakeholders about the "right thing to do" take on greater weight and more persuasive power.

For donors, these complexities create real challenges and require that difficult choices be made among four main options. The first option is to accept the idea that there are certain objective, positive human needs that are manifest and must be met, and to rally others around solutions to these needs. The inability of society or politics to satisfy all these needs creates a demand that can point the direction for philanthropy. To argue that there are objective public needs is to hold that there are certain social facts that rise above the level of debate and are objectively true. One can make such claims based on a hierarchy of needs ranging from the most prosaic to the most critical. The difficulty in insisting that social problems can be objectively determined is that politics appears to contradict this stance. The rising polarization of the country around a whole range of issues—from abortion to gun control to environmental protection—suggests that far from inching toward a consensus on many of the most important issues of the day, the public appears to be growing further and further apart in its views. However, amid all the noise, some problems rise up and simply demand attention. Although deep divisions remain on how best to fashion interventions in areas such as poverty, drug abuse, and illiteracy, there is still a sense that some issues or causes are patently important. Philanthropy may feel compelled to deal with these pressing problems, although the method used will be open to dispute and hearty second-guessing. Wanting to work collectively and collaboratively on defining public needs and holding a positivistic perspective on the nature of public needs can make declaring a mission of purpose fairly quick and painless: It reduces the task to studying the social research, consulting with the community of experts and thought leaders, and acting in areas in which needs are documented and enthusiastically accepted by all.

The second way for a donor to approach the question of public needs is to seek agreement among others but to give up on the positivistic dream. With this approach, even if it is hard to create a scientifically valid case for a hierarchy in public needs, it may still be possible to recognize that different communities attach different priorities to different issues. Donors committed to having their philanthropy address locally "constructed" public needs often start their philanthropic journey by commissioning in-depth neighborhood assessments and community surveys. By listening first to how others define needs, many donors hope that their philanthropy responds not to their own intuition about what a given community's needs might be, but instead to what those on the street level say is really the problem. This is not a guarantee that the claimed need is the most pressing, only that it is something that is wanted by those in the community in which the donor has chosen to operate.

The third option for donors is quite different. Rather than looking out into the world and either talking to researchers or the potentially affected population, it is possible to turn inward and argue that public needs are best determined by individual donors, not by some collective other, and that needs are ultimately a function of the persuasiveness of the normative claims made on their behalf. Many wealthy donors take this personalistic route and do not ultimately care whether there is broad agreement about the significance of the public need they choose to work on. They hold that their wealth is private and the significance of the public purposes they seek to address should not be judged by others but only by themselves. While it may be tempting to hypothesize that rural poverty, access to health care, and environmental degradation are each connected to more significant needs than are public gardens or social science research, for many donors, there is ultimately little evidence to support such claims. The actual criteria for defining the relative urgency of a public need is so nebulous that it is hard for many donors to even find much use in engaging in the exercise. Indeed, the actual distribution of philanthropic funds does not reveal any real discernable hierarchy of social needs. Money is distributed across many fields with religion, higher education, and health receiving large portions of the philanthropic pie. Within these broad categories, it is very hard to ascertain what percentage of donated funds are used for social justice concerns or to aid the most needy.[2] Politics has taught philanthropy that a rational hierarchy of social needs is very hard to construct and defend in a way that everyone will accept. Because the concept of need is so contested, some donors simply accept that there will never be enough money to meet all needs—pressing and not so pressing—and that all donors can do is focus on what they personally believe is normatively important and meaningful.

A final option for the donor confronted with this difficult challenge is to look inward and to define needs independently of the affected communities, and to make hard choices based on personal research aimed at grounding philanthropic decisions in as much objective information as possible. Providing a positive definition of a need individually is the most demanding approach. It places huge burdens on the donor to do large amounts of due diligence and to try to keep some semblance of detachment in a situation in which outside checks and balances are not present. For this reason, it is the least common response to the core problem of defining a public need in philanthropy.

In practice, many of the wisest donors pursue a compromise position that is a hybrid of these four models, one that combines both the expressed desires of the local community and their own convictions, balancing, at the same time, the latest research and science with the most powerful and compelling moral arguments made on behalf of others. One good indication that no clear, compelling hierarchy of charitable causes can be defined, based on either of these two central dimensions to public needs, lies in the enduring reticence of the tax code about treating any particular type of nonprofit differently from all the rest. Soup kitchens receive the same tax treatments as avant-garde theaters. Community health clinics working in desperate urban settings have no advantage over suburban historical societies. All public-serving nonprofit organizations are treated the same because the alternative, a differentiated treatment of charities based on their social contribution, is simply unworkable.[3]

If the nature of public needs defines one side of the conceptual playing field of philanthropy, the other side is marked by the character of the private values and commitments enacted through giving. Philanthropy allows donors to speak to the world about what they believe is valuable. Starting with the heartfelt beliefs of the donors, it is possible to construe philanthropy as an expressive activity that allows individuals to project their values into public space. Having earned or acquired money legitimately and not having to give any of it away, some wealthy individuals simply conclude that the primary factor driving their giving should be their own personal satisfaction. Seen from this perspective, giving is a way for donors to feel better about themselves. This may lead donors to support organizations that have been personally significant—a college that the donor attended or a hospital that prolonged the donor's life. When the private values of the donor are a starting point, charitable giving takes on an expressive character that is quite distinct from the espoused needs and desires of the broad public. Reciprocity and the sense of giving something back does not necessarily lead to the most pressing public needs being selected for funding. Rather, it often leads straight into the personal life experiences and values of the donor.

For every donor, there are some causes that pull on the heartstrings and then tug on the purse strings. The transition from appeal to action is often based on the strength of the donor's private values, commitments, and beliefs and how they relate or do not relate to the appeal being made. Rather than seek to sublimate the personal connection and passion of donors, it may be best to simply acknowledge it and seek to capture its capacity to mobilize giving. After all, on almost every major issue or topic, there are usually forces arrayed on both sides, each supported by their own group of dedicated donors. For philanthropy to work, donors need to be matched to the issues that speak to them so they can see their giving as a form of expression and action on behalf of causes or missions that matter.

The beliefs of donors range from being very strongly felt and central to a donor's philanthropic thinking to more marginal inclinations. Faith is certainly an important driver of many philanthropic decisions. Large numbers of donors come to their giving through their churches. They understand charity as a requirement or expectation of their religious community.[4] From Abraham's tithe to the priest Melchizedek's "tenth of everything" he brought back from battle to Islam's principle of zakat, which calls for 2.5 percent of savings be given away when wealth reaches certain levels, charity is a fixture in the world's religions. While faith is a dominant force behind the giving of many donors, sometimes the animating force is even more immediate and personal. Gifts are often given to remember loved ones and to honor an institution that had a profound impact on the life of the donor or the donor's family. The personal side of philanthropy is not lost on fund-raisers, who understand that donors with strong personal ties to institutions are more likely to give than those with little or no direct connection. In making gifts, particularly large ones, donors are often seeking to affirm a belief or value that is deeply felt.

Political ideology may also shape the values expressed in philanthropy. On the left side of the political spectrum, young, progressive donors have rallied through groups like Resource Generation to support grassroots organizing and the social change movement. On the other side of the political spectrum, conservatism has animated a large amount of giving, some with very clear political intentions. Richard Mellon Scaife gained a fair amount of recognition for his willingness to use his giving to advance his political beliefs. Scaife made grants to *American Spectator* magazine so that it could investigate and publish a series of embarrassing stories about President Clinton's Arkansas years.[5]

No matter where the donor lies on the political spectrum or where the donor's personal attachments might lead, values and beliefs are critical forces that both animate and direct giving. The satisfaction that donors receive from making gifts and their ability to see their values transformed into institutional and programmatic forms constitute the supply-side push that continues to drive philanthropic funds from donors to recipients.[6] Without donors feeling some satisfaction from their giving, it is hard to imagine how the long-standing growth of giving in the United States could be sustained. In contrast to taxes, which are taken involuntarily and used without specific taxpayer approval to cover a range of routine government expenditures, philanthropic funds can be directed to causes that matter to donors and that affirm their values. This is a powerful point of differentiation that gives philanthropy its powerful pull.

Not everyone is willing to embrace the private nature of the philanthropic impulse so quickly. Rather than accept the passions and commitments of givers as a source of strength and vitality for the field, some attempt to construe the private values as a threat to a rational and effective philanthropy. The sometimes bizarre and extreme ideas of donors must be held to some kind of account so that publicly subsidized giving can meet its full potential. Interestingly, those who tend to have reservations about the role of private values in philanthropy tend to overlap fairly consistently with those who believe that philanthropy should be directed at the most pressing human needs or who want to see communities have a greater say in the allocation of philanthropic funds. Only when one is willing to take a more nuanced point of view on the nature of public needs does the potential value added of a donor-driven, personalistic philanthropy come into full focus. Not only is it impossible to take private values out of individual philanthropy, but to do so would surely weaken the performance of philanthropy and undermine its ability to mobilize large amounts of money.

The private values of donors interact with public needs, and philanthropy is enriched when the two find some overlap. It is an elusive and complex intersection in which private values need to find resonance with community desires. Dueling perceptions of public needs can collide and make the location of this intersection elusive. What is striking about philanthropy is that in the cases where this confluence of forces has occurred, impressive results have been achieved for all parties. Nevertheless, in the many cases where this intersection is not achieved, philanthropy can and does take alternative or mixed forms that are greater or lesser approximations of strategic giving.

Four Forms of Value Creation

Although the concepts of public needs and private values are highly contested and problematic, it is still possible to sketch out a framework that allows one to understand the main forms of philanthropic value creation. To do so, it is necessary to introduce a somewhat different, though related, distinction. Giving can be understood to possess two very different dimensions, one of them instrumental and the other expressive. First, philanthropy is an important instrument for the accomplishment of public purposes, no matter how or by whom they are defined. Donors play an important role in supporting nonprofit organizations in a broad array of fields. Gifts and grants can be a central support mechanism that allows nonprofits to offer the services on which their clients depend. When they succeed in achieving public purposes, defined in any of the many possible ways, donors deliver something of instrumental value. As such, giving has an instrumental dimension that is measured in terms of the concrete outcomes it produces. In a search for validation and learning, the programmatic outcomes are increasingly being measured and evaluated using metrics borrowed from business. That philanthropy is valuable because it is a useful tool for the accomplishment of public purposes is the core of what I call the instrumental dimension of giving.

Second, giving can be seen as valuable because it allows donors to express their values and commitment through gifts to others. The very attempt to act publicly can be a satisfying end unto itself. The value that is created may be entirely psychic, arising simply from expressing commitment, caring, and belief.[7] The expressive quality of giving suggests that a narrow focus on programmatic outcomes distracts from what may be the deeper meaning of philanthropic action, which springs from the self-actualization experienced by those who give or volunteer. This is what I call the expressive dimension of giving.

The expressive and instrumental dimensions of giving can complement one another or they can create tensions. Under the right circumstances, the values that drive donors can be harnessed to produce better and more effective grantmaking. In some ways, this connection seems obvious. Committed donors are more likely to work hard to create value through their giving than donors who feel detached and removed from their philanthropy. When the values, commitments, and beliefs of the donor find expression in philanthropy, they can become at odds with the instrumental purposes that the donor is seeking to achieve.

As donors deliberate over how to balance these two critical dimensions, four main options emerge. First, giving can be purged of private values and be aimed at very narrow and specific public needs; what will result, however, is a form of giving that resembles old-fashioned charity, in which money simply passes quietly and uncreatively from one person to another through an intermediary organization. Second, giving can be infused with donor values and passions and be directed at a purpose that neither the community nor the donor can reasonably argue is urgent or important. This will generate a form of expressive giving that privileges the donor's needs, but that does not meet the test of effectiveness. Third, giving can be directed at the public needs of affected communities in ways that are potentially far reaching, with the donor's values and input screened out of the equation. In such cases, a kind of instrumental giving will emerge directed at delivering results, even if innovation and passion are missing. Finally, there is a kind of giving in which public needs are successfully married to deeply held beliefs and commitments of donors. It is this strange and elusive combination that I seek to illuminate here.

To better understand the interaction of these two dimensions, one can construct a map that tracks along two axes the critical difference between the instrumental and expressive dimensions of giving. The four forms of value creation presented here (see figure 5.1) are ideal types, in that they represent pure concepts. In practice, the boundaries around these types are almost always loose and shifting. More often than not, giving combines two or more of these types, either because the donor's approach to giving has multiple dimensions within a single chosen field of activity or—when the donor's substantive interests are diffuse—the donor's approach is different across the multiple fields of activity in which giving takes place. In the first instance, where giving is focused, for example, on education, donors may experiment with highly expressive forms of giving when supporting a class gift to the undergraduate institution they attended, while at the same time wanting to make a more instrumental gift that will create institutional change at a leading teaching hospital with which the donor has no affiliation. In the second instance, where philanthropic interests are broad, giving may combine, for example, charitable support for disaster relief in the developing world with expressive giving for an advocacy organization working on an issue close to the donor's heart. Even with these caveats, it is still possible to begin to sketch the landscape of value creation in philanthropy by distinguishing the kinds of private commitment and public purpose that is pursued.

More Charitable Forms of Giving

In its purest form, charity starts with the recognition that not all giving is or needs to be strategic giving. A large amount of giving by individuals and even institutions is simply uncomplicated benevolence that takes the simple form of a gift. Even though I have noted earlier that charity has fallen on hard times, the concept has a long and venerable history stretching back into the earliest societies. Charity is central to almost all religious traditions and connects faith with worldly deeds.[8] Today, the perceived problem with small-scale charity is grounded in the assumption that giving needs to do more than provide assistance as crises arise in the lives of individuals and communities. As the scale of human needs on both a national and an international stage grows, there is a sense that the size of the problems is enormous compared to the capacity of small-scale, traditional charitable giving. Charity is simply too modest and local for some donors, especially those with big ambitions focusing on complex problems.

Charitable giving takes many forms. Today, large amounts of charitable resources are mobilized through direct mail fund-raising. Frequently raising money for programs serving the disadvantaged or disabled or medical research, these appeals ask for small contributions. The appeals are mostly intended to get the attention of those who receive the letters, perhaps even targeting people whose families have been touched by the disease in question and want to do something to help others. The use of direct

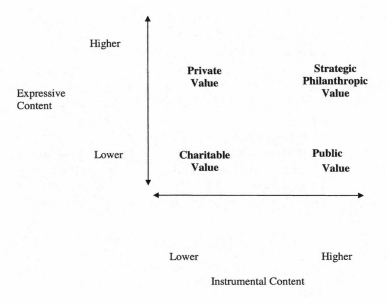

Figure 5.1 **Four forms of value creation in philanthropy.**

mail has become a very sophisticated business over the years, with appeals directed with increasing precision at those likely to be inclined to support a particular cause. One of the real attractions of this kind of fund-raising is that it tends to produce supporters who can be counted on in subsequent years. Thus, while the cost may be high in terms of finding donors within the broad universe of possible supporters, the long-term benefits of building a base of small contributors should not be underestimated. At a time when other sources of support—foundation and government grants, for example—tend to come and go over time, small donors can be counted on to supply critical unrestricted support for years.

When making small contributions by mail, few if any donors ask questions about the use of their funds. Most often the funds are simply given to the charity with the expectation that the funds will be used wisely.[9] With little investigation or follow-up from donors, the mobilization of large numbers of small contributors is attractive to organizations, providing them with unrestricted support that can be used to cover critical infrastructure expenses that institutional funders may balk at underwriting.[10] In exchange for their donations, small direct mail givers do receive something significant in return: a sense of having done something to help others. This is a feeling that can be bought for relatively little money and with no real commitment of time or energy. It is a form of charity that is admittedly superficial, but one that satisfies the needs of a large number of givers. It is built on a traditional model of charity, one in which the cause is preeminent and the donor is secondary. Billions of dollars are raised this way, with organizations routinely sending multimillion-piece mailings across the country. Because they tend to have a low response rate and the gifts that are produced tend to be small, direct mail seeks to compensate by increasing the volume of appeals. Direct mail fund-raising by nonprofits has gotten very sophisticated; it now times and directs its appeals to capitalize on such things as natural disasters, special holidays, event anniversaries, and local and national policy debates.[11]

One of the most ubiquitous forms of charity takes place during the holidays. Every year between Thanksgiving and Christmas, the Salvation Army stands on street corners shaking bells and collecting contributions from people walking by. The amount of the average contribution is small, often only pocket change, but the intention of those who give is clear: to help others who are less fortunate during the holiday season. The Salvation Army is able to elicit this kind of simple and direct giving because it has a reputation for lean operations and a devotion to mission. Those who contribute small amounts to the organization do not do so with any real illusion that their individual contribution will make a major difference, but rather that the totality of small contributions may amount to something significant. In fact, the Salvation Army raises millions from its bell-ringing campaigns. Thus, when small-scale charity is channeled and organized effectively, it can reach beyond the limitations of charity and seek out larger and bolder solutions to public problems.

Over time, a significant amount of small-scale private giving has been moved from the private realm of the household into the more public realm of the workplace. Many groups, including the United Way, seek small contributions from workers on an annual basis.[12] Often taken as a payroll deduction, these gifts go to causes in the community over which the donor has either little control or, with some intermediaries, a fair measure of control. Because they tend to be small contributions made without recourse to very detailed analysis, workplace gifts to federated funders look more like charity than anything else. Still, this form of giving has remained popular due to the collective nature of the enterprise and the stigma attached in some workplaces to not participating in these campaigns.

Although there is certainly a lasting place for charity in the broader landscape of giving, it continues to have its limitations, both as an effective instrument of change and as a vehicle for the expression of private values. When it is small and local, charity—practiced through workplace giving or in response to direct mail and seasonal appeals—may succeed in reaching populations that others have ignored. However, the scope of the intended benefits of this kind of giving is generally limited. For this reason, donors with greater levels of resources tend to seek out opportunities that will allow them to have a broader impact and more clearly measurable effects that can be attributed to the donor's own giving. These considerations set aside, there is still no denying that on the map of value creation, a fair amount of all giving occurs with little expressive content and with very modest instrumental purposes.

More Instrumental Forms of Giving

Sometimes giving has a purposeful or instrumental rationale. Donors may give simply because they spot a problem or need for which philanthropic resources represent a solution. The substantive topic can be less important than the quality of the philanthropic opportunity and the possibility of doing good. For such donors, achieving an outcome, not enacting their private values or beliefs, is particularly attractive. The instrumental side of giving is often accentuated by the fact that many wealthy donors do not have strong passions about any particular issue, and are more interested in being useful than anything else. For such donors, the instrumental side of giving looms large. It represents a relatively straightforward way to score their philanthropy, one that is not enmeshed in their personal or family lives.

Madison, Wisconsin, a city of about 200,000, recently received a massive gift to fund the creation of a major downtown arts district. Jerome Frautchi came from a family who had been in Madison for five generations and was known for the combination furniture business and funeral parlor it operated. Frautchi and his wife, Pleasant Rowlan, founded their own business and quietly built the Pleasant Company, which manufactured the popular American Girl doll collection. The company was sold to Mattel in 1998 for $700 million. Frautchi's father had always been involved in civic matters and helped raise money for the original Madison Arts Center, and Jerome Frautchi wanted to follow in his footsteps. He put aside $50 million for the arts in Madison in his newly created Overture Foundation and then raised that commitment to $100 million. The gift was equal to more than half of the city's annual tax revenue. More symbolically, the gift was larger than the entire annual grants budget of the National Endowment for the Arts. The funds were designated for the renovation of existing arts buildings and to erect new ones. To launch this complex effort, Frautchi hired the city's planning and development director to oversee what became known as the Overture Project. Eventually, the internationally known architect Cesar Pelli was hired to create the plans for the project, which would meld old and new into a world-class arts complex for the residents of Madison.

Several aspects of this gift are noteworthy. First, there will be no Frautchi Arts Center, no Frautchi Hall, nor even a Frautchi rotunda in the new complex. The donor consciously chose to avoid any such arrangements. Second, the gift does not enact the values of a real arts aficionado; the donor's favorite forms of culture include the tunes of Andrew Lloyd Webber and adventure novels. Third and most significantly, the gift does seek to address an important civic need, one that local government has long neglected. Wisconsin ranks among the bottom states in terms of state and local support of the arts. In rationalizing his philanthropic decision, Frautchi chose to focus on something that the public sector has neglected because of its other pressing commitments. Recognizing that a division of labor between the public and private sectors was inevitable, Frautchi believed that his gift was simply taking care of something that many taxpayers would not prioritize yet that many would enjoy.

Not surprisingly, given the activist reputation of Madison, this public-spirited gift met with a fair amount of resistance. The local wish list of the arts community included exhibition spaces, dance studios, concert halls, and a theater—not all of which were being addressed by the proposed plan. Second, because the plan involved a major renovation of the existing Civic Center arts building and the construction of new buildings around it, many residents thought that the planning process needed to be more open to community input and control. A People's Arts District group was founded to slow down the fast-moving project and ensure that what was built met the community's needs, and that not only the performing arts but also the broader cultural arts were assisted. A central point of contention was whether the Overture Project was a public project or a "civic gift." Although the funds were from a private source, the project involved the condemnation of the entire block on which the existing arts center stood so as to allow for full development. While the project continued to move forward toward completion, the boundary issue raised by even the most instrumental and public-oriented forms of philanthropy underscore the tensions that arise whenever private parties seek to act on the behalf of the public.[13]

The instrumental dimension of giving can be highlighted by the choice of the philanthropic vehicle through which giving takes place. Rather than work individually, many donors seek to collaborate with others, a move that signals a willingness to sacrifice some of the expressive possibilities of acting independently in exchange for the chance to have a larger and more meaningful impact by working in a coordinated manner with others. In New York City, Brazilian expatriates gather monthly to hear about the efforts of all sorts of nonprofit organizations working in their home country. The meetings are called "Ideas That Transform Brazil" and are sponsored by the Brazil Foundation. Since its inception in 2000, the foundation has been channeling resources to nonprofits that operate in five broad areas: education, health, human rights, citizenship, and culture. The purpose of the gatherings is to attract the resources to support those organizations. Leona Forman founded the Brazil Foundation and organized the early meetings. Forman worked for twenty years at the United Nations and had considerable experience bridging national boundaries. With over one million Brazilians living in America—many with an interest in supporting their home country—Forman identified the opportunity to connect potential donors with community efforts in Brazil. The foundation has donated over $1.5 million to twenty-two projects in Brazil. As a consequence of its collective character, the effort is not guided by any single ideological position or value claim, but rather works at a more technical level to address important problems abroad. Given the size of Brazil and the variety of programs that the foundation supports, $1.5 million might not seem like enough to accomplish substantial change. However, the efforts of Forman's organization are about more than just moving money from one place to another; the gifts are concrete pieces of a plan to build a tradition and culture of giving. What makes this effort more instrumental and less expressive is the fact that it focused so much on the needs of Brazil and much less on the needs of the donors for personal identification.

Instrumentalism finds its most common manifestations not in the megagifts of individuals or in the collective action of expatriates, but rather in the detached and often value-neutral giving practiced by major institutional donors. Many of the largest independent, corporate, and community foundations today are highly proficient when it comes to the technology of grantmaking; they efficiently process grant applications, conduct site visits, assess the merit of proposals, make recommendations to trustees, and process checks to recipient organizations. Throughout this process, grantmaking professionals work on behalf of boards that in turn owe some

allegiance to the donor's intent.[14] The twice removed principal-agent relationship that lies at the heart of institutional giving creates the conditions
under which grantmaking staff attempt to affirm process values—not substantive values—such as transparency, accountability, and fairness. The
privileging of process is a natural function of professional staff's attempt to
discharge their duties with detachment and in a way that puts institutional
interests first. While foundations all have donors in their past, the strength
of the donor's values in guiding the institution tends to diminish over time,
as the founder's vision is translated and interpreted by successive generations of agents, often first by family and friends, and then by persons who
are increasingly distanced from the founder. While professional staff and
outside directors may make every effort to respect the mission of the foundation as defined by the donor, this does not mean that the donor's values
will be preserved over time.

Artifacts of instrumentalism in foundation philanthropy are not hard
to locate. One of the most obvious manifestations is in the annual reports
of large foundations, which lay out the purposes and missions of these
institutions. What is most striking about these mission statements is the
breadth of the proclaimed missions and their generally noncontroversial
and nonexpressive character. The mission statements of the largest foundations reveal that, at least in the understanding of their purpose and goals,
these institutions rarely seek to enact or publicly affirm a set of strong value
commitments that may once have been held by the donor. In fact, most of
the stated purposes of large foundations, which control the preponderance
of philanthropic assets in the field, are entirely free of value claims. In table 5.1, the mission statements or descriptions of grantmaking priorities of
older billion-dollar foundations are displayed. What is striking about this
assemblage is its uniformity, its broadness, and it value-neutrality. The one
major exception to this trend is the Ford Foundation, whose stated goals
have a more normative and value-filled quality to them, invoking as they do
democracy, poverty reduction, and justice.[15]

The tendency of large foundations to pursue broad purposes is largely at
issue in these tame generalities. There is a long-standing tradition within
foundations that one scholar has even termed the "philanthropic standard."[16]
It dictates that the purposes and geographical reach of foundations' work
should grow as the size of philanthropic resources increases. In other words,
the largest foundations have the broadest mandate precisely because their
resources are so substantial that a donor must give plenty of leeway to future generations to find the best possible uses for the funds entrusted to the

Table 5.1 **Missions of select large American foundations.**

Name	Mission and Philanthropic Goals
Alfred P. Sloan Foundation	"to support projects in science and technology, living standards and economic performance, and education"
Carnegie Corporation of New York	"to promote the advancement and diffusion of knowledge and understanding"
John D. and Catherine T. MacArthur Foundation	"seeks the development of healthy individuals and effective communities; peace within and among nations; responsible choices about human reproduction; and a global ecosystem capable of supporting healthy human societies"
Lilly Endowment, Inc.	"supports religion, education, and community development, with special concentration on programs to benefit youth"
Pew Charitable Trusts	"contribute to the public's health and welfare and strengthen the communities in which we live"
The Andrew W. Mellon Foundation	"to aid and promote such religious, charitable, scientific, literary, and educational purposes as may be in the furtherance of the public welfare"
The Ford Foundation	"to strengthen democratic values, reduce poverty and injustice, promote international cooperation, and advance human achievement"
The Robert Wood Johnson Foundation	"making grants to improve the health and health care of all Americans"
The Rockefeller Foundation	"to identify, and address at their source, the causes of human suffering and need"

institutions. Sometimes breadth is achieved through geographical span, with foundations giving across the country and around the world when the substantive mission, like promotion of health care or scientific research, is more precise. Other times, breadth of purpose is achieved by selecting a mission that is all encompassing and that is entirely open to the interpretation, such as the Rockefeller's Foundation's mandate to address the causes of human suffering. No matter how it is achieved, breadth of purpose commensurate with substantial resources tends to lead away from personalization and the enactment of private values.

One additional reason why many large foundations have gravitated away from the expression of the personal values and commitments of their donors can be traced to the way work has long been organized in foundations. Foundation staffers have never understood their work to involve expressing their own personal beliefs or values or even those of a donor they never knew. Rather, staff members see their work as involving the technical task of improving the foundation's effectiveness. As a consequence, passion and personality are rarely central to institutional philanthropy over the long run. This allows it to be cool and technocratic, and at times to achieve interesting results, but rarely does it startle or surprise with challenging and controversial philanthropic initiatives grounded in personal experience and strong value commitments. By focusing on developing coherent plans for the disbursal of funds, by choosing recipient organizations carefully, and by tracking results dutifully, program staff in institutional philanthropy are able to pursue at least one part of the core challenge of giving, namely the achievement of instrument ends.

Over time, as donors leave the scene and as trustees and staff naturally take on greater responsibility for the disbursement of philanthropic resources, the capacity of institutional philanthropy to maintain a healthy balance between private values and public purposes is challenged. In the absence of clear and specific guidance from boards, staff struggle to interpret and act on the donor's intent, especially when it becomes difficult to ascertain the exact nature of the intent or to remain true to it as circumstances change and as time puts more and more distance between philanthropic principals and agents.[17] In the end, the move to institutional philanthropy that many donors commit to when they form a foundation leads eventually to a kind of broad, detached, and technical form of philanthropy emphasizing instrumentalism over expressivism.

More Expressive Forms of Giving

For all the claims of the professional grantmakers to rationalize and normalize giving, large segments of philanthropy retain a strong emotive side. The trigger to giving is often the private passions and convictions of individuals. Drawn to philanthropy by a desire to do something significant that will give greater meaning to life, donors want their giving to reflect their values and identity. For younger donors, philanthropy can be a potent way to construct a public identity and to attach oneself to an issue or cause, a way to discover and manifest latent interests or engage problems that otherwise appear too large or complex to tackle. For others, giving is a way to link private values and personal faith with real-world problems.[18] Many small and large donors seek to make a statement through philanthropy, either to the public or to themselves about what they believe in and what their priorities truly are.

Not surprisingly, religious giving constitutes the largest share of all giving in the United States. It is animated and encouraged by faiths as diverse as Catholicism, Judaism, and Islam. Though usually small and local in character, faith has at times inspired large and ambitious philanthropy.[19] One of the most far-reaching efforts to translate faith into philanthropic good works is that of Thomas Monaghan, the founder of Domino's pizzas. Monaghan was four when his father died, and two years later his mother placed him in a Catholic orphanage where he was raised by nuns. Monaghan was an altar boy who considered the priesthood, but then drifted away from religion after joining the Marines and starting his pizza empire. Over time, he slowly became more and more involved in Catholic matters. He made a grant to an antiabortion group that eventually led to a nationwide boycott of Domino's and funded the construction of a special chair for the pope to sit on while celebrating mass during his visit to Detroit. Over time, Monaghan developed a close relationship with Cardinal Edmund Szoka of Detroit, even underwriting a new computer system for the Vatican to help organize its finances when the cardinal was called on to help in Rome. However, it was only after Monaghan sold a large stake in his pizza chain for $1 billion that he began to give ever more aggressively and broadly. By putting $200 million into his Ave Maria Foundation and retaining plenty to give directly, Monaghan's giving has spanned a range of activities—mostly with a conservative Catholic purpose. One grant that attracted controversy was a $2.5 million donation to support the construction of a large cathedral in Managua, Nicaragua, at a time when Monaghan worried about the spread of communism throughout Central America. While even his local priest urged him to find a way to use his wealth to help the poor with needed services, Monaghan's approach has consistently been to focus on the spiritual and moral lives of individuals.[20]

Monaghan's Catholic philanthropy has been centered on higher education. One of his most ambitious undertakings has been the founding of Ave Maria School of Law, located in Monaghan's office park outside of Ann Arbor, where the 270-acre headquarters for Domino's and surrounding office buildings are built in the style of Frank Lloyd Wright's Prairie School. Seeking to enact his faith and his belief in the importance of education, Monaghan's law school serves students who are interested in the moral dimension of the law. His critics contend that the law school is simply a tool for training the next generation of conservative lawyers, who will go about trying to dismantle liberal jurisprudence. None of this concerns Monaghan, who has plans for a business school on the same campus.

Beyond starting this substantial undertaking, Monaghan has constantly sought out opportunities to fund projects that build spirituality. While other funders want to focus on critical material needs, Thomas Monaghan's philanthropy consciously focuses on faith. He even bought a fraternity house that was for sale on the campus of the University of Michigan, and after removing all the vestiges of party life and self-indulgence, converted the house into a dorm for Catholic girls, including crucifixes on the walls of every room. In addition, he has created several Catholic schools for girls that he believes make faith a more central part of learning than that of the existing Catholic schools. Monaghan's far-ranging but consistent philanthropy has not gone unnoticed. In fact, he is one of the most visible Catholic philanthropists in America, whose giving has earned him the privilege of taking communion from the pope and having his daughter married in St. Peter's Basilica, with Cardinal Szoka presiding.

Other donors use their giving not to express their faith, but rather to honor other things that have meaning in their lives. The case of David Duffield, the founder of the computer software firm PeopleSoft, is a case in point. Duffield and his wife had a very deep and important relationship with Maddie, a miniature schnauzer that lived with them before their fortune was made. The dog was a profound source of happiness for the couple, who could not have children of their own. Maddie's strong personality and affection were important to Duffield as he worked hard to build his business. He pledged to the dog that if he ever made a large amount of money, he would give it back. Maddie died in 1997 of cancer after ten years with the Duffields, but the dog would not be forgotten. Duffield became a billionaire and made the largest commitment to animal welfare in history through Maddie's Fund: a $200 million endowment to support animal welfare and create a network of no-kill shelters.

Giving away millions a year to fund animal welfare proved difficult to do effectively. Duffield hired the head of the San Francisco Society for Prevention of Cruelty to Animals (SFSPCA), which operated the nation's largest and most prominent no-kill shelter, to run Maddie's Fund. SFSPCA's shelter was known nationwide as a model that provided great care to stray animals. Seeking to illuminate the practice of euthanasia in a country that annually puts to sleep five million cats and dogs in overcrowded shelters was an ambitious goal. However, drawing on experience in the technology field, in which revolutionary ideas are regularly turned into successes, Duffield and his team forged ahead with their plan to offer grants to shelters that pledge to find homes for all animals within five years. Making grants that escalate as the shelters improve their performance, Maddie's Fund awards a $1 million grant when a shelter has fully reinvented itself into a no-kill facility that places all animals regardless of age, appearance, or physical disability. To achieve its goal, the fund also strives to reduce birth rates among animals and to ensure that families who have pets are able to keep them over the long run.

Many donors have explicitly connected their giving to their passions and interests. Peter Norton made a fortune in computer software and at fifty, after selling the company, turned his and his wife's attention to philanthropy. Unlike some donors who start out with a focus on the world and the needs that confront communities, a significant part of the Nortons' giving has consciously focused inward on what interests him most, namely contemporary art. The Nortons filled their large home with cutting-edge, socially conscious art by new artists, and even enlisted the help of two curators to help them locate the art and give it away to museums. The Nortons' philanthropy is not limited only to art, but encompasses a wide variety of untested and risky propositions across a range of fields including social service and education. The gifts share a willingness to break boundaries and experiment. One of the Nortons' most well-known philanthropic acts involved the letters of famed writer J. D. Salinger. Long a recluse, Salinger had written very personal letters to a young woman who had originally corresponded with the author while she was in college and then later became Salinger's lover. The woman placed the letters from Salinger up for auction. Norton bought the letters for $156,500 and returned them to Salinger.

Some donors give because their memories are strong and philanthropy is a way to leave a visible imprint on society that is more lasting and universal than a personal recollection or private feeling. Mary Ford Maurer grew up in Kansas City. One of her fondest memories was going to Union Station to visit her father's office at the Fred Harvey Company, where he was secretary-treasurer. She would often go out to lunch with her father in the station, where the two would talk. Four children, ten grandchildren, and two great-grandchildren later, she returned to Union Station for a hard-hat tour of the ongoing renovation. When asked to support the project, she offered $200,000 to pay for the renovation of the grand old clock in the station. Married to a successful businessman, Maurer ran the investment company for thirteen years following her husband's unexpected death at the age of sixty-six. She conducts much of her giving from a donor-advised fund in a community foundation and likes the fact that she can accumulate charitable assets in her account, save them for a major gift, and think about all the options before committing to efforts such as the clock restoration project. Other gifts by Maurer have been spread across the arts, education, and social services. Though not a member of the Community Christian Church, she was enraptured by its steeple of light, formed by light beams projected into the sky during weekends, and helped maintain it with a grant driven mainly by emotion and visceral attraction.

Charitable, instrumental, and expressive philanthropy overlap with one another, creating more blended forms. Moreover, few donors remain absolutely consistent across all their giving over time or even at any given point in time. Donors may hold a diversified portfolio of philanthropic commitments that may include, for example, some local charity around the holidays, a few detached donations to worthy organizations with strong reputations, an expressive gift to their church, and, if they are thoughtful and deliberative, a few commitments that tend toward the more strategic, linking private commitments and significant community or public needs. There is also an evolutionary dimension to the four main forms of value creation in philanthropy. The philanthropy of those who start out doing instrumental or expressive giving will often evolve into more strategic forms as time and experience allow them to sharpen their focus and gain clarity of purpose. On the other hand, many of the most strategic grantmakers consciously allow themselves to engage in more traditional forms of charity when the circumstances call for it. As donors move in and around the matrix presented earlier, working within and between the forms and experimenting with different philanthropic tools and techniques, they sometimes achieve the kind of fit and alignment that is a required element of strategy.

Bringing the Two Dimensions of Philanthropy Together

Giving that marries instrumentalism and expressivism is difficult to clearly delineate and can take many forms. It is not defined by the substantive issue that it happens to embrace, but rather by the quality of the fit achieved and by the melding of public purposes and private values. In formulating a grantmaking agenda, some donors attempt both to reflect the values that were important to the donor and to produce broad benefits for the public. When successful, these donors come closest to practicing strategic giving. A major philanthropic commitment by the F. W. Olin Foundation can serve as an example. Over the years, this foundation funded the construction of over seventy engineering buildings on college campuses around the country to reflect the donor's abiding commitment to engineering education. Born in 1860, Franklin W. Olin received little formal education, but was determined to study engineering and eventually graduated from Cornell University. Olin played in forty-nine games during two years of major league baseball with the Washington Senators and the Detroit Tigers, but his engineering skills proved greater than his athletic ability. After designing textile mill machinery, Olin began to work on powder mill construction. Olin founded two profitable munitions companies around the turn of the twentieth century. In 1938, he created the F. W. Olin Foundation, to which he donated most of his fortune upon his death in 1951. Over the coming decades, the trustees of the foundation sought to honor Olin's dedication to science and engineering by making major grants to support the advancement of engineering education around the country.

In 1997, the F. W. Olin Foundation attempted to make an even bigger impact on engineering education by creating the Franklin W. Olin College of Engineering, a new undergraduate school that would be located just outside of Boston. The foundation committed $300 million of its $500 million endowment to the effort, with the promise of more if needed. In a creative move, the foundation's board looked at a number of different undergraduate education models and found the Claremont Colleges' approach very appealing. Under this approach, a group of independent colleges shared major facilities such as a gymnasium and library while maintaining their own academic independence. The Olin Foundation eventually struck a deal with Babson College to purchase seventy acres of land that Babson owned next to its campus. The partnership was appealing to the board of Olin because it would connect the engineering school to a college that has a national reputation through its business school for teaching entrepreneurship, something that well-rounded engineers eager to translate their ideas into products truly need, something that the donor understood and believed in deeply.

The new Olin College will break some old rules in higher education. Tenure will not be offered to faculty. Instead, they will be given five-year renewable contracts based on peer review. In addition, students will not pay any tuition or room charges. To attract the very best students, who otherwise might attend MIT or CalTech, Olin decided to differentiate itself by both waiving tuition and by giving the first class of students the chance to work with faculty on designing the school's campus, its curriculum, and its teaching methods. To date, the college successfully recruited an initial class of students and, after receiving over a thousand applications for a maximum of sixty teaching positions, a dozen initial faculty committed to undergraduate engineering education were hired.

How well this risky and innovative philanthropic effort turns out will not be known for many years. But what is significant about it is the scope of its ambition and the fervor to enact the donor's values that mobilized the foundation's board to depart from their traditional grantmaking procedures that supported existing institutions. In this case, the board of the foundation decided to act in a way that a major individual donor might, by taking a substantial risk and investing in something that has a potentially high return rate. In seeking to develop a new model of undergraduate engineering education, the F. W. Olin Foundation has attempted to produce both expressive and instrumental value, and to satisfy both the intent of the donor and the needs of society for well-trained engineers.

Some donors are moved not by causes, but rather by a personal attachment to communities; they build a strategy accordingly. Dean Mathey, a partner in the investment firm Dillon, Read, created a foundation that would work to improve the small town of Grafton, Vermont. The Windham Foundation has three main goals: to restore historic buildings and promote economic vitality in Grafton; to provide limited financial support to educational and charitable causes in the area; and to develop projects that will benefit Vermont and Vermonters. These broad purposes have been pursued through an operating foundation, which uses the foundation's resources both to operate programs and to make some grants. Since its founding in 1963, one of the foundation's main accomplishments has been the restoration of the grand old tavern and inn in the center of the village, which now hosts visitors year-round, and a host of smaller buildings around the village that date back to the early decades of the 1800s. To preserve the character and integrity of the town, the foundation owns approximately 1,600 acres of land around the village. An interesting difference between Grafton and places such as Colonial Williamsburg, the village that is a museum, lies in the desire of the Windham Foundation to make Grafton a vibrant working community. Today, the foundation employs around one hundred people in the various for-profit enterprises that it operates, including a sheep farm, a cheese factory, a nursery, and a ski center.

While donors may start with an issue or problem that they want to address or solve and then work to build a philanthropic response, Mathey's philanthropy started with a commitment to a village and a way of life. Grafton faced problems of economic viability and historic preservation, but these social problems were not what animated the giving. Instead, it was the idea that the village was a special place that moved the donor to seek to help. Using an operating foundation to restore and protect a picturesque village in the Vermont hills is certainly quite different from funding a program to assist the urban poor or preventing the spread of disease in a foreign land. It is a form of giving that starts with the experience and passion of the donor and then projects this feeling onto a broad public purpose, in this instance the preservation of rural Vermont's way of life and heritage.[21] Mathey's use of an operating foundation was interesting because it signaled a more hands-on, local approach to giving, one in which the funding of programs would not be left to outsiders, but instead be directed to enterprises controlled by the foundation and employing town residents. Given the need of the residents for stable employment and the desire of the donor to preserve the historic character of the town, it represented a well-aligned strategic choice, one that has served the town and the donor's vision well.

Although it is difficult to draw a clear line between instrumental giving, expressive giving, and giving that blends the two, what should be clear is that finding a synergistic point of contact between worldly effects and the personal beliefs of a donor can be understood as a continuum leading from less to more joint forms of value creation. Donors may not always want to produce joint value in their giving and may at times experiment with other forms of value creation. In the end, philanthropy needs to be understood as being about both the production of public benefits and the enactment of the donor's beliefs. While these may be accomplished separately from one another through serial acts of more or less instrumental and expressive forms of gifts, there is something powerful and compelling when both are part of a single philanthropic act. The power of strategic giving comes from the infusion of private visions of the public good into society, which can have significant and often unanticipated effects. Unfettered by the need to secure the support of others and capable of acting in ways that government cannot even contemplate, donors are in a position to bring eclecticism and innovation to the public sphere. How well and how responsibly donors grasp the opportunities available to them is a function of the quality of their strategic vision.

The capacity of philanthropy to bring these two elements together has been both challenged and renewed over time. As major donors have turned their philanthropic fortunes over to foundations and entrusted others to carry on their philanthropic legacy, the expressive content of philanthropy slowly but steadily dissipates from giving. Boards turn over and become less and less familiar with the donor, and staff diligently but ultimately seek to carry out their responsibilities, focusing often on honing the grantmaking procedures and ensuring that funds are used sensibly and for their intended purpose.[22] This gradual drift challenges the capacity of philanthropy to maintain the dual focus on private values and public purposes. But there are countervailing forces at work that are renewing the field. Every year, new donors enter the scene and begin to project their visions of the common good into the public sphere. Sometimes they stumble and find that producing social returns through philanthropy is far harder than generating financial returns in the business world.[23] Still, the field benefits from a constant flow of new donors who enter with fresh ideas and distinct assumptions. Whether the ossification that occurs in some parts of the institutional landscape of philanthropy is exactly offset by the infusion of new funds and ideas is impossible to know. What is certain, however, is that the field of philanthropy experiences regularly both the birth and death of expressive and instrumental forces. Somewhere in this complex process of transformation, all four main forms of value creation are pursued.

Decisions donors make about the remaining four elements of the philanthropic prism will substantially impact the ability of donors to find the elusive point of overlap between instrumental and expressive giving.[24] Settling on a good logic model, an appropriate vehicle, the right time frame, and a sensible giving style will all significantly affect the likelihood that the choice of value to be produced will turn out to be one that has strong strategic potential. Looked at from the other perspective, having a purpose that connects private passions to public purposes will not itself be sufficient to overcome the many roadblocks to donors seeking a greater level of alignment and fit in their strategy. It does, however, constitute a necessary piece of the puzzle.

6. Logic Models: Theories of Change, Leverage, and Scale

As donors turn their attention to the world and seek to create value, they inevitably confront the question of how best to achieve their intended objectives. At the heart of this question is the idea of philanthropic effectiveness. Most donors, even those animated by values and the desire to express their convictions, are committed to doing so in a way that produces results. In searching for ways to give money effectively, donors have many options and confront a wide range of theories about how to achieve impact. It is possible to think about these theories as falling into three main categories: theories of change, theories of leverage, and theories of scale. Of course there are strong connections linking these theories to one another, and choices made in one realm have consequences for choices made in others. All three pieces actually fit together into what is known as a logic model.

Elements of a Logic Model

A logic model (see figure 6.1) can be understood as a formal explication of how a philanthropic intervention proposes to achieve its ends. Logic models

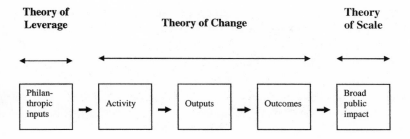

Figure 6.1 **Elements of a logic model.**

can take the form of the specification of causal linkages, which together articulate the steps that must be completed for an intervention to succeed. Sometimes, they take the form of path diagrams with arrows connecting boxes, leading to the ultimate desired outcome. To construct a logic model, donors need to be clear about their ultimate goal or objective. Without clarity about outcomes, it is almost impossible to construct a coherent logic model.[1] Donors also need to understand their starting point and the steps they will take along the way to their goals. One of the most common problems with logic models that are used in philanthropy is the mistaken belief that they include all the relevant determinants in a causal chain leading from intervention to social outcome. In reality, the vast majority of social interventions have built within them a substantial amount of noise outside the system that affects the outcome. This large residual factor may well dwarf the programmatic elements in the logic model in terms of its relative explanatory power. Still, all donors, like all researchers, need to proceed in the face of substantial uncertainty about what statisticians call the residual problem. While not crippling to donors seeking to construct logic models in their chosen fields, the residual problem should at least lead to some humility.

Clarifying a logic model usually starts with defining a theory of change that commits the donor to a set or class of giving targets. Theories of change can be very broad and define the level—ranging from the smallest societal units to the largest ones—at which the philanthropy will work. At one end of this spectrum are theories of change that focus on the training and development of individual leaders who might someday transform a field of practice. At the other end are theories that seek to bring change by shaping public policy at the national or even international level. This hierarchy of change theories merely spells out for donors a set of initial choices about how to direct their giving at a particular unit of society. Choosing the right theory of change depends on a host of considerations, including the field in which the donor is working and the nature of the outcome that the donor is seeking to produce.

Theories of leverage are different from theories of change in that they focus not so much on the grand idea of how impact is best created, but rather on the mechanics of the process. Leverage is something that allows donors to increase the effectiveness of their giving. It is a concept grounded in the physical principle, familiar to many, that a long lever may be more useful than a short one in dislodging or raising fixed objects. When a lever is placed under an object and a fulcrum is located, the lever allows one to exert greater force on the object one is seeking to move. The idea of giving grants and seeing—through the strategic construction of leverage— an impact greater than the amount of philanthropic funds expended has long been a powerful attraction to donors. Thus, many donors spend a fair amount of time experimenting with different philanthropic tools designed to create leverage or a greater impact. Not surprisingly, the need to achieve leverage increases as the social problem the donors are seeking to address grows in size. The need for leverage also increases as the amount of philanthropic funds at the donor's disposal decreases.

Beyond developing a theory of change and locating points of leverage, donors concerned with increasing the impact of their giving tend to focus on a third element: the theory of scale that will guide their philanthropic work. While some donors are content with making small, targeted gifts designed to meet episodic needs, many donors want to see their philanthropic work broadened. An intervention, when properly understood and documented, can be brought to scale through a variety of means so that the number of people who benefit increases. For many donors, achieving scale represents the final piece in the operational puzzle that starts with the development of a change theory and continues with the pursuit of greater levels of philanthropic leverage.

Theories of change, theories of leverage, and theories of scale can be understood as a set of interconnected concepts, all pointing toward the idea of increased programmatic effectiveness and impact. Theories of change are the heart of logic models and strategy development. Theories of leverage and scale are the supporting tactics at the front and back ends of the logic model that allow the donor to maximize impact. Donors able to sketch out some clear notion of any of these three elements will be in a better position to maximize the public benefits of their giving. While there is no guarantee that getting better at giving will increase a donor's personal satisfaction, there is a large body of experience in philanthropy that suggests that donors who manage to achieve their objectives are often motivated to give more than those who are thwarted. For this reason, getting better at the mechanics of giving is an important element in the philanthropic prism.

Theories of Change

To begin to sketch a framework for thinking about the theories of change that animate philanthropy, it may be helpful to focus on a single field to see how donors have variously constructed approaches to a complex philanthropic challenge. One can see embedded in some concrete philanthropic efforts in the field of K–12 public education a broad set of categories and distinctions that can help define a framework for the kinds of theories of change that are most often at play in philanthropy.

The first education reform to consider is the Broad Residency in Urban Education, which provides an entry point for young, talented leaders who are not currently working in public education to train and prepare for senior positions in urban school districts across America. Sensing that public schools lacked quality leaders with the skills needed to carry out broad reform, the Broad Foundation created the residency to develop an effective entry point for talented managers from outside the world of education who were interested in moving into this field. The underlying intent was to grow talent for the future and to transform education by inserting these new leaders into the establishment. The program consists of an intensive two-year management development program designed to get people from varied backgrounds ready for work in public education.

Taking a different tack, the New Schools Venture Fund focuses much of its attention on building strong, sustainable, and scalable organizations that will be potent battering rams for change in the world of public education.[2] NSVF provides management assistance to the organizations that receive grants and attempts to deliver extensive hands-on assistance where its experience indicates that new education ventures need it most urgently. In the area of governance, a NSVF representative occupies a board seat on all its grantee organizations and assists in further board development. When it comes to planning, NSVF provides guidance on the development of a strategic plan for the organization. If the need is present, NSVF helps with market analysis and guides its grantees in positioning their programs. One of the most significant ways it helps is related to fund-raising; NSVF actively introduces and connects its grantees to other sources of funds. Finally,

NSVF connects the organizations that receive its funding with qualified potential team members with expertise in both the business and education sectors. In all these ways, NSVF tries to do more than just write a check. It focuses much of its efforts on finding ways to strengthen the operational capacity of nonprofit organizations.

When the Annenberg Foundation sought to bring some change to the public school establishment, it focused a fair amount of resources over time on the Coalition of Essential Schools, a network of schools and centers that work together to "create schools where each child is known well and learns to use his or her mind well." A key part of the model is the creation and maintenance of a vibrant, collaborative community of educators, parents, students, and policy makers. Although no two schools in the network are precisely the same, affiliated schools do "share a common set of beliefs about the purpose and practice of schooling." By knitting schools together into a strong national community in which best practices can be shared and through which a strong movement toward change can be developed, the Annenberg Foundation waged a philanthropic bet that change required coordination, collaboration, and the forging of a movement. The Annenberg Foundation also used a network approach for its "Challenge," which delivered $500 million to fund school improvement, largely through large interorganizational collaborations in selected major cities around the country.[3]

In 2000, businessman Tim Draper decided to spend $20 million of his own money on a ballot initiative that would have given an educational voucher worth $4,000 to every child in California. Frustrated with obstruction by teachers unions and inaction in state government, Draper tried to use his private wealth to fund ads and a field operation aimed at winning a critical political fight. He spent heavily on ads and even took an active role in the campaign, but ultimately fell short in his efforts. Had he succeeded, he would have, with a single effort, sent a massive shock wave not only through California's entire public education system, but through the entire country's approach to funding and delivering education.

In Washington, D.C., the drive to reform has taken a different shape altogether. The Thomas B. Fordham Foundation focuses on driving change in American public education through the financing of research and policy analysis aimed at illuminating the performance of schools, the causes of their problems, and the development of new solutions. While the Fordham Foundation has been critical of public school teacher unions and of some of the trends toward more progressive school curricula, it has focused a lot of attention on the power of choice, both through charter schools and vouchers, to bring positive change to the American public school establishment. One of this foundation's most visible tools for getting its message out is a national magazine, *Education Next*, which has captured a large audience with its accessible yet rigorous articles on school reform. The editorial policy of the magazine is clear: "In the stormy seas of school reform, this journal will steer a steady course, presenting the facts as best they can be determined, giving voice (without fear or favor) to worthy research, sound ideas, and responsible arguments. Bold change is needed in American K–12 education, but *Education Next* partakes of no program, campaign, or ideology. It goes where the evidence points." By getting ideas out into the public debate, the magazine and the Fordham Foundation aim to move reform forward.

What differentiates these five philanthropic approaches to school reform? The answer lies in the underlying theory of change behind each. With some simplification, it is possible to define five broad varieties of change theories corresponding to the five examples. Each has its own logic and purpose, although all five tend to intermingle in practice. First, donors have experimented with an approach to philanthropy that focuses on training individuals for leadership in a field (Broad Foundation), with the assumption that change occurs one person at a time. Second, donors have looked at ways of building stronger organizations (New Schools Venture Fund), with the goal of creating greater and more sustainable capacity. Third, donors have established new networks (Annenberg Foundation) connecting organizations with common purposes. Fourth, donors have sought to influence politics (Tim Draper) and to shape the legislative agenda at the local, state, and national levels. Fifth, donors have generated new ideas and proposals for a field (Thomas B. Fordham Foundation) with the goal of shaping the underlying paradigm and conversation. If pursued simultaneously and implemented cleverly, these theories of change can reinforce one another and lead to interesting synergies. When choices among theories of change are needed because of resource constraints, donors must decide which of these approaches represents the most sensible starting point for action—given the field or problem within which the donor is working. It might be helpful to look at each of these five theories of change in greater detail.[4]

Individuals

One place to look for impact is at the individual level. Many funders concerned with maximizing effectiveness focus on training and developing individuals for leadership in fields in which change is needed. Focusing on building skills and creating opportunities for individuals is appealing because it promises to create an army of agents, ready both to change practice in the field and to lead efforts to change public policy. There are important issues of independence and control that arise when funders seek to change a field by training and developing new leaders. After all, the individuals taking part in such efforts need to be able to pursue an agenda that is their own, not one that is seen as advanced by the funder. Still, many donors have attempted to walk the fine line between neutral professional development programs and initiatives that advance a fixed agenda through the cultivation of leaders. When done well, leadership development, training, and professional education programs can help build the human capital in a field, cultivate new skills, and motivate the people to continue working toward the missions that matter to them.

Training and developing people in a given field requires a long-term perspective, especially when the field already has entrenched leadership or when the field is young and still evolving. Often such efforts take the form of summer institutes, seminars, executive programs, distance learning, fellowships, sabbaticals, and other efforts to identify and encourage talented people to take on greater responsibility for shaping a field. Beyond the work of the Broad Foundation in the area of public school reform, several funders have sought to generate change by establishing a large selection of training and management programs for teachers, principals, and superintendents, all designed to provide the tools to advance a reform agenda. By starting with individuals within a large and complex system, funders are making a conscious strategic choice, one that is built on the belief that change starts at the level of the individual and then percolates up through the organizational level. It is an approach that demands patience and a strong attraction to the ideas of working from the grassroots up.

A variation on the individual-level focus is the emphasis many funders place on supporting programs that require individuals to help themselves. From early scientific philanthropy's focus on self-help to contemporary community-based leadership training and empowerment programs, philanthropy has long aimed to create opportunities for self-advancement. The assumption behind this theory of change is simple. Programs that help people help themselves are more likely to have a lasting effect than those that offer only a short-term intervention. For this reason, many donors are attracted to nonprofit programs that build skills and confidence within individuals and that allow people to take part in economic and political life. Job training, career planning, and internship programs, particularly those aimed at young underserved populations, are an example of philanthropy's interest in giving individuals the tools they need to succeed, rather than just transfering payments.

The individual-level approach to change has also found its most visible—and in some ways controversial—manifestation in a whole series of award, fellowship, and grant programs designed to assist outstanding researchers, artists, journalists, practitioners, public servants, religious leaders, and other individuals do their work. The number and range of such awards and prizes is enormous and includes the Pulitzer Prize, Guggenheim Fellowships, MacArthur Fellowships, the Nobel Prize, the Balzan Award, and the Templeton Prize. In addition to these large and notable cash awards, a bevy of smaller prizes and fellowships are conferred each year to help individuals pursue new plans and visions.[5] These programs include, for example, the Ashoka and Echoing Green fellowships, which give young people the chance to create new nonprofit entities in countries around the world, a range of sabbatical programs aimed at helping experienced and potentially burned-out nonprofit managers, and many other programs designed to kindle or rekindle the fires of individuals across different professional fields. The Nieman Fellowships, which allow journalists to spend a year at Harvard taking classes and reflecting on large issues, are another example.

Underlying the individual-level theory of change is an interesting assumption, not always clearly articulated, on how society works and how it changes: an assumption that society is substantially influenced by individuals, even in the face of ever larger and more imposing social structures and institutions. There are both conceptual and practical consequences for those holding this view. It means that the units of change are small and require sustained attention over long periods of time. Working at the individual level demands that donors accept a fair amount of indeterminacy between their philanthropic intentions and the ultimate impact that is achieved. There is no guarantee that anyone who goes through a professional development or training program will use the imparted skills in a way that accords with the donor's ultimate desires. Individuals can be screened before selection, but there will necessarily be a fairly loose coupling between the intended and actual use of any skills taught in the program.

Organizations

Another way to bring change to a field is to create and support strong organizations. In the search for ways to build capacity within nonprofits, many foundations make an initial round of grants aimed at providing nonprofits with technical assistance, planning, and capacity-building advice—so as to position nonprofits to move ahead on a larger scale with their programs. Often this assistance takes the form of consulting on topics ranging from board development to marketing to capital construction. While some nonprofits bristle at any intrusion into their planning and operations, foundations often see capacity building as critical to positioning nonprofits to have broader influence and visibility. Working to support stronger organizations can be seen as a theory of change that prioritizes institution building as a critical ingredient in broader efforts to change a field.

Sometimes existing organizations cannot be reformed through technical assistance or consulting. A few large foundations have taken the drastic step of stepping outside the existing market of nonprofit service providers in order to set up independent organizations to carry out the foundation's agenda. The move to create new organizations represents a return to the idea embodied in operating foundations, namely that there are some missions that are most effectively and efficiently pursued through internal operations rather than through the external market of nonprofit providers. Most often, the decision to set up a new organization is related to an effort to coordinate a group of existing organizations working in a common area, or to carry out some function not currently being offered.

Donors often wrestle with the question of whether their giving should focus on building the existing capacity within organizations or whether it is wiser to seek opportunities to create new capacity, either in the form of new projects in existing organizations or through the formation of entirely new organizations. At one level, creating a new initiative or organization can be exhilarating. It offers the possibility of taking an idea from concept to reality, while shedding the baggage that almost all established organizations carry with them. Decisions about staffing have far more flexibility when the organization chart is a blank piece of paper. Without a dominant culture or a set of standard operating principles, new nonprofits are free either to scan the environment and focus on best practices or to consciously seek to do things differently. Starting without a history also potentially opens the door for the donor to place a large and enduring mark on the organization.

Still, there are important drawbacks to starting from scratch. The first is that the nonprofit sector is rife with duplication and excess capacity. In almost every American city, there are multiple nonprofits doing the same work; parallel projects often proceed for years in total ignorance of one another, even if the target population is quite small. Rather than start new programs or organizations, many experienced donors believe that existing nonprofits need to be consolidated or, at a minimum, encouraged to collaborate more fully with one another. Accordingly, donors need to assure themselves that the new organization or project is really needed and that existing efforts, if any, are simply unsalvageable or too costly to reform. The second drawback relates to operational efficiency: building something new will usually have higher start-up costs and may require more time.[6] Donors thus need to judge the cost and time delays that starting from scratch may bring against the benefits that come with such an approach.[7]

Networks

Facing limited resources and a long list of worthy causes, donors have sought to support collaborations and the creation of strong networks among organizations. These networks can support the sharing of best practices, the pooling of resources, and the mobilization of advocacy efforts. Funding the creation of systems of collaboration is appealing because it appears to resolve some of the most glaring shortcomings in the nonprofit sector, namely the duplication of effort and the inability to learn from others what works. Recently, the idea of building networks of capacity within all different fields of activity has gained even more currency because it appears to be a promising way to take small programs and local innovations to scale. By bringing people together and creating lasting networks of communication and collaboration, philanthropy is ultimately able to create the building blocks for broad movements and to overcome the isolation that many nonprofit organizations experience. Of course, networks of communication and collaboration can be transformed into policy and political movements when events create opportunities for action.

While the business world has experienced multiple waves of consolidations and mergers, very seldom do nonprofits merge, even when they have similar missions and operate in the same geographical area. This makes collaborations and communication even more important. The autonomous and disconnected character of large areas of nonprofit practice creates an opportunity for funders to have an impact. By locating groups with common values and goals, it may be possible to create a movement, or at least a coalition that did not previously exist. One example of this sort of philanthropy in action is the effort by the Kellogg Foundation to bring research centers focused on nonprofit management together to learn and exchange ideas. The "Building Bridges" initiative not only provided these centers with funds to carry on their work, but also required that participants in the effort meet periodically to exchange best practices. Other networks have been constructed in the philanthropy field itself through the establishment of special affinity groups, which unify funders with specific concerns such as education, health, arts, or environmental issues. When donors seek to build networks in the provider world, they sponsor conventions, symposia, and meetings in which emerging issues can be discussed by practitioners.

The construction of social networks can lead to the creation of social movements, although the link is anything but certain. Funders can encourage interaction and collaboration, but the interaction of individuals and organizations can take unpredictable directions. In this sense, it is easier to support a network than it is to construct a network with the expectation that it will be used or applied for a specific purpose or end. Nevertheless, when donors commit to building a network or fostering collaboration, they are betting that the power of many is greater than the power of one. This is often the case, but there are significant challenges to overcome in the building of these networks. The most obvious is the extra work—in the form of greater communication and coordination costs—that multiparty action demands. Unless there is a high level of consensus within the network, the construction of ties can be expensive. However, in the right context and with boundaries placed on the necessity of reaching consensus or taking joint action, network building can produce results that span boundaries between individuals and organizations.

Politics

Philanthropy has attempted to shape policy by entering the political arena and exerting pressure on the political process through at least three different approaches. First, donors support projects that stimulate civic engagement by exposing citizens to politics and mobilizing them to take action. Often civic engagement is translated into direct political action by organizing at the grassroots level around interests and causes, whether it's through registering voters and get-out-the-vote efforts, organizing communities, or any number of other activities to promote political engagement.

Second, donors often turn to nonprofits and ask them to play an important role in informing and educating the public and policy makers. Advocacy efforts take place at the local, state, national, and transnational levels, and often take the form of policy research and public information campaigns. Significant outlays of philanthropic funds have been made to support national advertising on reproductive rights, the dangers of tobacco, and other causes. One of the most visible efforts to engage the political process was undertaken by the Robert Wood Johnson Foundation, a private foundation created by the heir to the Johnson & Johnson health care products fortune. Sensing that the public lacked adequate information on the policy issues related to reforming health care in the United States, the foundation funded the controversial series of town hall meetings convened by Hillary Rodham Clinton during the period leading up to the announcement of her commission's recommendations. Afterwards, the Robert Wood Johnson Foundation bought two hours of prime time television on NBC for $2.5 million with the stipulation that the network would produce through its news division a program explaining the policy choices connected with reforming the American health care delivery system. In addition, the foundation bought $1 million in promotion and advertising time to ensure that the program would be viewed widely. While the foundation claimed that it was acting in a nonpartisan way and that the network would have complete editorial control over the program, it was soon attacked by conservatives for providing secret political support for the White House's health agenda.

Donors also support policy research that has the potential to shape public priorities.[8] During the 1980s, a group of conservative foundations, including the John M. Olin Foundation and the Lynde and Harry Bradley Foundation, provided an important part of the funding that fueled the creation and institutionalization of conservative public policy research institutes and think tanks.[9] Some of these organizations, like the Heritage Foundation, went on to have a profound political influence, especially during the early 1980s, at a time when government was searching for new policy ideas. These conservative foundations took a very high-risk approach to producing change and impact, one that could have failed given the difficulties of translating ideas into policies. The importance of their success is best seen in the efforts of the more progressive foundations to focus more on the war of ideas and the need for creative policy solutions, not just the creation of small model programs.[10]

Third, donors make grants to nonprofits that engage in direct lobbying around specific legislative issues. Different from advocacy in that it focuses on specific bills of legislation, support of nonprofit lobbying is a way to translate philanthropic dollars into direct political action. While there are legal constraints on foundations when it comes to lobbying, individuals and corporations face few limits. Working to shape the writing or to block the passage of a bill can be a potent and far-reaching intervention, particularly if the legislation appropriates or denies substantial amounts of public funding for causes of interest to the donor.

Ideas

Donors can engage with problems at even higher levels of abstraction. They can support the production of new ideas and paradigms that can reorient entire fields and lead to important breakthroughs in basic knowledge— breakthroughs that can lead to new ways of understanding problems and of seeing the world. If these new perspectives penetrate the field broadly, they can usher in changes that will have lasting effects not only on the further production of ideas, but on the way practitioners do their work. Being able to judge what constitutes promising research is a challenge, particularly because most funders are not deeply enmeshed in the disciplinary debates across fields. For this reason, many funders working to increase the flow of new ideas into a given domain ask the researchers within the domain to referee the applications and report to the foundation board and staff. With the right choice of author and topic, donors supporting the production of new concepts can generate significant change, whether by disrupting dominant assumptions or by catalyzing the reorganization of work to conform with a new understanding of the problem at hand.[11]

If funding the production of transformative ideas were easy to do, many funders would attempt to do it. Unfortunately, it is not easy to do well or with a high level of confidence that the results will either prove paradigm altering or even be easily translatable into new practices.[12] For this reason, donors often have a hard time letting go of their strong attachment to grassroots programs that deliver help directly to clients in a myriad of fields, ranging from drug counseling to emergency shelters to job training and beyond. These efforts have the advantage of producing measurable and visible outcomes. Thus, when a donor provides support for a program to assist battered women, it is possible to go out into the field, observe the services being delivered, and hear testimony from clients on how the services have helped them improve their lives. Many donors find this form of giving particularly satisfying because of its clarity and immediacy. The contrast with the funding of research and theory building is stark. Not only are there few outcomes that can be predicted and expected, but also there is no real guarantee that anything productive will result. If the funders of Jonas Salk, David Ho, or other leading researchers had examined the odds and gone with the option that had the highest likelihood of impact, it is probable that major breakthroughs in our understanding of diseases would have been missed. Similarly, had careful risk assessments been carried out by social scientists before funding important research and analysis of human problems, it is unlikely that we would have made much progress in understanding and being able to address such complex issues as sustainable development, school reform, and any number of other issues weighing heavily on the public agenda.

The support of basic research and breakthrough ideas often intersects with politics. Funding policy research can have a tremendous impact when successful, as ideas from nonprofits filter through the public realm into politics. By funding efforts aimed at shaping both public opinion and elite policy opinion, grantmakers can achieve substantial influence. Informing policy debates in fields ranging from health insurance to welfare policy can turn modest philanthropic investments into major interventions in public life. For this reason, many funders see "idea philanthropy" as a far more potent tool for effecting broad change than the incremental improvement of small segments of the service delivery system. Creating new and powerful ideas depends not only on being right, but also on finding ways to ensure that the ideas gain currency and infiltrate the political process.

Unresolved Issues

Donors have invested heavily on the back end of philanthropy, spending considerable amounts of money on evaluation and assessment of the impact and effectiveness of funded programs. Comparatively little time and money has been devoted to the front end, especially to thinking systematically and creatively about the full range of interventions available and the underlying causal claims that are embedded in giving.[13] If philanthropy does indeed operate across all five of the levels described here—individuals, organizations, networks, politics, and ideas—at least two major questions impose themselves and continue to hover above the field, visible to all but not readily answerable by anyone. The first relates to the interaction of these levels. The second concerns the relative effectiveness of each level. Neither question has been answered, nor even been posed very clearly. Yet donors continue to struggle with the whole question of how to chart a change theory because the field has still not clearly defined its underlying assumptions and demonstrated the robustness of its causal claims.

At first glance, the five levels at which change is pursued in philanthropy appear to be neatly nestled, starting at the micro level of individual, moving up to the meso level of organizations and networks, and finally culminating in the macro level of politics and ideas. But the interactions among these levels need not be and likely are not linear and aggregating. In fact, many funders operate simultaneously at two or three levels and attempt to capture synergies across levels, regardless of whether the intervening levels are fully fleshed out and supported. Foundations with multiple programs will typically identify for each field of activity a basic set of claims about the causal linkages they believe lead to the goals and outcomes they have defined. Within and across program areas, many if not all five levels of change will be pursued over time. The difficulty lies in specifying how these disparate attempts at driving change within and across fields add up to the kind of broad impact that donors usually aspire to achieve. This is a version of the old problem in social science of establishing the "micro-macro link,"[14] with many of the complexities increased because the problem is no longer a theoretical one, but a real-world challenge of practice.

Still, foundations, and the broader field of philanthropy, do not have a clear and compelling way of understanding the change produced by giving at each of these five levels. More important, the field still lacks a well-defined theory of how change at multiple levels builds toward significant effects and whether impact and causal inferences established at one level contribute to and build greater rigor and impact at other levels. This means that while a donor may believe, for example, that a training and professional development program for ministers in the inner city will help build the local leadership needed to move neighborhoods forward, they rarely have a clear sense of how leadership development will connect to the kind of capacity building that is needed in order to have strong nonprofit organizations that can bring broad change. Moreover, in this example, even if the donor were supporting a few organizations that work alongside the churches, the donor may not have thought through how networks of collaboration can be built and maintained to increase the impact of the work. This shortcoming works its way through all levels. Donors simply do not understand the ways in which levels of change interact and intermingle with one another, sometimes creating powerful synergies and at other times leading to unconnected and unsustainable interventions.

Understanding the basic interaction patterns among change theories is critical to philanthropy because these inter-level forces can be either productive or destructive. A well-conceived set of philanthropic activities operating across the spectrum of intervention levels can produce powerful connections, as new leaders connect to stronger organizations, which are in turn woven into tight networks of capacity, while policies are shaped by the development of new ideas. The interactions need not proceed up the levels in a linear fashion. New leaders can be policy shapers, and big ideas can transform practice within organizations. The critical challenge for donors is to chart and understand these interactions, even if they prove hard to predict, so that learning and growth are possible over time and with experience.

Beyond the uncertainty about the interaction of these levels, there are deep and unresolved issues relating to the relative effectiveness of these approaches to driving change. While the largest foundations have hundred of millions of dollars in grant funds available each year, many smaller donors, particularly those working outside foundations, have relatively modest resources. For these donors, knowing under what circumstance and for what reason each of the five levels is likely to lead to the desired result is critical to making the most of limited resources. Being able to bet correctly on advocacy work in one context, training programs in another, and network building in yet another would allow smaller donors to apply their philanthropic resources efficiently and effectively. Unfortunately, information about the relative effectiveness of the five levels of change is hard to locate because few donors think in terms other than the tired dichotomy between direct service and advocacy. Moreover, it is not clear that universal rules and dicta are even possible to develop in this area or, if they are possible, what kind of data would be needed to create some dependable knowledge.

Although there is little consensus about which approach is most likely to yield results in a range of different substantive fields, there probably is a fair degree of agreement that risk and return are related in philanthropy. It is hardly surprising that both risk and reward increase as one moves from small units of change (individuals) to much larger units (ideas).[15] Beyond this bromide, the field of philanthropy lacks much basis for adjudicating between competing effectiveness claims related to change theories. Even if effectiveness could be gauged, it would be hard to establish the inherent superiority of any single change theory across contexts. As a result of this knowledge gap, individual donors and professional staff typically end up falling back on what they know and what they are most comfortable with. It is far easier to fund what one understands, and given the demands and pressures placed on those who give, it is often more difficult to learn enough about new modes of driving change than simply to operate within the comfort zone that experience provides. Funding political work is easier than funding basic research if one has years of experience in the world of public policy. Human nature simply guides donors to what they know and often makes it hard to break new ground.

The search for the most effective change theory is also truncated by the political commitments that donors bring to their giving. Some donors simply believe, or want to believe, that change is ultimately achieved from the bottom up. This means starting with the training of leaders, moving on to building stronger organizations, connecting these organizations into strong networks and collaborations, mobilizing these actors to lobby the political system, and finally producing new ideas and policies. This is generally a progressive vision of change that seeks to empower individuals to frame and solve problems. Other donors have taken the opposite approach and sought to bring change from the top down. This means starting with the production of new ideas on the national scene, attempting to introduce these ideas into politics, building networks of dissemination, assisting organizations with the implementation of new programs, and then training individual leaders to bring change at the local level. This approach demands a higher level of confidence and even philanthropic hubris, because the core problem to be addressed does not emerge incrementally through the initiative of committed local leaders, but rather it starts with the donor pursuing an intellectual or political agenda and then driving this down through the system.

Theories of change do not operate in a vacuum. Other social, economic, and political forces contribute to shaping the ultimate outcome of an intervention. Still, many donors find it useful to be clear about the underlying theory of change that they are employing if for no other reason than to deal with the number and scope of antecedent and intervening forces shaping the social outcomes that giving may attempt to produce. All too often donors believe that they must completely diagnose the underlying issue or problem before embarking on grantmaking. Often this entails commissioning consultants or having foundation staff draft elaborate white papers describing the underlying logic of a given philanthropic agenda. Theories of change are best tested and refined over time through practice, however. To get better over time at constructing and applying theories of change, donors must be willing to watch closely how their philanthropy evolves across a wide variety of fields and contexts. The donor can use this information to gain a deeper and more comprehensive understanding of how to produce desired outcomes. In this regard, although the idea of building a theory of change may seem abstract and removed from practice, just the opposite is true. A theory of change should shape the activities of the donor, not hover above it. A good theory of change is developed over time through the interaction of the donor's planning and philanthropy experience.

Theories of Leverage

Donors have long relied on many tactics to create change. All these tactics—in one way or another—aim at creating leverage. By leverage, donors usually mean a way of maximizing the impact of their contributions, ideally by creating significant activity or change with the modest use of grant dollars. To do so requires turning grants from closed-ended commitments into catalysts for greater productive work. Finding ways to achieve such results is important in philanthropy because the amount of money available to most funders is limited, especially when compared to the scope of human problems awaiting attention. Within the context of the needs and resources available, the idea of philanthropic leverage has understandably only gained greater appeal over the years. Even though huge amounts of money are at stake, philanthropy's tool box—its ideas about how to generate leverage—is surprisingly full of old, rusty, and blunt implements. What follows is a brief taxonomy of the most prominent tactics for producing philanthropic leverage that have emerged over time. These tactics are divided into two main categories: those that depend on the development of new grantmaking techniques and those that involve the construction of special kinds of interventions and programs.

Grantmaking Tactics

In seeking to build leverage, foundations employ tactics that are centered on the nature and character of the grant itself. By adjusting the procedures and conditions connected to their grantmaking, many foundations believe they can achieve substantially greater impact and leverage. I focus here on ten prominent grantmaking tactics that have at various times held out great promise for improving the ability of foundations to achieve change and impact: project grants; short-term grants; matching grants; loans and program-related investments; large grants; grants driven by requests for proposals (RFPs); high-engagement grantmaking; overseas funding; joint funding; and technical assistance, planning, and capacity-building grants. Each of these tactics focuses on the grantmaking process, not the kind of program that is being supported.[16]

Project Grants, Not General Operating Support | Leverage may be gained by increasing the control and oversight that donors are able to exert over donees. One way control is established is through the narrow circumscribing of purposes for which grants can be used. Many donors seek to target their giving to specific programs or projects within organizations, believing that these constraints make accountability, reporting, and assessment easier. By focusing grants on projects, donors are able to pick and support specific activities within an organization's portfolio of programs. Because of the greater accountability that is possible when the terms and purposes of a grant are focused on specific activities, donors generally believe that project giving is particularly effective. For nonprofits, the rise of project grants has been a mixed blessing. It has allowed proposals to be narrowly targeted and encouraged detailed planning. However, it has made the securing of unrestricted general operating support increasingly difficult. As more and more funders have sought leverage through project giving, some nonprofits have complained about the difficulty of sustaining core activities.[17]

Short-Term Grants | "Get in and get out" is the motto of many large institutional funders. Long-term financial commitments have become less and less popular as donors have developed a theory of leverage related to the length of philanthropic support. By not getting involved with recipients for more than three to five years, many institutional donors attempt to "seed" activities, then move on to other efforts. Short-term support allows the funder to direct money to a larger number of organizations and thus increase the overall reach of its grantmaking. The assumption behind this approach is that shorter commitments counter the tendency of nonprofits to grow dependent on a single funder. By limiting giving to a few years, donors communicate to nonprofits that they need to plan on achieving a diversified and flexible system for generating revenues. Again, this theory of leverage has posed problems for nonprofits in that seed funding terminates before replacement funds are located.

Matching Grants | One of the most obvious ways to create leverage is to make a grant contingent on an organization's ability to raise additional funds. Matching grants can take many forms. They can require a one-to-one match, a three-to-one match, or any other ratio desired by the funder. Often, matching grants are a critical part of large annual fund drives at major cultural institutions. Solicitations are made to individual contributors with the assurance that every dollar contributed will be matched and made to go further. For some donors, the existence of a matching program makes donating funds more appealing. Matching grant programs are premised on the idea that philanthropy can catalyze further giving by offering an incentive that increases the impact of additional fund-raising.

On the surface, these contingent grants look like carrots dangled in front of nonprofits that cannot help but motivate. There are at least two main problems with this approach to leverage building, however. First, matching grants often reinforce behavior that would have occurred even without the introduction of the funds. That is, it can be very hard to establish that the presence of a matching grant actually led to greater levels of giving by others or that others were attracted to giving because of a match. Ironically, if a challenge is met by a nonprofit, this may be evidence that an organization already possesses the breadth of support and fund-raising capacity needed to mobilize significant amounts of funds and that a matching grant simply added to sources that would have been received with or without the presence of the offer. Second, while they are intended to stimulate the mobilization of resources, matching grants can actually impose significant costs and burdens on nonprofits. Soon after the receipt of a matching gift, nonprofits must scramble for contributors willing to make gifts that will be eligible for the match, which can lead to new fund-raising expenses, create a sense of false urgency, and distract the organization from its regular pattern of activity and long-term agenda.

Loans and Program-Related Investments, Not Grants | Why give away money once and forever, when it can be loaned and recirculated over and over again? The starting premise of loans, be they for capital building or program expansion, is that leverage can be achieved by using philanthropic funds in a way that maintains grantmaking resources and allows for a much greater range of assistance over the long run. Loan funds also build accountability and create a sense of responsibility that grants cannot duplicate. Program-related investments (PRIs) go one step further and attempt to achieve synergies between the investment needs of large institutional donors and their grantmaking objectives.[18] By drawing on investment assets, PRIs achieve leverage by bringing endowment assets into the service of social objectives.

Large Grants | Suspicious of the impact of small grants spread widely across a large number of recipients, many foundations have sought leverage by making fewer but larger grants. The goal of such a strategy is to move away from disjointed and dissipated gift giving toward an approach that puts significant resources behind selected initiatives. The larger the grant, the larger the stakes become. For donors wanting to achieve leverage, concentrating giving on a few large initiatives has at times been difficult, given expectations among recipients and the difficulty of rejecting many requests in order to accept a few. After all, making a small consolation grant has long been a way of avoiding tough choices and alienating community groups. Beyond the politics of saying no many times in order to say yes a few times, an important question that this theory of leverage raises is whether recipient organizations have the capacity to absorb large commitments of funds all at once, or whether large grants need to be built up over time in order not to overwhelm the capacity of smaller recipient organizations.

Grants Driven by Proactive RFPs | Many funders refuse to sit quietly in their office for the mail to arrive each day with ever more requests for grants. While there is never a shortage of demands on donors, often the proposals that arrive over the transom disappoint, either in terms of subject matter or sheer coherence. As a result, donors have begun taking a more proactive stance in soliciting grant proposals. This sometimes involves contacting specific nonprofit organizations and encouraging the submission of the proposals, particularly if the donor has had a positive grantmaking relationship with the organization in the past. Other times, proactive donors simply open the door more widely through the creation of a request for proposals (RFP) that is advertised and open to any organization willing to deliver a proposal meeting the guidelines.[19] RFPs spell out in great detail what the donor wants to accomplish and how the program should be carried out. There is at least one controversial aspect to the leverage achieved through RFPs and other proactive approaches: it appears to assume that the donor knows more about how to solve a given social problem than the service delivery community in the field. Given the pressure to be responsive, listen to needs, and fund from the bottom up, RFPs and other proactive top-down approaches can ruffle some feathers.

Some large donors have taken the proactive approach to a different level and sought to stimulate competition among a small number of very large potential recipients. Larry Ellison, the founder of Oracle and one of the richest men in the world, announced that he would make a $150 million gift to fund an institute focusing on the connection between technology, society, and politics. Rather than go directly to one institution or send out an open-ended request for proposals, Ellison approached Stanford University and Harvard University and played the two institutions off each other, making them vie for the funds. The idea is that competing for funds may be helpful if it forces institutions to present their very best proposals and ideas, knowing that someone else will receive the funds if they fall short. Other big donors to higher education have taken a similar tack, seeking out a limited set of institutions for a specific project. Donor Patrick J. McGovern, Jr., the founder of International Data Group, gave the Massachusetts Institute of Technology $350 million for an institute to study the brain, after giving six other potential host institutions the chance to make their case.

The introduction of competition into philanthropy need not be restricted to large donors focusing on research. Many smaller donors can also use competitive processes for their giving, although this approach can become problematic if the amount of funds is too small or if the competition is too broad. Some nonprofits simply are not willing to expend the considerable effort that preparing a special proposal entails without some sense that it has a decent likelihood of securing the funds. One way to deal with the transaction costs associated with bidding for philanthropic dollars is to provide nonprofits with planning grants that enable them to assemble full-fledged proposals and plans. The funder can use these small grants to overcome some of the reticence that smaller nonprofits often feel about dedicating substantial staff resources to responding to requests for proposals.

High-Engagement Grantmaking | Philanthropy has traditionally been driven by detailed paperwork and a certain hands-off etiquette. Grantmaking starts with the submission of elaborate proposals by nonprofits, which are read and reviewed by donors. Site visits and meetings may occur during the grantmaking process, especially if additional information is needed to arrive at a fair decision. Once the decision is reached and a check is mailed to the recipient, donors and donees rarely speak again for a year or until the period of the grant is over and a report is due. Sensing that this low level of engagement may not be optimal, some individual donors and foundations have begun to experiment with higher-engagement grantmaking. Based on a theory of leverage that holds that donors have something more than money to contribute to nonprofits, donors have been trying to reshape donor-donee relations in order to construct active, consultative relationships that start before proposal review, that build during program implementation, and that continue after the grant cycle is over. High-engagement grantmaking requires that the donor have skills (managerial, legal, accounting, or other) useful to nonprofits and that recipients are open to receiving this nonmonetary input. Not all relationships can or should aim toward a high-engagement model, especially if the amount of funds involved is relatively modest. However, in cases where the financial commitment is high and the skills are needed, this model of engagement can be an appealing alternative.

One of the most misunderstood aspects of the high-engagement approach to leverage is that it often masks a donor's honest interest in making a personal connection to the causes that the donor supports. In this sense, the collaboration, consulting, and coaching that often goes on between donor and recipient on programmatic matters may involve increasing impact and producing leverage, when in reality, donors are simply engaging in an activity that increases the quality and meaningfulness of their philanthropic experience, while also hopefully contributing something to the success of the initiative or project at hand. Thus, even if confused by personal needs, donors can and do contribute more than money to nonprofit organizations. The problem arises when the motives of the donor are neither about increasing the effectiveness nor even about satisfying psychic needs for a deeper connection. In some cases, high engagement is actually a product of a lack of trust between giver and recipient. In such cases, assistance begins to blend into oversight and consultation turns into micromanagement. Donor engagement has some hidden pitfalls and dangers that must be attended to before it can be embraced enthusiastically.

Overseas Funding | Geography can be a major factor in determining how much leverage is possible, particularly for American donors. A grant of $3,000 in New York might allow an education group to pay rent for a few weeks or cover the cost of one foundation executive's salary and benefits for a week. However, the same $3,000 when donated in India or Peru can make a huge difference in terms of the way people live and the assistance it can make possible. Thus, one way to achieve leverage in philanthropy is to choose a location that allows a maximum amount of buying power. While it would be wrong to let buying power alone determine the area in which one chooses to give, geography does become a more and more significant factor, particularly for small donors. It is a factor that needs to be weighed along with all the others to ensure that philanthropic resources are being used productively.[20]

Joint Funding | Facing limited resources and a long list of worthy causes, foundations have long sought out philanthropic collaborations. These partnerships pool resources from several donors and direct them at a common cause or project. Collaboration occurs both nationally and locally.[21] Some large foundations work together on issues of policy, while local funders often collaborate on local or regional problems. Although collaborative funding can be a useful tool for increasing the amount of support available to a cause, some issues of control and independence can arise.[22] Often funders that take part in such collaborative efforts are asked to contribute an amount that is commensurate with their resources. This arrangement often works well as long as the large funders have significant control over the direction of the effort. However, when smaller donors either initiate or attempt to direct these philanthropic collaborations, questions may arise as to why larger funders should hand responsibility and decision making over to parties with less at stake. Thus, while the idea of pooling philanthropic resources is very appealing, especially for funders with limited resources, philanthropic collaboration can create some tensions. It assumes alignment of interests that is not always present.[23]

Technical Assistance, Planning, and Capacity-Building Grants | Few nonprofits will ever admit that they are not "ready" to receive philanthropic resources or that there is a limit to their ability to grow. However, many funders have long believed that project grants alone do not lead nonprofits to plan and develop strategy and capacity.[24] Therefore, before making large commitments, funders sometimes make an initial round of grants aimed at providing nonprofits with technical assistance, planning, and capacity-building advice—so as to position nonprofits to apply later for larger grants, or simply to move ahead on a larger scale with their programs.[25] Often this assistance takes the form of consulting on topics ranging from board development to marketing to capital construction. While some nonprofits bristle at any intrusion into their planning and operations, funders often take an important step in making sure that this approach to leverage does not end up causing nonprofits undue concern. Grants for technical assistance, planning, and capacity building usually leave the selection of the consultant or personnel to carry out the work in the hands of the nonprofit organization. When this simple step is taken to protect the autonomy of nonprofits, these grants have a higher likelihood of being received positively.

Programmatic Tactics

A second set of leverage tactics is connected to the kind of program that is funded. These tactics aim to increase the effectiveness of grants by restricting the use of philanthropic inputs to a special class of activities. This approach to leverage begins to bleed into the theory of change in that it seeks greater impact by conditioning donations on certain kinds of activities that are thought to be high leverage. I identify here seven main tactics that have either received substantial public attention lately or that have already channeled substantial philanthropic resources: support directed at geographical communities, not program areas; funding for new initiatives and pilot programs; support for collaborations, not isolated work; private funding for public programs; support of commercial ventures within nonprofits; funding for organizations designed and set up by grantmakers; and funding for independent evaluations. All of these tactics focus on the kind of activity that is funded, rather than on the nature and terms of the grant itself.

Communities, Not Program Areas | Most foundations today organize their grantmaking around program areas such as social services, health, education, the arts, and environment, or narrower fields such as community development, early childhood development, and youth violence prevention. While foundations may focus on the needs of a city or state, most grantmakers think about their programs in terms of subject matter. Program staff are hired to work in substantive areas and are expected to become experts in their fields. A new theory of leverage has emerged recently to challenge this basic way of organizing philanthropic work. A few foundations have recently jettisoned traditional program areas in favor of a broad, cross-functional focus on specific geographical communities. The logic behind this move is simple enough. Problems are not categorical but rather adhere to communities in ways that make their resolution dependent on addressing a full range of interrelated issues within communities. By focusing on specific counties, towns, and city neighborhoods, funders believe that they can get leverage by focusing activity in confined areas. The move to geographical areas is intended to conceptualize social problems in a more realistic and holistic way. Rather than reify problems by categorizing them through traditional programmatic labels, this new way of thinking about grantmaking activities aims to achieve leverage through the coordination and concentration of effort.[26]

New Initiatives and Pilot Programs | To increase their impact, some foundations believe that nonprofits need to be coaxed into experimenting, innovating, and expanding. To encourage organizations along these lines, funders often seek out proposals for activities that represent a new activity or a strategic expansion of services, rather than a long existing activity. This theory of leverage is particularly popular in the foundation world, in which newness is a critical ingredient to any successful proposal. Foundations want to employ their funds in ways that encourage change, and one way to do so is to favor grant requests for activities that are not currently ongoing. Of course, for nonprofits, the emphasis on novelty, innovation, and expansion can be problematic, especially when maintaining existing activities can, in itself, be a challenging proposition. This theory of leverage has led to a set of clever counter moves within the nonprofit community, moves designed to repackage existing activities in ways to make them appear novel. To the extent that such strategic gaming is going on, the effectiveness of funding new initiatives is diminished because it saps considerable energy from nonprofits and makes the donor-donee relationship more dysfunctional.

Philanthropic leverage has also come to be associated with the funding of pilot programs, which are intended as models that government and other private funders can replicate and take to scale. The lure of pilot or demonstration programs is that they do not start and end with specific funded activities, but instead hold forth the promise of having lives of their own. By attaching the term "pilot" to an initiative, funders can, without much cost, express a desire to see their efforts evaluated, recognized, and expanded if they turn out to be successful. The main drawback with this theory of leverage is that all too often it is just that, a theory. Few projects ever get replicated and the moniker "pilot project" has come to be attached to just about any new project. Nonprofit organizations have also wised up to the name game. Many proposals are described as pilots in order to excite funders and play into their desire for leverage. The gap between the rhetoric and the reality of pilot and demonstration programs is best seen in the huge number of pilot efforts that are routinely announced, and the paucity of replication efforts that funders have embraced.

Support for Nonprofit Collaborations, Not Isolated Work | One of the earliest principles of Victorian charity was to make all necessary services available to the poor in one place. This place was often a settlement house in which poor immigrant families could turn for assistance with their problems, be they educational, financial, or social. Over time, as many parts of the nonprofit sector have become increasingly dominated by professionals, boundaries between service delivery fields have emerged, making integrated programs harder to find. Some foundations in recent years have seen a possibility for leverage through a return to these earliest philanthropic ideas about one-stop shopping for services—albeit now presented in the more fashionable language of collaboration and program integration. The fostering of collaboration among nonprofit organizations is appealing because the specialization of nonprofit services has made navigating the system increasingly difficult for many clients. To encourage collaboration, some foundations give preference to grant requests that include plans for cross agency coordination. Leverage is achieved by reducing the redundancy and isolation of providers, and thereby improving the effectiveness of the entire service delivery system.

Collaboration can occur either horizontally or vertically. Horizontal collaboration demands that organizations with similar missions work together in a coordinated way. In the field of homeless services, this may require that shelters share data and resources when needed. The desire to see similar organizations work together more closely poses some challenges when the two agencies see themselves as competing either for donor support or public contracts. To overcome this issue, funders can structure collaborations that bring together agencies with substantially different missions but a common client base. This means fostering vertical collaboration and integration of services, finding connections among programs that complement one another.

Private Funding for Public Programs | Not content with funding nonprofit organizations, a few foundations have begun to make grants directly to state and local government agencies. On the surface, such a tactic would appear to be leverage-free given the ability of government to raise revenues through taxation. However, times have changed. Many state and local governments are strapped for cash and can do little discretionary spending. Enter foundations offering grants with the stipulation that government carry on the program (birth control clinics in schools, for example) after the grant period is concluded. Significant leverage is achieved by locking government into funding an activity that private funders underwrite for a short period of time. There are significant questions about democratic accountability related to these tactics, because they do appear to compromise local decision making. However, aggressive funders do not shy away from putting such conditions on grants to government, seeing an opportunity to press an agenda in the long run by funding it in the short run.

Funding of Commercial Ventures within Nonprofits | One of the most important changes in the nonprofit sector in recent decades has been the rise of earned income as a source of agency finance. Unlike contributed income, revenues from fees and ventures have no strings attached, and thus are attractive to many organizations. At the same time, funders have become aware of the entrepreneurial skills present in some nonprofits and have responded with an approach to building leverage that targets the commercial impulse of nonprofits. A growing number of donors now make grants to help nonprofits start or expand commercial ventures. While these activities are often substantially related to the mission of the nonprofit, at times they are unrelated. By supporting a nonprofit's ability to generate a stream of commercial income, funders see significant leverage. Philanthropic funds are not only converted into one-time programmatic activities, but are also used to build income-producing capacity that will continue long after the grant funds are gone. For nonprofits, an emphasis on commercial revenues is both potentially liberating and distracting. Running successful ventures demands staff time and resources. Still, the availability of philanthropic funds to build capacity to move away from a dependence on contributed income is a potentially empowering proposition.[27]

Funding for Organizations Designed and Set Up by Grantmakers | The continuous search for leverage has led a few large foundations to take the drastic step of stepping outside the existing market of nonprofit service providers in order to set up independent nonprofits to carry out the foundation's interest and agenda. This move represents a return to the idea embodied in operating foundations, namely that there are some missions that are most effectively and efficiently pursued through internal operations, rather than through the external market of nonprofit providers. Most often, the decision to set up a new organization is related to an effort to shape public policy, coordinate a group of existing organizations working in a common area, or carry out some other function not directly related to service provision. Few foundations set up new organizations explicitly to compete with existing nonprofits. Instead, the leverage often comes from creating an umbrella organization that meets a need not currently met by other nonprofits. Sometimes the organizations that are started have a limited life, while at other times they evolve into enduring entities.

Funding for Independent Evaluations | By monitoring closely the work of a recipient, it may be possible for foundations to achieve significant leverage. A grant gives the funder access to the recipient organization that can be used to diagnose performance and make recommendations. Systematic evaluation is often anchored in a theory of leverage, one that sees grantmaking as a first step toward building knowledge and expertise.[28] Of course, one of the problems with using evaluation and access to achieve leverage is that not all nonprofits are eager to have funders or evaluators poking around their programs. Moreover, while it might seem obvious that evaluation data can help foundations make better future decisions and use funds more effectively, it is not clear how often this occurs in practice, given the often anecdotal and nongeneralizable quality of evaluation reports. Large amounts of evaluation data are collected, much of it of mixed quality, while little of it is actually used creatively to improve practice. Even if practice lags behind theory, supporting quality evaluation work can produce insights and spread models to large numbers of public and private funders.

It is unclear whether any of these strategies, tactics, schemes, and dreams improve the effectiveness of giving and increase its social impact substantially. What is clear, however, is that the greatest opportunity for philanthropic impact has been neglected for far too long. This opportunity lies in new basic research on ways of generating change and achieving leverage. All of which comes back to answering the not so simple question posed at the outset: "How do donors have impact?" This is definitely worth *trying* to answer. The fact that the history of philanthropy has been filled with so many attempts at reform and renewal is both encouraging and depressing. On the one hand, while it is unlikely that any one of the theories of leverage described here has or will in itself transform philanthropy, it is encouraging that past donors have struggled to improve their giving. On the other hand, given the huge amount of resources controlled by institutional and individual donors, these theories of change are surprisingly primitive and tired. Given the tremendous freedom that individual and institutional donors enjoy, there is really no reason why philanthropy has not done more in recent years to advance the core premises of the field beyond the ideas that have been circulating within the public and business sectors for a long time.

Where should donors begin their search for leverage? A modest start would be to sharpen the existing tools of the philanthropic trade. To date, many of the theories of leverage outlined here have been pursued in isolation. The field of philanthropy might benefit if some thought were first directed at finding mutually reinforcing approaches to leverage that could be pursued in combination. For now, donors are faced with a menu of isolated ideas for how to improve the effectiveness of their giving, backed often only by anecdotal evidence of effectiveness. Refining existing models of giving can only be a first step, however. Perhaps the greatest opportunity for any single donor lies not in the achievement of narrow programmatic successes through clever application of existing philanthropic techniques, but in the development of new, sharper, and hitherto untried tools that can be added to philanthropy's toolbox. Building new theories of leverage would be the equivalent of performing new basic research for the field of philanthropy and, if successful, could create more leverage than any other kind of philanthropy. With the projected growth of philanthropy over the coming fifty years, the stakes in philanthropy will only rise and make improving its underlying ideas more pressing.

Who will develop these new tools and do the conceptual heavy lifting needed? One possibility is the generation of donors that is just now beginning to make its presence known. The new philanthropists, baby boomers approaching retirement, appear interested in finding their own direction for giving. Not committed to existing vehicles like private foundations and community foundations, they are pushing out in new directions and using new vehicles for their giving, including charitable gift funds such as the popular one now offered by Fidelity Investments. Unwilling to simply hand the reins over to grantmaking staff and consultants, the new donors are taking greater responsibility for their giving, sometimes even expressing a preference to doing all their giving while alive. To date, however, we have just begun to identify these new donors and observe some of their initial gifts. Entrepreneurs and nonconformist baby boomers have pushed philanthropy toward new fields of activity and substantive agendas. For the moment, it is too early to tell whether the next generation of major donors will succeed in the broader and more challenging task of changing the theory and practice of philanthropy. This will mean not only supporting new causes but rethinking the assumptions of philanthropy and developing new models for achieving leverage. Given the aggressive and creative entrepreneurship that generated the new philanthropic wealth, it is unlikely that these individuals will sit idly by and accept business as usual in their philanthropy.

One nagging problem that may hold back the search for new and effective philanthropic tools is the issue of measurement and two very different understandings of the meaning of leverage. Financial leverage mobilizes resources above and beyond what was committed by the donor. Social leverage creates public benefits above and beyond the size of the gift. The main problem is that donors talk about social leverage, but are usually able only to track and measure financial leverage. This would not be an insurmountable problem if financial leverage were a good proxy for social impact, but often it is not. Creating financial leverage simply means that more resources have been mobilized. It does not mean that the resources are used wisely. Thus in working to improve the tools available to donors interested in the idea of creating leverage, one central task must be to clarify the boundaries and meaning of financial and social leverage and to become clearer about which is being created and what this means. If successful in the search for and clarification of the meaning of leverage, the next generation of major donors will move the field of philanthropy forward and generate change in a broad and profound way.

Theories of Scale

Assuming that donors are able to create coherent and compelling theories of change and leverage to guide their giving, they are still left with the difficult task of building on proven successes so as to reach as many people as possible. Being effective means more than just carrying out an initiative well and meeting the needs of a small group of people. Effectiveness also involves reaching many people and taking the social leverage that an intervention creates and amplifying it even more broadly. Given the interest in having a real impact, donors speak variously of taking program to scale, going to scale, and scaling up. The idea of scale focuses on creating a lasting and significant impact. Beyond the broad idea of greater impact, the idea of scale becomes more enigmatic when it is subject to sustained scrutiny.[29] Scale has at least five overlapping meanings in philanthropy, which are often collapsed in practice: (1) financial strength; (2) program expansion; (3) comprehensiveness; (4) multisite replication; (5) accepted doctrine. The first two meanings connect to the organization-based theory of change. The third and fourth meanings operationalize the network-based theory of change. And the fifth meaning of scale is built on the theories of change that privilege ideas and politics.

Scale as Financial Strength

The first meaning of scale is related to organizational strength and sustainability.[30] Large institutions such as museums and universities have achieved scale because they have visible institutional profiles and reputations for excellence across the nation, occupy large buildings or campuses, and possess the financial wherewithal to persist indefinitely.[31] Scale on this account is equivalent to financial strength and sustainability, often secured by endowment or by large operating budgets with dependable revenue streams. In a sector in which financial crises are commonplace, scale is the ability to withstand the test of time by being big enough to ride out the storms. The number of nonprofits that have gone to scale under this definition remains small; many are concentrated in a few categories of nonprofit activity.

In principle, there are very few obstacles to taking any single organization to scale. Though philanthropic resources are limited, funds are now available to create a new cadre of a small number of very large and durable institutions. In practice, many of the organizations that have achieved financial scale have been and continue to be supported by individuals or family foundations with living donors. Many recipients of this sustained largesse, such as private colleges and cultural institutions, are the beneficiaries of support from elites and provide benefits to them in return. Interestingly, in the case of private educational and cultural institutions, it is often the visibility, prestige, and competition with other donors that encourages supporters to give, and give more, year after year.

Large private foundations do not seem to embrace this notion of scale as readily as individuals, though there are some notable exceptions to this. Picking any single nonprofit organization as the one that will be taken to scale may appear unfair and capricious. It implies that a single donor should be able to disturb the competitive landscape and decide who wins and loses in the nonprofit arena. While this may be precisely what an individual would like to achieve, few foundations want to be perceived as inequitable and heavy-handed. As a consequence, they shy away from tipping the scales completely in favor of one organization over another. Moreover, foundations may be less likely to bring an organization to scale because their interests are not in the organizations they fund per se, but in the specific programs and outcomes that these organizations deliver. The foundations have priorities that overlap somewhat with those of nonprofit organizations. When these priorities change, funders can and do find new organizations.

Another reason that individual nonprofits are not often brought to scale through the infusion of large amounts of money may be connected to efficiency concerns. While giving a nonprofit the ability to withstand the vicissitudes of the nonprofit marketplace sounds reasonable, it may not be the most efficient way to use philanthropic resources. Endowments are often established with a projected 4 or 5 percent draw rate. Funding a large programmatic agenda from an endowment therefore becomes an expensive proposition. There is also the concern that taking a single organization to scale will eliminate the leverage that funders have over nonprofits, because the funds will free the organization from the usual relationships of dependence. After all, if a nonprofit has enough money to conduct its programs without the continuous input of new contributions, an important performance incentive may be removed.

Scale as Program Expansion

The second meaning of scale refers to the breadth or scope of service, usually measured by the number of clients served. Going to scale in this sense is thus roughly equivalent to program expansion and reach. When a pilot or project is launched, the goal is often to take it to scale by funding it at a higher level and by bringing the program to more people. There is a sense that a good program can never serve enough people. As soon as an initiative seems to achieve significant results, one of the first impulses of nonprofit managers and funders alike is to ramp up the effort and find a way to identify and serve more clients. In the past, the ultimate ambition has often been to get local, state, or federal funding after a launch with private money.

There are a number of powerful forces propelling nonprofits and their funders toward program expansion. First, funding scale as expansion appears fair and equitable in that it rewards past performance. Funding decisions can be justified by the results that are actually achieved. Second, growing a program will allow it to achieve greater operational efficiency, as the *marginal* cost of administration decreases as the program expands. Third, this approach creates incentives for nonprofits to develop and deliver successful projects. If nonprofit managers know that funding to grow their programs depends on how well they work, the managers will work harder to make them succeed. Fourth, it allows funders and recipients to work together over longer periods of time than they otherwise might.[32]

Nonprofit organizations are especially comfortable with the idea of scale as program expansion. It represents a natural way to evolve a nonprofit from a small community organization to one that has a broader presence and impact. For nonprofit managers, aiming toward scale as program expansion is important. Because general support funding is scarce in some fields, program growth is essential to achieving some level of financial stability. Growing programs is seen as equivalent to professional success and can be a key to advancement. Moreover, the financial incentives in the sector provide a strong correlation between budget size and salary, with managers earning more depending on the scale of the program they oversee. Thus, both as a signal of success and as a tool for advancement, scale as program expansion is thus attractive to many nonprofit organizations.

From the perspective of the funder, allowing an organization with a proven track record to expand its operations represents both a high return activity and a relatively low-risk proposition. After all, the nonprofit has already demonstrated its ability to implement a given program. All they are seeking is funds for program expansion so that they can do more of one particular activity. This is a proposition that can be considerably less risky than the design and creation of a new initiative.

Scale as Comprehensiveness

The third meaning of scale refers to a set of programs that are closely linked and constitute a coherent set of resources for clients or communities.[33] Under this definition, the coordination problems inherent in the nonprofit sector's division of labor and proliferation of programs is overcome by bringing under one roof an integrated set of activities and interventions. Comprehensive community-based initiatives are seen as a remedy to the problems of categorical funding, one that aims at system-wide reform.

Comprehensive community initiatives began in the twentieth century with the settlement houses. From Hull House to the modern community-focused initiatives launched by large private foundations, there does not seem to be any decrease in this type of initiative. The belief that comprehensiveness is the critical ingredient to scale emerged from years of experience with isolated project funding. Seeking to create synergies by funding integrated sets of services, many donors see scale as being closely linked to building a dominant local presence. Viewing scale as comprehensiveness is thus embedded in the idea that program linkages are at least as important as the creation of new programs. By focusing resources in one geographical community, some funders see bridge building as the best way to create a sizable presence and a more fundamental and lasting impact.

Achieving scale by weaving together disparate programs and efforts into a cohesive whole requires that four important problems be overcome. First, interagency collaboration requires that difficult governance issues be worked out so that all parties can work together productively. Second, this approach emphasizes the goals of inclusion and diversity, and those leading such an effort must show leadership in this area and be sensitive to the heterogeneity of many community groups, programs, and networks. Third, comprehensiveness depends on the effort gaining legitimacy and support from the grassroots, not only from community elites. Fourth, any focus on collaborative strategy must address the issue of sustainability and the development of new funding streams. Inevitably, due to the size and ambition of many of these programs, government is often involved, which can be a source of support or frustration.

Scale as Replication

When a particular initiative or service model proves successful, many dissect its essential elements in order to reconstruct it. Replication, a technique that has long been tried and tested in the business sector, is one way to achieve scale.[34] Replication can proceed in two quite different ways: (1) within the organization through a set of more or less closely linked chapters or through a franchise system linking independent organizations;[35] or (2) outside the organization through independent efforts to create similar programs.[36]

The chapter or affiliate way of replicating services has proved critical to the expansion of many of the older and more established service organizations and civic associations. Opening chapters in cities around the country enables an organization to achieve scale quickly yet maintain some degree of control through centralization. Often, chapters are established in a hub-and-spoke arrangement, in which funds and resources flow back and forth between the center and the periphery. One obvious problem with this approach is that it can be difficult to achieve uniformity across chapters so that the mission is clear and consistent. Not surprisingly, one of the biggest questions that this approach raises is the amount of autonomy that should be granted to the affiliates. Some organizations have successfully implemented loose confederations, while others have long operated tightly controlled networks.

The competing franchise approach to replication is based on the simple assumption that once a model has been established, the real work involves copying and multiplying the model in as many places as possible. Franchising has become popular with younger social entrepreneurs who see this model as providing swift action. By licensing a "brand," nonprofits can go to scale quickly. A key challenge of the franchise approach is locating people who can take a model into a new community and implement it. The brand name must be protected by some form of quality assurance. Achieving consistency and measuring quality are both difficult propositions in the nonprofit sector, however.[37]

There are some clear difficulties to both chapter and franchise replication. Replication is not an approach that can easily be initiated or directed by funders. Although funders may be able to foster some replication through the use of grants and incentives, most externally directed replication efforts will struggle with the vast idiosyncratic tide of nonprofit organizations that resist imitation and convergence. While some innovations and ideas have been replicated, large numbers of projects are unable to find any takers, even when they have shown great promise. Replication may rest on the shaky assumption that nonprofits are amenable to cookie-cutter duplication. Moreover, some funders who experimented with replication strategies discovered that some initiatives successful on a small and local scale defy replication when they are taken out of their initial contexts. This seems especially true when the nonprofit is working with disadvantaged populations, where trust and credibility are crucial.

Replication also ensues if the philanthropist creates a pilot or model program and then allows government or other funders to take the effort to scale. The philanthropist Eugene Lang, for example, had the novel idea of "adopting a class" of middle-school students at the inner-city school he attended years ago. Lang promised all the students in one grade that if they worked hard and stayed in school, he would guarantee to pay for their college education. When New York State got word of this offer, it did not take long before a scholarship program was devised for other disadvantaged students. This proved to be problematic. Critically missing from this public sector imitation was the direct personal involvement that was a central part of Lang's innovative educational gift. Thus while it is tempting to think that the replication model involves the simple multiplication of existing programs and institutions, in reality, this process is more labor intensive. Embedded in many successful programs are the vision and commitment of an individual. When the program is replicated in other sites, this personal connection is often missing; the organizations may pass from being an expression of one person's values and beliefs to a more instrumental attempt to produce certain public benefits.

Scale as Accepted Doctrine

A fifth dimension of scale focuses on the power of creating a new and accepted doctrine within a given field. Scale can be achieved by formulating and diffusing an idea or concept. Precipitating a major shift in the way people think about their work and carry out their programs in a given field creates a wide-ranging and lasting impact. Creating a new doctrine is different from other forms of scale because it seeks to infiltrate broadly by changing the conceptual frame surrounding a particular field. A successful effort at doctrine building will lead to a wholesale reevaluation of a field's standard operating procedures and assumptions. While an operational model may be associated with a new doctrine, new ideas can and do triumph in the absence of clear applications.

Pursuing scale through doctrinal shifts is appealing to funders for a number of reasons. Unlike other ways of going to scale, this approach is not limited to the organizations receiving funding. It is possible to propagate an idea or theory and to change service delivery models without spending money on implementation, but one should be able to point to at least one concrete application of the doctrine. One key to successful paradigm building involves the penetration of small networks of policy elites and nonprofit leaders. Once an idea is embraced by opinion leaders, it can filter through a field quickly.[38] Influential doctrines have emerged from think tanks and university researchers and from practitioners who can articulate a clear theory supporting their work. One significant shortcoming to this approach to scale is that the outcomes of such efforts are very hard to predict. Sometimes ideas and frameworks emerge as powerful tools for transforming practice, but ultimately find no audience or willing adopters. At other times, second-rate ideas spread like wildfire within fields and are broadly adopted. The process of spreading a doctrine is not amenable to a great deal of control.

Although many funders like the idea of going to scale, the number of initiatives accomplishing scale under any of the three definitions remains small. Only around 200,000 nonprofits out of some 1.5 million have revenues above $25,000. The number of very large and successful nonprofits is considerably smaller than 100,000 and probably closer to 10,000, the majority of which are universities and hospitals. The achievement of scale thus remains an elusive goal and one that raises a number of questions: When and why should any of these five scale strategies be applied? Why does scale sometimes fail? Does the ideal of scale fit better in the business sector than in the nonprofit sector? Can commitments to scale and equity be embraced simultaneously? Are the less successful attempts at scale simply examples of domains in which public policy should be allowed to operate? Most of these questions remain unanswered even though scale has become a major target of organized philanthropy. It is far easier to simply fall back on arguments about spreading the benefits more broadly and achieving efficiencies than it is to engage these difficult questions.

The fundamental problem with the concept of scale, as understood in the philanthropy field, is that it assumes that the scope of public impact achieved through philanthropy correlates with the public value created. Scale seems an obviously desirable objective by virtue of the simple math seeming to lie behind it, namely that assisting 10,000 clients, all things being equal, is better than assisting 1,000. This assumption is particularly hard to defeat in the context of philanthropy because it is difficult to measure the quality of nonprofit programs. With all the obstacles preventing precise measurements of effectiveness and program quality in the nonprofit sector, it is very easy to use size as a proxy for impact and to embrace the idea that programs serving large numbers of people are contributing more to public welfare than those targeting smaller populations. In this sense, scale is much easier to measure than effectiveness, and it represents an appealing way to change the conversation. But the danger of such a move lies, of course, in the fact that scale is not a particularly good proxy for effectiveness and that many large programs do not deserve the support they receive, while many smaller programs deserve great acclaim. When scale is pursued without adequate evidence of efficacy or sufficient quality controls, it can undermine the entire coherence of a logic model.

While a theory of scale typically comes toward the end of the process of perfecting a logic model, it should be conceived, along with a theory of change and a theory of leverage, as part of an integrated system aimed at producing significant social impact. One way to visualize this system is to move away from the linear representation of the value chain in philanthropy presented earlier and toward the image of a triad, one in which all three elements are connected to one another (see figure 6.2).

As donors look out across the philanthropic landscape at all the many opportunities, many will want to include in their fundamental logic model a theory of change, a theory of leverage, and a theory of scale. These can help donors focus their understanding and render explicit some of their assumptions. One thing is certain: there are no universally applicable theories of change, leverage, and scale. Depending on the field within which the donor is operating and the choices that it makes in other parts of the philanthropic prism, choices vary considerably in terms of social benefits produced. Donors who attempt to take a logic model from one field and impose it crudely on another will be sorely disappointed. The context is critical in determining not only the logic model, but all the other elements of the philanthropic prism.

One additional caveat that bears on all three parts of a logic model concerns causality. In drawing up a logic model, donors will surely be tempted to simplify as they proceed, purposively bracketing certain complex issues and simply overlooking other elements. To a certain extent, this simplification is both necessary and productive; it allows donors to begin to sketch out the pieces of their program and how they will create change. There is, however, a substantial risk involved. Causality will tend to appear stronger and more certain than it really is. In almost all cases where philanthropic funds are used to address significant public problems, many factors that donors cannot possibly control will ultimately impinge on the results.

Take, for example, a donor who spots a promising after-school tutoring program in the high school he or she had attended. The school has fallen on hard times and now suffers from low test scores, poor discipline, and high drop-out rates. The donor approaches the nonprofit that carries out the program and offers to fund an expansion. Before cutting a check, the donor decides to lay out the logic model that is at play in this endeavor (see figure 6.3). Staring at a blank piece of paper, the donor decides to start at the left-hand side and sketch a box for the grant that is being contemplated for its promised leverage. In this case it's a matching grant that requires the program to raise two dollars for every one that the donor provides. The donor

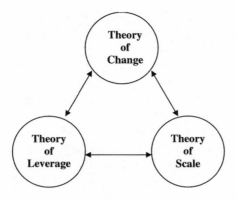

Figure 6.2 **Three elements of a philanthropic logic model.**

then connects this first box to a second one containing the main funded activities—more tutoring programs. This second box is in turn linked to a third containing the expected output, an increase in the number of youth receiving mentoring services from the provider. Pausing to think through what follows, the donor defines the outcome that is being sought as something manageable: improved academic performance by students in the program. This relatively short-term outcome is linked in the donor's mind to longer-term outcomes, such as greater opportunities and life chances, but for the sake of this exercise, the outcome is specified more narrowly. All that is left is the final box containing the theory of scale. In this instance, the donor hopes to see the project expanded and replicated with government funding once the program results are publicized. Having sketched a logic model, the donor feels a certain level of satisfaction for having taken such care in making this decision.

The problem with this imaginary planning and strategizing scenario is that it fails to take into account the real-world complexity surrounding philanthropic interventions, particularly those involving effects to shape human behavior or redress complex social problems, such as uneven academic performance in schools. The most glaring problem with this model has nothing to do with its contents, but rather with the fact that it represents a closed system. In fact, almost every logic model is a profoundly open system—shaped, distorted, and overdetermined by the vast array of forces and conditions surrounding the system.

Thus the donor's work is not done. It is incumbent on anyone sketch-

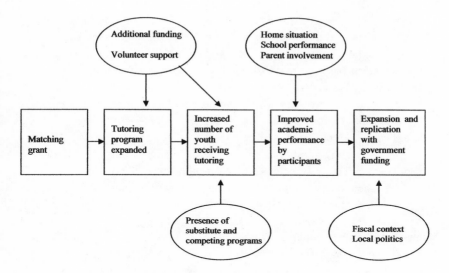

Figure 6.3 **Logic model for tutoring program.**

ing out a logic model to take into consideration the external factors that impinge on the causal claims being made. It may not be possible to control for, or even account for, all of the factors, but they still need to be confronted even if only for coming to terms with the model's limitations. In this example, external factors that lie outside the donor's immediate control include such things as the availability of additional funds and volunteer support. These will have a major effect on the breadth of the possible expansion. The presence of competing or substitute programs will also be a factor in determining how much expansion is possible. When trying to establish the net impact of the intervention on the children, a whole range of competing factors must be considered, including the home situation of the children, the amount of parental involvement, and the quality of the school in which the child is enrolled. All these factors and many others will impinge on the net change in academic performance. Finally, a whole range of broader economic and political considerations, including the availability of local revenues and the commitment of public officials, will ultimately determine whether the program is expanded and supported on a larger scale.

At one level, large amounts of "noise" in philanthropic systems is disconcerting in that it weakens the causal linkages that lie at the heart of all logic models. Part of the problem stems not from the mere presence of exogenous forces, but from the inability to ever assess the amount of impact wrongly attributed to philanthropic interventions. In some cases, exogenous factors will be enormously important and render claims about net philanthropic effects basically meaningless. In other circumstances, the problem of exogenous factors will be far more manageable, especially when the noise is matched up against a very substantial philanthropic intervention. There is a clear connection among causality, the nature of the intervention, and the scope of the program.

One interesting question is whether sound strategy demands that donors focus their giving on situations where causal linkages stemming from philanthropic action are strong and compelling. The attraction of such a decision rule is that it controls exogenous factors at the outset by guiding donors away from problems where causal claims of progress are difficult to make. Although it would simplify some aspects of philanthropy, such a decision rule would likely lead donors to focus on problems far too limited in character and whose solutions are far too obvious. One of the real tests of philanthropy actually comes down to crafting interventions in areas where others have failed. These tend to be areas where there are ample amounts of noise in the form of existing support programs and where public policy can shift in an effort to address the problem. The last thing that donors should want is to remove from their list of potential targets the long list of intractable human problems simply because they are subject to multiple and interacting factors. However, when sketching logic models it is important to confront the fact that there are many intervening and competing variables at work.

The presence of confounding factors around a logic model could discourage a donor from trying to achieve some conceptual clarity. This is especially the case if the philanthropic object at hand is an enduring human problem that others have attempted but failed to fully address. The right response in taking on a large and challenging issue is simply to act with a fair amount of humility. Some donors do not give up easily and attempt to confront these intervening forces head-on through the implementation of experimental evaluations with control and treatment groups, which allow some control for factors outside the program. These efforts are expensive, difficult to execute effectively, and usually have some significant limitations to their generalizability. Thus, while it may be possible to "control" for some of the factors that influence an intervention, there is no real substitute for a clear understanding of the weaknesses inherent in much causal modeling.

The last issue to be resolved is that logic models are very useful for planning and describing programmatic initiatives, but are less useful at depicting the overall strategy of multiprogram organizations. Logic models tend to be very specific in their focus. As a consequence, funders who operate simultaneously in multiple program areas will find that one model rarely tells the whole story of how the funder is attempting to achieve its specified goals. Assumptions about methods and drivers will vary greatly across program areas and require the simultaneous elaboration of multiple models within program areas. This is the approach that the Hewlett Foundation has taken in its grantmaking.[39] Each Hewlett program area is asked to elaborate and defend its fundamental assumptions about how change happens in fields as diverse as population, neighborhood revitalization, and the arts. While this situation creates a certain amount of incommensurability and may highlight some potential contradictions between the causal assumptions related to effectiveness in the program areas, it can also open up a number of fruitful opportunities for dialogue. Lining up competing logic models next to one another within a foundation could be a useful exercise, especially if supplemented by reliable and usable performance data. This work could lead to important forms of organizational learning related to building stronger and more robust models in the future.

In the end, the real justification for a powerful logic model is not its ability to provide the framework for evaluation, although it can certainly do that well. The ultimate rationale for the kind of reflection and modeling described here is that donors need to render clearer in their own minds the objectives driving their giving. By formalizing the donor's beliefs and assumptions through a logic model, one meaningful step can be taken on the road toward greater strategic clarity. In some sense, it is important to judge philanthropy not only by the effects it produces or, to put it another way, for what comes out of the logic model. It is important also to take stock of the quality of thinking that lies behind giving and the plausibility of philanthropic intentions. A logic model can be a telling representation of the donor's best judgment about how to address a human problem. Getting beyond the narrow measurement of the net effects of philanthropy to the donors' underlying aspirations would be productive for the entire field. It would reorient the field's attention from something that can often be only indirectly connected to giving, namely the outcomes made possible by philanthropy, to something that is at the heart of responsible decision making, namely the care with which a donor disburses funds. This is something over which donors have complete and absolute control and for which they should be held accountable.

There is a final irony in this entire discussion of logic models. Much of the argument in this book has been *against* the overprofessionalization of philanthropy and its rendering of the art of philanthropy into a dry arid technical chore, and *for* a more expressive, personal form of giving that connects the donor's passions and values to community needs. The discussion here of logic models might ultimately seem a bit out of place, or at least at cross-purposes, in that it turns the human complexity of giving into something more akin to the arid schematics of an electrician's circuit map. This conclusion is wrong for the simple reason that the construction of logic models is not, and never can be, a substitute for the inner exploration and search for fundamental commitments that lie at the core of strategic giving. Logic models of the sort described here can be helpful, however, in assessing how plausible and well conceived the plans are that emerge from this process. In this sense, the pursuit of robust and predictive logic models is best thought of as a kind of preliminary warm-up exercise for donors seeking a way to both act on private values and meet public needs.

7. Institutions and Vehicles

Giving can no longer be conceived only as an act linking isolated individuals to social causes. Today, much philanthropic funding is delivered by institutions and vehicles that stand between the donor and the recipient. The organizational landscape of philanthropy has grown increasingly crowded, as more and more organizational forms have come to populate the terrain. The decision to conduct one's giving in part or completely through an institution, and the choice of the appropriate institution, must be guided by a careful consideration of all the dimensions in the philanthropic prism. Decisions about institutions can quickly either make giving more satisfying or turn it into a painful exercise. For some families, the creation of a foundation is a powerful vehicle for teaching and conveying values from one generation to the next. In other situations, the formation of a foundation simply provides fuel for long-standing family conflicts and may lead to greater strife among children, especially when large amounts of money are involved.[1] In some contexts, the use of federated funders is a powerful and satisfying way for individuals to be part of something greater than themselves. In other contexts, reliance on federated funders provides an alienating buffer between donors and the world they seek to influence. In many cases, the choice to create an independent or family foundation that will operate in perpetuity gives donors a comforting sense that their philanthropic legacy will live on long after they are gone.[2] In a few isolated but visible instances, decisions to form foundations have led to the slow and controversial drift away from the donors' values and intent, and eventually to the existence of institutions that would be barely recognizable to their philanthropic creators.

The choice of the right institutional vehicle for giving is thus not something that donors can or should take for granted; it is an element of strategy building that demands constant and careful consideration. All too often, the choice of vehicle proceeds in a kind of conceptual vacuum. Creating a foundation, for example, is not a complex process. It requires a modicum of legal work up front and then entails that certain legal and regulatory requirements be met regularly. Because major donors have from the earliest days of modern scientific philanthropy had a particularly strong attraction to foundations, due at least in part to their perceived permanence and professionalism, the default position for many donors with substantial means has long been simply the creation of a private foundation. Moreover, having a foundation has become a way that the wealthy signal to one another that they have significant financial and philanthropic means.

Beyond the obvious choice of a private foundation established in perpetuity, donors have an ever expanding range of options.[3] They can contribute to a community foundation, an operating foundation, or, if their wealth is tied up in a business, a company-sponsored foundation. For smaller donors, federations such as the United Way beckon, as do new vehicles such as gift funds and giving circles that promise alternatively great administrative efficiency or peer counsel through collaboration. These options are supplemented by a range of more complex choices involving various forms of trusts. According to tax lawyers, sorting out these options involves a complex calculation focused on tax savings and estate planning issues. In reality, the decision about the vehicle to be used, if one is to be used at all, involves a whole group of considerations that have little to do with finances.

If one accepts the premise that philanthropy involves more than just the instrumental pursuit of public benefits, since it also includes the expression and fulfillment of the donor's values and commitments, then the choice of institutions needs to be judged by how well it supports both these dimensions. In order to improve the benefits of giving and maximize the personal satisfaction that giving can bring, it is important for donors to make an informed decision about the institutional form. By exploring some of the trade-offs and opportunities that donors face in the choice of philanthropic vehicles, it may be possible to begin to identify how and why institutional forms coincide—and at times conflict—with the process of attempting to move toward strategic giving.

Four Forms of Foundations

In common parlance, "foundation" has become shorthand for a private or independent foundation, an endowed institution that makes grants to nonprofit organizations using the interest and appreciation from its investments. Constituted by a board and sometimes a staff, a foundation reviews grant applications and disburses funds to those applicants deemed most deserving.[4] Not all foundations fit this image, however. Aside from the generic private, independent foundations that simply make grants, there are operating foundations (which use endowment interest to fund program activities carried out by foundation staff), community foundations (which solicit endowment funds from residents of the surrounding city or region), and corporate foundations (which businesses contribute to annually based on a share of corporate profits or a percentage of endowment, if one exists). These three new philanthropic vehicles are all based on the model of the private foundation, although each has a distinctive organizational structure and practices. Table 7.1 lays out some of the differences as well as some of the similarities among philanthropy's four main organizational forms.

Where did these four basic forms come from and why did they emerge when they did? Looking at changes in society, the nonprofit sector, and the tax code, we may give a credible historical account of why private foundations and operating foundations were created around the turn of the twentieth century and why corporate foundations and community foundations have emerged as major philanthropic players over time. But such an account—no matter how detailed in terms of historical facts—would tell only a small part of the story. The emergence and spread of philanthropic forms has not been driven exclusively by the convergence of social forces or events. Philanthropy's four main forms have established themselves and gained currency because each represents a different strategic response to a combination of external pressures and internal management challenges.

Table 7.1 **Four main foundation forms.**

	Primary activity	Financial base	Use of funds
Independent foundation	grantmaking	endowed	grants to nonprofit organizations
Operating foundation	program administration	endowed	operation of internal programs
Community foundation	grantmaking and fund-raising	seeks to build endowment	grants to local nonprofit organizations
Corporate foundation	grantmaking and community relations	unendowed or endowed	grants to nonprofit organizations

Operating Foundations

Operating foundations are endowed philanthropic institutions that use investment income to operate programs run by the foundation's own staff, rather than to make grants to outside organizations. The idea of an operating foundation is simple enough. Whenever possible, an operating foundation pursues its stated mission directly through the foundation's own internal programs, thereby reducing the need for outside agents or nonprofit middlemen. Within American philanthropy, operating foundations occupy a conflicted position. On the one hand, they are endowed institutions that exist in perpetuity, which makes them look like conventional foundations. On the other hand, they rarely make grants to outside organizations, preferring instead to act like a nonprofit by carrying out their mission directly through the work of their own staff—something that an independent foundation would never do. Operating foundations have both endowments and substantive programs and thus have characteristics of both conventional foundations and more generic grantseeking nonprofit organizations.

What is the logic that underlies the decision of an operating foundation to conduct its own programs rather than contract out? The concept of transaction costs turns out to be very useful in understanding the hybrid structure of operating foundations and the place they occupy in the philanthropic landscape. Economists have long been attracted by the idea that organizations are efficiency maximizers and that decisions represent the rational calculation of the best course of action. It is therefore not surprising that rational action is at the core of transaction costs economics (TCE).[5] In attempting to give an account of why giant firms have emerged and replaced smaller, more specialized firms, economists tend to fall back on the claim that this move represents the most efficient way to produce goods for an industrial society. Using the basic logic of transaction costs analysis, one can see that all organizations are really sets of contracts that collectively determine governance structure. In managing their affairs and the complex web of agreements and contracts that hold an organization together, firms seek to minimize transaction costs to gain a competitive advantage. This can be done in two basic ways. First, firms can work through the external market and seek out the best possible deals. Second, they can operate through internal hierarchy and control the production process from start to finish.

Economists argue that a key determinant of how organizations obtain needed resources is the relative specificity of the asset. When a particular physical or human asset becomes specialized and difficult to obtain in the market, firms will attempt to secure the asset through ownership rather than through spot contracting. The need to minimize transaction costs, manage uncertainty, and secure assets leads firms to buy out suppliers or subcontractors. This leads to a small number of larger firms organized as hierarchies, rather than a large number of small firms contracting with one another in the market. All things being equal, hierarchy will tend to replace markets when there are long-term contracts in an uncertain environment and the barriers to entry are reasonably high, because costs can be reduced by substituting an authority relationship for a contractual one.

The TCE perspective provides a good explanation of how and why organizations assume the structure they do, and it presents a plausible set of hypotheses about the nature of interorganizational relations. The ability to distinguish spot contracts from long-term contracts, many bargainers from only a few, and the degree of substitutability of goods and services constitutes a major advance for scholars committed to studying organizations within the rational actor model. These concepts are pertinent to the institutional landscape and allow one to understand why operating foundations frequently carry out their missions with their own staff rather than contract out. Operating foundations are able to fulfill their missions most efficiently through internal hierarchy because of the high transaction costs associated with working through the external grants marketplace. Both the structure and practices of operating foundations can thus be usefully understood from a TCE perspective.

A couple of examples may prove helpful. The Liberty Fund in Indianapolis is an operating foundation with a large endowment that uses its resources to promote libertarian principles through a range of publications and conferences. The fund uses its philanthropic resources to produce and distribute at a subsidized price copies of the works of political writers with a commitment to liberty. The fund also publishes a series of volumes called Liberty Classics that offer to students, scholars, and the general public handsome editions of all the work of Adam Smith at low prices. The interest generated by the endowment is also used to host a series of conferences around the country each year where works in the classical liberal tradition are discussed. These conferences are held at resorts from coast to coast and participants have all their expenses paid by the fund. Rather than contract out all of the work of organizing these meetings, the fund has a number of full-time support staff who work on hotel and travel arrangements for participants. In addition, the fund's professional staff travels to each of the seminars and helps organize the meetings and guide discussions of the selected texts.

The Century Foundation in New York City is also an operating foundation, but it functions more like a think tank than the Liberty Fund. Using its endowment to pay the salaries of its staff of researchers, the fund seeks to spread information and research on public policy issues such as housing, welfare reform, and international trade. The foundation could easily make grants to academics around the country to carry out the desired research, but this would entail paying the enormous overhead costs associated with university-based research. Thus, the impulse is born to bring the research within the organizational umbrella of an operating foundation. The foundation hires policy analysts to conduct research and provides residential fellowships to researchers working on books and papers. This method of sponsoring research can be readily contrasted to that of the large independent foundations, many of which fund a great deal of research on public policy subjects, but it does so mainly through universities and nonprofit intermediaries such as the Social Science Research Council and the Aspen Institute. The Century Foundation is different in that it brings the research within its own organizational umbrella and then publishes it under its own imprint.

What the Liberty Fund and the Century Foundation have in common is the decision to move—within the nonprofit economy—from markets to hierarchies. Rather than have their publishing, conference planning, and research needs met by individuals and organizations competing in the grants market, operating foundations internalize these functions and solve their problems through hierarchy; researchers, editors, and conference leaders are employees of the operating foundation and serve at the pleasure of the foundation's executive director. This allows operating foundations a great deal of control over their programs, something that is not usually possible in a grantmaking relationship. For once foundation money is disbursed, only a nonprofit organization's goodwill and concern for its reputation ensure quality work. On the other hand, operating foundations can take steps to reduce this uncertainty. The Liberty Fund can control every step of the publishing process from title selection to distribution to price rather than allow them to be determined by the market. It can also shape and control more easily the content of the conferences it subsidizes when the conference planners are regular Liberty Fund staff members.

If operating foundations represent an efficient response to a changing philanthropic landscape, the following question naturally arises: Why haven't all grantmaking foundations turned into operating foundations? The answer lies in the tremendous variety of charitable missions that exist in American philanthropy. For large foundations pursuing broad social agendas, such as improving the education of children or providing job training for the unemployed, working through a hierarchy is often impossible or impractical. For such philanthropic organizations, grantmaking is the only alternative. Not only does grantmaking allow foundations to pool resources through jointly funded projects, but it also gives foundations the ability to move quickly in responding to changing social needs. Only when the mission is more narrow and related to research does the structure of an operating foundation become more attractive.

The decision to form an operating foundation must be linked not only with the value to be produced through giving, but also with the identity and style of the donor. Being able to design and carry out programs without having to rely on grantees is attractive to donors who want to control their giving from start to end. The operating foundation form also gives donors a chance to do more than just write checks and read reports. It puts the donor at the center of the philanthropic equation and demands not only good judgment but also sound execution. For a donor wanting to maintain substantial control over the use of funds, operating foundations are attractive in that they internalize the process of translating financial resources into publicly valuable purposes. Yet because operating foundations demand that the donor think through the entire process of moving from a mission to a set of programs and outcomes, few ultimately choose them.

Operating foundations are frequently viewed as aberrations on the philanthropic scene, strangers who have abdicated the traditional arms-length relationship between grantmaker and grant recipient. They are, however, better viewed as efficiency maximizers that fulfill their philanthropic missions through hierarchy rather than in the traditional grant market. When the Century Foundation brings research within its organizational walls rather than funding research within a university setting, it gains some control while eliminating the transaction costs of grantmaking in the university setting. Similarly, the Liberty Fund is able to fulfill its mission of spreading information on libertarianism most efficiently through hierarchy rather than in the market. In this way, the emergence of operating foundations can be interpreted as a response to the rising costs of grantmaking; operating foundations represent an organizational form that permits a high level of control, low transaction costs, and—in certain program areas—increased efficiency. For some donors and for some missions, operating foundations are an option that can help achieve a high level of strategic fit and alignment.

Community Foundations

Community foundations are philanthropic institutions set up in cities or regions that allow residents to make contributions and give their estates to one large foundation.[6] Unlike most private foundations that grow simply by wisely investing their initial endowment, community foundations depend on a steady stream of inputs or contributions to grow their corpus. This is especially the case with new and emerging community foundations, which often start with very small endowments and then attempt to attract local gifts. In this way, continual dependency on donors is a central feature of community foundations that is not present in independent foundations.[7]

The dependence of community foundations on outside donors for philanthropic resources does have one positive feature: it makes the foundations accountable for their decisions, because every grant is reported in an annual report and can be reviewed by potential donors. Community foundations in this sense are more "public" than independent foundations, whose grantmaking is not shaped by a need to attract resources. Community residents can review past grants, talk to foundation staff, and work out arrangements that meet their philanthropic interests—all before committing their funds to a community foundation. This gives donors a high degree of control over the disbursement of their funds while forcing community foundations to make grants that cover a broad range of areas, from the arts to environment to health to education to child welfare. Their dependence on outside resources thus invariably breeds broad grantmaking programs, as community foundations become large department stores where donors can find the philanthropic wares they are seeking.

Interestingly, community foundations have experienced a period of phenomenal growth over the past few decades, with hundreds of new institutions sprouting up in small and midsized cities around the country. One of the reasons for the popularity of community foundations is precisely that they are easy to start. All that is needed is an initial gift, which sometimes comes from local government, from a large private foundation, or even from an enterprising individual. Once the first funds are located, the foundation must launch a strong campaign aimed at attracting gifts from others who might otherwise consider setting up their own private foundation. Since they must secure funds from local residents to survive, the long-term viability of community foundations is not always assured. To succeed, they must attract and manage resources ably. Community foundations may be established in perpetuity, but to be effective and to have meaningful grant-making ability they must build their endowments. Soliciting new contributions shapes not only the staffing of community foundations, but also their programs. Community foundations must employ development officers to locate donors. At the same time, program officers must identify and support high-profile grant applicants capable of generating good publicity for the foundation. In both staffing and programming, community foundations are oriented toward garnering resources from the community of possible donors that lies within the geographical bounds of the foundation. From all of these characteristics, it should be apparent that the defining features of community foundations can be usefully understood from a resource dependence perspective.

The resource dependence model starts with an emphasis on the raw volume of resources controlled, the need for these resources, the number of alternative sources for these resources, and the degree of control that can be exercised over the flow of resources.[8] Resource dependence applies these concepts to interorganizational relations and argues that organizations are defined by their need to secure and distribute resources. Organizations are not self-sufficient because they almost never possess all the resources needed to survive. As a result, organizations engage in exchanges with various entities. It is the need to establish and maintain these exchanges that creates dependency between organizations. The resource dependence model stresses the role of interdependence as a mechanism for adaptation to changing conditions.[9] Most organizations depend on resources from the outside and must establish structures and implement strategies to ensure that the flow of goods and services entering and leaving remains open. According to the resource dependence model, it is possible to understand organizational structure and development by looking at the organization's environment. The complex patterns of resource flows—and the relative degree of control exerted over these flows—are central to understanding which organizations are in positions of power and which are weaker.

The quest for endowment gifts is the driving concern of administrators of community foundations. Without resources, the foundation's mission cannot be pursued. Given these constraints, community foundations must commit significant amounts of both staff time and administrative expenses to fund-raising. Community foundations also frequently pursue high-profile grantmaking, funding public radio and television, in order to gain publicity and increase their profile within the community. On the staffing side, someone must focus on securing new gifts. The Kansas City Community Foundation, for example, has full-time employees whose sole function is to solicit contributions and manage relations with donors. To encourage donations, it has initiated a range of programs that make contributing to this community foundation an attractive alternative to setting up an independent foundation. First, the foundation allows contributors to maintain considerable control over the disbursement of grants generated by their gifts. These donor-advised funds create significant accounting complexities, since many of the funds within the foundation must be tracked and administered separately. Donor-advised funds also undermine to some extent the foundation's ability to control its own grantmaking programs. Catering to the donor's desire to have some control over the use of its gift has paid off well, however, for the Kansas City Community Foundation; it has been able to counter the trend toward greater giving through new vehicles by making the community foundation form appealing to donors who want to take an active role in disbursing their philanthropic resources.[10]

The community foundation field has been anything but static over the years. Hundreds of smaller community foundations have sprouted up in small and midsized cities around the country and in regions (or clusters of cities) that have experienced substantial growth, such as Northwest Indiana, Lorraine County, Ohio, and Research Triangle, North Carolina. In many of the smaller cities and rural regions, funds for the start-up of community foundations have come from the large independent foundations. The Charles Stewart Mott Foundation, which has an endowment of over $1 billion, has been a major funder of small, start-up community foundations through special endowment grants. These grants are intended both to leverage other funds in the community and to overcome the free-rider problem. When a community foundation has no endowment, there is little reason for the first donors to give to a foundation bearing the community's name rather than set up a charitable organization in the donor's own name. There are no economies of scale to be taken advantage of during the early stages of a community foundation; hence, for individual donors, the incentives to make one of the first contributions are weak in the face of considerable overhead rates when funds are scarce.

By making the initial grant to endow a community foundation, many independent foundations believe they are getting a very high return on the philanthropic dollar, however. For foundations, early endowment gifts—if they are successful—can be seen as highly leveraged philanthropic choices, since they not only fund an organization's early programs but also stimulate giving by individuals. Early support is never enough because community foundations need to continually attract new money, to replace funds given away, to keep grantmaking resources growing faster than inflation, and to ensure the long-term well-being of the institution. There is a sense that any community foundation that does not have a constant flow of resources into it may come to be perceived as failing to meet the needs of its philanthropic clients. Hence, growth in the world of community foundations is often taken as a sign of success.

Community foundations are often able to attract donors by offering themselves up as hosts for family philanthropy. Donors also have used a community foundation to house their own family foundations as "supporting organizations." This arrangement allows families to have their own board of trustees (usually with minority board representation from the sponsoring community foundation) and carry out philanthropy in a group fashion.[11] While organized and run like a family foundation, supporting organizations within a community foundation can avoid a lot of the paperwork associated with an independent foundation and rely instead on the structure and support of the community foundation on administrative matters.[12] However, like donor-advised funds, community foundations are rarely able to exert much control over the direction of these supporting organizations or integrate them into a broader, community foundation–driven philanthropic agenda.

Resource dependence theory illuminates the way power in community foundations is shaped by relations with outside donors. Because they must have gifts in the form of estates or trusts to survive and flourish, community foundations are forced to engage in a complex game of courting and supporting current and new donors, which places those who give in a position of considerable power. In practice, donors to community foundations have gained increasing power over time and now exert substantial influence through the establishment of donor-advised funds, which represent an ever larger percentage of giving to community foundations. Whether pursuing unrestricted gifts, donor-advised funds, or supporting funds, community foundations are similar to universities and other nonprofit organizations that must solicit funds; the money chase invariably leads to a loss of at least some autonomy. Decisions are not made solely on the basis of merit and need, but instead on the way gifts will appeal to important donors or potential donors.

Corporate Foundations

Corporate foundations operate much the same way as private foundations do, with one large exception. While a few corporate foundations have modest endowments, most operate with little or no resources committed in perpetuity to charitable causes.[13] Rather than lock up a large amount of money in an endowment, most corporations make annual contributions to their foundations based on a percentage of profits. To be sure, there is usually a small reserve fund maintained to pay administrative expenses and make emergency grants. But this amount pales in comparison to the multibillion-dollar cash reserves of many of the larger private foundations. Because the annual grants of a corporate foundation are linked more or less directly to the performance of the firm, substantial fluctuation in the level of charitable giving occurs from year to year as market conditions change. The fact that corporate philanthropy is shaped by the competitive position of firms ultimately defines the unique character of this form of philanthropic activity.[14]

The growth of corporate philanthropy over the past decades is the product of a growing sense that it is good business to give something back to the communities in which a corporation operates.[15] It is hardly surprising that many corporate contribution programs and foundations are run by people with backgrounds in marketing, public relations, or corporate-community relations. For this reason, some critics charge that corporate philanthropy is not "independent"; it is very closely tied in to the other functions of the firm and plays a strategic role.[16] While in the past some CEOs might have quarreled with such charges, today the fact that corporate giving supports the core business functions of the firm is openly trumpeted. Indeed, a fair amount of resources are devoted to finding ways to extract contributions to the bottom line from corporate philanthropy. Companies may invest substantially in measuring the impact of their giving if for no other reason than to demonstrate to corporate leadership that spending money on corporate philanthropy creates real returns in the form of positive perceptions of the company in the eyes of customers, community residents, and public officials in the towns where the company is located or does business.

Unlike independent foundations, corporate foundations are not chartered and then sent on their own idiosyncratic route, never seeking or needing another infusion of endowment funds. Nor are corporate foundations immune to changes in the financial world around them; they exist by virtue of their parent company's ability to compete in the market.[17] The philanthropic activity of a firm increases when it is successful, with profits being "distributed" back to the people who made the success possible in the first place. Microsoft's charitable giving, for example, has increased in recent years as the firm has experienced exponential growth. Its presence within the nonprofit community in the Pacific Northwest has grown to reflect the software company's increasing profitability. By the same token, however, corporate philanthropy almost invariably shrinks—sometimes to the point of being eliminated—when a firm's profits decrease. Thus, for example, the Borg-Warner Foundation was closed down when the firm experienced severe financial problems. In very short order, the foundation's small reserve fund was spent down, the executive director was terminated, and the foundation's grantmaking was suspended. There is more than a little irony in this aspect of corporate giving; when recessions hit the nation, corporations almost always are forced to scale back their charitable activity—a reduction that occurs precisely when nonprofit service agencies most urgently need grants.

Some corporate foundations manage to persist while others die or fade from prominence. Not only is the list of the largest corporate giving programs reshuffled regularly, but new entrants continuously appear. Large corporate foundations have been established in recent years by manufacturing companies such as Hitachi and Mitsubishi and banks such as Sumitomo and Sanwa. In one sense, the appearance of these corporate foundations is the product of competition between American and Japanese firms, a competition in which the Japanese fared very well in the 1980s. Among large American corporations such as ExxonMobil, General Motors, and IBM, patterns of corporate philanthropy change from year to year as market conditions shift and as foreign competition increases. Because of their unique ties to market competition among firms, corporate foundations can be usefully understood by using the tools of population ecology.

Population ecology looks at the development of groups of organizations and emphasizes the role natural selection plays in organizational dynamics. It holds that organizations succeed or fail based on how well they meet the demands of their environment. The key factor in this life-or-death struggle is organizational form: Environments differentially select organizations for survival on the basis of the fit between organizational forms and environmental characteristics. Selection, not adaptation, is the central process that needs to be studied in organization research. Organizational inertia—stemming from bounded rationality, sunk costs, and turnaround time—may make it impossible for organizations to react to change quickly enough to meet new environmental demands.[18] Accordingly, organizations are not always able to search out optimal solutions to the never-ending stream of environmental challenges that arise. Furthermore, powerful forces weigh against adaptation; change often produces inefficiencies that may weaken a firm's competitive position, gained through economies of scale and well-established procedures. Moreover, there is the liability of newness, which makes change difficult in a turbulent environment. For these reasons, populations of organizations are often helpless in the face of environmental selection pressures.

Population ecologists generally believe that organizations approach an environment by choosing one of two types of niches: a generalist niche that tries to meet diverse needs of the environment, or a specialist niche that addresses one component of the environment. What determines the kind of niche an organization chooses? The answer lies in the frequency with which changes occur over time. In fine-grained environments where many small changes occur, organizations will tend to survive if they operate in a specialized niche. Conversely, in a coarse-grained environment where a few big changes occur, firms operating in a generalist niche are well positioned to survive when wide fluctuations occur over long periods of time.

Other variations of the ecological perspective have shifted the analysis toward organizational communities and evolution.[19] For all their differences, however, the ecological models all share a few assumptions. The ecological perspective rests on the notion that organizations are not maximizers capable of swift and rational adaptation to the environment. Instead, organizations are beholden to standard operating procedures and have limited ability to collect and digest information in the face of powerful environmental forces.

Ecological theories all focus on competition as the key to understanding why some organizations survive and others die. In corporate philanthropy, competition manifests itself in an important—albeit indirect—way;

the firms that sponsor corporate philanthropy are locked in a life-and-death struggle, one that directly determines who will be a major contributor and who will be cutting back on grants. This competition, though not oriented at philanthropy, determines grantmaking options because most corporate foundations operate without substantial endowments. Each year, the corporate sponsors inject funds into the foundation's account, and this contribution is then distributed by the foundation. Competition in the market and the search for earnings thus have a profound impact on the shape of corporate foundations.

The lack of substantial endowments in corporate philanthropy means that an important buffer between philanthropy and the prevailing economic trends has been removed. Not only are corporate foundations sensitive to changes in the economic environment, they must also be sensitive to the interests of the corporate sponsor. Corporate foundations cannot and do not make arbitrary grants. Every grant has some instrumental value, even if this value is relatively small. Thus, for example, while the Dow Chemical Foundation has a broad range of philanthropic interests, it does spend a good deal of money on improving science education for minorities. Students receiving Dow scholarships are then invited to intern at the company and are recruited into the company after graduation. A more powerful example of business interests shaping corporate giving can be located in some of the Coors Brewing Company's recent philanthropic activity. Throughout the 1980s, Coors was a generous supporter of the American Enterprise Institute and the Heritage Foundation, two conservative and free-market think tanks in Washington. Coors's interest in the public policy research of these organizations (and their congressional connections) may well have been shaped by the company's decade-long struggle against unionization in its plants and by the conservative values of the company's leadership. More often, however, corporate self-interest is simply shaped by geography; firms tend to do their grantmaking in the cities or regions where they operate, with the simple goal of building goodwill and appearing as a good corporate citizen.

Corporate philanthropy is more complex than any other form of grantmaking because of the intrusion of outside interests and the contingency of funds on the competitive struggle between firms. The ability of corporations to make grants through their foundations is linked more often than not to the competitive success of the firm in the market. Thus, corporate giving is shaped less by forces within the nonprofit sector than by forces in the broader national economy.[20] Population ecology captures this feature of corporate giving and helps understand when and why corporate foundations are created, expanded, and eliminated.

Using a corporate foundation can be a way for donors to connect their business interests to their social concerns, although there are features of corporate philanthropy that make this link sometimes hard to establish. Chief among these is the tension within corporate foundations between the desire to do good and the desire to look good. While companies and their leaders can have powerful social commitments—and some companies, like Ben & Jerry's, are actually known for their political positions—many companies do not want to get too deeply enmeshed in controversial issues for fear of alienating their customers. The competitive pressures of the market have oriented corporate philanthropy in recent times more and more toward the task of demonstrating that giving and community involvement actually contribute materially to the bottom line by supporting key business functions such as marketing, sales, and public and government relations. As the demand for proven value has risen, the ability of corporate foundations to give without consideration to the "return" has been commensurately diminished.[21]

For the individual donor, the question of whether to use a corporate foundation arises only when the donor has a corporate or business interest large enough to make this possible. Corporate foundations can enhance the reputation and community standing of the company, but may not reflect as directly on the donor. For this reason, corporate giving programs tend not to be substitutes for the other forms of individual philanthropy, but rather an additional vehicle through which charitable impulses can be channeled.

Private Foundations

One of the most distinguishing features of private or independent foundations is their ability to function and survive regardless of the environment around them.[22] Since they are endowed and do not seek additional funds, private foundations have a level of independence that is quite unique in American society. Private foundations are not beholden to outside groups that hold needed resources, nor are they subject to pressures to locate a market niche in order to survive. On the contrary, private foundations have an independent position from which they can experiment in ways that are impossible in the public sector or business world. Free from worries about constitutionality or political feasibility and unbeholden to the bottom line, private foundations can—with only a few exceptions—do as they please. What then shapes the action of private foundations? What is the defining element of their organizational form? I argue here that it is the quest for legitimacy and the emergence of strong professional norms that have been the key feature of American private foundations. One tool for understanding these features is the new institutionalism in organizational analysis.

In its present form, the new institutionalism is a big tent that accommodates a broad range of theoretical, methodological, and substantive interests. And while much work has been done to sort out and classify the many strands of institutional research, the theory remains more of an orientation than a settled doctrine. Differences among institutional arguments are considerable, but a few central themes do unite the approach. Early statements of the theory emphasized the symbolic and ceremonial transformation that organizations undergo, changes that reflect myths in the institutional environment, rather than a detached calculus of costs and benefits. The focus of this early theoretical work was on processes such as isomorphic transformation, legitimization, structural decoupling, mimesis, homogenization, professionalization, and organizational field construction. Organizations in the institutional world are—within their fields or sectors—remarkably stable and similar. The few changes that do occur are rarely abrupt. Instead, the field is shaped by incremental learning and copying, with organizations engaging in a complex game of peek-a-boo aimed at appropriating ideas and practices from other organizations that appear to be effective.

Institutional theories of organizations provide a complex and penetrating perspective on organizational structure and development. In its broadest sense, institutionalism argues that organizations are driven by outside pressures to legitimize their work, professionalize the workplace, and copy what other organizations are doing. With its emphasis on legitimacy, satisficing behavior, and symbols, institutionalism presents a major departure from such rival theories as transaction costs economics, population ecology, and resource dependence theory. Neoinstitutionalism emphasizes the role external coercion plays in shaping organizations. The coercive pressures that drive organizations to adopt legitimized practices come mostly from external sources connected to the state, such as regulatory, licensing, and accrediting agencies. Once new practices are adopted by a few organizations working in a common area or field, these ways of doing things spread among similar organizations, as the desire to fit in and avoid further conflict with the environment increases. The pressure to conform and the need for legitimacy ultimately lead to isomorphism and homogenization within fields. With its emphasis on symbols and legitimacy, neoinstitutionalism has often been described as representing a radical and complete rejection of rational action theory that uses utility maximization as its touchstone.

Private foundations have long engaged in many of the highly symbolic and ritualistic behaviors that neoinstitutionalism predicts. Large private foundations have elaborate financial accounting systems, structured evaluations of their grantmaking programs, and a whole host of other internal controls aimed at making the foundations appear well managed and accountable. Many of these behaviors are just as much aimed at building public support and legitimacy as they are at meeting real world management needs. Indeed, philanthropy is an amazingly simple activity that has been complicated by foundations' drive to demonstrate that they deserve their tax exemption. There is a profound decoupling within many foundations between the internal management practices and the intended goals of the organization. Many times, layer upon layer of controls—over grantmaking decisions and over financial strategy—are instituted to ensure that legitimacy and public confidence are maintained.

By building layers of oversight that typically start with the program officer and move up to the program director and then to the executive director, foundations are not necessarily seeking efficiency. Multilayered decision-making structures in philanthropy are anything but efficient because they stop foundations from acting quickly when grantmaking opportunities arise that require immediate action. But they do allow private foundations to make the case that their decisions are the product of expert opinion and careful review. This is an ironic development, given that one of the oldest justifications of private philanthropy is that it is free of the constraints that burden both government and business enterprises. Bureaucratic structures do nothing but build in delays and limit the ability to act.

Bureaucracy in philanthropy also tends to produce compromises and safe decisions. As decisions are reviewed over and over with the professional staff and final recommendations are taken up by the board of directors, the inevitable consequence is that most controversial and risky grant applications are rejected. The grants that large private foundations typically make are thus filtered to such an extent that little emerges at the end of the decision-making chain that anyone could possibly find objectionable. The sanitizing of all decisions through bureaucratic structures is also ironic given that philanthropy has traditionally prided itself in being innovative and experimental, thus willing to fund solutions to social problems that others would not.

Why then have many of the larger private foundations added substantial numbers of staff and built in multiple layers of decision making? One reason is that private foundations are extremely sensitive to outside criticism and challenges to their legitimacy. To avoid the appearance that grantmaking decisions are capricious or shaped by personal relationships between foundation staff and grant recipients, philanthropy has instituted a range of controls aimed at legitimizing the grantmaking process. Those who scrutinize the grants of private foundations are less likely to question the privileges enjoyed by these foundations if their grantmaking decisions appear objective, professional, and subject to oversight. These appearances are purchased at a cost, as organizational structure is radically decoupled from function in many private foundations.

While bureaucratization and professionalization have hit most of America's largest private foundations over time, the last two decades have seen the rapid spread of these processes to foundations with only modest resources. Among large private foundations, the MacArthur Foundation, with assets of over $3 billion, has been subject to profound isomorphic transformation and professionalization. MacArthur's administrative staff has grown exponentially during its first two decades. When John D. MacArthur died and left his fortune to the foundation, a minuscule staff was hired to administer the foundation. The board of directors made many of the grantmaking decisions and the staff simply processed the paperwork and issued the checks. But over the years, the foundation's staff grew to the point where it now has over 200 employees, possesses a large downtown office building, and enjoys every technical amenity and luxury one would find in a major corporation. Administrative expenses at MacArthur, particularly staff salaries, are high and have even been the subject of criticism for diverting too many resources to noncharitable purposes.[23] By creating multiple layers of professional staff to support its grantmaking work, the MacArthur Foundation and other large private foundations have succeeded in legitimizing themselves and making their decisions appear to be less a function of board interests and values and more a function of comprehensive and fair review by professional staff. To further ground its decision, staff at large private foundations interact regularly with grantseeking organizations. A chief responsibility of these staff is to say no far more often than yes and to do so in a way that appears fair and impartial and the product of careful professional review leading to a decision that is based on the merits.

There are countless examples of bureaucratization and professionalization within the world of large private foundations. The general move to professional staffing was discussed in some detail in chapter 3. At this point, it is important only to emphasize that many of the central tenets of neoinstitutionalism—the return to legitimacy as a central organizational problem, the emphasis on structural decoupling, and the tendency toward isomorphism within fields—have clear application to private foundations. While institutionalism has been criticized as seeing all organizational behavior as symbolic rather than purposeful, the theory remains a good tool for understanding the structure and practices of private foundations. As one of the few organizational forms that are forever resource independent, private foundations enjoy both the freedom that endowments provide as well as the buffering that shields these institutions from pressures to perform.

Connecting Theories

So far, philanthropy's four forms and functions have been neatly aligned with the four classic explanations of the behavior of organizations. While this approach has the merit of drawing out the central feature of each organizational form, it does obscure the connections that exist between the forms. Although the four types of foundations may appear substantially different in structure and in mission, a number of similarities actually exist. The association of a theory with a particular organizational form is limiting, in that it chooses to overlook the explanatory value of rival theories for each of the different forms. Thus, for example, resource dependence may well capture the most central assumption of community foundations, namely the need to attract resources from local donors. But community foundations also require legitimacy, in that the flow of contributions to the endowment is contingent on the foundation being perceived as fulfilling the community's interests. At the same time, community foundations in the same geographical region can be seen as locked in a competitive struggle with one another for a philanthropic niche. Community foundations define their missions in a variety of ways, each with a different target population of donors and each directed at building assets and increasing grants.

Similarly, corporate foundations also seek to build legitimacy, though not always for the sake of defending the privileges of tax exemption. Corporate philanthropy often simply attempts to make the corporate sponsor appear as a responsible member of the community, thereby legitimizing its profit-making activity. Another function of corporate giving is to build ties between local firms and the community in which they operate. Grants create dependence on corporate largesse within the grant-receiving community, a resource dependence that can be managed and shaped to a corporation's advantage. This dependence can create a reservoir of influence and goodwill that can be tapped at critical moments for the sponsoring company. Corporate philanthropy might well be driven by the fight for profitability that characterizes the business world, but there are in fact many drivers behind the impulse of companies to act charitably.

Operating foundations are best defined as a philanthropic form that emphasizes hierarchy over markets, but other perspectives can usefully be brought to bear. Because they do not disburse grants to outside organizations, operating foundations must be careful that their internal programs meet the test of tax exemption, namely that they fulfill a real charitable or educational mission. Elaborate public information and education campaigns are consequently quite common. Operating foundations also compete, in some sense, with other nonprofit organizations without endowments, but the life and death of the foundations do not hang in the balance during this competition. Operating foundations may be outdone by think tanks, research institutes, publishing houses, and universities, but they almost always carry on with their work because their endowments allow them to resist challenges from the market.

Finally, independent foundations are not one-dimensional mavens of legitimacy, which an excessive emphasis on neoinstitutional theory might have one believe. At times, private foundations attempt through their grants to restructure the nonprofit marketplace, encouraging hierarchy over markets when this is the most efficient way to achieve an end. By giving a small number of large grants in a particular programmatic area, private foundations frequently give a select group of nonprofit organizations the resources needed to dominate their field by bringing a broad range of services under a single organizational hierarchy. On the other hand, private foundations can encourage market competition by spreading their grants broadly and evenly across organizations working in a common area. This kind of philanthropy will breed specialization and competition within a broad range of nonprofit service providers. The decision whether to support markets or hierarchies is one of the most important ones that a foundation can make. While staff judgment plays an important role in this decision, the size of resources controlled by a foundation often determines how effective the effort will be. The larger the private foundation and the more grant money it has at its disposal, the easier it is for it to reinforce hierarchies and undermine markets. There is at least one other chink in the armor of institutional explanations of private foundations. While most organizations within this field are and have always been private foundations, the level of institutional isomorphism is far from perfect. Of the 60,000 foundations now in existence, over 90 percent are private foundations. The very existence of three alternate philanthropic forms—many of which were also caught up in the move to professionalize philanthropy—complicates this account by showing that convergence has not been complete.

In the end, the juxtaposition of organization theory and philanthropy may be a handy antidote to the current overabundance of historical studies of the evolution of organized giving. Looking at changes in society, in the nonprofit sector, and in the tax code, many researchers have provided credible accounts of why private foundations and operating foundations were created around the turn of the twentieth century, and why corporate foundations and community foundations emerged as major philanthropic players soon thereafter.[24] These accounts have drawn on a wide array of explanations, though most return to some broad historical trend, be it changing orientations in public policy, the sway of religious movements, or the growth of a new class of wealthy individuals in major cities. No matter how detailed these accounts have been in terms of historical facts, they have succeeded in illuminating only part of the picture. For the emergence and spread of philanthropic forms have not been driven exclusively by the convergence of social forces or events. The historian is ultimately ill equipped to explain the endurance of organizational forms over time. Drawing on the tools of organization theory, I have suggested that philanthropy's four main forms emerged and continue to find currency because each represents a different strategic response to a combination of internal management challenges and external demands.

Philanthropy's four main forms have emerged not simply because of the convergence of historical factors, but because each form has presented a strategic option that is more or less appealing, depending on a donor's philanthropic intent and resources. Over the past century, as individual donors have confronted the task of using their accumulated wealth for philanthropic purposes, three of the four organizational forms have been available. Depending on the breadth of their philanthropic intent and shaped by the amount of resources available, various paths have been chosen by donors. When they have put a premium on name recognition and lacked a single clear philanthropic intent, many have chosen to start private foundations. When their resources have not quite been sufficient to justify setting up a private foundation, many have made gifts to community foundations. When the charitable mission has been well defined and when it could best be pursued through foundation-administered programs, many donors have decided to create operating foundations. Corporations acting as donors have chosen to start corporate foundations for similarly strategic reasons, rather than administer an ad hoc giving program, when operations and profits have reached a certain level of size and stability.

The existence of four distinct organizational forms within philanthropy ultimately bodes well for the future of the field, at least when it comes to choices about institutional arrangements. The ability of these forms to cope with a variety of internal management challenges and external environmental pressures will ensure the long-term viability of the field, particularly if major individual donors continue to turn in large numbers to foundations to execute their long-term philanthropic visions. For as donors search for vehicles to fulfill their diverse intentions, the existence of philanthropy's four main forms ensures that a viable organizational solution will always be present. Choice among the main forms will be a function to some extent of the priorities and needs of the donors, and the match of the institutional structure to the donor's broader strategic direction.

Alternative Vehicles

One of the most popular variations on the four main institutional forms is the family foundation, which is identical to the private foundation with one major exception: it is governed by family members, and its goals include both grantmaking and the enactment and inculcation of values across generations.[25] The line between an independent foundation and a family foundation is nebulous, although it might be simplest to define a family foundation as an independent foundation in which the descendants of the founding donor control a majority of the board. Beyond this basic characteristic there are considerable differences between family foundations that are professionally staffed and managed, such as the Surdna Foundation in New York City, which is still controlled by the Andrus family ("Surdna" is "Andrus" spelled backwards),[26] and unstaffed family foundations that are run informally by a group of relatives who come together to talk about social issues and purposes.[27] One of the many arguments for family foundations is that they provide a vehicle for keeping relatives talking and working together, while also teaching the values of service and generosity. Donors are drawn to family foundations because they appear to be a tool for bridging differences, teaching about money, and building social consciences in the young.[28]

Not all plans for family unity and learning through philanthropy are realized. J. M. Kaplan founded the Kaplan Fund with little experience in philanthropy. He built up his fortune from nothing, eventually amassing over $100 million from his leadership of the Welch's grape juice corporation. Kaplan greatly admired families such as the Rockefellers that put their wealth to good use and trained its younger generation to do good. But by the account of his own heirs, Kaplan did not have a clear ideology of what he wanted his foundation to aggressively pursue. His grandson Matt Davidson, who served as executor of the estate, noted that if somebody came to Kaplan and he took a liking to that person, he would fund their project. Kaplan's giving was very much a direct response to an immediate impression. There was no real definition or program to the philanthropy. Kaplan's children and his grandchildren served on the fund's board but were plagued with the challenges of weak governance structures and an unclear programmatic mandate. After Kaplan passed away, the heirs to his fund have found it increasingly difficult to work together as they have moved away from New York and become attracted to diverse and contradictory causes.

When J. M. Kaplan gave up control of grant and program management in 1977, the leadership job went to one of his four children, Joan Davidson. She established the fund's long-term commitment to New York City "liveability." The Kaplan Fund has been widely recognized for signature initiatives in historic preservation, parks, and arts funding in New York. There was some dissension among Kaplan's children about Joan's strong leadership. Some complained that Kaplan put Joan in charge to offset her disappointment after losing a post in the state government. Joan's three siblings sat on the board of trustees but were reduced to rubber-stamping her decisions. As another generation of Kaplan's descendants became involved with the fund, the problem of a unified purpose worsened. The Kaplan Fund's mission was unclear from the start; to make matters worse, Kaplan gave mixed signals on his intent for the fund as he approached death. At times he talked about dissolving the foundation within ten years; at other times he told people that he could see the foundation going on forever as a way of preserving family unity. After Kaplan's death in 1987, the foundation started coming apart at the seams. Davidson gave up her role, and professional help was brought in to get the foundation back on track.

Divisions were hard to overcome. The board was eventually divided into two groups. One group consisted of J. M. Kaplan's four children. They were given control of 35 percent of the grant budget and could each make about $450,000 in grants annually. The second group consisted of the second generation of Kaplan heirs. They could make grants by consensus and also could each award up to $25,000 in Trustee Initiated Grants (TIG). If

Kaplan's intent as a donor was for the fund to bring his heirs into a working relationship and enforce family unity, then it has been a hopeless failure from the start. The first group of heirs has always been divided, and giving each of the four children their own funds to disburse has failed to bring any unity. The second generation briefly considered just splitting their annual budget eight ways to fund grants that they felt passionate about individually, but ultimately decided against individual grants in favor of consensus-based grants, spearheaded by the foundation staff, focusing primarily on their interpretation of the fund's main issue area, liveability in New York City. The ability of the members of this group to abandon their pet interests for the sake of coherence can be viewed as a victory for professional grant-making, but it did lead to general apathy among the younger generation. In the name of focus and impact, the group gave up their private passions and their ability to use philanthropy to act on their personal commitments and convictions. The result was that the fund had a credible program, but few of the board members were interested in it. As staff took on greater responsibilities, some board members lost interest in attending and thought the process was now out of their hands.

The Kaplan Fund's experience highlights the enduring tension between private values and public purposes. Being able to express and enact one's values is critical to donor satisfaction. This is what the first generation of Kaplans has chosen to do and all four family members seem quite satisfied with their philanthropy, even if the collective impact and significance of their giving is not readily apparent. The second generation has chosen to focus on the other half of the philanthropic equation, namely the orderly pursuit of meaningful public purposes. The younger Kaplans have not experienced the same level of satisfaction as the older generation in part because they have willingly sublimated their personal interests and passions in order to achieve a measure of professionalism, focus, and order. Family foundations are useful vehicles for donors to consider, although, as the Kaplan family's experience highlights, achieving some kind of strategic fit between private values and public purposes can be difficult when family dynamics and family issues are added to the already contentious issues of how to distribute charitable funds responsibly.[29]

Federations are another long-standing option to donors seeking a vehicle through which to carry out their giving. Ranging from the secular federations such as the United Way to the more religiously grounded ones such as the Jewish federations, donors seeking assistance in making the right choices about what causes to support have options that require very little effort. Federations will often approach donors through various campaigns and seek a contribution with the promise to disburse the funds raised to worthy causes and organizations. At the core of the federated giving model is the argument that funds pooled together can have a greater impact and that expert selection of recipient organizations can lead to greater community benefits. Federations also create a sense of solidarity among those who give, particularly in the workplace settings where the United Way, for example, focuses. Giving can become the norm and a friendly competition among groups to deliver the largest gift can emerge.

While this simple vehicle is appealing to smaller donors, it has fallen on somewhat harder times lately when it comes to major donors. The whole process of disintermediation, which swept through the financial industry and led to millions of individuals taking control of their own investments, has found a correlate in the world of philanthropy. Donors have begun to ask why they need such intermediaries as the federations to filter their giving. Shaken by a series of scandals involving mismanagement and fraud, the United Way has struggled in recent years to regain its footing and the confidence of donors. As donors in the United States have gotten more interested in controlling their own philanthropy, the United Way has turned to new markets in foreign countries to sustain its growth. For the Jewish federations, the challenge has been different. Many younger donors have come to view the federations as an artifact of their parents' philanthropic inclinations, one that is not in touch with the broader understanding that many younger Jewish donors have of what "Jewish philanthropy" really means.[30] For them, tikkun—the calling to heal and repair the world—involves just as much working in poor minority communities to address unemployment and inadequate housing as it does setting up Jewish day schools or supporting hospitals and schools in Israel.[31] The federations are thus caught in the difficult position of wanting to be a place where giving is made easy while also offering services that are in tune with the changing needs and interests of donors.[32] As a result, the federations are no longer viewed as the logical and inevitable vehicle through which young donors will make their gifts, and their claim of expert knowledge has been effectively challenged by a new generation of givers that is willing and interested in getting more engaged with philanthropic decision making.

Beyond the changes that are rippling through the world of federations, new forms have emerged in the institutional landscape of philanthropy, old forms have evolved, and the field has consistently sought to adapt to the needs of donors. One of the newest vehicles open to donors is the product of large mutual fund companies, which have become eager to meet not only their clients' investment needs but their philanthropic needs as well. Rather than sit idly by as philanthropic funds are transferred out of mutual fund accounts into family and community foundations, several large firms have established their own charitable organizations that act in many ways like community foundations, although they often offer reduced fees, practically no regulations, and less paperwork than many other vehicles. Gift funds have attracted billions of dollars in a very short period of time. One reason for their surging popularity is that they speak directly to the desire of donors to make their own charitable decisions. Gift funds simply take the names of the organizations submitted by donors, check their tax-exempt status, and then send a check in the amount specified by the donor. These funds typically operate with lower expenses than community foundations, a fact that has caused some in the foundation community to worry about this new competition. In many ways, gift funds represent a clear response to the desire of some donors for efficient support for philanthropy that focuses on the mechanics rather than the substance of giving. Gift funds also mirror the broader trend in the financial services industry toward disintermediation and the empowerment of the customer as chief decision maker and strategist.

The community foundation world has not greeted the emergence of this new vehicle warmly. In fact, for several years, leaders of the community foundation field lobbied and worked through the media in an attempt to close down these funds.[33] One reason the established community foundations felt threatened by the gift funds was the perceived lower costs associated with having a financial services company, not a nonprofit, administer a donor-advised fund. In fact, when Fidelity Investments' costs are compared to those of full-service community foundations, the comparisons are not always flattering. More significantly, the gift funds were a threatening development because they represented a complete repudiation of the idea that foundation professionals added value for the costs associated with them. The gift funds presented their services as a more efficient solution for donors seeking to make their own charitable decisions. The community foundation field was forced to go through some very extensive self-examination as huge amounts of funds flowed into these new accounts. Two questions emerge. The first was whether the market for a full-service community foundation with all its attendant costs was shrinking. The second was whether the donor population was turning away from unrestricted grants—that put decision making about community needs in the hands of professional staff—toward a model that emphasized donor control. In many ways, these questions continue to reflect some of the most important and unresolved issues in contemporary philanthropy writ large.[34]

Gift funds are but one alternative to the conventional community foundation. Native American tribes have experimented with another alternative. Because Native Americans have a deep-rooted philosophy of sharing community resources, a tradition of only taking what is needed, and strong ties among tribe members,[35] the community foundation model has long appeared to be a good fit for their culture. Most tribal foundations have 501(c)(3) status and are independent of the tribal councils, albeit with primary support and oversight from members of the tribe. Cultural and regulatory boundaries around philanthropy remain daunting, and some tribes have chosen to go in an entirely different direction and eschew the standard legal structure of conventional community foundations. For example, the Cowcreek Umpqua Indian Foundation, which is incorporated under tribal law—not under any IRS classification—devotes its grantmaking mostly to education and youth development in the seven counties of Oregon occupied by Cowcreek lands. The vast majority of its grants go to nonnative organizations. Despite forgoing federal recognition, the tribe has been forced to follow the guidelines of a state compact requiring that 6 percent of net profits from gaming enterprises be given away to charity. The Cowcreek Band of Umpqua Indians resisted the trend of incorporating their community foundation as a public charity because of an aversion to federal regulation. In so doing, the Umpqua demonstrated that not all forms of institutional giving need to take place within the narrow confines of the standard institutional options with which most donors are comfortable. It is possible to operate through an institutional vehicle that is not part of the mainstream philanthropic menu of institutions.[36]

For donors not wanting to place their funds into any kind of institutional resting place on the way to disbursal, a range of intermediary institutions for channeling funds directly to causes have emerged. The philanthropic landscape has seen the emergence of a host of new Internet-based virtual foundations that connect causes to donors.[37] One example of a charitable cause finding its way to a new audience is Trees for Life, an environmental project located in Beijing, Sichuan, Hebei, and other cities and towns in China. How does a small nonprofit in China connect with donors around the world? The answer lies in the Internet. Environmental donors can make their gifts through the Virtual Foundation, which encourages small-scale giving by individuals in support of grassroots projects in the fields of environment, health, and sustainable development. The Web site is a way for nonprofits around the world to showcase their work for donors. Though the gifts are often small, the Virtual Foundation allows for otherwise improbable connections between donors and nonprofits. The Virtual Foundation is a project of ECOLOGIA (Ecologists Linked for Organizing Initiatives and Action), an organization that provides technical support and training to grassroots environmental efforts worldwide. Given its global perspective, ECOLOGIA is also able to connect individuals and organizations that might share information and resources to improve their local efforts. The Virtual Foundation allows donors to take advantage of ECOLOGIA's global network of grassroots environmentalism. Projects seeking funding through the Virtual Foundation must first meet with the approval of a local intermediary organization—there are thirty worldwide—that recommends projects to the Virtual Foundation. Once the Virtual Foundation approves a project, it is posted on the Web site with a description and budget. The ultimate screening process, of course, is left to the donor who chooses to contribute. For a donor interested in making a small gift to a local organization in another part of the world, the Virtual Foundation model is ideal.

The Internet offers some important advantages in terms of breadth of exposure and the capacity to link people who would otherwise not be able to find each other. Research has shown that one of the principal reasons people give is that someone asks them to. Internet-based giving allows a larger number of smaller organizations to gain access to donors that would otherwise be difficult to reach. For donors comfortable with technology and who enjoy using the Internet, virtual foundations are an appealing intermediary. There are some real limitations in terms of the depth of interaction that is possible with this model, however. In the absence of someone playing the role of independent arbiter, some donors will surely find it hard to trust information that is simply set forward on a Web site by an organization or cause with which they are not already familiar. In fact, direct Internet giving—making a donation directly through the organizational Web site of a charity—is popular primarily because it facilitates a streamlined transaction that donors have already decided to make. Virtual foundations are an attempt to do more than just render philanthropic giving more efficient; they have the added goal of bringing new causes to the attention of donors. The success of this process is conditional, to a substantial extent, on the comfort level of the donor with the quality of the independent screening that determines which organizations make it onto the Web pages of virtual foundations.

While the Virtual Foundation seeks very small contributions to support small projects around the world, other groups, like the Acumen Fund, seek much larger commitments. The Acumen Fund adopts many of the principles of venture capitalism and applies them to the world of international grantmaking. It seeks partners who will give—or "invest"—$100,000 in one of several grantmaking portfolios, including health technology, economic development, and water resources. Using expert advisors in these fields, the fund selects and profiles a small group of projects that meet a set of criteria including whether the project meets an unmet need, has an innovative approach with the potential for broad impact, has strong leadership, and has a plan for long-term sustainability. Its work includes the distribution of long-lasting antimalaria bed nets in Africa, the building of affordable housing in Pakistan, and the implementation of new drip irrigation systems in India. Contributors to the fund get regular updates on the progress of the projects they have chosen to support and access to special events and travel opportunities to visit the supported projects. The fund charges donors a fee of 10 percent of their contributions for these services. The Acumen Fund thus has features of a virtual foundation, a community foundation, and a membership organization.

Donors do not come together just to get the best possible expert advice to guide their philanthropy. Sometimes they seek out a connection related to philanthropy with broader purposes in mind. One such multipurpose group, Mama Cash, was founded in the Netherlands; it seeks to protect and expand women's rights and opportunities across the globe. With individual and foundation support, the group invests in women-initiated projects to protect women from violence, promote women's art, support economic equality, fight homophobia, and work for peace. Five women started Mama Cash in 1983 as an expressly radical funding organization. One Mama Cash initiative, called Women with Inherited Wealth, is a network of female inheritors in the Netherlands. The operating assumptions of the effort are that money that one inherits is not the same as money that one earns and that often there are conditions attached to inherited wealth. To overcome these obstacles, the organization assists women to safely navigate their way through what they see as a male-dominated, conservative financial world. The goal of this network is to increase the self-confidence of women so that they can take full responsibility for their inherited wealth and to encourage them to use their inheritance in a socially responsible manner. This approach to educating donors is about more than helping women make smart philanthropic decisions. The feminist perspective of Women with Inherited

Wealth assumes that a woman faces inherent obstacles when dealing with money and that philanthropy can be a tool to explore one's values and set a life direction.[38]

There are other new vehicles that have emerged with even more distinctive assumptions about what donors really want. Giving circles—local clubs in which donors act as one in doing philanthropy—are based on the belief that there are donors seeking a vehicle that will embed giving in the process of forging social ties among individuals. They are particularly attractive to donors who want company as they make their philanthropic journeys. Typically, such groups are local coalitions and networks of individuals that support local causes. The Hestia Fund in Boston, for example, is a group of women that seeks to pool funds and work together to find worthwhile projects. With an evolving membership of about forty members each giving $5,000, the group works with charities in and around the Boston area so that participants can see firsthand how their funds are used.

With the launch of the Engaged International Philanthropy Program (EIPP), however, the concept of the giving circle was applied globally. The EIPP is an effort by the Clarence Foundation, a Bay Area philanthropy that supports innovative nonprofits across the globe in areas including education, health, and human rights. The foundation recruits ten to fifteen donors to join a giving circle; each participant is asked to commit $3,500 and attend eight meetings over one year. The approach emphasizes "engagement" throughout the project, and participants will review proposals, communicate with prospective grantees, and decide which groups will receive funding. The Clarence Foundation has teamed up with Ashoka, an international nonprofit focused on supporting social entrepreneurs, Grantmakers Without Borders, an affinity group interested in international giving, and other partner organizations in order to identify potential grantees and educate the donors. In addition to attracting new dollars to global giving, the EIPP seeks to leverage those dollars by combining donor education with the hands-on process of group grantmaking. The group meetings include presentations by leaders in the field of global philanthropy.

There will always be donors who do not want to transfer their assets all at once, or at the expense of providing support to family members or other beneficiaries needing income. Donors seeking some combination of income and estate tax reduction have a range of planned giving options open to them. When Jacqueline Kennedy Onassis died, much of her estate went into a charitable lead trust, which permitted both her heirs and the selected charities to receive a significantly larger portion of her estate than would otherwise have been possible because of estate taxes. The benefits of a charitable trust are not limited, however, to the glamorous and the affluent. Charitable trusts can be important vehicles for accomplishing more modest philanthropic objectives. They permit an individual to make substantial gifts to a favorite charitable organization without giving up all rights over the property either currently or at a later time. Through a charitable trust, an individual can make an irrevocable future gift to a charity and still claim a current income tax deduction for the gift.

Trusts are often the product of both careful estate planning and the pursuit of charitable purposes. Charitable trusts come in two main forms: the charitable lead trust and the charitable remainder trust. The mechanics of these trusts are fairly straightforward. A charitable lead trust delivers a stream of income for a set period of years to the designated nonprofit organization. When the period is over, the property held in trust returns to the donor or to a beneficiary designated by the donor. The operating principle is thus one of giving away funds over time resulting in a tax-advantaged transfer of the remaining assets at a later date. Under a charitable lead trust, the donor receives an immediate federal income tax deduction when making the gift, equal to the present value of the future income stream. The donor is taxed each year, however, on the value of the income interest that is payable to the charity. A donor may set up a charitable lead trust while alive or at death through instructions in a will, with the assets returning years later to the heirs the donor designates. There are other options for the donor seeking both a vehicle for giving and a solution to some of the vexing estate tax issues many individuals face. A charitable remainder trust allows a stream of income to reach the donor for a specified period of time, which is often defined as the donor's lifetime. At the conclusion of this time period, a gift of the assets is made to a charity.

Whether donors commit to family foundations, select gift funds operated by investment houses, use the Internet to reach out and find causes, connect with others through giving circles, or decide to work through the use of trusts, there can be little doubt that philanthropy provides an ample array of options. In evaluating the many vehicles available, donors need to pay special attention to the mission that is being pursued, the appropriate time frame for the giving, and the grantmaking style sought by the donor. Selecting the appropriate structure through which to give requires a conscious effort aimed at overall fit and alignment. While choosing an appropriate philanthropic vehicle must be integrated into the broader task of setting a coherent philanthropic direction, it is still possible to clarify a couple of the key considerations that go into choosing a vehicle before this choice is subject to the rigors of being aligned with the broader purposes being pursued.

One way to think about the many options available to donors is to array the institutional landscape of philanthropy along two major dimensions of concern to donors: the specificity of the mission to be pursued and the amount of donor resources available for philanthropy (see figure 7.1). These two considerations will of course vary greatly from donor to donor. Some donors have a very precise idea of what they want to accomplish, while others will have only the most general and ill-defined philanthropic objectives. Some donors will have immense fortunes to disburse, while others will only have modest amounts of funds available.

In surveying this space and the options contained therein, donors face a number of challenges. The first is that their philanthropic intentions may not be static, but instead may be highly dynamic. In fact, it is likely that over time the donor's interest will evolve as time passes. Sometimes the progression will be from wide open and undefined to precise and narrow purposes as events and personal interests evolve. Many major donors have spent the vast majority of their time and effort building successful businesses and have not really been able to focus on the question of what issues and causes excite their passions. Philanthropy can be something that is sprung upon them without much context or preparation. One donor likes to tell the story of working so hard at a software start-up business that he

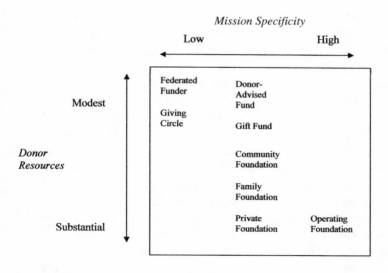

Figure 7.1 **Selected institutional options for individual donors.**

was stunned to learn when looking at the receipt from an ATM that his personal checking account had $6 million in it. Up until then, he knew he was making money and the account was the place the money was landing, but he had no real sense of the scale. Over time, as the amount escalated quickly, especially after the sale of the company, the entrepreneur knew it was time to find some real productive use for these funds and has thrown himself into philanthropy as a full-time occupation. Some donors think about philanthropy a lot while making money and have strong opinions from the outset, but then lose interest once the reality of seeking to address a particularly difficult social problem becomes clearer through philanthropic experience. For these donors, philanthropic focus can go from very clear to nebulous in a short period of time. The problem with either of these natural shifts is that they can confound and render problematic the choice of philanthropic institution. And it may not be just the underlying purposes and objectives that change; it can be the time frame or personal style of the donor, or some other factors.

One way to address the challenge of achieving fit and alignment between vehicle and philanthropic purposes is for donors to have multiple vehicles at their disposal. While there are some considerations related to ease of use, overhead expense, and resource dispersal, donors can call on multiple vehicles to meet their complex interests and needs. Thus, a donor may want to take part in a giving circle in order to enjoy the benefits of peer learning and network building, while also having a donor-advised fund in a community or family foundation. Or a donor may set up a private foundation to make grants in a particular field or area with the benefit of advice and counsel from staff and other trustees, but also choose to have a gift fund at a brokerage house in order to support a favorite set of charities. Vehicles for giving do not require exclusive commitments, and they can be used in combination to create a portfolio of instruments.[39]

Nevertheless, one important consideration arises: philanthropic vehicles, particularly with private and operating foundations, tend to be harder to alter than any of the other elements of the philanthropic prism. Changing the stated mission of a private foundation dramatically from what is spelled out in the original filings can be an expensive and time-consuming matter, demanding expert legal advice and even the consent of state charity regulators. While it has certainly been accomplished, such efforts at mission redefinition must usually first demonstrate that the original mission is impractical, inefficient, or impossible to accomplish. Because of the safeguards set up to protect the intent of the donor after funds are placed into foundations, many donors define their philanthropic intentions in very broad terms when creating a perpetual foundation, even when they have a good sense of the direction they want to pursue in the short run. Legal barriers are not the only difficulties entailed in changes in missions of perpetual foundations; just as significant is the problem of placating nonprofit organizations and other stakeholders following a change in focus that renders existing grantees ineligible for future funding. Mission changes in foundations create winners, losers, and strife.

It is not only the mission or focus of a donor that can change and lead to second thoughts about institutional choices. Donors may change their minds about the amount of involvement they want, or the donor's family may have a very different level of interest than the donor in the actual disbursal of funds. In Chicago, the descendents of pharmaceuticals magnate Gideon D. Searle eventually sued the Chicago Community Trust in order to get greater control over the actual choice of causes that the family's $250 million trust would support. While the founder thought a community foundation an appropriate and a good fit with his philanthropic interests, those who followed did not and sought successfully through a three-year legal battle to get a modification that would allow the family greater say in what kinds of grants are made. There have been many other instances in which changes of heart have occurred in the opposite direction, instances in which donors have started off believing that they want to bring to philanthropy the same level of deep engagement and involvement that characterized their work in the business sector, only to learn through experience that a very different and less engaged philanthropic style is appropriate. For these donors, creating an operating foundation requiring large amounts of hands-on work can be a major false step and an albatross that must be worn around the neck for years before it is finally shed.

While almost all the mistakes donors make related to their choice of vehicles for their giving are reversible, there can be little doubt that when committing to an institutional arrangement for one's philanthropy, it may be wise to have much of the broader strategic mix well defined. And while it is possible to enter the philanthropic prism through the hurdle of institutional selection, such a strategy may have real costs if the other elements of strategic giving have not been given careful attention. With little reason to make this kind of commitment quickly and with much flexibility preserved by direct giving, donors need to locate a compelling and lasting rationale for a decision to shift to a philanthropic vehicle or combination of vehicles. While there can be peer pressure in elite circles to either form a family foundation or to set up a donor-advised fund or even to join a giving circle, these sorts of commitments should never be driven by trends or concern over appearances. Commitments to philanthropic vehicles need to be made carefully and with as much information as possible about the donor's broader philanthropic objectives and preferences. Only when the vehicle of choice for giving is well fitted to the mission that is selected, the kind of change that will be pursued, the donor's own identity, and a defensible time frame will the move to institutional giving contribute to rather than detract from the ability of donors to produce value through their giving.

8. Giving Styles

If philanthropy were purely science, then the task of the donor would be largely a technical one, consisting of learning the rules and laws governing giving, studying the key tools and systems needed to get from charitable intent to desired social results, and then simply applying all this knowledge to the resolution of human hardships. This is obviously not the case, and the field of philanthropy is better off because of it. Philanthropy cannot be reduced to a narrow set of technocratic directives or even to a single set of prescriptive claims. In its natural form, philanthropy is full of art and personality, bursting with idiosyncratic visions, unsupported claims, and deeply held passions. The great mistake that many donors have made is to aspire to turn their giving into something purely efficient, precise, and consistent. The impulse to strive for a more scientific approach, I argued earlier, has been aided and abetted by the rise of a class of professional grantmakers in the foundation segment of the field, who have sought to normalize and rationalize giving. In the vast majority of large private foundations, the donor is no longer living, and the professionals carrying out the grantmaking do not feel authorized to insert their own values, but instead attempt to interpret fairly and neutrally the mission that has been given to them—all with an eye to maximizing public benefits. One of the recurring themes in this book has been that professionalization in philanthropy is problematic because it saps giving of the critical expressive dimension that makes it an original contributor to the public debate.

Not all of philanthropy has been neutralized and homogenized. There are still many philanthropic principals who have not delegated the work of giving to agents. The many purposes pursued by individual donors and the multiple logic models they concoct are testament to the field's capacity for pluralism and diversity. No part of the landscape of philanthropy, however, is as diverse as the giving styles of individual donors. The history of American philanthropy is full of colorful characters including religiously motivated helpers, politically connected operators, scoundrels from the world of business and finance, unapologetic egomaniacs and self-promoters, safety-seeking incrementalists, restless social innovators, and quiet but curious thinkers. What is stunning about the huge field of principal-led giving, filled with people attempting for one reason or another to accomplish some philanthropic purpose, is the sheer diversity of the backgrounds, belief systems, and basic identities.[1] Although it would be tempting to believe that the act of giving cleanses and reinvents those who choose to engage in it, in reality philanthropy more often than not simply magnifies and transposes the personal characteristics of the donor into a new and usually more public domain than was the case before the decision to give was reached. Philanthropy brings out the latent personality traits of individuals and provides a channel to connect commitments to causes.[2]

Giving is public, while motives are private. While the goal here is to spell out the many different styles of philanthropic giving and to connect this element to the broader challenge of crafting a coherent strategy, it is useful to explore briefly the issue of motives and determinants of giving, if for no other reason than that it is helpful in framing the breadth of personalities and intentions that crowd the field. Although it is always easier to think about and analyze philanthropic deeds than about philanthropic motives, there is an important part of giving that can be understood only by looking beneath the surface. The multiple explanations of the motives for giving produced by social scientists over the years render more comprehensible the huge array of philanthropic styles.

Motives and Ethics

While comparatively little has been written to date of the nature of philanthropic strategy, there is a sizable literature across the social sciences on philanthropic motivations, which range from caring and moral obligation all the way to a desire to reduce exposure to personal income taxes.[3] Most of what we know about giving indicates that no matter what drives giving, it is clear that most giving proceeds from a mix of interacting motives that shape not only the decision to give but also the cause to be supported and the manner of the giving.

Understanding why individuals choose to engage in giving requires a general explanation that takes into account both the supply of and the demand for philanthropic funds. The demand side brings the needs of people to the attention of those who can supply the resources necessary to meet those needs. From a small contribution made on the spur of the moment based on perceived need to a large gift driven by considerable study and a full needs assessment, philanthropy connects social demand with the supply of private resources. The supply side is driven by the individual's desire to engage in helping behavior and by the presence of funds that can be directed to giving.[4] Clearly, the simple existence of an authentic public need does not, in itself, always, or even usually, create a response in the form of an activation of the supply of philanthropic resources. After all, individual charitable giving requires that donors purposively shift their preference away from other possible uses of their resources toward the one that is presented to them by those seeking a contribution. In this sense, the chief task of the fund-raiser is to help donors see the attraction of shifting their preferences so that they give. When the demand for and supply of philanthropic funds do intersect and find common ground, the connection will be powerfully felt by both sides and giving will likely ensue.[5]

What then moves donors closer to placing themselves in a position where demand and supply will have a chance to converge? There are several specific factors that motivate people to be more charitably inclined and to be open to charitable appeals. Psychological, sociological, and economic studies have pointed out three broad factors that appear to be important in the determination of whether people will act in a charitable way. From the perspective of each of the disciplines, these factors relate to (1) the individual's personal values and inclinations, usually conceived as being altruistic and embedded in complex psychological frameworks that draw individuals toward helping behavior; (2) the presence of broad social norms and expectations that together constitute the environment within which individuals operate; and (3) the more direct economic considerations that drive and result from philanthropic activity. While the activation of these different factors cannot *guarantee* that charitable giving will take place, they can and do increase the probability that giving will occur. These drivers will also help predict the kind of philanthropy donors will practice and the missions they will chose to focus on.

When psychologists attempt to explain giving, they gravitate to analyses of the different mental states or frames of mind that lead individuals to charitable and helping behavior. Research into the psychological determinants of charitable giving has variously isolated personal characteristics, deeply held values, and beliefs that are common among givers. One approach has sought to isolate three core characteristics that lead to helping the behavior of individuals. The first is empathy, which involves recognizing and opening oneself to others' needs.[6] The second is obligation, which stems from a commitment to moral rules that often result in a feeling of wanting to help other people. Both of these characteristics are important motivators of helping behavior. The most important characteristic, however, is what researchers have termed *prosocial value orientation*, which simply refers to feeling positively about being part of a community, group, or collectivity. This means seeing oneself not as an isolated being, but one who is connected to others and who derives meaning from these attachments. Having lots of social capital or personal ties to others thus turns out to be critical to feeling inclined to give. And being embedded in a network of relations also naturally influences the style that the giver will eventually adopt when giving.[7]

Another common starting point in explaining how and why people give is the concept of altruism.[8] Not surprisingly, the degree to which individuals have altruistic feeling shapes their charitable behavior. For the altruist, giving can be a form of expression that is activated by the individual's values and concerns about other people's well-being.[9] Even though there are strong arguments in favor of altruism as a potential source of motivation for helping behavior, there is, in the end, no clear evidence that the underlying motivation in much of philanthropy is altruistic.[10] In place of the reassuring idea of a caring and socialized giver simply seeking to help others, the alternative school of research starts with the more hardened assumption that individuals are, for the most part, self-centered and self-interested. That is, they value others only *instrumentally* and care for their welfare only to the degree that it affects their own well-being. On this account, individuals are capable of caring for the welfare of others only because it makes givers feel good about themselves.[11] For those skeptical of the idea of altruism, psychology has created a threefold typology that categorizes the motives for helping behavior in more self-interested terms, including "aversive-arousal reduction" in which the individual finds that helping others in distress relieves their own distress; "punishment avoidance," in which the individual is moved to help in order to avoid the feeling of guilt or embarrassment; and "reward seeking," in which helping leads to personal gratification.[12] None of these conditions requires that givers care for anyone other than themselves. Recipients of philanthropy become means to the donors' own self-serving ends.[13]

In the real world of practice, it is ultimately difficult to ascertain whether these egoistic explanations are correct and exhaustive in explaining philanthropy. The psychological research on giving thus leaves one with an enigma that is really not amenable to resolution. The arguments put forth in defense of "social egoism" claim that helping a person in need is a means to the ultimate end of donor gratification.[14] The donor in this account will want recognition and will seek out a level of engagement that will meet his or her personal psychic needs. The argument for altruism, on the other hand, posits that the intentions of givers cannot be questioned merely because they may reap some benefits as a result of seeking to help others.[15] A belief in pure altruism can help us understand why some donors may keep a distance between themselves and those they support, and why some donors choose to operate in complete anonymity, not wanting any recognition or attention for their acts of generosity.

Thoughts and feelings can lead individuals to giving as a form of commitment and action in the name of a cause. The move from psychological framework to charitable action is often shaped by the additional impetus of religion, political ideology, and social norms. There is no sharp demarcation between what donors do because of their "framework of consciousness" and what they do because of their membership or participation in groups or communities. Hence, it is hardly surprising that a parallel body of research and theory has focused on the social and cultural factors that drive philanthropy in conjunction with the many complex psychological factors that are at play.

Like most behavior, giving, and how much is given, is subject to social norms and expectations. Philanthropy is often both public and personal. Rarely do donors give to causes about which they care little or to which they have no personal connection. Giving typically takes donors, often from relative obscurity, and places them squarely in the public arena. The choice of a purpose or cause and the decision to give represent a declaration by at least one person of what public needs are. With the stakes set high, there are social expectations about giving and helping behavior that, depending on the context, can be relatively light or extremely strong. These pressures may reflect the individual's desire to fit in and find acceptance, all of which reflects the normative influences of friends, family, and other significant associates who are themselves likely to be givers.

Normative altruism, as some have termed it, is controlled by social rewards and punishments. Potential givers may want to or be obliged to help, in order to conform to social norms, or to fit into the reference group. Helping may also provide an opportunity to expand one's social network and access new social opportunities. By giving, donors can buy entrée into social groups and communities that have social prestige, political power, or business ties.[16] The decision to give and the amount given may be shaped by seeing other people engage in charity and the awareness of a social norm connected to the behavior. In many situations, the failure to give does carry a significant and negative distinction, the burden of norm violation, and the need for justification of not having maintained a minimum obligation that people expect of one another. Moreover, the decision of how much to give can also be shaped by the norms for the social groups within which donors find themselves. This fact is most evident in elite circles in which the amount that is given often serves as a form of "social reproduction," a way of reinforcing one's class position and maintaining one's social power. In such cases, donors do not need to feel empathy for the recipient in order to be motivated to give. Giving is driven by the potent desire to announce and project publicly one's social position and power.

While researchers have found potent effects of elite networks on giving,[17] studies have also found that membership in nonhierarchical groups may lead individuals to trust one another, which in turn leads them to be more charitable and civic minded. Positive interaction with others outside the personal sphere, and engagement in shared work and activity, is likely to lead to additional forms of engagement, including charitable giving. Membership creates familiarity and bonds of reciprocity within which the individual is made aware of needs that require response. Additionally, it is more likely that the individual or group will be asked to give in highly socialized settings, and being asked to give is a critical determinant of giving. Many appeals for support entail direct requests for contributions of time or money from friends and acquaintances who share common values and concerns. Being asked to contribute by someone known personally, or by a representative of an organization in which the individual is a member, is a major driver of giving. One prominent form of this type of socialized giving is exchange philanthropy; individuals give to a cause at the request of an associate in anticipation that in the future they would be able to call upon the associate to contribute to their own cause. In this system of logrolling, individuals, located in networks of friends or associates, feel free to call upon others to support a favored cause or project knowing that the favor may need to be returned in the future. In such cases, it is not the needs or demands of beneficiaries that motivate philanthropy, but rather the web of social ties that shape individual charitable behavior and the desire of individuals to be seen as contributing their fair share.

One thing is clear about giving: the propensity to give increases as social status increases. Education is a key determinant of income and an important determinant of charitable giving as well. Research has documented time and again that rates of volunteering are higher among college graduates, married persons, and people living in higher-income households who are employed and who own homes. One explanation for the link between social position and volunteering is that status brings with it networks of acquaintances, and networks bring a greater likelihood of being asked to volunteer. Similar forces are at work when it comes to giving, which suggests that giving is not a spontaneous behavior that occurs in a vacuum, but rather an activity that is socially conditioned. Personal identification with causes may be the catalyst for giving, but the catalyst for identification is association.[18] Many empirical studies have established that people who volunteer as youths are more likely to volunteer as adults. This reflects the formative impact of the environment surrounding early other-regarding behavior.[19]

Social conditions shaping giving include the myriad of formal and informal communities of participation in which donors learn about people in need and come to identify with them. It is not surprising that the greatest portion of giving and volunteering takes place within a donor's own community and helps support activities with which the donor is directly associated. This means that the basis for giving and volunteering is in large part a function of the network of formal and informal associations in which the donor is situated.[20] Differences in levels of giving of time and money are due to more than differences in income, wealth, gender, and race. These factors may shape, however, the networks within which individuals find themselves, which are critical. Put differently, when it comes to explaining how and why people give, differences are rarely a function of differences in financial capital or even moral capital, but rather the intensity of *associational capital,* which takes the form of social networks and close identification with causes.[21]

If the links between association and identification and giving are clear,[22] that still leaves a number of complex cultural factors to be reckoned with. A very significant source of norms relating to giving is found in religion.[23] The causes that donors select and the way they go about supporting their chosen causes are deeply conditioned by religious conviction. Religious organizations not only teach compassion but they also mobilize congregational members to take on charitable activities to help the needy. All major religions teach their members to care for others. Religious ties also help members to construct situation-specific personal norms, both by encouraging them to internalize values of justice and compassion and by explicitly connecting such values to helping behavior. One important way in which religious organizations give personal meaning to abstract ideals of compassion is through telling stories and parables and other examples of selfless behavior, which have the effect of mobilizing members to help the poor.[24] Once the values of justice and charity are linked to helping people in need, a person who wishes to maintain a positive self-image may find it difficult to ignore the pull of religious communities. When a church or community organization tells its members about specific needs, the members learn that potential recipients depend on them, and this knowledge activates the norm of social responsibility. Religious teachings are often directed at moving individuals to apply the values of justice and charity to problems in the community.[25] The process of helping others through charity is not a one-way street, however; the more a person identifies with a cause or need, the more acting increases the vicarious rewards that are experienced.

Religion affects behavior not only through the teaching of values that promote helping behavior, but also through the institutional arrangements of congregations and the interaction of people and communities that these institutions foster. Religious congregations establish the context that moves members to improve community services through volunteering and giving. While there is some disagreement over the degree to which affiliation with religious organizations encourages helping/charitable behavior in general, much of the research holds that people begin by volunteering and giving for the benefit of the religious organization and move on to being charitable towards other causes.[26] Membership and participation in religious organizations provide people with information about who the needy are and how to help them, and religious leaders also make direct demands for volunteers, raise people's consciousness, press people to implement their values, and provide them with opportunities to do so.[27]

Psychological and sociological explanations of giving are critical for filling in part of the huge black box that is the concept of philanthropic motives. However, economics has something important to say about this topic, as usual. The economists have taken a more materialistic view of the process of giving, emphasizing the importance of services and commodities that individual donors obtain from the provision of public goods supported by charitable donations.[28] While the dominant economic perspective on giving is one that takes it to be a form of consumption, a few economists have recognized that altruism plays some role in the giving process and have attempted to account for it in their analysis. The main thrust of the economic perspective is that giving may arise out of some tangible or immediate benefit to the giver. In contrast to altruism, the model of reciprocal giving requires that a consideration be offered in return. According to this view, people act charitably for the same reason they buy insurance or equities: giving brings the benefit of a potential return even if not clearly specified at the time the initial gift is given.

Sometimes the return that donors realize is the recognition granted by the recipient organizations in the form of a name placed on a plaque or building. The return can be in the form of an invitation to serve on an influential nonprofit board. Or it can be something as petty as an invitation to a special gala celebration where good food and conversation can be had. From the economic perspective, donors are buying something when they give, although the nature of the purchase varies considerably. The extent to which self-interest lies behind philanthropic activity is difficult to fully gauge accurately, but there can be no doubt that donors often do benefit through the making of business contacts and the receipt of favorable publicity in return for their charity. Having a library, park, or classroom named after the donor can be viewed as simply public philanthropy. By the same token, it can also be viewed as the acceptance of a reward for making a donation, and a form of consumption.

Governments have historically supported philanthropy through a variety of means, one of which is a set of incentives designed to encourage private philanthropy through special provisions of the tax system. The U.S. income tax has provided incentives for private philanthropy by allowing people to deduct charitable gifts from their gross income. This deduction is widely thought to encourage giving because it decreases the amount of other consumption people must forgo at the margin. For those individuals and households who itemize their deductions on their personal income tax returns, the net cost of donating a dollar is one minus the marginal tax rate. This arrangement is thought to lead to an increase in charitable giving as the tax rate rises.[29] To measure the incentive effect of the tax deduction, a spate of empirical studies have modeled giving by individuals.[30] The studies measure the elasticity of demand for giving with respect to tax-defined "price" of giving. If one were to generalize, empirical studies have found that giving is income inelastic but somewhat price elastic.[31]

It is important to make a distinction between deciding to engage in giving and how much money or resources to donate. It is tempting to assume that an individual's decision about how much to give is driven by the same factors that determine whether or not to give. Research has shown, however, that this is not the case.[32] Several studies reveal that income, for example, has no real effect on the decision to give, but has a significant effect on the size of the donation once the decision to give has been made. Furthermore, an individual's level of altruism or caring about others positively influences the decision to give, but has no real effect on the size of the donation. In considering the multiple and competing psychological, social, and economic explanations of charitable behavior, it is therefore important to examine separately how each factor may or may not lead an individual to give something and how each factor may or may not determine the size and nature of the gift.

While psychologists, sociologists, and economists have devoted considerable time to the study of what leads people to give, there are still some difficult and unclear questions lurking around the issue of philanthropic motivations. While social scientists are naturally drawn to descriptive and explanatory work that helps model and predict behavior, there is something missing in this approach. One of the most obvious questions set aside by psychologists, sociologists, and economists is whether there are good and bad motives for giving or, put differently, whether motivations really matter. Normative claims about motives may ultimately be difficult to define with any real precision, but they may turn out to be important in understanding the consequences and implications of different approaches to giving. Asking whether there are any normative claims to be made about giving can be challenging, in that it opens up a whole set of complex questions related to human intentions that may not be readily answerable.

These normative questions move the discussion clearly out of the realm of social science and into the domain of ethics. There are countless ways in which the ethical dimensions of philanthropy could be analyzed, and many different ethical and moral philosophy traditions could be brought to bear on the subject. I will simply choose one of the very earliest attempts to wrestle with these issues, which highlights how the motives and ethics of giving may intersect. The twelfth-century philosopher Moses Maimonides described giving as having eight levels, each with different moral consequences. Starting at the bottom with the lowest form of charity and moving up to higher and more righteous forms of giving, these levels are: (1) giving reluctantly; (2) giving cheerfully but not sufficiently; (3) giving cheerfully and sufficiently but only after being asked; (4) giving cheerfully and sufficiently and without being asked, but to put the gift in the recipient's hand in a way that makes him feel ashamed; (5) not knowing the identity of the recipient of one's gift, but letting others know the giver's identity; (6) knowing the identity of the recipients of one's giving, but remaining unknown; (7) giving in such a way that neither the donor nor the recipient knows the other's identity; and (8) working with others in partnerships or making loans in order to allow others to provide for themselves and to live independently. Maimonides' examination of Jewish law led him to organize the tradition's perspectives and directives into this graded hierarchy of *tzedakah*, from the least to the most praiseworthy and righteous forms of giving, and to conclude that the motives and methods of giving matter considerably.[33]

Beyond this early emphasis on a hand up over a hand out, a theme that would reappear centuries later as the centerpiece of American scientific philanthropy's flight from charity, what is intriguing about this ladder of giving is that the ranking is based on the way giving affects both the recipient and the donor. The ladder places significant weight on secrecy both in giving and getting. The tradition of anonymous and blind giving in which the giver's and recipient's identities are hidden throughout harks back to the form of charity in which the wealthy would secretly place funds in the courtyard of a temple and the poor would secretly take what they needed from this place, or to the giving that is mediated through a donation box that connects givers and recipients but does not let either party know the other. Maimonides differentiates between types of giving based on the degree of separation maintained between gift givers and recipients because of two factors. First, the more contact there is between the two sides, the more humiliation the recipient will likely experience.[34] Second, anonymous giving ensures that the donor's motives are pure and that the giving does not proceed from motives other than altruism. In some ways, the ladder is an attempt to wrestle with some of the complex problems that are raised by the presence of multiple motives in philanthropy. By privileging anonymous giving, Maimonides points to the problems that arise when donors act out of anything other than a desire to help. When donors try to get more directive when they attempt to make a connection with the persons they are helping, the result is only pain and humiliation for the recipient who must look his benefactor in the eye.

Maimonides' interest in keeping donors and recipients apart has been realized to some extent by the rise of the nonprofit sector. With professionals in service agencies doing the fund-raising and working with clients to deliver needed services, the donor is now, more often than not, distanced from the clients of the services that are funded. Nonprofit organizations mediate with the philanthropic exchange and protect ultimate recipients from having to confront their benefactors. One ironic element of this broad trend toward distancing is the growing amount of interaction between givers and the organizations they support. As donors have become distanced from clients, they have grown increasingly close to the nonprofit organizations that they support. The impulse to reach out and form a connection in giving is now focused not on the clients who ultimately benefit from the giving, but on the organizations that deliver the services. By seeking to build capacity and by offering advice and counsel to grant recipient organizations, modern donors are often trying to get more out their giving in terms of personal satisfaction than a hands-off approach would afford. This solves one problem but creates a new one. It liberates the client from the embarrassment of having to look the donor in the eye, but it places the nonprofit leader in this potentially compromising position. Of course, there is a difference between seeking alms to survive and seeking grants to deliver programs that help others. But the rapprochement between donors and nonprofits has in many ways replaced one undesirable form of giving in Maimonides' ladder with a different but potentially equally problematic form of delivering philanthropy.

As donors have accepted the idea of working through nonprofit organizations rather than directly with those in need—which has made them less connected with clients but more engaged with nonprofit leaders—the appeal of actual anonymous giving appears to be waning. Donors routinely seek out press attention and publicize their giving, both before and after the fact. They do so for a number of reasons ranging from a desire to increase public understanding of their giving to simply wanting to be seen as exercising a leadership role in their community. No matter why publicity is sought, the act of rendering public one's philanthropy has consequences for the nonprofits that are the recipients of the giving. While there is rarely any shame involved in receiving grants—in fact, there is some honor in being an effective fund-raiser—the fact remains that nonprofit leaders must on a regular basis and as a central part of their work look donors squarely in the eye and ask them for money.[35]

As donors have increasingly defined giving styles and engagement strategies that call for close collaboration between themselves and nonprofit organizations, it is not always obvious that the needs and dignity of the organizations are taken seriously. While those who work for charitable organizations are different from clients, the act of asking for funding and the challenge of managing a relationship between a nonprofit and a funder can be difficult. Some of the shame and humiliation that were part of charity may be dissipated, but other problematic elements of the relationship remain, including a gross differential in power. Thus, while few donors today actively seek out the lowest rungs of the Maimonides ladder, modern donors do create new ethical challenges related to how they interact with the people and organizations that represent and serve the disadvantaged.

In the end, getting to the motives of donors may or may not be of great consequence, depending on which of philanthropy's many stakeholders one asks. From the government's point of view, it may matter very little why someone has decided to support a particular program or initiative. What matters is that someone stepped forward to help those in need. Motives may be mysterious and intriguing, but the real question is whether public benefits were generated without public expenditures. Government will want to know this so that it can in turn recalibrate its priorities to take into account the work of private donors. For the community in which the program operates, motives may matter a bit more in that few will want to be part of something that has impure motives embedded in it. For example, there may be some reluctance to accept something from one who is seeking to rehabilitate his reputation and gain some visibility among the next generation in a given neighborhood or area, even if the benefits are mediated though a charitable organization. There may also be an issue of community pride that could make the motives of the giver pertinent, especially if they conflict with local values. For the recipient organization, the motives of the donor may matter even more, since they have implications for how the organization will be seen in the future. Taking funds from someone who may not have the best interests of others at heart could damage the reputation and integrity of a nonprofit organization while also potentially alienating other existing and future donors. For the clients and users, the motives of donors tend to be off the radar screen, though few individuals would want to benefit from a program with a heavily stigmatized benefactor. In practice, clients of nonprofit services rarely inquire about the donors supporting the services of which they avail themselves.

In sorting out some of these issues surrounding motives and methods, two key signposts will be the level of engagement or involvement of the donor and the amount of public profile the donor seeks. Before, during, and after funds are conveyed by donors to recipient organizations, a core challenge is to come to an agreement about the ultimate purpose that both sides have in mind; this purpose may represent the amalgamation of many, if not all, of philanthropy's complex functions. While the donor holds many of the cards in this game, recipient organizations are in a position to assert at least some control. In this give-and-take process, donors need to make important choices about how much engagement and public profile they want. No matter why a donor gives, the act will demand that answers be given about how exactly the gift will be made and how philanthropic intentions will be translated into action. In important ways, the engagement and profile of donors will be shaped by the motives that lie behind the gift. If all a donor wants is to do some good, the profile sought will be low and the level of engagement will be appropriate to the project at hand and subject to definition by both sides of the transaction. If, on the other hand, the donor has strong views about either engagement or profile based on personal considerations that have little or nothing to do with the actual project, there will likely be problems ahead. A key element of good strategy thus comes down to calibrating the appropriate level of engagement and profile in one's giving.

Engagement

In assembling a plan, including an engagement strategy, donors need to think about who will carry out their philanthropic work and how this work will proceed. In some cases, donors will seek out the advice and counsel of family members, friends, lawyers, and consultants. These parties may be brought in to assist with planning or implementing a philanthropic agenda. A trend toward philanthropic disintermediation has, however, emerged in recent years; younger donors increasingly have decided to cut out all philanthropic middlemen and instead look to themselves as the principal agents of their own philanthropy. This do-it-yourself turn is, of course, the simplest solution to the agency question in philanthropy, one that removes the threat of deviation from the donor's intent that delegating responsibility can create.

Engagement styles range from very hands-off approaches, in which nonprofit autonomy and expertise are privileged, to a more deeply engaged approach, in which the donor and recipient work together on program development and problem solving.[36] There are donors who are involved in all aspects of their giving and with the work of the organizations that receive their funds. Often stemming from a sense that philanthropy must be about more than check writing, involved or engaged donors want to feel a connection and offer advice and input above and beyond money.[37] This may lead the donor to talk to and toil alongside the inner-city community activists as they weed out a plot in the community garden that has gone untended in order to understand the community better. It may entail listening in on a board meeting of an organization that is attempting to overcome a challenge and offering some suggestions where appropriate. It may involve the regular introduction of independent evaluators into the program to advise both the organization and the donor on the strengths and weaknesses of the program design and implementation. There are many ways that donors can and do more than just send checks. The important question is why donors at times become engaged and how they go about adding value through engagement.

Why would a donor seek a high level of engagement with a recipient organization, rather than simply maintain a more traditional and distanced philanthropic relationship? High-engagement donors may want to get involved because they are reaching for the highest rung on Maimonides' ladder: helping others to help themselves and gain independence. Or they may seek a high level of engagement simply because they believe they know better than others how to manage a project, even if they lack the specialized training and experience of the leaders within the recipient organization. This impulse to micromanage and meddle can be a product of years of managerial work in the business sector, which may have led to substantial wealth creation and success. It is often just a small—though sometimes unwise—leap to assume that these patterns will lead to success in philanthropy. It is also possible that the drive to engagement can be related to vanity, overblown self-confidence, or a desire to impose one's will on others.

On the other extreme, an increasingly smaller number of donors are happy to withdraw from the grantmaking process and let recipient organizations do their work as they see fit. Such deference may stem from a recognition that in many cases it is the nonprofit that truly understands the problem at hand. It can also be the painful result of experience in attempting to be highly engaged, leading only to the recognition that nonprofit managers prefer to have plenty of leeway in how they operate their programs. There are other reasons to resist jumping too quickly into the philanthropic fray. Low engagement has been justified in the name of professional detachment and as a necessity for maintaining objectivity. It is also far easier and less time consuming to limit the scope of the giving relationship to pre- and postgrant evaluation than it is to expect the donor to take partial responsibility for the execution of a program or the recipient organization's performance. In fact, the more engaged a donor is with a project the harder it may be to exit or terminate the relationship if the facts so dictate. Engagement can muddy the philanthropic waters by placing the donor into the program that is being funded, a position from which it is hard to render tough and objective judgments about quality and impact. For this reason, there are cases in which donors need to actively resist the temptation to throw themselves into the fray and get their hands dirty.

As they become more and more comfortable with giving, donors choose an engagement style somewhere between a totally hands-off approach and a deeply engaged one. For nonprofits, these decisions about style can have significant consequences. High levels of donor engagement may mean access to resources and talents of great value to the nonprofit. It may also entail a tremendous amount of extra work, as donors need to be handled and satisfied. For this reason, some nonprofits prefer to receive general operating support with as few strings attached as possible. Over time, however, almost all nonprofits learn to work with the different engagement approaches of their donors and understand that considerable variation is to be expected.

In thinking about philanthropic engagement, two critical dimensions to any relationship between giver and recipient impose themselves. The first dimension is the one just described: the level of donor engagement, which can vary from very light oversight to heavy-handed control. The level of engagement will vary not only with the style of the donor but also with the nature of the work being carried out by the recipient. Some work, such as scientific research or the arts, makes it hard for donors to be engaged directly in the funded work because it simply requires a certain amount of independence. Other kinds of projects, such as youth programs and scholarship funds, are far more wide open to donor involvement and even reengineering. After all, everyone has an opinion on how to help young people, but few people know enough about genetic research to get deeply involved. The second dimension is simpler and only describes the level of congruence or match between the values and intentions of the donor and the recipient. In some situations, donors and recipients think alike and share common aspirations, while in other cases, the two parties are very far apart, even if this is not apparent at the time of the grant. In either event, it is possible to view congruence, overlap, and coincidence in outlook and underlying values between donors and recipients as central to the formation of a strong working relationship. When these two dimensions are joined, four types of philanthropic relationships emerge (see figure 8.1): contractual relationships in which donors and recipients simply give and get under narrowly circumscribed terms and then go their own way; delegating relationships in which donors delegate responsibility freely to those doing the work; auditing relationships in which trust is low and oversight is extensive so as to monitor the precise use of grant funds; and, finally, collaborative relationships in which the two sides work together closely to achieve a set of mutually agreed-upon goals.

What do these different engagement strategies look like in practice? When writer James Michener came to Texas in the early 1980s to research the novel he was writing that would eventually bear the state's name as its title, he was given tours of the biggest ranches, an office at the University of Texas, and special attention from the governor. Michener came to love the state and bought a house in Austin. He volunteered, in his words,

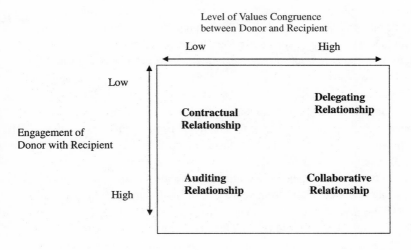

Figure 8.1 **Forms of philanthropic relationships.**

as a "teaching assistant" in the graduate fiction workshops at the university. Michener worked closely with students, commenting on their work, encouraging when necessary, and giving them career advice. In 1988, he gave $1 million to create a interdisciplinary master of fine arts degree at the university, which would provide students with training in fiction writing, poetry, playwriting, and screenwriting. The goal of the programs was to develop multidimensional graduates who could work across a range of writing professions. Michener was not an absentee donor. Instead, he worked with the students and helped set the direction for the center. Within a couple of years, he made another gift of $3 million, followed by a $15 million contribution to fully fund the new Texas Center for Writers, including fellowships for writing students. Michener was very involved with the program until his death in 1997. Collaborative relationships involve not only the gift of money but work together based on shared values and mutual interests.

Collaborative relationships need not be based on large gifts. The financial scale can be modest while the personal involvement can be intense. Rebecca Berman is a retired New York City schoolteacher living in Teaneck, New Jersey. Not wealthy but frugal, Berman has pursued her philanthropic passion of helping children and families in the poorest areas of Guatemala. A sixty-nine-year-old widow and three-time cancer survivor, Berman first went to Guatemala through an exchange program in 1992. Though she had always been committed to public service and philanthropy, the opportunity to make a difference in Guatemala was striking. On her trip, she heard that $1,000 could build a school. Following the trip, she raised money from friends to build three schools in remote areas of the country. Her commitment, however, is about more than raising money and writing checks. Berman has visited Guatemala nearly every year since, bringing everything from basketballs to books as well as money raised for new schools and health care. Back home in New Jersey, Berman convinces friends, stores, and hospitals to donate goods that she brings to Guatemala. She seeks out deals at yard sales, and takes goods that others might throw away. She has found or been given clothing, wheelchairs, and school supplies at little to no cost. In Guatemala, she is connected with the schools, clinics, and families, which allows her to target her efforts to the needs of the communities. Giving across national boundaries creates cultural challenges and requires more than check writing. Berman's small-scale approach to giving allows her to meet these challenges by engaging very directly and deeply with the schools she has founded and supported.

There are many examples of gifts that move away from deep personal engagement to a more delegating relationship in which values are aligned, but in which the donor simply does not have the time nor the inclination to really get involved in operational details. One of the largest gifts ever recorded fits this description and it turned out to be also one of the most controversial. Media mogul Ted Turner shocked many when he announced that he was giving $1 billion to the United Nations over ten years. The gift provoked both admiration for its size and scope and ridicule for focusing on an agency that some argued had a reputation for bureaucratization and inefficiency. Still, for Turner, the gift represented a fulfillment of his commitment to international cooperation. For years, he had flown the UN flag above the offices of CNN and had sponsored the Goodwill Games at a time when international tensions were running high. After its initial announcement, Turner's gift went through a number of changes. First, Turner created the nonprofit UN Foundation to receive some of the shares of Time-Warner stock he acquired following the sale of the TBS broadcast company. The UN Foundation was not a foundation, but rather a public charity that would solicit outside funds to help support its activities. The gift was not limited only to the United Nations but was also directed at "UN causes," which include the UN Commission on Human Rights and a range of nonprofit environmental and advocacy organizations. The exact amount of the gift would also depend on the performance of TimeWarner stock and would be capped at $1 billion, or less if the stock performed poorly. Regardless of these changes, the gift sent a major shot across the bow of philanthropy by virtue of its size and ambition. To run the UN Foundation, Turner chose former U.S. Senator Timothy Wirth, an experienced actor in international politics. Interestingly, Turner pondered a different use of his philanthropic funds before settling on the UN Foundation; he inquired into paying off the UN membership dues of the United States, which were in arrears, but decided against it.

At the other extreme of engagement approaches are donors that do little other than monitor progress, review financial statements, and ensure that the terms of the grant agreement are fulfilled.[38] Depending on how closely values are aligned, this can produce a respectful contractual relationship or a more tense auditing relationship. These auditing models often arise in smaller foundations, where large numbers of small grants are made. Unable to do more than a cursory monitoring of grantees, these underresourced foundations are led to simply set a group of procedural hurdles in place to maintain some semblance of accountability. Nonprofits must submit to these periodic audits and remain in compliance. Since it is far easier to monitor financial matters than mission fulfillment, it is no surprise that much of the auditing that goes on in philanthropy is over the expenditure of and accounting for funds.

Contractual relationships are frequent in the world of corporate philanthropy, where gifts are conveyed often with relative detachment, but where there is some assumption of alignment of values—or at least of interests. Companies that give are reluctant to get too closely connected to the organizations they support for a range of reasons. Chief among them is the fear of exposure to negative publicity should charitable programs backfire or fail. While executives may want to see their employees involved in community volunteer projects that aim to rehabilitate buildings or clean up beaches, they may not want to get too deeply involved in designing a community program aimed at tackling a tough problem such as crime or drug abuse. Moreover, the focus on arts funding[39] that is often present in corporate philanthropy makes engagement more difficult, because there are few real opportunities for company executives to help design an exhibition or a theater production—although there are ample opportunities at each to fly the corporate banner. The engagement level of corporate donors is generally lower than that of other donors for another reason: few company foundations have large enough staffs to really do more than process requests and focus on making sound grant decisions. Real engagement requires a substantial commitment of time, resources, and people that are not always available in corporate philanthropy. Many corporate giving programs are set up more to negotiate and structure issues related to profile and recognition than to rigorously intervene in the work of nonprofits.

Engagement is a critical part of the style defined by a donor. Not only does it have implications for the overall fit and alignment of the giving strategy, but it also has very clear implications for the nonprofit organizations that are on the other side of the table. Finding a level of engagement that both satisfies the donor and adds value to the recipient organization is not always easy. Sometimes there will be a misalignment between a donor that wants a lot of publicity and a cause or organization that simply cannot mobilize the attention. Other times, donors will want a relatively low level of engagement but end up funding an organization that continuously seeks to draw the donor into the organization's governance.[40] Engagement levels are thus like many other elements of the strategic puzzle in philanthropy: they are variable and contextually defined by the interplay of public purposes and private values. Engagement is something that must neither be declared by donor fiat nor postulated by a recipient. Instead, engagement needs to emerge from communication between the two parties and should aim toward finding a level of fit and alignment that will satisfy both sides of the philanthropic exchange.

There is a second element to the idea of a giving style that is somewhat different from the element of engagement. Either actively or passively, donors define a profile for themselves and their giving that shapes their identity. While the level of engagement will determine to some extent how active a donor chooses to be, there remains the difficult issue of when, whether, and how, if at all, to assume a public profile in philanthropy. This means carrying out a philanthropic agenda in such a way that it projects an image to the public about the donor, preferably an image of the donor that reflects well.

Profile: Anonymity and Acclaim

Philanthropy attracts two extremes—and everything in between—when it comes to profile: those seeking anonymity and those seeking acclaim. Just as with engagement, there is a broad distribution of styles. There are donors who believe that it is very important to maintain a highly visible public profile,[41] if for no other reason than to publicize the recipient to other donors and attract additional funding. For every donor angling for media attention and recognition, there is a donor who prefers to maintain a very low profile and do most giving quietly and without much fanfare. For these givers, public attention given to the donor only risks wasting precious resources and diverts attention from the underlying mission and cause. Although personalities will dictate to some extent how much of a public profile a donor wants to assume, there is no doubt from the comparative scarcity of anonymous giving that donors usually want some kind of recognition and profile. Striking the right arrangement can test a nonprofit's ability to read and respond to the funding environment. This can be a complicated task since donors may want plenty of recognition but not want to ask their recipient organizations to provide it. In such cases, it falls upon the nonprofit to "read" the donor.

While engagement connects the donor to a nonprofit organization in ways that can be either productive or destructive, profile has implications that are far less transparent and immediate. Recognizing a donor may not "cost" a nonprofit much—at least as long as the demands are modest and the donor has not been engaged in any activity that reflects badly on the recipient institution. There are in fact many cases in which donors have had their gifts returned because of scandals, including a university that named its convocation center in honor of its chief donor and only later learned he was a central figure in international arms dealing. Donors may request that their names be included in lists, honor rolls, and commemorative plaques, or they may want to be mentioned in press releases, advertising, and other outreach efforts. In all this jockeying, some valuable resources may need to be diverted from mission-related work to donor satisfaction work. There is at least one more troublesome element in all this. When a donor decides to go public and seeks to cultivate a public profile connected to its philanthropy, questions will always lurk related to motives. Of course, visibility can be defended on a number of strategic grounds, particularly for new funders that are eager to announce their presence to the broader field in which they are working and for already well-known donors who choose to work in new areas that are not well known to the public. High profiles can shed light and attention. However, concerns over ego and ambition will lurk near any claim about strategy or leverage related to profile.

The drive for a high philanthropic profile can sometimes be the product of a desire to escape an existing identity and to change public perceptions. For some married women, high-profile philanthropy is a way of defining themselves and creating some separation from the long shadow cast by their husbands. Such was the case with Sheila Johnson. Within the span of one year, Sheila Johnson divorced her husband, split with him a $1.5 billion windfall from the sale of the television network they cofounded, Black Entertainment Television (BET), and moved to Middlesburg, Virginia, with her two children to start a new life, which includes a leading role as a philanthropist. Johnson soon made a number of significant donations in her new incarnation as philanthropist and has plans for a $100 million foundation to pursue her philanthropic vision. Johnson established herself as a leading citizen of Middlesburg, Virginia, just by buying a vulnerable piece of property. The mayor and many long-time residents were relieved when she bought a 342-acre estate previously owned by Pamela C. Harrison. There were fears that the estate would be converted into unattractive subdivisions, but Johnson declared her intention to turn the entire estate into a high-end lodging called Salamander Inn. She also underwrote lavish fundraising galas for the Loudon Hospital Center's health vans, which travel to the underserved pockets of her adoptive county, and gave $2.5 million for a performing arts center at the Hill School, a private school where her son is a student. The style of Sheila Johnson's giving is intertwined with her own personal goals and is, at least partially, a function of a drive to distinguish herself from the business she and her husband created. She has also used her influence to make a connection at the Parsons School of Design and has been actively involved with the school's governance, serving on the school's board. Her involvement in the school may be fueled as much by a desire to break into the fashion and design industry with her own new business venture in fine linens as it is by a desire to get more philanthropic visibility. Nevertheless, Johnson's search for a new identity and the role philanthropy has played in it are significant because they demonstrate how giving can transform more than just the recipient.

Other donors have sought out the philanthropic spotlight in more controversial ways. Catherine B. Reynolds tells her story as an embodiment of the American dream. She was hired as the comptroller of EduCap, a small student-loan company in Washington, D.C., and saw it turn into a giant in the field. Reynolds got her start in philanthropy after the sale of EduCap to Wells Fargo. From its inception, however, Reynolds's philanthropic career has been clouded by controversy. EduCap was started by a Washington priest, John Whalen, in the 1980s, but did not take off until Reynolds was hired from an entertainment business in northern Virginia. Reynolds helped EduCap develop and market a clever way of selling bonds on Wall Street to raise capital to finance student loans. Proceeds of the loans secured the bonds and over time more than 300,000 families took out loans worth $2.5 billion. This success did not come without criticism. The company was criticized for charging higher interest rates than other nonprofit student-loan providers and giving its executives more lavish perks. EduCap also set up a for-profit partner, Servus, and gave its executives generous stock shares in the new company. When EduCap was sold to Wells Fargo, by law, the profits could not go to an individual. Instead, they were put into a foundation that became known as the Catherine B. Reynolds Foundation, a move that raised some flags. Some have argued that EduCap was never Reynolds's creation and the foundation should have been named after Father Whalen, who was the founder.

Amid the controversy, Reynolds received attention for major gifts to the Kennedy Center, Morehouse College, and other institutions, but not everyone understands that the foundation's endowment is not really her own wealth. In her defense, Reynolds has explained that she wanted to name it the LuckyStar Foundation, after a nickname favored by her daughter, but that name was already registered to another organization.

All of which has led Reynolds and the Catherine B. Reynolds Foundation to be the subject of sustained criticism. She herself has been accused of social climbing because of a series of large and visible donations. She has also organized highly successful fund-raising galas that have been criticized as being too slick and entertainment oriented. Most famously, her proposed gift to the Smithsonian of $38 million for a Hall of Achievement, planned with her husband and American Academy of Achievement director Wayne Reynolds, was turned down. The Smithsonian's rejection surprised many, especially since the Smithsonian recently blamed a fund-raising shortfall of over $30 million on a lack of major gifts. Reynolds wanted to create a Hall of Achievement that would feature shrines to noted American citizens. Controversially, she wanted to personally select ten out of fifteen famous Americans to be featured in the exhibition. Her initial suggestions included Oprah Winfrey and Martha Stewart, women who, like herself, had risen from humble beginnings to dominate an industry. Both had taken part in earlier American Academy of Achievement galas organized by her husband. And like most of the honored guests, they also, in turn, had become generous donors to the American Academy of Achievement.

Reynolds has been sharply criticized both on the grounds that her choices represented a conflict of interest and because of the curatorial role she wanted to take in the planning. She endured considerable criticism in the media, including an article suggesting that the entire project was déclassé for an institution like the Smithsonian, comparing Reynolds's planned exhibition to a Madame Tussaud's wax museum for celebrities. In a letter to the Smithsonian chief, Lawrence Small, Reynolds finally wrote, "This gift to our nation has become impossible to give." Throughout the whole controversy, Reynolds appeared to be trying to celebrate in a very public way a version of the American dream that has a strong hold on her mind, the self-made American who rose from nothing. By drawing so much attention to herself and by staking a rather controversial claim to the name of a foundation, Catherine B. Reynolds ultimately made it difficult for the institution named after her to achieve some of its objectives.

Given all the complications that a high profile can create, donors have at times sought to remain anonymous. For many reasons, anonymous giving is a special case in philanthropy. Anonymous giving is a subject that is difficult to research and explore in great detail precisely because it is done anonymously and often with little public recognition. Furthermore, it raises all kinds of issues for those who believe the main driver of human action is utility maximization. By giving anonymously, donors are foreclosing any "return" other than the personal satisfaction that arises from doing a good deed. A few examples of this rare form of giving that actually heeds the hierarchy of giving defined so clearly by Maimonides are still useful, if only to contrast them with the more dominant, higher-profile approach to giving that modern donors have embraced.

For years, an anonymous donor in Denver, Colorado, has donated $10,000 to the homeless. Seeking to honor the late Monsignor C. B. Woodrich, the city's celebrated defender of the poor and founder of the city's largest shelter, the donor delivers a thousand $10 bills to the Holy Ghost Catholic Church. Each year, the church gives the money away after holding a short prayer. As the homeless pass in front of the altar they are given an envelope with a picture of the monsignor on it and a $10 bill inside. How they use this money is entirely up to them. While some undoubtedly use the money for essentials such as food, others may well end up using the funds for alcohol or drugs. The donor, however, chooses this form of direct charity because it assures that funds reach those in need, rather than help organizations. While this anonymous donor could support the shelter that the monsignor helped found, this direct form of charity is clearly more satisfying in that it allows the donor to ensure that the funds reach those in need without intermediation.

Some anonymous donors give behind a veil because they want the public to focus on the cause or issue, not the benefactor. Thus, when Johns Hopkins University received a gift of $100 million for a new center on malaria, the focus was on the issue of malaria and the need for a cure to the disease that kills one million people each year. The new research center will bring together scientists from a range of fields including immunology, biology, population studies, vaccine development, and molecular parasitology. By starting fresh with an interdisciplinary team of researchers, Hopkins hopes to make progress on a disease for which there are presently only ineffective and expensive preventative medicines, which are becoming even less able to combat new drug-resistant strains of the disease. One interesting feature of this large gift was that the donor was known to be an impatient, high-risk financial investor. Unwilling to wait for the National Institutes of Health to fund the center progressively as results were achieved, the donor decided to place a large bet on the university from the start, and then allow it to do whatever it thought would most quickly and significantly generate progress.

The most famous anonymous donor is Charles Feeney. This unassuming New Jersey man quietly gave away hundreds of millions of dollars before anyone knew he was the donor behind a Bermuda-based foundation. His veil of secrecy was pierced only when the sale of his company forced him to go public. Feeney created Atlantic Philanthropies from the proceeds of the duty-free business he created in airports. The foundation's assets have been declining lately due to Feeney's decision to spend his multibillion dollar foundation out of existence over the course of a decade and a half. He wanted to see his funds put to productive use now, rather than be held in perpetuity. Uncomfortable with donors who fail to take responsibility for their own charity, Feeney's approach to giving while alive is anchored in the simple notion that money spent solving human problems today is better spent than money given away off in the distant future. Moreover, giving while alive ensures that the donor experiences the pleasure of seeing good work being done with their philanthropic funds. Brought up in a working-class neighborhood in Elizabeth, New Jersey, Feeney studied hotel administration at Cornell, which he attended on a GI scholarship. The breakthrough for Feeney came when he and a partner opened duty-free shops in Honolulu and Hong Kong, then expanded around the world to capture growing tourist travel. Feeney's share in the business became worth over a billion dollars, but he had transferred his interest to Atlantic Philanthropies, a foundation in Bermuda. To avoid detection, Feeney chose not to claim a tax deduction. Part of his decision to maintain a low profile stemmed from his desire to live a normal life and not create security problems for his family. Atlantic Philanthropies' giving has spanned a range of issues from improving the quality of higher education in Ireland to the support of nonprofit infrastructure organizations in the United States to health programs in countries around the world.

When money moves from the hands of donors to those of recipients, questions about reciprocity arise, especially when the veil of anonymity is raised. Donors range greatly in their desire for acknowledgment and acclaim. A small number of contributors insist on complete anonymity in all their giving. Sometimes, donors insist on anonymity because they do not want to take the spotlight away from those delivering services or from the social problem being addressed. Other times, donors seek a low profile as a way of protecting themselves from an onslaught of requests for charitable support. Whatever their motives, anonymous donors appear to some to occupy the moral high ground. Philanthropic profile is an element of strategy that can be managed, but only to a small extent. There are times when profile simply is determined by others. In New York, a taxicab driver decided to use the money he earned in the United States to engage in philanthropy back in his hometown of Doobher Kishanpur, India. By contributing $2,500 a year, Om Dutta Sharma is able to run a school for girls in the small house where he was raised. Because teachers earn only about $50 a month, Sharma is able to educate almost 200 girls in grades one to five. His plans for the expansion are keyed to the sale of his taxi medallion, when he retires from his regular driving schedule of twelve hours a day, seven days a week. Sharma's decision to give back in India was fueled by two major factors. First, he wanted to do something to honor his illiterate mother, so he named the school after her. Second, he realized that he did not have the funds needed to make a major difference in the United States. However, his modest contributions could go a lot further back in India. Thus, Sharma took the calculated step of applying his modest philanthropy to a place where it could create maximum impact. He did not seek any real public recognition for his giving. However, he was the subject of stories in the major media and was thrust into a highly visible position.

There are many donors who do not want to operate in the shadows, but instead want to be acknowledged and thanked for their gifts, sometimes in very public ways. In fact, visibility can be a critical factor driving some donors' giving. The range of ways in which donors seek a public profile is broad, from having buildings named after them, to hiring public relations firms to get the word out about particular gifts, to taking part in special events to celebrate and recognize their gifts. Exacerbating this inclination is the fact that changes within the field of professional fund-raising have turned donor relations and donor acknowledgment into an increasingly elaborate and extensive activity. Structuring a giving opportunity so as to meet the profile desires of the donor is now a routine part of securing a major contribution. It is not uncommon for donors to be approached about gifts with an explicit menu of naming opportunities and a clear offer of quid pro quo. However, when giving turns into a simple exchange of money for visibility and publicity, something important about philanthropy is threatened, namely the balance between private and public priorities. The search for recognition and public profile can go too far and move philanthropy into a position in which the private satisfaction of the donor, not the search for creative solutions to public problems, becomes the primary element driving giving.

Where do philanthropic styles, which include both a desired engagement level and a preferred public profile, really come from? They tend to be a product of the life experiences of the donor before philanthropy rather than the result of a careful consideration of the strategic considerations at hand for any particular gift or series of gifts. Style is more fixed than other elements of the strategic framework, which can be readily adjusted and calibrated to circumstance. In fact, the most common approach is to categorize donors based on a fixed typology of philanthropic styles. Attempts to sketch the landscape of philanthropic identities into archetypes has yielded only modestly helpful distinctions. One approach defined seven major donor identities: the dynast who gives inherited money as part of a family tradition, the communitarian who seeks to sustain ties to the place where he or she lives and does business, the repayer who gives after receiving service from organizations, the devout who gives from religious conviction, the investor who has an eye to tax issues, the socialite who is driven by norms of a social class, and the altruist who gives in order to find meaning. There are two problems with this kind of typology. The first is that it renders philanthropic identities far more clear-cut and static than they are in reality. Many of the most visible donors over the past century have had very complex and overlapping identities that span several of the categories suggested here. Moreover, donors are often driven by different motives when they make different gifts. Thus, after a particularly meaningful college experience, a donor may decide to pay the institution back with a large gift, particularly if the donor sees the college experience as critical to life success. This same donor may also make gifts to religious organizations out of a deep faith and a desire to contribute to the work of the church. Thus, as donors give different gifts over time, it is all but certain that they will give for very different reasons. The second problem with a rigid typology of donors is that it conveys a false sense that donor identities are subject to strategic analysis and marketing efforts by nonprofit organizations designed to part donors from their wealth. In fact, a fair amount of energy has been devoted to profiling exercises, all in the name of giving fund-raisers a small edge in shaping and perfecting their pitches. In practice, none of the clever ploys and pitches to donors will succeed unless there is a fundamental alignment between the donor and the cause at hand. In this sense, style needs to be understood as just one piece in the strategic puzzle.

The selection, testing, and adaptation of a distinctive style is like most other parts of the strategic challenge in philanthropy; it requires continuous reevaluation and adjustment in order to achieve a level of fit and coherence with the other elements of the philanthropic prism. Engagement level and profile need to be able to adapt to the distinctive demands of specific circumstances, even if changes in style are difficult for the donor. The style adopted by the donor must meet the dual test of adding value to the philanthropic effort in question while also producing the kind of personal satisfaction that leads the donor to continue to give. Striking the balance thus requires both a considerable amount of introspection and knowledge of the funding environment. It also can be overtaken by new trends that sweep across the philanthropic landscape and make particular styles appear appealing. Unfortunately, style alone can never be a substitute for good strategy, only an element of it.

A New Style: Venture Philanthropy

One of the most popular styles in philanthropy in recent years has been the one that transposes elements of the hard-nosed businessman or investor into the softer world of nonprofit activity. Donors have embraced the idea that there might be significant value added if the philanthropic relationship between grantmaker and grantee were refashioned to look more like the relationship between an investor and an investee. It is fair to say that few ideas in philanthropy have gotten more attention over the past decade than that of venture philanthropy, which has codified this shift and given it meaning. What exactly is venture philanthropy? What makes it different from traditional philanthropy? What innovations has it introduced into the field? To begin to answer these questions, it is important to step back for a moment to consider the political and intellectual context within which the idea of venture philanthropy emerged.

Over the past decade, two broad developments, one in business, the other in politics, have quietly elevated the word "investment" to new heights. The 1990s saw the rise of Silicon Valley and the vast fortunes that were made by the creators of new Internet and computer hardware and software companies. The technological revolution that was ushered in by these new upstart firms gave the old practice of venture capital investing fresh exposure and currency. The capital flows that fueled the high-tech boom came from a relatively small group of firms, many located in California, that brought to their work a set of practices designed to increase the odds of success for their young and often inexperienced investees. These practices included heavy amounts of due diligence during the screening process, long-term financial commitments designed to overcome the problem of undercapitalization that cripples many start-up firms, and extensive advice and consulting on how to develop and manage the new company. The ultimate goal of this investment process was to build large companies from scratch, take them through an initial public offering in as short a time as possible, and for all sides to make large amounts of money in the process.

The powerful pull of the investment approach to achieving results was impossible to confine to business and soon entered the political arena. Starting with the presidential campaign of 1992, the Democrats shifted the language of their party's policy arguments in a distinctive way. Rather than call for higher *taxes* and more *spending*, the rhetoric of the Democratic campaign was about the necessity of greater *contributions* to make possible higher levels of *social investments*. The contemplated investments in education and health care were nothing other than greater levels of public spending in long-standing domestic health and education programs. But the change in language ushered in by the New Democrats was significant; it represented a repudiation of the idea of wasteful government, and the rise of a new tougher, more savvy fiscal policy, one that would take a more rigorous, businesslike approach to public problems by making "critical infrastructure investments" that were capable of generating social returns.[42]

The rhetoric of the New Democrats and the practices of Silicon Valley were ultimately wed in the field of philanthropy, and the result is what is now generally termed "venture philanthropy." It was a marriage made in heaven, in that sophisticated donors have long sought to turn their gifts and grants into something more concrete and scientific. Rather than simply being a purveyor of charitable funds for deserving organizations of all sorts, venture philanthropy promised to turn donors into hard-nosed social investors by bringing the discipline of the investment world to a field that had for over a century relied on good faith and trust. Two major differences still separated the new philanthropic investors from their government and business counterparts: first, while government was able to make social investments that affected millions of people through the funding of entitlement programs, philanthropy struggles to marshal enough resources to have a major impact; second, while business firms had a clear way of determining whether their investments pay off, namely return on investment, philanthropy has long struggled to develop performance measurement tools to assess the impact of philanthropic investments.[43] The search for solutions to the problems of impact and measurement has been at the center of the conversation about venture philanthropy, as the approach has taken hold and begun to spread, especially among younger donors who have made their money through entrepreneurship. The attempt to transfer wisdom across sectors galvanized a small group of individual and foundation donors who have now declared themselves to be venture philanthropists.

Venture philanthropy's approach and language have penetrated the private and community foundation world, the small giving circles and clubs that help guide new donors, and the territory of corporate philanthropy. The idea of turning philanthropy into social investing has been tried in a whole host of fields such as early childhood health, environmental protection, and community development, to name just a few. However, one of the most popular fields of focus for venture philanthropy efforts has been K–12 education. Many businesspeople see the failure of large parts of the public school system as a crisis that has the potential to erode the long-term economic growth potential of the United States. The challenge of getting public schools to perform better has been taken up by many of the high-tech entrepreneurs who have shown an affinity for the venture philanthropy model and for education reforms across the country.

It is difficult to pinpoint the exact size of the venture philanthropy movement today, although one recent survey estimated that there are some forty institutional funders committed to the approach, investing about $60 million a year. Although venture philanthropy remains small today, particularly when compared to the total $200 billion given away each year by all donors, its influence is considerable. It has been the subject of growing media attention and the profile of its early practitioners has risen within the field. Most significantly, several of the largest foundations, such as the W. K. Kellogg Foundation and the Pew Trusts, have recently begun to experiment with the language and practices of venture philanthropy. Because of the powerful appeal of the metaphor on which it rests, it is critical to understand what the approach has to offer philanthropy.

At its core, venture philanthropy can best be seen as being built on three main intellectual pillars, each of which is seen as a solution to a problem in traditional philanthropy. The first idea is that of bringing nonprofits to scale by providing large blocks of financial support to nonprofits over longer periods of time. The second idea is the development of new metrics of organizational performance. The third is the establishment of a close relationship between funder and recipient, one in which the donor engages with core strategic and operational issues and seeks to act as an advisor and problem solver for the organization. In combination, the three define a distinctive style, one in which both engagement and profile are high.

Venture philanthropy has developed tools for increasing the likelihood of success in nonprofits, including the provision of a different kind of capital flow than nonprofit organizations are used to receiving. From the vantage point of nonprofit service providers, private foundations and corporate donors have long engaged in any number of practices that seem designed only to frustrate grant recipients. High on the nonprofit list of grievances is the move to increasingly narrow forms of project support, often delivered for short periods of time, and almost never for general support for operational capacity. In a search for greater levels of accountability, many institutional funders have in fact developed a strong preference for project grantmaking, in large part because they believe that these grants can be monitored more actively than unrestricted support. One problem with general operating support is that it has come to be associated with "nonessential" items like support staff, rent, and other basic expenses. Providing funds to cover these is less attractive to many funders because these costs seem extraneous to the core mission and public purposes of nonprofit organizations.

As a consequence, many institutional funders have come to insist on funding projects and activities, not organizations. In recent years, generating operating support has constituted only about 15 percent of all grants. Much of the rest is being disbursed as project-specific grants. To make matters worse, many funders limit their project support of particular nonprofit organizations to two or three consecutive years. Fearing that they will create a dependence that cannot be sustained indefinitely, traditional institutional funders have settled on a short-term approach to grantmaking that allows them the flexibility to change direction quickly should community condition or board interest change. The consequences for nonprofit organizations of this pattern of funding have been predictable: financial instability, programmatic uncertainty, and wasted effort, all of which make the achievement of real scale and impact very difficult.

Venture philanthropy has keyed on this pattern and come forward with a different approach to funding, one that builds on the venture capital model and offers longer-term support and larger amounts of unrestricted financial support. Instead of pulling the plug quickly and moving on to fund other organizations, the venture philanthropy model emphasizes long-term funding commitments designed to help organizations develop and grow. Unlike most grantmakers that trickle out support in small installments, the venture philanthropist seeks to get into projects with a large initial investment that signals real commitment. In New York, for example, the Robin Hood Foundation, an early venture philanthropy entrant, has long focused on building lasting relationships with the organizations it supports, with some engagements lasting up to a decade. In a few cases, this has translated into very large financial commitments, while in other instances, the amounts have been more modest. By providing large blocks of capacity-building support to nonprofits over longer periods of time, venture philanthropy believes that it will be possible to overcome one of the biggest drawbacks in the nonprofit sector, namely the inability of nonprofit organizations to achieve real scale and impact.

Before delivering these blocks of support and committing to an organization over the long haul, the venture philanthropist engages in a heavy dose of what they refer to as "due diligence." While it is not entirely clear how this review differs from what all donors have always done (reviewing financial disclosure documents, requiring the presentation of a strategic plan, and performing a site visit), the new language is designed to draw attention to the fact that great care needs to be devoted to the decision-making process leading to a commitment.[44] In making the choice of which organizations will be supported, venture philanthropy groups, like New Profit Inc., view the ability of a nonprofit organization to achieve scale as a critical consideration. New Profit's long-term investments have focused on organizations like Jumpstart, a prekindergarten program designed to help disadvantaged children get ready for school, which is expanding to sites in over a dozen cities around the country.

One of the most visible efforts to apply business know-how to the reform of public schools is being undertaken by John Doerr, the Palo Alto venture capitalist. In 1998, Doerr founded the New Schools Venture Fund (NSVF) with the intention of providing seed capital for promising new for-profit and nonprofit organizations that had the potential to bring movement in the public education field. In choosing organizations to fund, Doerr applies a clear set of criteria. He seeks to support organizations that have strong leadership and could have a direct impact on school achievement. What made his approach different was that he also insisted that the organizations that would receive support had to have a concept that could be brought to scale. Like any business investor, Doerr assembled a team of partners who invested in the fund. In all, some $20 million was raised to fund both nonprofit and for-profit initiatives. NSVF's early nonprofit investments included a comprehensive online guide to California public schools, both nonprofit and for-profit charter school management organizations, a school leadership training program, and a math curriculum development effort. On the for-profit side, NSVF invested in a network of charter schools operated by a for-profit firm. NSVF's approach to school reform continues to reflect a distinctive application of the venture philanthropy model. Drawing on the talents of a group of exceptionally successful entrepreneurs and CEOs, the fund has developed its own idea about getting to scale: beyond funding organizations that have real potential for growth and impact, NSVF also works to build a network of school reformers through which innovations and ideas can spread. Thus, NSVF both invests and convenes with the aim of maximizing the impact of its investees and moving them to scale.

Beyond delivering larger grants over longer periods of time, venture philanthropy also emphasizes the importance of evaluation or performance management. Funders such as NSVF and New Profit work closely with nonprofits to determine a set of meaningful objectives and a way of tracking progress. The premise of this work is that if a long-term relationship is to be sustained, nonprofits need to be held accountable for their performance. To this end, multidimensional tools for measuring performance have been adapted from the business sector, including the Balanced Scorecard and other attempts to go beyond simple measures of financial performance. There have been efforts to breathe meaning into the concept of social return on investment, but these have largely collapsed in the face of careful examination. While a few forms of nonprofit activity can be monetized and then subjected to financial analysis, the vast majority of nonprofits engage in work that cannot be converted into simple financial terms. Thus, after some delay and distraction, the venture philanthropy movement settled on more modest efforts to simply calibrate the quality of work and progress toward jointly defined objectives. In carrying out their evaluation work, venture philanthropists seek to encourage nonprofits to manage goals and to be ready to make adjustments in order to improve performance. This focus on measurement bleeds into both the first element of the approach, the idea of long-term, substantial commitments of funds, and the third, consultative engagement.

In its effort to reengineer the mainstream model of philanthropy and reorient it toward achieving impact on a broad scale, venture philanthropy has also focused on changing the relationship between the funder and the recipient. Looking at the way many institutional and individual donors carry out their giving, the proponents of venture philanthropy observed that a tremendous amount of effort was being sunk into the process of selecting grant recipients and very little effort was being devoted to helping nonprofit organizations succeed once the check was sent. Indeed, in many foundations, there is today very little follow-up or consultation between the two sides from the time the grant check is mailed to the time the final report on activities is due. One reason that most of the effort of philanthropy is directed at decision making about grants, not effective implementation, is that there is a real pressure on funders to be transparent, fair, and accountable for their actions. Given these demands, it is hardly surprising that many institutional funders have little time for anything other than careful review of applications, site visits before the board meeting, and the writing of recommendations for the board. As grant cycles roll around and around, it can in fact be very hard for funders to break this cycle and engage with recipient organizations in a sustained relationship.

Venture philanthropy takes a different approach to donor/recipient or investor/investee relations, one that extends the time horizon and deepens the contact between all parties.[45] Rather than cut a check and run, venture philanthropy believes that the work begins only once a financial commitment has been made. Given that the commitment is intended to be a long-term one, the new funders have set out to connect directly with the organizations in their portfolios. There are two perceived benefits to a high-engagement strategy. First, nonprofits may learn something that they do not know already, especially if the consulting that is rendered involves specialized skills not usually found in nonprofits. At New Profit, grant recipients receive hands-on assistance from the management consulting giant Monitor Group. Working with organizations that have received money from New Profit, Monitor's team of consultants assists with planning growth and tracking progress. For organizations such as Citizen Schools, an after-school program that uses adult volunteers to teach real-world teenagers skills through creative projects, this added service is intended to increase the likelihood that the organization will continue to flourish and grow. In lending the expertise of a management consulting firm to their investees, funders are attempting both to protect their investments and increase the social benefits that are achieved.

The second perceived benefit of a consultative and engaged relationship has little to do with nonprofit performance and everything to do with the satisfaction of the donor. High-engagement philanthropy is a social activity that satisfies the desire of many wealthy people to find meaning in their lives outside of business. Young entrepreneurs who are active in venture philanthropy enjoy taking a hands-on approach and view the process as one of learning and personal growth. At Social Venture Partners (SVP), one of the earliest venture philanthropy efforts, donors commit a minimum of $5,000 to the fund and in exchange they gain firsthand exposure to the nonprofits that SVP funds. Many of the investors in other venture funds get even more involved in the organizations they fund either by helping with fund-raising or by serving on the board.

There are several assumptions built into the engagement part of the venture philanthropy model: first, that nonprofit organizations want outside help in strategizing and carrying out their work; second, that those offering the consulting have skills that are missing in the nonprofit world and that nonprofits will run better once they have been exposed to these tools and models; and third, that engagement is ethical and appropriate in philanthropy. All three assumptions can reasonably be questioned. One recent survey of the recipients of high-engagement grants found that the process of working closely with a funder was often draining and added little value to their work. As one might expect, the generally tense relationship between benefactor and supplicant is hard to overcome. Many nonprofits believe that the best support is a windowed envelope carrying a no-strings-attached check. Second, there is no evidence that the people who control capital in the business sector or with expertise in for-profit management have any special claim on knowledge about how to create a successful non-profit organization. Nonprofit mission fulfillment does not always equate to satisfying the demands of clients or responding quickly to market trends. Sometimes, nonprofits need to lead by offering services for which there is little immediate support but nevertheless speak to important if overlooked social needs.

Finally, when it comes to the ethics of giving, the central tenets of venture philanthropy appear problematic. Over time, a recurring theme across such faiths as Christianity, Judaism, and Islam is that the donor and the recipient should be separated, so that the recipient is not shamed by having to take money directly from someone else. Anonymous giving promises to ensure that the donor's intent is pure and that the gift is aimed to helping others, rather than gratifying the donor. The venture philan-thropists' response to such objections is that they are making investments that are different from charity. Because funds are delivered under differ-ent initial terms, the moral problems associated with charity do not apply. Some might even go so far as to say that social investments are fundamen-tally different from grants and that this difference solves any ethical ques-tions that might be posed. Because they are demanding a return when they invest their dollars, venture philanthropists feel entitled to actively man-age and shape the programs that they support. This is an argument, how-ever, that ultimately rests on semantic hairsplitting and skirts the reality of the asymmetric power in all forms of philanthropy. Besides, there is good reason to believe that the whole idea of turning grants into investments is problematic given the absence of any coherent way of measuring return on investment. Still, venture philanthropy's secular, entrepreneurial turn may satisfy the current generation of entrepreneurial donors eager to express themselves through action in the social sphere.

Venture philanthropy remains something of a question mark. For now, it is very difficult to find authentic innovations that justify the new terms that have been introduced. Many of the "investments" made by venture philanthropists look just like the "grants" made by other donors. The best evidence of this is that many of the organizations supported by venture philanthropists regularly receive grant support from mainline philanthropic funders. In fact, only some of the highest-profile venture philanthropy investments represent substantial portions of the operating budgets of the nonprofit organizations on the receiving end. Similarly, the idea of "consultative engagement" that many describe as a trademark of venture philanthropy is hard to distinguish from the multiple forms of "technical assistance" that donors have provided to nonprofits for decades. Across many of the other terminological divides, the underlying practices do not appear significantly different from what has come before.

In one sense, the excitement and energy created by the language of venture philanthropy are positive. New people have been brought into the world of philanthropy and are being converted to the pleasures and challenges of trying to create public value. At the core, venture philanthropy's search for impact has enlivened the field. After all, the problems of traditional philanthropy are clear and undeniable. There is nevertheless something troubling about the frenzy of verbiage and social venture fund foundings. One thing is impossible to deny, however: By seeking to move concepts and language from the world of business to the world of nonprofit organizations, venture philanthropy must be viewed as a marketing triumph. It has sold a new higher engagement style of philanthropy to a whole class of new donors. As a set of practical philanthropic innovations, venture philanthropy's contribution to the field remains far harder to ascertain.

Philanthropic Relationships

Venture philanthropy's emphasis on engagement is not without precedent. With the exception of anonymous giving, the world of philanthropy generally does not afford donors the luxury of operating in quiet contemplative isolation. Giving almost always draws the donor and the recipient together into contact as money and missions intercept one another. Yet few relationships are as complex and as highly charged as the one between donor and recipient. Over time, both sides to this relationship have settled into a normalized pattern of professional interactions, although important challenges and tensions still exist in this asymmetric relationship. Lurking just beneath the surface are a large number of uncomfortable and unresolved questions about power, class, and race, as well as a fair amount of contempt and suspicion. The sad result is that too many donors and non-profits interact through a highly stylized form of kabuki theater built on a ritual of smiles, office chat, and elaborate paperwork. Interviews with nonprofit managers have confirmed that recipient groups have many complaints about their donors. Among the most prominent is the sense of fatigue and bitterness over having to constantly reinvent, recast, and reposition nonprofit activity to please donors and ensure financial survival. As nonprofits try to read donors and give them what they want, this process produces fund-raising appeals that have increasingly little connection to the lived reality of nonprofit organizations and are often a thinly veiled attempt to appeal to the interests and needs of the donor. By delivering giving opportunities that will allow donors to pursue projects of interest, at levels of engagement that are attractive, and with profiles that suit the donors' desires, nonprofits are led to sublimate their real needs and their own preferred ways of structuring philanthropic relationships. One of the most critical challenges in defining a philanthropic style thus involves taking seriously the distorting effects that a choice can have on the very organizations that donors are trying to help.

Why do the candor and quality of communication between grantmaker and recipient sometimes disintegrate during the funding process? It comes down to two main problems. The *language of needs*—be it for general operating support, capital construction, capacity building, or anything else—has been replaced by a *language of opportunities* designed to appeal to the interests of donors. Appeals for grants have increasingly come to be based more on opportunities for donors, rather than on the needs of recipient organizations, for two reasons. First, financial pressures and competition within the sector are rising quickly. As the sheer number of nonprofit organizations continues to escalate, there is a sense that there will always be a nonprofit organization willing to do whatever it takes to get a grant—even if it means accepting onerous terms. The result is that nonprofits do what they need to do in order to survive. There is also a cultural obstacle to stating needs that stems from the power imbalance in the donor-donee relationship. The guidelines defined by donors appear immutable and definitive to many nonprofits and the easiest response under financial pressure is to craft proposals that present funding opportunities that fit neatly within these parameters.

At the same time, donors have become increasingly pro-active in their grantmaking, often telling local nonprofit communities exactly what kinds of proposals they are interested in receiving. The rise of careers in philanthropy and the idea of grantmaking expertise have reinforced this trend toward an increasing role for foundation managers in agenda setting. By encouraging nonprofits to approach funders with requests for capacity-building grants, the venture capital model addresses one important aspect of the nonprofit sector's needs. However, the model ends up circumscribing rather narrowly the type of grants that nonprofits *should* seek. Of course, some nonprofits need assistance in building organizational capacity and infrastructure. Other nonprofits just as surely would benefit most from other kinds of support. Ultimately, the focus on project funding and the proactive methods of donors is problematic in many cases, because it shuts down authentic conversations about needs. Rather than direct funding into any single predetermined type of grants, donors and their recipient organizations need to aim for the broader goal of being able to fund a very broad array of grants that is limited only by the range of authentic needs.

Before embracing the elements of philanthropic style that are part of the venture capital and other business models, donors need first to take seriously the possibility that nonprofit managers may well have radically different goals and concerns that need to be both understood, cultivated, and respected—and that these goals may or may not fit within existing definitions of "impact." After all, many nonprofit workers are animated not only by the instrumental goals of service delivery and program performance, but also by a desire to act based on solidarity, commitment to community, and the need to express values through work. Donors need to find a way that nonprofits can safely include these goals, which are more difficult to document but important, in their proposals and communications.

Are there donors and nonprofits that have open and honest relations today? Of course there are. But are there many donors that are not hearing the truth from recipient organizations? Surely there are. Ultimately, all donors should be able to agree on at least one thing: Any proposal to reengineer philanthropic styles through the application of new business precepts can only be a second step in the process of improving philanthropy. Donors and donees must first work to improve the quality and candor of communication during the process of giving and getting grants. In this sense, one of the key tests for the appropriateness and effectiveness of a philanthropic style is whether it allows the kind of authentic conversation about organizational and community needs that is the basis for sound program planning and development.

How can such a style be crafted? While there is no simple answer, donors need to constantly remind themselves of two things. First, nonprofit organizations have a very broad set of needs that may or may not fit within existing foundation guidelines, and no one is served when authentic nonprofit needs are repressed. Second, nonprofits are moved by both instrumental and expressive goals, and while existing performance-based evaluation is important and must continue, other forms of evaluation need to be developed that acknowledge the important although less easily measured nonprofit contributions. Only after honesty is actively cultivated in foundation-nonprofit relations will donors and donees be in a position to act on some of the new models for grantmaking that are now capturing the field's attention.[46] More important, getting the relationship between nonprofits and their donors right is critical to the achievement of strategic fit and alignment.

In deciding upon a grantmaking style, one that includes both an engagement level and a preferred profile, donors need to do more than just assess their own private comfort levels. They must ask which form of agency is most aligned with the type of program that is being funded and the structure through which their giving is taking place. Only when the donor's style is understood in terms of its relationship with other points in the philanthropic prism is it possible to come to an assessment of its appropriateness. Viewing style as contingent and situationally defined is very different from the highly personalized perspective that assumes donors have fixed styles embedded in immutable personality traits, deeply held assumptions, and prior experiences. Instead of seeing the real challenge as one of finding a place in the philanthropic landscape where the donor's style finds acceptance, the task becomes one of adjusting and modifying the style depending on the nature of the philanthropic challenge. This is not only a strategically attractive approach in that it allows far greater flexibility in terms of the range of projects and issues that can be tackled, but it also has the merit of easing some of the power asymmetry between giver and recipient. If donors take seriously the idea that their giving style needs to be contextually defined, some of the imbalance in power in philanthropy can be attenuated. This would be a result that not only would satisfy and please nonprofit organizations, but might also give donors the chance to form more satisfying and balanced relationships with the organizations and causes that they support.

9. Time Frames for Giving

Timing is an important part of giving. Because philanthropic resources are always limited to some extent, donors have to decide how much to spend on current needs and how much to conserve for future needs. As a person's wealth and resources increase, the question of timing takes on a special meaning. The trade-offs of current use compared to future use become starker and the stakes rise substantially. At its core, the timing question in philanthropy involves a difficult amalgamation of complex conceptual issues, including a projection into the future of the evolution of a particular problem or issue, an assessment of the benefits of trying to intervene early, and a consideration of the appropriate discount rate. These conceptual tasks are complicated by serious limitations on the accuracy of any of these projections. However, donors who fail to engage the timing issue in philanthropy will have a hard time developing a coherent giving strategy. The timing of giving is inextricably connected to the value proposition, the vehicle through which giving will take place, the style of the donor, and the theory of change that is pursued. Thus, all donors must define an appropriate pace of disbursement, which will vary from a single day to perpetuity. The payout rate will affect both the impact donors will be able to achieve in the short run and the amount of resources that will be left for efforts in the years ahead.

More often than not, the time dimension within philanthropy is overlooked in the rush to implement innovative theories of change and leverage or in the quest for a meaningful and appropriate giving style. In planning a strategy, it is easy to set aside the question of the time frame because other matters appear more "substantive" and more determining of the success or failure of the giving plan to be enacted. Deliberations over the underlying mission or field of activity, explorations of different levels of donor engagement, even the choice of an appropriate vehicle for giving usually attract more attention, interest, and study. Yet the timing of the disbursement of philanthropic dollars is profoundly important because it speaks to the strategic challenge of pacing philanthropy in a way that will fit coherently with the other dimensions of the philanthropic prism. An undefined or ill-defined time horizon can singlehandedly undermine a philanthropic strategy.

Although some donors have committed publicly to carrying out all their philanthropy while alive, the majority of large donors opt to spread out their giving over a period of time reaching deep into the future. In making decisions about timing, donors must weigh how important their legacy and charitable intent truly are. Over time, experience has taught that it is very hard—though not impossible—to maintain control over the governance of philanthropic entities ranging from donor-advised funds in community foundations to private foundations to endowments given to nonprofit organizations such as universities and hospitals. The passing of time has a way of changing the world, the nature of public needs, and the memories and resolve of trustees to protect the intent of the donor. Not all donors accept these realities and many a deceased donor would be appalled to see how time has treated their philanthropic legacy. Still, when donors opt for perpetuity, they are affirming a desire to leave a permanent mark on society, an act that is at once a profoundly private expression of the donor's character and values and a strategic choice about how to address public problems. For in choosing a time dimension, donors make a decision both about the speed with which their philanthropic intent will be fulfilled and the pace at which resources will be directed to the fulfillment of public needs.

Social Problems and Time

Just as there is substantial variation in the personal time horizons of donors, so too do public needs have a range of contours over time. The contour of a public need simply refers to the projected evolutionary path of a need or problem over a long period of time. In some cases, the need will be more acute. In other cases, it will diminish. In still other cases, it will remain the same or will vary unpredictably. The task of thinking about the contour of problems is thus complicated by the fact that some social problems that attract philanthropic attention may have fairly simple and transparent forms, while others are far more difficult to diagnose. The contour of problems and issues is important because the pace of giving over time must be chosen with at least some reference to the contour of the problem being addressed. At a high level of abstraction, it is important to understand how the time frame that guides a donor's giving fits or does not fit with the projected development of the issue to be addressed. In cases in which the costs of delaying action are great, as is the case with major diseases, famines, and intense social crises, donors may need to consider a time frame that privileges current giving. However, when the issue that the donor chooses to address is likely to be present for decades or centuries, as is the case with many global health problems, a longer time frame may well be called for.

There are at least two other major challenges associated with thinking about the public purposes addressed by philanthropy over time. First, it is difficult to project into the future and know with any certainty how trends will play themselves out. There is tremendous uncertainty when predicting social and economic trends and this uncertainty only increases the further one looks out into the future. While models can be developed to chart trend lines and help estimate future needs in a broad range of social areas, the accuracy of these models diminishes as years turn into decades. Moreover, when the social problem is conceptualized very broadly (global warming) rather than narrowly (air quality in Denver), more and more uncertainty is inevitably introduced into the equation. Put simply, as the scope of the issue broadens, the amount of noise in the logic model increases, rendering considered judgments into guesses.

The second problem with projecting the shape or contour of a problem relates to what one might call "the endogeneity problem." It is not clear whether the curves merely represent the shape of a social problem in their ideal and pure form or really reflect the systemic effects of current and future public and private priorities. In other words, a need that is rising may be the result not only of the objective demand of people for a particular good or service but also of expected inadequacies in the levels of that good or service over time. However, since it is hard to project the level and quality of response over time, it is easier to predict the shape of a social problem by assuming that all other intervening factors—including philanthropic expenditures—are stable and do not materially affect the trend line. This is an assumption that is not entirely realistic given the changes that occur in social and political priorities—and how these shifts affect the contour of social problems and the responses that are fashioned. The endogeneity problem thus simply draws our attention to the fact that the "true" future shape of problems must—but ultimately cannot—take into consideration the full range of factors that may change that shape. Since so little is known in the present about future actions, the trends donors consider come with an important simplifying assumption that all other factors are being held constant and that trends will continue.

Still, as one looks across the landscape of social problems, it becomes clear relatively quickly that time affects the evolution of problems dramatically. Take, for example, the global environment. If one were to plot over time the trend line for environmental problems, it would look like a relatively steep ascending curve, at least as measured by greenhouse gases, air and water quality, and other global indicators of environmental stress. Linked closely to population growth and industrialization, the data on the global environment are such that any informed donor would rightly conclude that action is likely to be needed both now and in the future. Yet in making a decision about when to give, now or far in the future, the donor must make a difficult judgment about the probability that his charitable intervention is likely to significantly change the steepness of the curve. If it will not and if philanthropy is by a simple order of magnitude irrelevant to the future contour of the problem, then there may be good reason to save resources for when they will be needed even more urgently. Yet there is something troubling in this sort of analysis. If donors with limited resources can have no effect on the future shape of a social problem, then one might well ask why to give at all. Of course, the answer lies in the way the breadth of a social problem is defined. One donor might reasonably seek to take on the issue of urban sprawl around Chicago, while another might be able to push for international agreements on carbon dioxide emissions. In this sense, strategic giving starts with and demands not only thought about the timing of giving but also in the boundaries around the problem to be addressed. Only when donors choose areas in which it is likely that their giving will have an effect on the future course of events can they truly claim to be doing anything remotely strategic.

Consider next the reverse situation. If environmental problems are getting more serious, there are many areas where the severity of the problem is diminishing. Since the development of the polio vaccine, the scale and human toll wrought by this disease has been shrinking (see figure 9.1). Over time, the number of children victimized by polio has dropped precipitously in developed countries, and has been reduced significantly in developing countries. The Gates Foundation today is spending hundreds of millions of dollars on vaccinations in those parts of the world where the disease is still present. It is useful to consider the issue of endogeneity in this work. In the case of polio, while the trend is in the right direction, donors remain active in this field precisely because they believe it is a field where it is possible to draw a link between the future shape of the problem and the level of current philanthropic activity. That is, giving today will allow the problem to recede faster than if nothing were done. On the surface, social problems exhibiting a downward sloping curve appear to be low-leverage opportunities, in that, even in the absence of giving, the problem will likely diminish. In reality, such situations do offer opportunities, especially when even small increments of change are meaningful due to the high stakes involved.

Some public needs have more complex and variable shapes than either a declining or rising curve. Take, for example, the case of AIDS in the

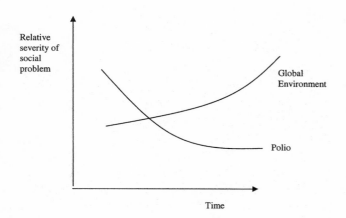

Figure 9.1 **Projected evolution of the problems of global environment and polio over time.**

United States. As the disease spread in the 1980s at high rates, the need for interventions was acute. Today, the rate of infection is lower and the range of treatments is far greater. The curve for AIDS in the United States thus has a convex shape (see figure 9.2). For donors, this raises an interesting issue in terms of the timing of their giving. If active public and private funding of research and public information efforts in the 1990s helped turn the curve downward, are future philanthropic efforts in this area likely to be as valuable as ones made in the short term? The answer lies in where along this line one situates the present. If one believes that we are somewhere just past the apex of the curve, then more giving in the short run will likely help to drive the curve downward in a significant way. If, however, one believes that we are well past the apex and already into the decline, giving in the present or in the future may be harder to justify, especially if other causes are calling. Here the endogeneity problem is very severe, because it is hard to construct a scenario in which interventions did not play a role in turning the tide in terms of the severity of the problem. To be sure, some problems come and go as demographic shifts work themselves out, but in most cases, bending the curve is likely to be the product of intervention and investment. Thus, in the case of polio, it is unlikely that the bend would have occurred in the absence of substantial public and private investment in research and public information. The best evidence of this endogeneity is the course the disease has taken overseas, where efforts to combat the disease started later and were far weaker than in developed nations.

Of course, there are some problems that remain relatively constant in

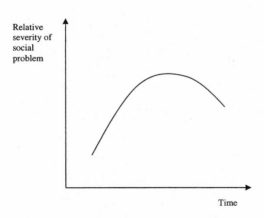

Figure 9.2 **Projected evolution of the problem of AIDS in the United States over time.**

terms of their intensity over time. In the case of rural poverty, the rates have varied little over the past five decades, even with the introduction of many publicly funded initiatives aimed at helping the rural poor (see figure 9.3). Variations in the rural poverty rate have proven to be closely related to the state of the national economy, with recessions imposing a fair amount of pain on the most vulnerable workers. For donors interested in combating poverty, the presence of a relatively flat line is once again conceptually challenging in terms of defining a time frame for giving. One strategy might be to acknowledge that the issue is driven heavily by macroeconomic trends and that the role of philanthropy may simply be to respond consistently over time to need. Under such a strategy, conserving funds in order to be able to respond over the long run would be one plausible course of action. Another approach might be to seek to minimize the social stress by undertaking broader, more integrated steps to move people out of poverty. By acting aggressively in the short run, donors might be able to tilt the trend line downward. Again, the timing of giving depends heavily on other mitigating factors within the system.

An additional scenario is possible. There are some social needs that become extremely acute for short periods of time, then recede only to re-emerge. The most obvious example is disaster relief. Organizations such as the American Red Cross are constantly going through periods of heavy activity aimed at helping devastated communities following hurricanes, fires, and floods. While there is a general ability to predict the timing of this work

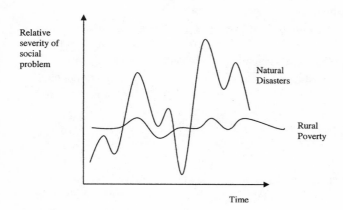

Figure 9.3 **Projected evolution of the problems of natural disasters and rural poverty over time.**

based on years of experience, it is impossible to know with any real certainty when these periods will occur and how closely grouped together the events will be. This can make planning charitable activity extremely difficult and requires a capacity to mobilize to render assistance well before the financial support for the particular intervention has been secured. Another trait of disaster relief is that it requires a very short response time. While some donors deliberate for weeks, months, or years before beginning a charitable initiative, any donor seeking to work in a field as unpredictable as disaster relief must be willing to make decisions quickly.

In considering the shape of the problem that a donor will tackle, it is important to set clear boundaries around the geographical scope of the issue. Depending on the breadth or narrowness of these boundaries—local, regional, national, international—the timing of philanthropic strategies will vary considerably. As the focus broadens, the time horizon, to some extent, must extend outward. Dealing with youth violence on the South Side of Chicago is a formidable task, let alone focusing on the whole city. Dealing with the issue nationally is another matter altogether. And trying to work on youth violence on an international scale is an entirely different proposition. As a donor's focus broadens, two things must happen. First, the amount of money devoted to a problem must be increased and the time allocated for action must be extended. While there are a few areas where substantial economies of scale are obtained and where the client bases are relatively easy to access across the board, in the vast majority of cases, the time horizon of a donor will be conditioned by the way boundaries are drawn around the problem to be addressed.

The assessment of the severity of social problems is highly subjective and imprecise, in that few are likely to agree exactly on the relative threat of global environment change compared to continued levels of rural poverty. The first poses a long-term risk of unknown dimensions to the planet's entire population. The other involves self-evident erosion of human potential and short-term pain of considerable dimensions. However, how one assesses the comparative severity of these problems is less important than is a realistic assessment of the temporal contour of the problem and its relationship to the pace of disbursement chosen by the donor. The rate at which a donor spends its philanthropic capital is often referred to as the payout rate.[1] It is a subject that is at the center of the regulation and oversight of private foundations, but it is also an issue for donors operating free of institutions.

The Payout Rate Decision

The time dimension of philanthropy is translated most often into the operational question of setting a payout rate, expressed as the percentage of assets to be devoted each year to charitable purposes.[2] For individual donors, the payout question can be a simple function of the willingness of donors to part with funds sooner or later, and the resulting speed with which their giving unfolds. For private foundations, the payout rate is the rate of expenditure from the endowment, which is mandated by law to be a minimum of 5 percent of the monthly average value of the endowment over the previous year.[3] In thinking about the rate at which philanthropic funds are spent, there are at least three significant issues: effectiveness, equity, and values expression.[4]

The oldest argument for faster rates of philanthropic disbursals harks back to scientific philanthropy's early claims over Victorian charity and is grounded in beliefs about effectiveness. Giving away larger amounts of money today rather than in the future is attractive because it could make it easier for donors to actually solve social problems within communities, rather than merely treat the symptoms of social disorder. The idea of nipping a problem in the bud rather than waiting years for it to fester has strong intuitive appeal, especially since organized philanthropy for over a century has sought to distance itself from never-ending almsgiving. To be effective, donors need to perform preventive giving, which involves intervening before problems become so acute that no amount of philanthropic support is likely to have much effect. By getting to the root causes and by committing large blocks of philanthropic capital in the short run, donors can in principle avoid having to spend ever larger amounts of money over longer periods of time. In some fields, such as medical research, funding work today has considerably more value than funding research twenty, fifty, or even a hundred years from now. In cases like this, in which problems are likely to grow in the absence of philanthropic interventions, it may actually be more efficient to act in the present and to pay out large amounts of grants in order to tackle a problem aggressively.[5]

Of course, this whole line of argument assumes that philanthropic interventions are likely to be able to get to the root causes of such problems as poverty and not just relieve the visible symptoms (e.g., unemployment) by offering short-term programs (e.g., job training). For this assumption to be plausible, donors would need to commit not only large amounts of funds in the present, but continue to devote resources to the pursuit of the underlying causes of problems. Unfortunately, there is little evidence that even if donors could spend funds in a concentrated and focused way on targeting root causes, they would be able to solve problems that in many cases have persisted for centuries. Moreover, there is even a good case that particular social problems may become more acute than they are today—regardless of how much short-term effort is devoted to addressing the problem. For the fatalistic donor, it is hard to see many problems becoming smaller and less daunting in the future. In fact, some donors might reasonably argue that many areas are likely to grow substantially in their urgency over time, and that charitable funds should be spent cautiously today in order to ensure that large amounts of philanthropic dollars are available in the future, when the problems may become even more pronounced.

There is at least one other dimension to the claim more should be spent in the present in an attempt to reach the root causes of problems. If donors were to push large amounts of money out into the nonprofit sector, rather than place it in perpetual endowments, it is unclear whether nonprofit organizations could absorb and use effectively substantially larger amounts of money in a short period of time. The payout question in philanthropy involves not only the interests and needs of donors, but it also has clear practical implications for the broader nonprofit sector, which uses charitable funds to deliver services. For some donors, substantially increasing the flow of grants to nonprofits is not an obviously efficient way to increase social impact—especially if smaller, local, and less sophisticated nonprofits lack the infrastructure to use these additional funds productively. Moreover, there is always the question of whether growth and scale are universally desirable ends, with many believing that nonprofit agencies are most effective when they are small and tightly linked to local communities. In some areas of activity, there may well be diminishing returns on philanthropic investments. In the area of public policy advocacy, for example, funding new research and public information in those fields already saturated by well-funded groups may not be particularly effective. Nor would it be particularly promising to seek to turn a small community service organization into a national nonprofit through one sudden large infusion of cash. In some cases, funds need to be provided at a pace that matches the capacity of nonprofits to grow and use the funds most effectively.

Another, more subtle argument for current use over future use touches on equity concerns.[6] The whole question of philanthropic payouts has serious fairness implications, especially given the exponential growth in the size of philanthropic assets expected in the coming decades. For some, a higher payout rate may make sense if intergenerational equity is a concern. To be sure, money earned in one generation does not entail a moral or legal obligation to help those who either contributed to one's success or who did not fare as well. Some donors are nevertheless interested in returning some of their wealth in the form of helping others. For this group, the idea of deferring giving until old age, or even further off in the future through the establishment of a foundation, is unappealing. It would create an intergenerational gap that would make it hard for the donor to recognize and thank others. Thus, for individual donors, the temporal dimension of giving raises the difficult question of just who is entitled to receive the public benefits that philanthropy can create. Some donors answer this question by giving out their funds faster and sooner in order to concentrate the effect of their giving on the most proximate circumstances surrounding the creation of the wealth.

The equity issue is somewhat different for private foundations, most of which are established in perpetuity. Foundations have long represented one of the few alternatives to paying high estate taxes, which for many years exceeded 50 percent on large estates. When a foundation is created today, the burden of lost tax revenue is borne by citizens now in the form of a tax expenditure. However, the benefits of any particular foundation's giving largely do not accrue to the citizens who made the tax expenditure that allowed its establishment. Research has shown that the vast majority of private foundations give out each year close to the minimum defined by law, namely 5 percent of the value of their assets. By giving the wealthy the opportunity to create foundations in perpetuity, taxpayers today are in essence being asked to subsidize the welfare of future generations at a time when many current social needs continue to be unmet. This ever-evolving intergenerational transfer of resources would be unproblematic if each generation made tax expenditures of roughly equal size. This is likely not the case, however. As demographic waves of different sizes and with different levels of resources age and convey their wealth into foundations, the unequal intergenerational distribution of foundation assets will become pronounced. Just as the burdens and benefits of Social Security are not distributed equally across generations, so too will low foundation payouts in perpetuity create intergenerational inequities with some generations reaping more benefits than others. Higher payout rates may be needed to even out the costs and benefits of foundation giving.

The problem with this argument is that new money is continually entering the field of philanthropy to replace what might be spent in the short run and to ensure that the philanthropic pie continues to grow. Philanthropy's projected growth should make it easier for donors today to spend their funds on current needs, since future needs will surely be met by other donors who will come of age in the future. Money disbursed by donors and foundations may indeed be lost to endowments forever and may not be entirely available to citizens who made the tax expenditures that encouraged these funds to find homes in foundations. But new funds are entering philanthropy through the creations of new fortunes and new generations of donors, through additional bequests to existing foundations, and through the formation of new foundations. For donors pondering whether higher levels of giving will lead to a long-term diminution in the availability of funds and to the inequitable allocation of benefits across generations, these new sources of funds offer some reassurance that philanthropy's future is secure. Just in the last five years, two foundations created with technology fortunes have leaped to the top of the list of the largest foundations. As a result of recent infusions of funds, the Gates Foundation and the Packard Foundation, both relatively new entries in the foundation field, now control over 5 percent of the assets of the entire field comprising some 60,000 foundations. Other substantial fortunes, including those created by the growing ranks of billionaires, have been pledged to philanthropy, although the funds have not yet arrived at their final institutional resting places. The availability of these new funds for giving in the future should make higher levels of giving today more appealing for any donor concerned about the depleting philanthropic resources or unjustly favoring one generation over another.

The third rationale for prioritizing current needs and current giving stems from the fact that philanthropy is more than just about the satisfaction of public needs. Spending today rather than saving for tomorrow has the benefit of allowing the donor to take part in and enjoy the act of giving. Many donors find tremendous satisfaction in giving away their wealth, recognizing institutions that have touched their lives, and connecting with organizations that are pursuing causes of interest. The satisfaction of giving one's own money away may also be connected to a concern about allowing others to make the decisions in one's stead. The desire to carry out a donor's philanthropic agenda has led some foundations to pursue a payout strategy that will eventually lead to the liquidation of assets. Bob Buford, a major donor in Texas interested in assisting churches and faith-based charitable work, has declared that he intends to do all his giving himself so that he can enjoy translating the fruits of his business success into actions helping causes that are important to him. While this is an extreme position, many donors have begun to do more of their giving while alive simply because they want to enjoy their giving and see their aspirations fulfilled while they are still here. For such donors, giving today oneself makes more sense than giving in the future by someone else.

This may ultimately be the most compelling argument for paying out funds sooner rather than later. Given the tremendous uncertainty over whether greater levels of impact will be achieved by attempting to root out problems in the short run, and given the very unclear question of whether intergenerational inequities are created by the founding of large numbers of foundations today holding enormous amounts of wealth for future disbursement, there is little doubt that calling on donors to spend their funds faster rather than slower (during their life rather than afterwards) creates at least one clear benefit for all: it ensures that philanthropy is animated by the kinds of passions and convictions that only individuals hold. From the perspective of the public interest, having philanthropic principals, not their agents, carry out philanthropy should be a priority since this is the best way to ensure that philanthropy's unique voice in the public sphere continues to be heard loudly and that it speaks in ways that are different from and less constrained than government.

Yet there is and will always be resistance to this argument. Centering principally on the question of particularism and elite control, having donors do their own giving while alive will appear to involve a large unproven assumption that this kind of giving will, in the long run, prove more beneficial for society than giving that is moderated by disinterested agents working within the regulated confines of a foundation or other institutional context. The flaw in this counterclaim is simply that it misses the point that philanthropy is not only about the efficient satisfaction of public needs but also about the satisfaction of the donor. The timing or payout question in philanthropy thus cannot be understood strictly on the basis of how it affects the public in terms of net benefits realized; it must also be understood in terms of the expressive character of philanthropy, which allows it to contribute to pluralism. Alongside the arguments related to effectiveness and equity, the timing of philanthropic giving ultimately brings the discussion right back to the fundamental question of what is truly the underlying purpose of philanthropy. I suggested earlier that while there are many answers to this question, the affirmation of pluralism through expressive acts of caring may be different and more universal than the other more narrowly instrumental functions of philanthropy.

The Idea of Discounting

If the question of how much to give today and how much to give tomorrow appears complex, it gets even more challenging as soon as one begins to unpack the analytical issues it raises.[7] A central issue is that of philanthropic discounting or how the value of giving is measured over time. In theory, discounting could be an useful analytic frame for donors who are planning to pay out philanthropic funds over time, a frame that points to how a sustained consideration of time must inform decisions about giving. If it could be applied to philanthropy, discounting would allow a donor to consider how much future giving will cost in today's dollars. Such information could inform the timing of gifts and the pace at which funds are disbursed. The case for some kind of discounting in philanthropy is straightforward enough. Discounting recognizes that all asset allocation decisions have opportunity costs.[8] To make informed decisions, be they financial or philanthropic, the alternatives need to be known and understood. Donors, formally or informally, routinely evaluate competing grant requests to determine the "best" possible allocation of a limited pool of money. The practice of discounting extends the notion of opportunity costs to broader decisions over time in a systematic and rigorous manner.

The idea of discounting is roughly analogous to the more familiar idea of compounding. While compounding tells us what investment funds will be worth in the future given a set of assumptions about rates of return, discounting tells us what grant funds at some point in the future are worth today, based on similar assumptions.[9] Discounting captures the importance of time in shaping the choices we face about how to use limited resources. When applied in the world of business and government, it is a means to confront methodically difficult questions about intertemporal choices that are wrapped up in many significant decisions.[10] As donors contemplate how to use philanthropic resources over time, discounting could be a tool that would remind them that the competing claims of future generations need to be weighed against those of the current generation.[11] If it could be adapted meaningfully to philanthropy, discounting would allow donors to plan the timing of their philanthropy systematically. However, complications present themselves quickly.

One critical consideration when weighing the value of a future philanthropic dollar against a current philanthropic dollar is the selection of an appropriate discount rate. Discounting is really just a concept until it is rendered operational through the specification of a discount rate. The higher the discount rate, the greater the opportunity cost is of spending today rather than in the future. Conversely, when the discount rate is low, future philanthropic giving appears to cost closer to the same as giving today. Since philanthropy prides itself on tackling difficult social problems that require sustained intervention, donors often must work methodically on those problems over long periods. As they do so, they might be wise to place their decisions in a framework that includes some notion that time matters. The problem is that it is very hard in practice to come up with a clear and compelling case for a given discount rate. Holding all else constant, donors might be tempted to begin their search for a philanthropic discount rate by looking to the rate that they would earn from their financial investments. Why would the rate of return on financial investments be relevant to a philanthropic discount rate? The answer lies in the fact that the rate of return earned by an endowment indicates what sensibly invested funds not donated today will be worth in the future. Any funds not given away today by a foundation with an endowment to be managed will be invested in an account where they will earn the financial rate of return. The opportunity cost of making the grant today rather than the following year thus begins to look like the forgone return that the retained funds would have earned.[12] But there are problems with this approach.

Since the expected rate of return varies dramatically depending on how much risk one is willing to assume in investing an endowment, it should come as no surprise that the discount rate would have to be different for different donors. Some donors have a higher tolerance for risk in pursuit of higher rates of return, while others have a low tolerance for risk. To peg the lower bound of the discount rate, one that has almost no risk and thus provides a very conservative estimate of the value of the future dollar, one might look to the interest rate on long-term U.S. government bonds. Given the fact that most donors are willing to assume some risk in their investments, the actual discount rate would more likely be calculated by taking a weighted average of the expected return from stocks and bonds. But the rate of financial return, while providing a tempting benchmark for setting a philanthropic discount rate, turns out to be an inadequate point of reference.

This basic decision about the value of giving now as opposed to later is complicated by at least three factors that would not be taken into consideration if the simple financial discount rate were applied. First, donors do not know the extent to which the social problems on which they choose to focus will become exacerbated or attenuated as a result of forgoing immediate action. In order to discount accurately, it would be necessary to have a firm understanding of how bad conditions are likely to be in the future. This is difficult to know; projections about social problems have often proven to be far off the mark. Second, donors do not know how the cost of administering and implementing nonprofit services will evolve over the years. Some fields will have high rates of cost escalation while others will be much flatter. Without being able to know the nonprofit inflation rate in particular fields, it would be very difficult to know what the costs will be in the future in order to accurately discount them.[13] Third, donors may be working on multiple issues over time, and each will have its own discount rate. Few donors devote all their resources to one particular issue or purpose over a long period of time. In practice, many of the larger institutional donors have tremendous freedom to change and adapt over the years, as social problems arise. In addition, many of these funders are operating simultaneously in multiple fields. To discount accurately, careful calculation across each field would be needed.

Like all actors facing a difficult intertemporal decision, donors are likely to be tempted to rely on reasonable simplifying assumptions: namely that social problems will evolve as they have over time, that program costs will rise modestly like everything else, and that differences across fields will even out in the long run. We know, for example, that many of the most pressing social problems are rarely subject to sudden reversal or dramatic decline. While there is no donor price index that can easily be consulted, the costs of delivering services in the nonprofit sector have not evolved demonstrably differently from those in the broader economy. Across fields, we know that all nonprofits face rising costs to some degree and that the difference between higher education, a notorious outlier in the sector, may not reflect the broader sector's more moderated trends. On the whole, the past gives donors a reasonable point of departure for thinking about how the context for philanthropy will evolve over the years. Only by making reasonable simplifying assumptions can donors begin to see and adjust to the undeniable fact that philanthropic funds spent in the present need to be valued differently from funds spent some time in the distant future.

This much said, there are still some large obstacles to making the idea of discounting applicable to the world of giving. Chief among them is translating a mathematical calculation into a strategic planning process. A first step might be to note that donors engage in some kind of calculus about social benefits each time they award a grant to one qualified applicant while denying a grant to another qualified applicant. In deciding what programs to support, donors routinely make judgments about the comparative value of different options based on the social benefits that are likely to accrue. This is an imprecise science, but one that is needed when trying to sort out the many competing claims on philanthropic resources. On the other hand, in deciding how much to give now versus in the future, it is more appropriate for donors to think in terms of the costs of competing intertemporal strategies. The discounting approach described therefore draws attention to the costs of the various alternative strategies available to donors while bracketing some of the measurement problems associated with the assessment of the benefits of specific grantmaking decisions. If some of the obstacles could be overcome or at least rendered manageable, discounting would make it possible to compare the cost of acting immediately versus waiting to make a grant and, in the process, allow one to attack some critical issues in grantmaking strategy.

Interestingly, the two most common criticisms of discounting—particularly prominent in the field of environmental policy—have traditionally been ethical in character and do not relate to the difficulty in setting a rate or implementing this mode of thinking.[14] The first is that discounting unfairly privileges the present generation at a cost to future generations. In the area of philanthropy, some might reasonably argue that equating the philanthropic discount rate with the financial rate of return would lead to an unacceptably low present valuation of future philanthropic benefits. This objection misses the point that discounting simply applies the logic of compounding and helps us recognize that funds that are invested, rather than spent now, will grow over time, which will make greater resources available for future generations. Discounting reflects this fact, makes no ethical judgment about who is more deserving, and thus puts all generations on an equal footing.

Critics of discounting might offer a second objection by asking how donors can reasonably apply a test to their giving that says that a life saved in the future is worth less than a life saved today. Since philanthropy often attacks difficult problems facing the most needy and vulnerable members of society, discounting might appear to cheapen philanthropy and subject its opportunity costs to a primitive comparison to the return on financial assets. The practice of discounting would thus seem like a questionable, if not untenable, proposition.[15] The difficulty of sustaining this moral position is that it simply does not answer the question posed by philanthropic discounters. In essence, the donor that refuses to discount on moral grounds substitutes a normative question—what do we owe future generations?—each time the foundation that discounts poses an analytic question—how do we balance the donor needs of future generations with those of the current one? These two questions are different enough to make one realize that defining a core problem in philanthropy as one of addressing issues of efficiency and intergenerational equity quickly pushes giving into the competing realms of analytics and ethics.

The conflicting analytic and ethical questions raised by foundation giving also demonstrate that thoughtful philanthropy involves confronting both obligations and opportunity costs. Philanthropic discounting is a first step toward finding a solution to the deeper and more politically charged questions of deciding how much donors should pay out in grants now versus how much they should pay out in the future, a decision that has multibillion dollar implications.[16] Discounting—even if only used as a tool for defining strategy and framing central questions and concerns—can be an important focusing device for donors who pay out philanthropic funds over time, a device that draws their attention to the complex time dimension in philanthropy.

Donors' Definition of the Time Dimension

Outside the world of private foundations, a growing number of individual donors have begun to seek answers to the question of when to do their giving. Some have taken bold and decisive steps to confront the issue of intergenerational equity; witness the rise of "mega-gifts," which in several cases have reached into the hundreds of millions of dollars. Many members of the new generation of major donors, drawn increasingly from the ranks of successful entrepreneurs, have declared their commitment to doing their own giving during their own lifetimes. The rise of these do-it-yourself donors and the appearance of new, more flexible vehicles for philanthropy for smaller donors (such as the charitable gift funds now offered by mutual fund companies) have helped open new channels outside of foundation philanthropy for exploring the responsibilities of wealth. This choice between giving while alive or after death is a personal one that depends on whether donors feel a calling for philanthropy or whether they believe they can best contribute to society by building wealth and leaving the giving to others.

Some very wealthy individuals have postponed their philanthropy precisely because they believe their greatest social contribution is building wealth that others can then disburse at a later time. The investor Warren Buffett, for one, has argued that his time is better spent on making his money grow than on giving it away. As a consequence, Buffett has declared his intention to create a foundation that will receive the bulk of his estate after his death. Trusted advisers and talented scientists will then administer the funds to maximize the social benefit that this wealth can create, with a possible focus on global population growth issues. Buffett has concluded that his philanthropic discount rate is considerably lower than the financial rate of return that he is able to realize in the business world. Other modern philanthropists have reached similar conclusions. Entrepreneur John D. MacArthur, who made a fortune in the insurance and real estate fields but left most of his wealth to others to give away, famously declared: "I figured out how to make the money. You fellows [at the MacArthur Foundation] will have to figure out how to spend it." In other cases, smaller donors have made the news only upon their death, when it is revealed that they focused on saving their money during their lives rather than spending it, so that others could later benefit. In these and many other cases, it is apparent that philanthropy beckons people in very different ways.

When wealthy people eschew giving during their lives, they may have a host of reasons that have little to do with a rational calculus of a discount rate. Instead, it simply may reflect an unwillingness to confront their own mortality or the inability to make a decision about what causes are worth supporting. Delaying one's giving in order to focus on asset accumulation has its dangers, however. The history of philanthropy is littered with tales of donor betrayal and the overthrowing of the charitable intent. As time has marched on, many donors who have sought to enshrine their philanthropic legacy in perpetuity have been rudely rebuffed by trustees and executors. The idea of perpetuity—that philanthropic institutions should exist forever—is a controversial part of giving today that most major donors will confront. The allure of perpetuity is strong. It promises to allow the donor to live—or at least have his or her legacy live—forever. By linking the donor's name to philanthropic institutions that are established in perpetuity, philanthropy can be one of the few salves to the gloomy reality of death. The idea of perpetuity is not a simple and uncomplicated one. After all, there is something at once very noble and very presumptuous about the idea of philanthropic legacies living on forever and good deeds being done in the name of someone long dead. Presumptuous, in that forever is a very, very long time. Noble, in that the impulse to establish a foundation in perpetuity represents a selfless and caring act to project good work across time to unknown legions of persons. It means that donors are able to project the benefits of their giving way off into the future and in the process separate themselves from the act of giving. Perpetuity also means that the donor is willing to trust others to act in keeping with a more or less clearly defined charitable intent and to do so in a way to benefit people who are not even born.[17]

There are several ways in which the idea of perpetuity can be realized. Among the most obvious is the establishment of a foundation that will operate in perpetuity and be governed by a board of trustees. This option has been chosen by thousands of donors in the United States. There are challenges to making such an arrangement work, chief among them preserving the donor's intent over time and ensuring that accountability systems are in place once the donor is no longer on the scene. Sometimes, donors will attempt to maintain some control and avoid mission drift by specifying either that family members should serve as trustees or that certain selection criteria should be followed in naming trustees in the future. No matter how much work is done to tether a foundation to its founder, perpetuity slippage will always be hard to avoid. Of course, one solution to the issue of mission drift is simply to define a mission that is so broad that there really is nothing that could be done that would ever be outside the parameters of the donor's stated charitable intent. Defining one's charitable intent in very broad terms may reduce the expressive content of giving and make it less appealing to donors, however. Trading away some or all ability to use philanthropic funds for distinctive purposes may turn out to be too high a price for the pleasures of perpetuity. In practice, few donors actually see a zero-sum game between the length of the time horizon of their giving and the specificity of the mission that will be pursued. In fact, the recent history of philanthropy is full of cases in which donors have set in place missions that have proved difficult to sustain over time. The result has been a series of battles, featuring both legal challenges from regulators on the outside and struggles for control among trustees on the inside.

The tension between time and control plays itself out within the context of the principal-agent relationship in philanthropy. Although it is clear that foundation administrators are agents, there has been in recent years increasing disagreement about who truly is the principal in philanthropy. Obviously, foundation trustees and staff have a responsibility to the donor, but the tax-exempt status of foundations has led some to argue that the public at large is the real principal to whom professional staff must act as loyal agents. After all, the argument goes, foundations are granted special status by government and must justify their tax exemption by meeting public needs.

Large-scale philanthropy requires organization and planning. Thus, when a donor establishes a foundation with substantial assets, the donor invariably selects a board whose job it is to oversee the institution's operations and ensure the long-term viability of the founder's philanthropic mission. The board serves collectively as the agent of the donor and brings to the grantmaking process a distinct set of talents and resources that are used to advance the donor's interests. Because the foundation board acts on behalf of a principal, it must scrupulously exclude its own interests when negotiating a myriad of philanthropic transactions with grantseeking third parties.

Donors seek out agents because they allow the philanthropic vision of the donor—in theory at least—to be pursued in perpetuity. The agent of the donor, who administers the foundation, provides the donor not only with technical assistance in the disbursal of funds, but also with a means to carry on philanthropic activity well into the future. Because of this element of permanence, donors often seek out persons whom they know and trust to serve as agents, including family members, long-time business associates and attorneys, and influential members of the local community. Members of the donor's inner circle serving on the foundation's board may in turn be asked to select professional staff members they believe can be trusted to act in good faith in carrying out the day-to-day grantmaking of the foundation.

While the principal-agent relationship in modern philanthropy might appear simple and straightforward, nothing could be further from the truth. The primitive model of agency portrayed in this brief account belies the complexity of the issues of duty and professional responsibility within the field of philanthropy. The question of whose interests foundation professionals are charged with representing has become increasingly difficult to ascertain in recent times. Although there may well have been a time long ago when matters of duty in philanthropy were fairly clear-cut, foundation workers today often find themselves torn between two opposing allegiances—one to the donor and the other to the public at large. The tax-exempt status of foundations has led many activists in the nonprofit community to argue that foundations have important responsibilities to the public they serve. Taken to its logical conclusion, this argument about the public responsibilities of tax-exempt organizations culminates in the view that the real principal in philanthropy is not the donor, but rather the public, and that money put in foundations is really part of a "public trust" to be directed toward public purposes. Under this view, once a donor sets up a foundation, his claim to full control over the funds is weakened by the countervailing public claim to these resources.

To complicate matters further, foundations have two distinct management levels, and each level has a distinct understanding of its responsibilities as an agent. Trustees who sit on the foundation's board are charged with defining long-term goals, hiring staff, managing investments, and approving grants. The level of trustee involvement in the actual grantmaking varies greatly from foundation to foundation. In all circumstances, however, trustees have a duty to protect the integrity of the foundation's mission and its compliance with all relevant laws. Professional staff, from the executive director down to the program officers, are charged with evaluating grant proposals and making recommendations to the board. They are the foundation's contact with the community and carefully manage relations with grantseeking nonprofit organizations.

For many years, the dominant view within the foundation community was that trustees are bound by the guidelines and institutional goals put in place by the donor. According to this view, trustees have a duty to protect the values, interests, and desires—no matter how outlandish they might be—of the donor who created the philanthropic institution that the board was subsequently entrusted to operate. For those who claim foundation trustees are nothing other than agents of the donor, the problem of what standards should be used when deliberating over the disbursal of funds and the programmatic direction of the organization could not possibly be clearer: trustees must seek to ascertain whether the donor—were they present—would support the work of the foundation. When the donor is alive (perhaps even serving on the foundation's board), the relationship between principal and agent is significantly simplified. But when the donor is deceased and only a vague institutional memory of the donor's interests and values survives, the issue of agency becomes more complicated. For just as in literary studies, there is a question as to whether authorial intent can—or should—ever be fully or accurately reconstructed.[18]

A foundation's professional staff members have a different set of responsibilities. Rather than worry about the donor's intent or program priorities, the staff is charged with effectuating the board's agenda. Staff members do this by locating those grant applicants that best meet the program objectives of the foundation. When it comes to the principal-agent problem in philanthropy, staff are less clearly responsible to the donor than trustees. In fact, after years of interacting with local nonprofit organizations, some foundation professionals believe that they are in fact agents of the grantseekers and the needy clients that these organizations serve. For this reason, professional staff members often define their work as being advocates before the foundation's board for the most deserving community organizations. Over the past three decades, this new, public-oriented view of the principal-agent relationship has also slowly been embraced by trustees in large, established foundations. Within this climate of deference to professional judgment, the charitable intent of donors has been challenged through the courts under what has come to be known as the "cy pres doctrine."

The Cy Pres Doctrine and Donor Intent

> What right has the State, or those called upon to administer a charity, to dictate conditions to its founder? Those conditions may seem to us foolish fancies; we may deem ourselves far more competent to establish such as will secure the general object, but it is not ours to say. When we see fit to create such a foundation out of our fortunes, we shall be at perfect liberty to show our wisdom, but it is out of place in administering the fortunes of others . . . One may do what he will with his own.[19]

This opinion, rendered by the Missouri Supreme Court in 1869, expressed the quintessentially American belief that private wealth, when lawfully gained, is subject only to individual control. Much of the history of legal rules governing trusts and foundations appears to support this belief. The sanctity of the donor's intent may be a centerpiece in American traditions, but there will be circumstances in which the donor's wishes cannot be carried out, in which the mission established is no longer practicable. In such circumstances, the courts may intervene and apply the doctrine of cy pres. The term "cy pres" comes from the Norman French *cy pres comme possible*, which means "as near as possible." The cy pres doctrine provides that a court may modify the express terms of a charitable trust whose specified purpose has become impossible, illegal, or impracticable to fulfill only if the donor had a general charitable intent. By making modification of the trust contingent on the donor's charitable intent, "*cy pres* suggests that, whatever the court does, it does with the consent of the phantom donor."[20] Thus, even after death, the intent of the donors is not only allowed to live on, but viewed as something to be protected as much as is reasonably possible.

The history of the doctrine can be traced back to English common law at the time of the American Revolution, when two types of cy pres—judicial and prerogative—were recognized. The power to invoke judicial cy pres was originally exercised in the English chancery courts by the chancellor in his capacity as a judge. Rulings were based on legal interpretation and judgment, with fidelity to the donor's intent pursued as much as possible. The power to call forth prerogative cy pres was invested in the crown and exercised at the discretion of the king by the chancellor as his minister. While judicial cy pres directed the court to carry out the testator's intention as closely as possible, the prerogative doctrine allowed the king to apply the property for any charitable purpose he might select without considering what the wishes of the testator might have been. In other words, it vested in the king the ability to usurp donor intent. In the frequently cited case of *Da Costa v. Da Pas*, a Jewish testator established a trust for an assembly to study Jewish law, but the king used his prerogative power to direct that the funds be used to teach children about Christianity. The purpose of the trust was deemed illegal because at the time it was unlawful to promote any religion other than that of the Church of England. For obvious reasons, there was resistance in America to the tyrannical exercise of prerogative cy pres. By the early nineteenth century, American courts began to show their distaste for redirecting charitable trusts to purposes that were clearly opposed to the donor's declared intent. These early rulings rejecting cy pres tended to overlook the difference between judicial and prerogative cy pres, seeing both as arbitrary exercises of power. Today, there are three common law prerequisites to the application of judicial cy pres: (1) the gift must be for charity; (2) the donor must have general charitable intent; and (3) the purpose of the gift must be illegal, impossible, or impracticable to further via the specified terms.[21]

Cy pres is the most visible and controversial point of contact between giving and government, but it is not the only one. The tax-exempt nature of charitable activity means that the private interests of the donor must be aligned, somehow, with the public interest. As a consequence, the state and its many regulatory powers have become active over the past few decades in all levels of philanthropy:

> The trust becomes operative only after a court has found, either specifically or by inference, that it is charitable . . . To encourage a continuous flow of funds into philanthropic enterprises, [the court] bestows privileges, of which tax immunity is only one. The state creates and defines charitable trusts, grants them perpetual existence, modernizes them through *cy pres*, appoints and regulates trustees,

approves accounts, construes ambiguous language in the trust charter and sometimes goes so far as to impose a less stringent standard of tort liability on such trusts than on their private counterparts.[22]

The cy pres doctrine is particularly important to philanthropy because it represents an enforcement mechanism aimed at preserving the covenant between the donor and those charged with carrying out the donor's mission and running the foundation. Cy pres limits the ability of boards and staff to change the focus of a foundation's giving programs, particularly if these changes run counter to the intent of the donor. In this sense, cy pres operates somewhat like a straitjacket. While there is room for some wriggling, foundation trustees are not completely free to disburse funds as they see fit as long as the donor has established a reasonably defined and feasible mission. Of all the ways that foundations come into contact with legal institutions, struggles over cy pres are particularly significant because they bear not only on the programmatic direction of foundations, but also on their management. The interpretation of cy pres, when broad and liberal, invests trustees and staff with real powers. By the same token, if cy pres is interpreted narrowly and modifications are discouraged, foundation trustees are limited in their ability to adjust an institution's grantmaking focus. Cy pres is the legal structure around the core issue of charitable intent, which the time dimension of giving invariably raises.

The very topic of donor intent continues to stir controversy, in part because it speaks to the line between the public and private dimensions of philanthropy.[23] By holding that donors actually have a right and interest in preserving their philanthropic legacy, defenders of the idea of donor intent are often viewed as mavericks or conservatives in philanthropy. Without a clear commitment to doing what is most efficient or effective, sympathizers with the goal of preserving the donor's intent can been painted as preoccupied with property rights and the prerogatives of the wealthy. The struggle for the moral high ground on this issue has led to the drawing of the parallels between the ideas of donor intent in philanthropy and the theory of original intent in Constitutional interpretations. Just as some hold that the only way to properly interpret the Constitution is to work back from the present to the intent of the Founders in writing the document, so too can a case be made that the meaning and purpose of a trust or foundation mission must be anchored in the concrete and fixed object of authorial intent. The significance of a particular charitable intent may change over time, but the actual meaning is unwaveringly linked to the intent of the founder.

Without having this reference point, meaning would be hard to establish with any reliability; arbitrating between competing interpretations would be all but impossible. When it comes to Constitutional interpretation, the alternative point of view to original intent doctrine is often grounded in the notion that texts such as the Constitution are in fact living documents and that their meaning changes as time passes. The traditional problem with this argument is that it becomes difficult to set boundaries on the potential meaning of texts if authorial intent is not a central criteria.[24]

To bolster their claims, those who argue that the permanence of philanthropic intent must be sacrosanct make two very practical arguments. The first argument is that the contract that donors draw up with eternity is what encourages them to leave their funds for future generations. Undermining this contract would have very negative effects on the willingness of future generations of donors to entrust their funds to others to administer. Thus, as a policy tool for encouraging future giving, protection of a donor's intent is needed to give future philanthropists the confidence they need to pass their wealth on to others to administer. The second argument relates to a perceived role of philanthropy. Those who take the idea of donor intent seriously believe that only by protecting the idiosyncratic and at times outlandish ideas of donors will it be possible for philanthropy to innovate and pursue ideas that are either ahead of or behind their time. The awkwardness—and even apparent inappropriateness and irrelevance—of some philanthropic ideas is a small price to pay for affirming the value of pluralism and diversity that respect for private visions of the public good entails. By arguing that the trust and confidence between donor and trustee will be eroded if the donor's intent is not respected, and by suggesting that the concept of protecting private visions of the public realm is a key element of a vibrant pluralistic society, the defenders of donor intent make a fairly compelling case.

Critics of the slavish pursuit of a donor's philanthropic desires counter with two arguments of their own. The first is that philanthropic funds are really public funds being held in trust for public purposes; thus, the guiding principle in the disposition of these resources must be the public's needs, not the desires of particular individuals. In making this claim, critics point to the favorable tax treatment given to philanthropic funds and refer to this treatment as a sign that the funds have passed into the public realm. Given the expectation that charitable funds will be deployed in ways that create public benefits, the argument for a more activist approach to overseeing charitable purposes over time rests on the assumption that the public has a legitimate interest in ensuring that these privileged funds be used sensibly and effectively. The second argument relates to the limited capacity of donors to see into the future. Under such circumstances, most donors want their trustees to use reasonable judgment in modifying their philanthropic intent so as to keep pace with changing times and social attitudes. Moreover, adequate legal protections are in place to ensure that these modifications are made only in extreme circumstances. Usually, a donor's philanthropic intent can be modified significantly only if trustees can demonstrate to a court that the current mission has become impossible or impracticable.[25]

Examples of conflicts over mission definition after the death of the donor are legendary and numerous. One of the most high-profile disputes pitted the friends and associates of Milton Hershey against each other in a struggle for the control of the chocolate magnate's philanthropic legacy. In Hershey, Pennsylvania, the company founder created a school for orphans that has grown and now serves 1,500 students, mostly from single-parent families. The school's most notable feature turned out to be its endowment, which rose to over $5 billion, greater than that of all but a small number of private universities in the country. The Hershey School, which serves children from kindergarten through high school, has 650 full-time employees, spends $60,000 per student, and is located on a plush campus with a new library, arts center, swimming pools, and the latest technology. Given these substantial expenditures, some alumni and community members believed that the school was not maximizing its potential and that it should enlarge the number of students it served, rather than spend lavishly on new facilities.

The leadership of the school created a controversy in 1999, when they proposed using some of the institution's wealth to fund a foray into research and training related to educating needy children. To make this important shift in priorities, the school took the unusual step of going to probate court to seek permission to divert $25 million to the construction of a Catherine Hershey Institute for Learning and Development and additional funds to support its operating budget in the coming years. In seeking permission to undertake this project, the school's board had to show that it was unable to use the funds left to the school efficiently and that the modification sought was in keeping with the general charitable intent of the Hersheys. The move created a major division within the community. Some argued that the creation of a research institute, far from allowing the school to help more children, represented an abandonment of the real values and commitments of the Hershey family. Citing evidence that Milton Hershey did not want his funds used by others to create monuments themselves, a group of nearby residential programs for disadvantaged children petitioned the court for part of the Hershey overflow.

The problem of maintaining Milton Hershey's charitable intent had been confronted at least once before. In 1963, the school received permission from the court to give $50 million to Pennsylvania State University for a medical center in Hershey. Over time, other conflicts have surfaced as the school's trustees have sought to interpret and enact Hershey's philanthropic desires. Over the years, the school deemphasized vocational training and began to put more and more emphasis on college preparatory work, which infuriated many graduates who learned trades at the school. They alerted the state attorney general to a possible violation of the donor's intent, and eventually a deal was struck to preserve some vocational education. As the controversy has continued to rage over time over the use of the large bequest of Milton Hershey, one thing is undeniably clear. The establishment of a perpetual trust has created the difficult challenge of interpreting and remaining faithful to the donor's intent as the world has changed and the amount of money in the trust has increased.

Acrimony and lawsuits seem to become more common as the amount of philanthropic assets in question increases. Determining how closely to adhere to the donor's intent was particularly difficult in the case of Albert C. Barnes and the display of his magnificent collection of Impressionist paintings.[26] Barnes was a Philadelphia chemist and businessman who made his fortune in pharmaceuticals. By 1910, he had made enough money to focus on three things that interested him deeply: philanthropy, radical politics, and art. Barnes used his money to support a broad range of leftist causes, including support to Leon Trotsky during his exile from the Soviet Union, and counted as his friends intellectuals such as John Dewey and Bertrand Russell, both of whom were hired by his foundation at one time or another. Barnes was a notoriously difficult man who engaged in lifelong disputes with most of the Philadelphia institutions, including the Philadelphia Museum of Art, the Pennsylvania Academy of Fine Arts, and Haverford, Swarthmore, and Bryn Mawr Colleges, with the leading art critics of the day, and with many of the newspapers and magazines that had dared to write about him. He wrote a vast number of insulting letters during his life using a range of different pen names, including that of his dog, Fidele de Port Manech.

Barnes's great virtue was that he was among the very first Americans

to appreciate the importance of French modernism. He bought master-
pieces by the dozens, eventually accumulating a collection of over a hundred Cézannes, sixty Matisses, and scores of Renoirs and Monets. In 1922,
he created the Barnes Foundation with the goal of both finding a reposi-
tory for his art and building an alternative to the modern museum. In the
course of his collecting, Barnes convinced himself that he had developed
a special way of looking at art and decided to use his collection to teach
others how to appreciate art. The paintings were, in his mind, teaching
tools. Barnes hated the idea of creating a museum that would be open to
the public, where people could simply walk about chatting and socializ-
ing, rather than seriously studying the art on display. In fact, a clause of the
foundation's bylaws explicitly notes that no "receptions, tea parties, din-
ners, banquets, dances, musicales or similar affairs" can ever be held in
the museum. To visit the collection on the few days it was open to the public, it was necessary to write in advance and request an admission ticket.
While alive, Barnes routinely denied admission to any person with an affiliation to any major Philadelphia institution or anyone who appeared to be
of means. The foundation bylaws also contained a provision that the collection should be open and free to "plain people, that is men and women who
earn their livelihood by daily toil in shops, factories, schools, stores, and
similar places."

Perhaps the most unusual part of the Barnes philanthropic legacy was
the strictures he put in the care of the collection. Not only could no painting
ever be lent to another institution, but no painting from another collection
could ever be shown in his building. Barnes also insisted that none of his
paintings should ever be moved from the positions he had placed them in
within the building. This was particularly significant because Barnes chose
to display the paintings very close to another, stacked high, often in strange
patterns. Moreover, Barnes did not want any catalogue of his collection to
be produced, nor did he want the school that would be connected to the
collection to teach painting, drawing, or sculpting. The school would simply
use the collection to teach art appreciation. To lock in all his philanthropic
intentions clearly and permanently, the foundation's bylaws included an
article that notes that the foundation's articles are "unamendable and shall
never be amended in any manner whatsoever."

Soon after Barnes died in a car crash in 1951, litigation connected with
the Barnes Foundation began over small matters, such as the number of
days it would be open to the public. Then over time the struggle reached
more important matters. While Barnes's friends and associates were able to

maintain control of the foundation for close to four decades, by the 1990s the board had turned over substantially and eventually included only persons appointed by Lincoln University, a traditionally African American university located nearby that had been given the responsibility of filling board vacancies. Over the coming decade, under the leadership of university-affiliated board members and a new president, almost all of Barnes's philanthropic intentions were reversed. One by one, the key blocks in the charitable vision of Barnes were knocked down by the courts. The board sought and received court approval to produce a color catalog produced by a major publishing house, to develop a CD-ROM of the collection, to send part of the collection on a worldwide tour where it would be shown in other museums, to charge a substantial admission fee, and to increase the operating hours. One effort undertaken by the new board did fail: an attempt to sell a number of paintings to pay for a major renovation of the Barnes Foundation building was eventually abandoned as public criticism mounted and as alternative revenue-generating activities were located.

Of course, some of Barnes's philanthropic ideas were strange and unconventional. They fit his personality and temperament better than the mood of the public. Still, with the possible exception of the early limitations on public access, most of the elements of Barnes's plans for his legacy were probably feasible and legal. But because he chose perpetuity as his time frame, was unable to control the board after his death, and did not foresee the changes that Lincoln University would seek to impose, his private vision was ultimately almost entirely thwarted. Today, while the paintings still hang in the places where he left them, the Barnes Foundation is a vastly changed institution, and even more changes are coming when a new museum for the collection is completed in Philadelphia. The experience of Albert C. Barnes makes clear that perpetuity requires one to have either a fairly broad philanthropic mandate or a willingness to allow time to reshape substantially the purposes defined by the donor. While not all foundations veer away from the donor's intent as dramatically as in the Barnes case, there is ample evidence that many philanthropic institutions have evolved pronouncedly from the original direction defined by their donors.

While struggles over intent are usually a function of the passage of time and the changing nature of society, they can take on more political overtones. Most people know that Henry Ford was a legendary businessman who built one of the largest and most successful companies in American history. What few people realize is that Henry Ford had very distinctive views about society and human nature. Having seen the way work could transform men, Ford believed that the best way to help people was not by giving them something but by giving them a chance to earn for themselves. Recipients of charity, he worried, were being trained to expect something for nothing, a practice that would cripple them over the long run. Ford once declared, "I believe in living wages. I do not believe in charity. I believe we should all be producers. Organized charity and schools of charity and the whole idea of 'giving' to the poor are on the wrong track. They don't produce anything."[27] Ford applied his idea during his lifetime to a number of major projects including a major effort to revitalize the town of Inskter, a town outside of Detroit with a large minority population that was in serious decline. Instead of providing grants, Ford offered jobs to the town's residents and helped them organize their own community revitalization effort. The episode was important because it exemplified Ford's deep conviction that traditional forms of charity were destined to fail and that the only way to truly help those in need is through employment.

If Ford had dim views about mainstream charity, including the early philanthropic foundations, he nevertheless confronted a major dilemma in 1935, when Congress enacted estate taxes that rose to over 70 percent. While there was some concern at the time about the effect these taxes would have on family-held businesses like Ford Motor Co., the desire to punish the rich and force them to share their wealth was stronger. Seeking to protect his family's control of the company, Ford created the Ford Foundation on January 15, 1936, and a will that provided that nonvoting shares in the company would go to the foundation upon his and his wife Edsel's death. The voting shares would remain in the family. This arrangement allowed Ford to place the bulk of his wealth in his new philanthropic institution while giving his son and grandchildren the chance to operate the business. For close to a decade, the Ford Foundation operated in anonymity and with minimal resources. Only upon the death of Henry Ford in 1947 did the Ford Foundation become the biggest foundation in the country.[28] From the outset, Ford's son Henry Ford II decided that the family would not attempt to control the foundation. Henry Ford II, chairman of the board of both the Ford Motor Company and the Ford Foundation, believed that the amount of money the foundation handled was so great that it needed outsiders in addition to the family members who would serve. It was a decision he would regret for much of the rest of his life.

The next thirty years of philanthropic activity were filled with adventures and misadventures, starting with the creation of the progressive Fund for the Republic, which the educator Robert Maynard Hutchins led into many controversial political battles, carrying on through the funding of voter registration drives in Cleveland, which helped Carl Stokes become the first African American mayor of a major American city, and culminating with the turbulent tenure of McGeorge Bundy as president, when the foundation's free spending eroded its endowment. During all this time, Henry Ford II could only watch as the board moved the foundation in ever new directions and with ever greater worldwide involvements. By 1976, Henry Ford II gave up and resigned from the board, declaring that he could no longer recognize the place. His letter of resignation pointed to what he thought was a troubling departure of the foundation from the values and intentions of its founder: "The foundation is a creature of capitalism, a statement that, I'm sure, would be shocking to many professional staff people in the field of philanthropy. It is hard to discern recognition of this fact in anything the foundation does." To be sure, Henry Ford was no staunch social and political conservative, but he was vehemently and unrepentantly probusiness. And Henry Ford II could not accept the substantial mission drift of the foundation over the years. Later, he would explain that he made a terrible mistake in not spreading the family's funds evenly among the Henry Ford Museum, the Henry Ford Hospital, and the Ford Foundation. The sheer size of the foundation led it inevitably into fields and areas that were simply beyond the intent of the founder. All of which alienated the founder's remaining family representatives involved with the foundation, eventually leading to an acrimonious parting of the ways between the family and the philanthropy it had spawned.

Much has been written about the story of the Ford Foundation. Some accounts have focused on the good work the foundation has done around the world, others have focused on some notable fiascoes underwritten by the foundation. Regardless of how one views the actual performance of the Ford Foundation over the past half century, the resignation from the board of Henry Ford II was troubling because it indicated that even if the Ford Foundation has produced significant public benefits, it fell radically short in terms of satisfying the intent of the donors and their family. By putting the vast majority of his wealth into a single perpetual philanthropic institution, Henry Ford gambled that his survivors would watch over his wealth as closely as he watched over his business. This did not happen, because the donor did not set up safeguards to protect his intent and also because Henry Ford's charitable intent was not transparently clear and, given the size of the assets, necessarily broad.

Even donors with more modest estates and relatively straightforward philanthropic ideas have had their intent thwarted over time. More recently, a 1995 lawsuit by a New York nonprofit organization against a community foundation rekindled the debate over the sanctity of a donor's intent. The suit was the strange product of an incorrectly addressed bank statement. In 1993, officials of the nonprofit Community Service Society of New York opened their mail and found a bank deposit slip for an account they did not know existed. The account had been started for the benefit of the society by a set of donors in 1929 and had always been controlled by the New York Community Trust, the largest community foundation in the nation. When the bank statement was accidentally sent to the Community Service Society because the organization's name was on the account, the society's director was surprised to learn of the account's existence and puzzled that no money from the account had been received by his organization for almost twenty-five years.

The reason no money had been forthcoming soon became known. In 1971, the directors of the New York Community Trust decided that the money in the trusts should be redirected to other organizations because—and this fact is now being disputed—the Community Service Society changed its focus during the 1960s from direct service programs for the needy to social change advocacy. Even though the donors had specifically designated the Community Service Society as the beneficiary of the trusts, the directors of the New York Community Trust decided that there was reason enough in 1971 to invoke a variance clause agreed to by the donors. Over the past twenty-five years, funds derived from the trusts were directed to other antipoverty groups in New York that the trustees of the New York Community Trust believed were more committed to providing direct services to the poor.

In its suit, the Community Service Society maintained that its mission has not changed and that the donor's designation of the charity as the sole recipient of the trusts' income should not have been contravened. The lawsuit sought to recover about $8 million that the organization would have received had the community foundation not rerouted the money. Responding to press inquiries, members of the foundation's board have argued that they did nothing wrong and that the rare invocation of the variance clause was necessary to ensure that a donor's philanthropic intent did not become obsolete or impracticable. After much legal wrangling, the courts found that the trust had abused its variance power but that the Community Service Society had been given adequate notice and had waited too long to bring suit.[29] More than anything else, the New York case raised questions about the bonds linking donors and community foundation trustees because in this case the intent was fairly clear and the reasons for the variance sought by the trustees were not overwhelmingly compelling.

These lingering questions—and doubts—have practical consequences for community and private foundations and for philanthropy more broadly. Put bluntly, if the relationship between donors and community foundation trustees continues to be weakened—or is even perceived as becoming weakened—some potential donors may consider one of at least two main alternatives. To combat the concerns stemming from variance cases, donors may well pursue a first alternative to perpetual foundations, namely direct charitable contributions. Donors who take more literally Andrew Carnegie's famous dictum that "to die rich is to die in disgrace" may eschew the foundation structure entirely and simply disburse all their philanthropic funds while alive. Of course, giving away an entire fortune during a lifetime— particularly when it reaches into the hundreds of millions or even billions of dollars—would require a fundamental reorientation in charitable giving. Today, many wealthy individuals begin thinking about philanthropy as they near retirement, when time for such matters becomes more abundant. However, for large fortunes to be liquidated effectively during the lifetimes of donors, the pace of individual giving would either have to increase dramatically later in life or begin earlier in life. Several major donors have already declared their intention to take care of their giving themselves. Rita and Gustave Hauser are committed to spending their foundation right out of business. One reason the Hausers give for doing their own giving is that they question the wisdom of professional managers running foundations in perpetuity, especially if the donors' intent is not respected. Other donors have followed New York society figure Brooke Astor, who decided that her foundation would spend itself out of existence by making large payouts over a period of years so that the donor could maintain some control of how her funds were ultimately disbursed. This approach removed the risk of mission drift that perpetuity posed while also allowing Astor to enjoy the act of giving and the recognition it brings with it.

A second option for donors concerned about community foundations and the problem of perpetuity is to establish a private foundation with a limited life span. Under such terms, a foundation can be established, allowed to operate normally for years, and then upon reaching a particular point in time or upon the death or retirement of the donor or a key trustee, must liquidate the remaining endowment assets and cease operation. While such self-liquidating provisions are rare, they have been used effectively on occasion, particularly when the donor's mission is focused or controversial. For donors concerned about maintaining control over resources, a self-liquidating provision is a reasonable alternative to not setting up a foundation at all or creating one that will be allowed to operate in perpetuity. A trend away from perpetuity may even be developing, as several major foundations have recently announced their intentions to liquidate assets or are in the process of doing so. One of the more interesting cases of a limited-life foundation is the John M. Olin Foundation, which was founded by a conservative businessman. Entrusting his friend, the former secretary of the treasury William E. Simon, with the task of leading the foundation, Olin provided that his foundation be spent out of existence when those trustees he knew best retired. After decades of funding academic centers and research by leading conservative policy intellectuals, the foundation began to close itself down soon after the death of Simon in 2000. John M. Olin was both committed to the ideas of free enterprise and constitutional government and certain that he did not want his name and fortune used by others in perpetuity for causes no one could foresee. For Olin, the choice of a limited-life foundation was a natural and effective means to preserve his intent.

The idea of creating a limited-life philanthropic institution as a way to split the difference between giving everything away during life versus leaving everything for others to give away in perpetuity can be traced back far into the past. Two American donors of the nineteenth century, the banker George Peabody and the Connecticut manufacturer John Slater, understood the problems associated with perpetuity. Both Peabody and Slater established funds to help newly emancipated slaves gain education and independence during Reconstruction. Although Andrew Carnegie is routinely credited with defining the original principles of organized philanthropy—and distinguishing it from charity—Peabody actually anticipated these ideas to some extent by creating the first modern American foundation and by understanding the importance of solving social problems, rather than merely providing alms. Peabody noted that "more good was done by striking at the evils of humanity at their root, than by providing for a few of their victims." After the Civil War, Peabody and his contemporary John Slater both established funds to assist with the education of the populations of the Southern states. Each charged a group of trustees to work on this mission for thirty years, to then reassess public needs, and, if deemed wise, to close down the funds by distributing the corpus to institutions of higher education committed to assisting people of color. So close were the purposes of the two funds that they decided to merge in 1914. Finally, in 1937, Peabody's and Slater's philanthropic work was further combined with that of other funds designed to assist former slaves, and the result was the formation of the Southern Educational Fund, which today operates a range of programs designed to assist African Americans.[30]

While neither Peabody nor Slater put a definite date for the closure of their funds, both realized that changes in circumstances might render their philanthropic intentions obsolete. Julius Rosenwald, who owned and built the mail-order catalog company Sears, Roebuck, amassed a fortune of $200 million by 1910. Rosenwald created the Julius Rosenwald Fund in 1917 to carry out his philanthropy. One of the most distinguishing features of the fund was that its trustees were instructed to spend all the principal and interest within twenty-five years of Rosenwald's death. Because he did not believe it was possible to foresee the needs of society way off into the future and because he believed that the intent of the donor would be ignored or thwarted over long periods of time, Rosenwald opposed the idea of perpetual foundations. In 1928, in a letter to the trustees of his fund, Rosenwald famously decreed:

> My experience is that trustees controlling large funds are not only desirous of conserving principal but often favor adding to it from surplus income. I am not in sympathy with this policy of perpetuating endowments and believe that more good can be accomplished by expending funds as trustees find opportunities for constructive work than by storing up large sums of money for long periods of time. By adopting a policy of using the [Julius Rosenwald] Fund within this generation, we may avoid those tendencies toward bureaucracy and a formal or perfunctory attitude toward the work which almost inevitably develop in organizations which prolong their existence indefinitely. Coming generations can be relied upon to provide for their own needs as they arise.[31]

By 1948, the Rosenwald Fund had spent all of its funds, a full nine years ahead of the deadline. The legacy of the fund is impressive to this day; it includes the construction of over 5,000 public schools, the expansion of the YMCA and YWCA, the relocation of Russian Jews following the Russian Revolution, and many other projects that provided assistance to disadvantaged populations in the United States and abroad.

The Challenge of Time

For donors confronting the challenge of devising a strategy for giving, the time dimension may not appear at first blush to be a pressing issue. After all, questions relating to purpose and institutional structure seem more urgent and technically challenging. To avoid thinking about the time dimension in philanthropy would be a serious mistake, however. For timing affects not just the rate at which funds are expended, but the way giving is organized, the identity and engagement of the donor, the use or avoidance of institutional arrangements, and even the very choice of fundamental purposes to be pursued. Meeting the challenge of time in philanthropy requires that donors think carefully about both the time horizon of the public problem they are interested in addressing and the significance and permanence they attach to their own charitable intent.

The time dimension to giving demands not only thought about the timing of a donation, but also the timing of the use of the gift. Donors need to make a judgment about when and at what pace their philanthropic resources should be consumed by recipient organizations. Some donors, particularly those who support universities, prefer to make endowment gifts that offer the promise of permanence. There is of course a high price for the stability that endowment funding offers; it often requires a commitment of more than twenty times the amount that is to be spent on an annual basis. This means that large amounts of philanthropic resources need to be transferred from the control of the donor to the recipient organization in order to gain the benefits of perpetuity. The rate at which funds are transferred from donor to recipient reflects to some extent the degree of trust between the two parties. With the exception of large institutions such as universities, hospitals, and museums, endowment funding is typically given only after an organization has proven itself through the wise use of annual operating support. Finding the right pace at which to transfer philanthropic resources will also be significantly shaped by the level of engagement the donor has with the recipient organization. With greater levels of personal contact with senior leaders in nonprofits and with full familiarity with programmatic content, donors will feel more at ease transferring funds sooner rather than later and in larger rather than smaller installments.

Construing the time dimension of giving properly is progressively more difficult as the underlying value to be produced through giving becomes more complex and multidimensional. For donors that have single-interest agendas, thinking about the right pace at which to disburse funds, varying somewhere between giving everything away immediately to giving slowly over a long period, will be a reasonably manageable task. It will involve some primitive attempts to think about how to adjust the future value of interventions against the present value of giving, taking into consideration a range of factors that impinge on how much discount should be applied. For donors with complex missions and with program operations spread across a range of subject fields, the discounting exercise will be less fruitful given the sheer complexity of the streams of expenditures and benefits that would need to be assessed. Still, even though discounting should be understood more as a heuristic device than as an actual operational tool, the time dimension of giving needs to be taken into consideration as a plan for giving is shaped.

These complications aside, the philanthropic challenge remains unambiguously clear: to fashion a strategy that takes into consideration the temporal dimension of giving; this dimension is inextricably linked to the other elements of the philanthropic prism. Witnessed in the phenomenal growth rate of the foundation field over the past decades, many donors start with the assumption that their giving will go on forever and the right institutional arrangement for them is thus a foundation. There are, I have suggested, good reasons, both from the perspective of the donor and from that of the public, to resist this impulse. The time dimension of giving can be the starting point for the construction of a philanthropic giving plan, but because time limits the options across the other dimensions of the philanthropic prism, it may be in the best interests of donors and of the public to resist this temptation. Choosing between current giving or the slow disbursal of funds in perpetuity is ultimately a personal choice for donors that has profound implications for the organizations and individuals that stand to benefit from the giving. One thing is certain: treating time as something complex and contingent—and not just simply accepting the default position of perpetuity—is critical to philanthropy moving toward greater levels of strategic alignment and coherence.

10. Measuring, Knowing, and Acting

Each of the previous five chapters focused on a distinct element of the philanthropic prism. By examining each element of the model separately, a very complex subject—strategy in philanthropy—has been explored in small and accessible pieces. The flaw in this mode of presentation is that it works to some extent against the underlying claim and argument, namely that the essence of strategy consists in the achievement of fit, alignment, and coherence among all five of the critical elements. While all five elements of the philanthropic prism must be brought into focus together, clear exposition has required that the elements be defined and developed independently. There is also the problem of "preferred" sequential ordering that might be inferred from this mode of discrete exposition, with those elements examined early wrongly appearing more central than those considered later. Thus, the presentation of the argument in manageable pieces and in one particular arbitrary order could lead one to forget the claim made at the outset of the book that it is possible to engage the challenge of philanthropy by entering from a commitment to any one or more elements of the prism and then elaborating and filling in the rest. It would be a mistake not to take advantage of this flexibility because so much of strategy in philanthropy is personal and dependent on the sometimes very distinctive and often inscrutable motives of donors.

How can one really know whether alignment has been achieved? One way is to take seriously the challenge to measure both what was defined in chapter 2 as mission effectiveness (how well the funder is doing at achieving its mission) and program effectiveness (how well nonprofits are doing at achieving their goals). Having good information about both aspects of philanthropic performance could in principle be very valuable to donors. It could allow for growth and learning over time and help a donor get better at the work of giving. While it never has existed in practice, imagine what a fully functional performance measurement system in philanthropy might look like. A donor could look up any nonprofit organization and find a detailed report on the programs carried out by the group, with their impact on the community measured with sensible indicators, and a series of scores that would allow the donor to assess the quality of one group's work compared to that of other organizations working in the same field. Such a system has never existed and likely will never be seen by donors. It is a fiction because so many of the dimensions of charitable activity cannot be clearly measured, because results are almost always incommensurable across organizations and across fields, and because the cost of developing and maintaining such a system would be too high.[1] What then is a donor to do? The answer lies in the search for imperfect but usable knowledge and the cultivation of the capacity to learn over time. The use of performance information to guide philanthropy is appealing because it promises to bring some reason and method to a world of giving that sometimes is driven mainly by reaction and impulse.

A successful philanthropic intervention. A good use of philanthropic funds. A catalytic grant. Whatever the language used to describe a positive result in philanthropy, the certainty of such assertions is usually a little bit suspect. The reason claims of success are often greeted with skepticism stems from the difficulty of ever really measuring impact and, even more problematically, directly attributing results achieved on the ground to philanthropic decisions. Still, the quest for knowledge about the effects of giving goes on unabated. In part, this search stems from the growing amounts of funds involved in philanthropy and the rising stakes involved. As philanthropy has evolved into a multibillion dollar enterprise, looking for signs that grants make a difference has become a common interest within the field, spawning a large evaluation and reporting industry that now produces large volumes of performance-related documentation. The search for certainty about impact is at its root a function of the desire of donors to make a connection between the instrumental and expressive components of giving. Philanthropy always has a goal in mind, even though it may sometimes be broad or amorphous. The quest for measures of impact represents the coming together of these two powerful forces in philanthropy. Donors do want to know if their gifts make a difference both because it adds to the satisfaction that giving engenders and because it authenticates the public service aspect of giving.

Functions and Forms of Evaluation

Evaluation can be pointed outward toward each of the organizations that receives a donor's grants or it can be directed inward at the donor's work itself. In either case, donors are in a position to do three important things through measurement. First, they may be able to improve overall program performance, both of the agencies they support and of the way in which they deliver resources. In principle, evaluation research can help donors adjust programs to remedy known problems and focus resources on the elements of an intervention that have proven most valuable. Evaluation data can be a potent tool for reengineering processes and improving operations in part because funders are in a position of power—in that they control the flow of funds—and this permits them to insist on programmatic changes. After a particular program is complete, the use of evaluation data is not over. Rather than starting from scratch and learning incrementally with each funding effort, donors can, by using program evaluations, shorten the learning curve and improve more quickly at allocating funds and managing relations with service delivery organizations. Donors then are in a position to use this information to design and fund better programs than they would without it. In this way, evaluation research can help donors both improve nonprofit operations and their own philanthropic operations.

The operational applications of performance data can be directed inward. Through studies of their own grantmaking procedures and systems, institutional donors in particular have been able to improve the overall efficiency of their grantmaking, all with an eye to making their otherwise forbidding institutions more approachable and easier to work with. At a time when many nonprofit managers complain about the costs—in terms of time and effort—that securing grants demands, these efforts simplify procedures and improve the overall quality of operations. Working on operational improvement has not always come naturally to foundations because their special status in the nonprofit sector as funders largely shields them from having to worry about the quality of their interactions with recipient organizations. No matter how badly they perform their work of selecting and supporting organizations, there will always be a queue of nonprofits seeking grants and willing to jump over whatever hurdles may be placed before them.

The second use of evaluation research in philanthropy is connected to the political and authorizing environment. At a time when funds for discretionary program spending are increasingly limited, the ability of donors to document programmatic success and point to recipient organizations that have proven effective can be a potent tool for mobilizing political support for further public funding for these organizations. Evaluation research allows donors to document programmatic effects and make the case not only for public support, but also for support by other donors interested in the problem or field in question. Using existing philanthropic networks and professional associations, grantmakers are able to use evaluation data to convince other funders and policy makers that their programs represent an effective approach to a particular public problem.[2] In microlending, for example, early evaluations of programs designed to get small loans into the hands of community entrepreneurs led not only to substantial public investment in the approach through international development agencies, but also to replication by private funders in countries around the world.

When directed inward at the actual mission effectiveness of the donor or foundation, evaluation data can be a first line of defense against criticism and calls for increased regulations. Private foundations control hundreds of billions of dollars in assets and use these resources to generate funds annually for grants. Over time, foundations have proven to be especially frequent and easy targets of Congress and state regulators, who see in these privileged institutions large untapped reserves of funds that could be used more aggressively for public purposes. To counter public criticism and to quell nonprofit activism directed at regulating more fully the foundation field, institutional donors can use evaluation data of their own performance to make the case that philanthropic resources are being used wisely and the public interest is ultimately being served. Meaningful performance data can serve as an umbrella for donors, shielding them from the changes in the political weather around them. Thus, evaluation data can be both a tool for building funding support for the best recipient organizations and an instrument to sustain public and government support of the philanthropy field itself.

The third use of evaluation research is the most important although often the least understood. Collecting, examining, and discussing evaluation research can be an important way of defining and reckoning the philanthropic value to be produced. Working with evaluation data can open up conversations about what is important to measure and, ultimately, what objectives are worth pursuing—both for donors and their recipients. Because evaluations are always about some aspect of performance, they can be tools for articulating and clarifying the nature of the philanthropic value that donors are trying to produce through others or the results they themselves are seeking to achieve. While this third function may appear less central than the first two, it can in many circumstances be more important. The act of defining what value is to be achieved can be a focusing exercise for a donor, one that demands that both mission and goals be clearly specified. In the context of foundations, doing this work can be a useful tool for building consensus and solidarity among staff about what the funding is intended to achieve and how any given program will go about achieving results. For individual donors, the process can lead to a greater clarity of purpose and understanding. When the conversation about ultimate purposes takes place within the context of a funded initiative, donors and recipients can clarify what ultimately is at stake and worth trying to accomplish. In this sense, defining the core purpose, which is essential if one is to measure whether or not it has been achieved, is a valuable exercise in itself because it cannot help but clarify and render more concrete the ends of philanthropy.

While each of the three possible functions of evaluation has its place and can contribute to the general progress of donors toward greater levels of effectiveness, there can be little doubt that a large amount of effort, time, and expense has been traditionally focused on the first two functions: improving operations and building support. Performance data can be expensive to collect well, especially if control group studies are undertaken to examine the effect of programs on clients. It also can take a long time to produce solid results; sometimes several years are needed to track and study programs. For donors with little patience, evaluation research can seem to be a large pit into which prodigious amounts of money can be thrown. In light of the time and cost involved, evaluations tend to be undertaken only either when they are absolutely necessary to diagnose and correct problems in program design or when the profile of the effort is high enough to make the outside world ask, "Did the program work?" Not surprisingly, motives behind evaluation tend to be practical and instrumental in nature.

Donors resist measurement not only because it is expensive and time consuming, but also because it is hard to use and apply. An immense volume of informal program reporting is generated each year by grant recipients. They vary from self-serving narratives to more or less independent accounts of the design and delivery of services. These reports lack the rigor and standards of professional evaluations, but are often relied upon to serve as proxies for true independent and systematic evaluations. This annual tidal wave of storytelling by grant recipients has had the unintended effect of making funders jaded when evaluating them. It is hardly surprising that, after seeing these reports as representations of the work of program evaluation and finding only marginal value in them, donors have not yet gained a real thirst for true efforts to measure performance. With vast collections of informal, nongeneralizable, and hard-to-use reports lining their offices, funders have developed a noticeable resistance to measurement, largely based on their negative experience with the dominant practice and their concern that quality performance measurement is too expensive and time consuming to undertake.

To break through this cycle of dread and avoidance, donors need to think more creatively about how to plan and execute evaluations to create knowledge that is usable.[3] It may be useful to sort out the range of options that donors confront when conducting evaluations to clarify some of the choices presented to donors seeking to use measurement to accomplish all of their potential purposes. Part of the complexity of thinking about the subject of measurement is that evaluations draw on a range of methods, focus on different subjects, and speak to different audiences. To make matters more complicated, there are two main targets on which an evaluation can focus, two broad evaluation strategies, three different candidates for who will conduct the evaluation, and at least two different potential audiences for foundation evaluations.

When setting out to conduct an evaluation, donors face an important first choice regarding the target or focus of their study. Philanthropic evaluations can focus—and the majority of them do—on the nonprofit organizations that received funding. The evaluation will target recipient organizations for study, sometimes to build accountability into the grantmaking relationship, sometimes to inform future grantmaking to the organization. In the best cases, the choice to focus on recipient organizations is part of a coherent strategy aimed at improving decision making by the donor. In the worst cases, it is a perfunctory process that merely fulfills a procedural requirement. To ensure that the evaluation speaks directly to and informs philanthropic practices, the target of the study sometimes shifts away from the recipient organization to the donor or the philanthropic vehicle doing the giving. This second possible target of evaluation is far more elusive, since it is difficult to build support for turning the focus of the evaluation away from recipient organizations and toward a foundation's activities. There are also substantial methodological issues raised by this approach, since it is more difficult to reach a global assessment about a foundation's performance than it is to see whether or not grant recipients have been successful in fulfilling the terms of their grants.

Which brings us to the question of methodology. Beyond selecting a target, donors have to make a decision about what kind of evaluation is needed. While there are myriad names for different types of evaluations, two main categories have emerged, each with a different goal and a different logic: one focuses on process and one on outcome. Process evaluations document and measure program implementation and seek to assess the capacity of the organization to achieve its stated objectives. They will often measure the quantity and quality of services delivered, sometimes through surveys of clients or through on-site observations of service delivery systems. In carrying out a process evaluation, it is not uncommon for the subject matter to be either complex or new and for the evaluation to be a key first step toward studying how services are delivered. In this sense, the goal of a process evaluation is to dissect and understand implementation, to provide a window into the program delivery world. In philanthropy, the processes studied are usually related to program delivery systems when the grant recipient is the subject of the evaluation. When donors turn the focus on their own performance, the process studied is that of grantmaking, from the fielding of questions all the way to the termination of funding relations. Although process evaluation can generate important operational insights, it sometimes lacks the depth that is needed to make the case either for or against the subject being studied. After all, what matters most is not always how things are done in philanthropy but whether they work and achieve intended objectives.

By contrast, outcome evaluations focus on what kind of results a program ultimately achieves. Since process evaluations are sometimes criticized for being too focused on the minutiae of service delivery and for missing the bigger picture, evaluators often include the measurement of impact and outcome. Whether the chosen outcome is defined in terms of short- or long-range objectives, it must adequately represent the underlying purposes that are being evaluated. The task of defining the desired outcomes for any given project is both difficult and critical, since this decision will set the terms for the measurement to follow. One of the challenges to defining outcomes is to fully think through what a program is really trying to achieve, beyond what may or may not have been explicitly stated when the program was first begun. Thus, for example, a new training program may initially believe that the outcome it is trying to achieve is the placement of graduates into full-time jobs in the months following their completion of the program. This short-term outcome may evolve, however, as the organization becomes more familiar with the terrain it is negotiating, perhaps to the point where the real outcome is redefined to be stable employment for three or more consecutive years. The success or failure of outcome evaluations depends very heavily on the quality of the defined outcomes. The further in the future the defined outcomes of a program are, the harder it is to control for all the other factors—outside the actual program or intervention—that may be affecting the results. This can be a major problem because the meaningfulness of the outcomes may increase as greater and greater time unfolds after the program or intervention. For this reason, donors and nonprofits negotiate a set of short-, medium-, and long-term outcomes that are to be tracked.

After deciding on whether to focus on the recipient organization or the donor's vehicle and choosing the appropriate type of evaluation, a decision must be made on who will conduct the actual evaluation. Here there are only three main choices. The first is to encourage the recipient organization to carry out the evaluation, using its own staff. This is often seen by nonprofits as the least threatening route, since control over the evaluation is never wrested away from the organization. For donors, this approach is often of little use, as evaluation blends into grant report, which in turn can mutate smoothly into requests for renewed support. Because it is hard to expect nonprofits to be objective and even critical of their own organizations with funders, nonprofit "self-evaluations" are of dubious value.

Donors, and foundations in particular, can pursue a second option, which is to conduct the evaluation with the foundation's own staff. While foundation program officers routinely conduct site visits and evaluate program performance, such activity is usually intended to supplement and verify information contained in the grant proposals. The main obstacle to having foundation staff conduct evaluations of the programs the foundation has funded is fairly simple: it is hard to find a way to remove the built-in conflict of interest that such arrangements entail. Foundation staff members have an interest in the programs they have recommended for funding performing well. Who would want to have to report to a foundation board that the organization they recommended failed to do what it said it would? Poor performance by grantees reflects badly on the staff. This problem is actually exacerbated by the growth of philanthropic careers, which have made foundation staff very conscious of the outcomes of their grants. With the possibility of professional advancement hanging in the balance, it is not entirely reasonable to ask foundation managers to evaluate major initiatives.

This points to the third option, the use of outside or independent evaluators. Many foundations currently engage professors, consultants, and practitioners to conduct independent evaluations of larger grant initiatives. By looking outside themselves for evaluative input, donors can break through the incentives of recipient organizations and foundation staff that run counter to the need of donors for a full and frank performance assessment. While there has been much written on the use of outside evaluators and while some significant independent evaluations of programs have been conducted, especially by larger private foundations, the results of this research have rarely been circulated widely or incorporated into the decision making of the field as a whole. Without meaningful channels through which to share knowledge, too much evaluation research remains proprietary information, consumed only by those closest to the subject matter.

To sum up then, as donors look at the question of evaluation, they need to answer three essential questions: What will be the focus of the evaluation? What kind of evaluation is appropriate? Who will carry out the evaluation? In making difficult decisions about evaluations, foundations must weigh the consequences of their choices for the audiences to which their evaluations will eventually speak. No evaluation will meet the needs of all audiences. However, by asking the core questions about what the evaluation needs to track, who is best positioned to conduct the evaluation, and what type of evaluation is most appropriate to the problem at hand, foundations can take a critical step toward doing more than just sending checks into the nonprofit darkness.

Part of the problem with getting evaluation to serve the advancement of the philanthropy field is that it must be focused not only outward on the organizations that receive funds, but also inward. Donors need to assess their own overall performance and make tough judgments. One of the most common ways that large foundations have interpreted the need for self-evaluation has been to commission surveys of grantee organizations in which questions about a foundation are posed to those most knowledgeable about the institution. The impulse of these efforts to construct "customer satisfaction surveys" for grantee organizations is well meaning and aims at the complex issue of mission effectiveness, even if superficially. While a foundation would probably prefer to have information on the aggregate impact it has achieved and its performance as a donor, grantee surveys at least provide feedback on the procedural side of grantmaking, including such things as program officer courtesy, promptness in handling correspondence and returning phone calls, and a host of other issues related to the fair and open disbursal of funds.

The relative claims of the expressive and instrumental dimensions of philanthropy are deeply affected by all the work that is done in the area of measuring performance. For evaluations, be they focused on recipient organizations or on the processes of grantmakers, tend to naturally tilt the balance of power toward the more purposive and instrumental side of giving. Measuring is often taken to be an activity designed to respond to the public responsibilities of donors. Tracking performance is a way of assuring the public that charitable resources are being used wisely and that programs are being operated effectively. The problem with these assumptions about measurement is that they largely ignore the fact that the expressive side of giving—that part of philanthropy by which donors enact their commitments and values—needs to be supported if the flow of funds to charitable purposes is to continue to grow. In measuring either the impact of grant recipients or the degree of mission effectiveness achieved by the funder across the board, evaluation research has a natural affinity for technical questions that lend themselves to quantification. However, what is important to measure is not always what is easy to measure. The whole question of how much expressive content giving achieves is almost never taken to be a valid topic for assessment. It may seem narcissistic to assess how well philanthropy actually matches the values and beliefs that lie behind the gifts; but without taking the expressive component of philanthropy seriously and giving it a place alongside the more mainstream technical questions about instrumental effectiveness, philanthropy risks becoming even more one-sided in its focus on the public benefits it generates. Evaluations should build universal knowledge that can advance a field's self-understanding, but it should also take seriously the question of how well programs align with the intent and commitments of the funders. Without some balance between instrumental and expressive dimensions in philanthropy, the capacity of the field to innovate and to sustain itself will likely be diminished.

There are at least two ways to ensure that the expressive dimension of giving is part of any evaluation. The first is to define the values that are both implicit and explicit in the delivery of a funded program and to compare how close these nonprofit values are to those of the donor. This approach is more difficult than taking a measure of technical performance, which often entails counting and accounting for the number of outputs generated by the program. Some of this work is presumably done before a grant is made, but there is still a need to check on the actual program that is delivered to ensure that it remains faithful to the promises and spirit of the proposal. Doing this work entails rendering a judgment on the way the work of a nonprofit fits in with the overall approach and vision favored by a donor. It is possible that a program could perform well instrumentally by achieving its stated objectives but fail miserably to align with the expressive goals of a funder, although much of the grant screening process is designed to avoid this possibility. Such cases will require tough choices by the donor and the recipient organization about what is more important and how to balance the sometimes competing claims of donors and communities.

The second way to assess the expressive aspect of grantmaking is to focus not on nonprofits but rather on the funder's work itself. By probing the quality of mission effectiveness that is achieved across grantmaking efforts of individuals and foundations, evaluations can help sort out the programs that support the underlying goals of donors from either those that are simply neutral or those that actually work against them. Turning the evaluation lens inward at the work of giving and the quality of decision making is difficult because it demands both that the values of the donor be made explicit to those carrying out the evaluation and, in the case of professionally managed foundations, that the work of staff be scrutinized in terms of its fidelity to donor intent, rather than to the more accepted standard of effectiveness. Still, the exercise of asking how well a donor or foundation is doing at achieving its mission is valuable if for no other reason than that it refocuses attention on what matter most, namely the underlying commitments and values that animated the giving in the first place. If evaluation can help do more than just track results and also help donors see where and how their giving connects with their fundamental beliefs, the field as a whole will likely be significantly strengthened.

The expressive dimension of impact is the easiest to overlook because instrumental goals are both easier to track and fit more closely with the norms of the industry that has established itself around the field. However, a good argument could be made that it is the plurality of values and ideas animating giving that constitute the raison d'être of philanthropy, give it its strength, and justify its special privileged tax status. For this reason, donors should consider focusing carefully on how well their values and those of the recipient organizations ultimately align. In the end, foundations must make clear decisions about which of the dimensions of impact is most important to them and then seek the most appropriate measurement strategies. To do less is ultimately to fail to act responsibly. After all, donors, nonprofit managers, and policy makers all stand to benefit from honest and open evaluation. In carrying out their work, foundations need to constantly ask themselves how they can best design a measurement strategy that draws on the right methodology, the right kind of evaluator, and the right target or focus for study. If successful in these tasks, philanthropy may well begin to define for itself a new and much needed variation on the old Delphic motto "know thyself," one that will stress the importance of the constant search for a better understanding of the many ways foundations shape society.

Knowledge Building

With pressure rising on foundations to process a huge number of applications for support, it is a miracle of sorts that the bigger foundations have still managed to carry out evaluations of their work. The expectation of results in philanthropy, while not as intense as in certain for-profit industries, is real—even if most of it is self-imposed. Failures are not always welcome and a culture of good news—grounded in close professional networks and peer relations—has emerged that makes it hard for any single donor to take the lead in producing honest assessments of its work. Even when good evaluations are conducted, either internally or externally, there is always the question of how the information will be used, whether it will be presented as an excuse to terminate funding if the results are disappointing or as the critical piece of evidence supporting major programmatic expansion. There is room for a fair measure of creative interpretation and rationalization when it comes to the actual meaning of evaluations, particularly when the findings are mixed. The best of efforts can be given in terms of getting to a clear conclusion about the impact and effectiveness of a program or organization, but sometimes the picture is simply clouded by the fact that there are positive elements coexisting with more negative ones, or that impact may be detectable using one set of measures but not another. In such cases, the consumers of evaluation data need to apply as much care in interpreting and using the results as those who actually designed and carried out the study.

Occasionally, donors actually carry out evaluations and then honestly confront the faults and false assumptions of their work. Such acts of humility and honesty are refreshing because they demonstrate that the loop between evaluation and understanding can be closed. One of the best examples of a closed loop is *The Path of Most Resistance: Reflections on Lessons Learned from New Futures*, a report written by the Annie E. Casey Foundation about its work in poor communities.[4] The foundation, founded in 1948, has long focused on supporting programs that assist disadvantaged children. Starting in the mid-1980s, its assets increased dramatically, providing great opportunity for the expansion of its mission and the scope of its philanthropic work. Room for rapid growth and the presence of substantial resources, however, often opens the door for greater errors and for lessons learned the hardest way of all.

In 1988, the Casey Foundation launched a highly ambitious, five-year initiative called New Futures, one of its first long-term, multisite systems and policy reform initiatives. New Futures offered each of its five selected cities $10 million paid over five years for the implementation of a deep systematic reform (as opposed to adding social services or improving existing ones) aiming to engage a diverse and complex group of stakeholders in problem solving; the group included community leaders, foundation staff, evaluation and technical assistance consultants, as well as school boards, parents, public officials, and business leaders. New Futures, by its results and the questions that followed its implementation, served as a basis on which to evaluate, modify, and refine succeeding initiatives funded by the Casey Foundation. *The Path of Most Resistance* is a good example of a philanthropic organization's candid evaluation of its own "incomplete success and some plain failure." This sort of honesty is useful because it leads to an imperative for change; the report explains how many shortcomings and misjudgments have been remedied in the initiatives that followed New Futures. Many of these realizations and lessons in the Casey Foundation report are intuitively obvious, but still deserve attention. The general lesson learned from New Futures was that "comprehensive reforms are very difficult." While this might appear somewhat obvious and trivial, the report provides a closer, fairly detailed, and constructive look at the factors that caused difficulty, beyond the inherent complexity of the work.

Time and timing play a major role in planning and implementing social reforms. The foundation found that it should have devoted more time to the project overall, to allow significant time for all stakeholders to build strong mutual trust and respect (which was lacking in New Futures) for effective cooperation. As the report stated, "The bottom line . . . is that there is no substitute for adequate time." The foundation also learned that the *timing* of its involvement of the highly diversified array of stakeholders was off. It should have been started earlier to avoid excluding anyone from key planning decisions. Moreover, the timing of communication proved to be a missing piece in New Futures, and the report argued that if the foundation had developed a system of periodical checkpoints that could have demonstrated concrete progress to the community, both observers and participants of New Futures would have had a better sense of the value and direction of the program overall.

The study also reveals that there was also a very complex balance between local ownership of the initiative and the role of the Casey Foundation as the outside funder. In this case, the specific problem seemed to lie in the amount of money that the Casey Foundation distributed and the ineffective way in which the funds mobilized the commitment of grantees and stakeholders. The amount of $2 million per year for each New Futures's site city was largely meant as encouragement for the stakeholders to locate matching funds for New Futures aims and goals. The Casey Foundation hoped to ensure local financial commitments and in the process solidify local political support. While the initial commitment of funds attracted the attention of community leaders, the report suggests that the foundation's leverage strategy for New Futures sites to redeploy and redirect existing funds did not fully succeed due to difficulties in monitoring the matching fund requirements and in overcoming local resistance to making a high-risk financial commitment. This led the Casey Foundation to rethink and refine its leverage strategy.

In addition to the technical problems of New Futures, the foundation found that there were also psychological and substantive conditions that needed to be taken into account before embarking on social reform. First, some communities were just not ready for such deep systems reform because of a lack of core leadership that could galvanize local support and shift the community's commitments from their current priorities to those of New Futures. Second, in some communities and environments, "system reform efforts must be augmented by social-capital and economic-development initiatives." Often, the cycle of poverty among children and youth—even if all the "right" social services and institutions are in place for positive change—is perpetuated by the lack of visible and accessible examples of success, incentives, or viable opportunities. The Casey Foundation, in realizing this through New Futures, has since established a Rebuilding Communities Initiative, which focuses on human and social capital development in low-income neighborhoods in hopes of setting the stage for further institutional and systems reform.

The report ends on a positive note, reaffirming the foundation's "stay at it" attitude and commitment to constantly revising and improving comprehensive programming and reform. While many foundations and philanthropic efforts go through periods of modification, refinement, and restructuring to create sophisticated and effective programs, few impart to us a view into the growing pains that brought them there. The Annie E. Casey Foundation produced an honest and helpful self-evaluation, one that helped the foundation and other funders working in disadvantaged communities understand that failure should not drive philanthropy out, but rather motivate it to try harder and learn from experience. Not only did the foundation learn something, it shared the report with the public and senior foundation officials discussed it openly with the media and other funders.

Honesty in evaluation involves not only the frank appraisals of a project, but the actual methods used in conducting the evaluation. In 1991, the Chicago Community Trust began its planning for a multiyear project called the Children, Youth and Families Initiative (CYFI). CYFI's main objective was to reform the social service system within seven Chicago neighborhoods by broadening the scope of services and integrating existing components of the social service system to more effectively address and support the developmental needs of each community's children and families. It was an ambitious effort backed by considerable funds and managed by able foundation staff. Yet it produced disappointing results.

When the initiative began its transition from planning to implementation in 1994, the various stakeholders in CYFI—Chicago Community Trust (CCT), CYFI advisors, community representatives, and Chapin Hall Center for Children staff—met to formulate a vision and process for measuring the progress of the initiative. The result was Markers of Progress, a set of guidelines that described the vision of CYFI, the key elements of the initiative's implementation, and markers of the progress of the implementations.[5] It was agreed that each community would build its own list of "evidence" for use in charting progress for each of the markers presented in the document. The goal was to accommodate a multiple-stakeholder approach that would encourage and sustain a participatory process in evaluating progress and outcomes.

Even though the intention of this democratic process was clarified and even embraced from the outset, Markers of Progress was far from successful. One of the main factors in the failure of Markers of Progress was its time-consuming and demanding nature, especially for community representatives. As stakeholders were given a great deal of control in specifying what constituted evidence of progress, many found the task "conceptually and practically overwhelming" and struggled to make choices from what appeared to be an infinite number of items that could be used as "evidence." As a result, the time devoted to putting together these lists turned into a distraction from the actual implementation of the initiative. Moreover, the *timing* of the implementation of Markers of Progress caused problems. Had Markers of Progress been initiated and carried out well before the implementation of CYFI, it could have served not only as an evaluation mechanism, but also as documentation for a common vocabulary and clarification of terms for the goals and aims of CYFI. But this was not the case.

Another factor troubling Markers of Progress was traceable to the imbalance in power and influence among the funder, local community representatives, and other stakeholders. Community representatives questioned whether the evaluation process was for the community's sake or really for the benefit of Chapin Hall (the group primarily responsible for setting up Markers of Progress) and CCT. Although CYFI intended eventually to move the assessment process away from CCT and Chapin Hall's jurisdiction and to increase reciprocal accountability among all stakeholders, the community representatives' feedback indicated that they did not feel the evaluation process was being carried out in a balanced and collaborative manner. This perception in turn reinforced established patterns of interaction between stakeholders (e.g., funder being controlling, grantees needing to prove their worthiness), which were damaging to CYFI's overall goal of true cooperative effort for reform. Moreover, the stakeholders felt that if communities were to have influence in determining what items constituted evidence for progress, then the whole Markers of Progress process would have to be geared toward and willing to accept local decisions. There was a problem in all this, however. Too much local variation would make achieving a truly consistent and coherent effort impossible, because ideas of what constituted evidence would surely differ to a great degree across the different communities involved in CYFI. This problem in specifying prospective terms of evidence of progress proved much more difficult and time-consuming than Chapin Hall and CCT had expected.

While this unusually candid foundation report offered few concrete recommendations for the improvement of Markers of Progress, except to start the process well before implementation to allow for common language across stakeholders, the report did express its continued value in pursuing participatory evaluation processes. The Markers of Progress report's honest self-criticism offers real insight into both the difficulty of evaluating the success of any philanthropic endeavor and the complexity donors encounter when they seek to act, measure, and build knowledge. This episode in grantmaking and evaluation ultimately allows us to see that philanthropic failures and misjudgments are not only setbacks but opportunities to improve understanding and uncover the nuances of complex, often localized social problems.

Conceived carefully and executed with precision, evaluation research can be a critical tool in advancing the quality of philanthropic decision making.[6] However, evaluation findings must be robust and not subject to much second-guessing, at least when it comes to methodology. Substantial time and expense may be required to do this work correctly. While philanthropy has produced many quality evaluations and much usable knowledge, the transfer system for moving this information into the hands of decision makers remains poorly defined and systematized. Far too much data is hoarded by those who pay for it and far too little is pushed into the public sphere in a way that makes it accessible to others. At the same time, donors are drawn to reinventing the wheel and do not routinely seek out research data before launching philanthropic efforts. If some of these barriers could be overcome, the link between measuring and knowing in philanthropy would certainly be strengthened.

At the heart of the problem is the fundamentally asymmetric relationship that evaluation establishes between the organization being evaluated and the past, present, or potential future funder who reads the evaluation. Philanthropy is already burdened with asymmetric relations just by virtue of resource differentials and the fact that givers are in a position of power and authority over recipients. Evaluation exacerbates this situation and brings it out into the open. A common response to this tension by donors is to seek to bridge the gap and heal the wounds that these differences create by inviting recipient organizations into the evaluation process. By allowing those who are going to be evaluated to have some input on what the standards and metrics for measuring performance should be, donors hope to smooth over the rough spots that hard-nosed evaluation can create. The problem is that in so doing, donors may compromise the evaluation process itself and surrender a fair amount of rigor and control. By its very nature, measuring performance involves picking winners and losers, distinguishing good work from bad, and to some extent choosing sides. Philanthropy is not always comfortable with this fact and often seeks to stay close to the safe center. When donors do take chances and attempt either controversial projects or ones that are very ambitious, having the will to look realistically at the results of these efforts is critical if the link between measuring and knowing is to be strengthened.

The confessions of the Casey Foundation and the Chicago Community Trust apply evaluation for its most powerful and valuable purpose, namely to build knowledge and expertise and to help revisit ultimate purposes and assumptions. Unfortunately, these two documents are aberrations. The vast majority of evaluations and program reports tout successes and have as their end the other two functions of evaluation described earlier: building support and improving implementation. While there is nothing wrong with shining a light on success with an eye to protecting one's reputation and attracting other funders, and while understanding better the technology behind effective interventions is useful, far too little knowledge building and honest self-criticism are present in philanthropy today.

Crisis and Action

One of the larger assumptions of this book has been that reason and logic, when properly applied and combined with passion and values, can add value to philanthropy. The strategy model presented here is designed to guide the donor through a set of topics and issues that together will lead to the constitution of a more strategic philanthropy. In most cases, philanthropy operates in relative comfort and calm. Research can be conducted, proposals can be read and reread, decisions can be contemplated carefully, and donors can slowly edge toward their philanthropic objectives through incrementally increasing grants based on sound evaluation data. Unlike fields, such as commodities trading, where there is tremendous time pressure surrounding decisions, most giving unfolds in a relatively quiet and unrushed process. Donors are ensconced comfortably in the driver's seat in their relations with nonprofits, and the quarterly meeting schedule of most foundation boards adds a quiet and calming rhythm to the work of philanthropy. Within that rhythm, information on past performance can be analyzed and factored into decisions bearing on future support.

Time, study, and learning are sometimes luxuries that cannot be afforded, however. Under some circumstances, philanthropy cannot inch forward but rather must charge ahead without detailed planning or evaluation systems in place. One such circumstance is in the aftermath of crises and disasters. When natural disasters strike, there is no time for profound reflection; needs can suddenly be pressing and conditions can be precarious. Slow programmatic rollouts geared to tough ongoing evaluations are not always an option. Philanthropy is often the force behind the first response to crisis, supporting relief agencies and reaching out to victims. The impulse to help is very strong and the outpouring of support can be wide. One of the consequences of this reactive process is that there is often little or no time for thinking about how to assess and measure programmatic impact since the preponderance of giving is concluded quickly and not part of a long process that can be adjusted and refined in midstream. It would be tempting to assume that the time pressure of crises and the resulting truncating of strategy would mean that this kind of giving is dangerously burdened. In reality, however, there is a place for giving that is driven not by careful planning but by the presence of urgent need and time-sensitive opportunity. The philanthropic outpouring following the attacks on September 11, 2001, provides a good lens through which to view the challenges facing donors whose giving is driven by urgent needs. Emergency philanthropy also raises the interesting question of whether evaluation is needed if the likelihood of a similar event is remote and, even if it is probable, how to create usable knowledge from a uniquely tragic set of circumstances.

September 11 created tremendous human needs that called for an extraordinary response. While government agencies at the federal, state, and local levels moved quickly to respond, the first funds to reach those in need came from private sources. The response of private donors to the September 11 attacks was enormous and immediate. One survey reported that charities raising funds for September 11 relief and recovery efforts had collected almost $2 billion in gifts by February 7, 2002. This massive outpouring of caring did more than demonstrate the speed with which private giving can react to public needs. It showed that simple, old-fashioned charity, governed by caring and compassion, still has a place within a landscape of giving dominated by modern philanthropy and geared toward complex interventions and social experiments.[7] The giving also demonstrated that in times of crisis there is room and even a need for giving that can be driven by things other than proofs of effectiveness or detailed documentation.

The philanthropic effort spurred by the attacks can be understood in a number of different ways. At one level, it was the desire to simply demonstrate compassion and offer help to those whose lives were so tragically transformed by the death and destruction that the attacks brought. At another level, philanthropy constituted a currency through which many people sought to construct bridges between strangers and themselves to demonstrate that the national fabric was still strong after such a blatant and brutal attempt to sow discord and anger. Still at another level, those who gave were taking part in a personal exercise of confronting and dealing with the event. Giving was a way for some donors to overcome the sense of helplessness that this act of violence caused. Although there is no single, all-encompassing interpretation of the impulse to help following this tragedy, it is clear that philanthropy was both an expression of caring and an attempt to address some of the real needs that the event created. Probing questions about strategy and detailed needs assessments were never fully engaged as donors moved quickly to react. Major private assistance following September 11 came quickly and impulsively from private philanthropic foundations, corporations, and individual donors.

Two things are notable about the foundation grants made after the attacks.[8] The first is that they represented very large and open-ended commitments for institutions that all too often make smaller, targeted grants in support of clearly circumscribed projects. Clearly, the needs created by all the destruction changed the usual scale of foundation action and called forth very sizable and unrestricted grants, which in many cases were well outside the established grantmaking guidelines of many of the foundations. The second reason these foundation grants were significant relates to the way in which they were made. These donations broke down procedural conventions within foundations. Instead of going through proposal review and evaluation by staff, the standard operating procedures of foundations were largely abandoned so that funds could be delivered quickly. Many of the largest foundation grants were triggered by trustees, not professional staff. In this sense, the disaster funders broke through some long-standing procedural boundaries that vested grantmaking control in the hands of staff and left trustees with broader strategic duties, allowing foundations to act decisively in this moment of need. Evaluation plans were not carefully drawn up in part because much of the giving was to be in the form of cash assistance to families who lost a loved one in the tragedy. How one would even go about assessing the impact of helping the widow of a firefighter by giving her a large amount of money is also not entirely clear.

The corporate contributions that flowed soon after September 11 were distinctive in that they broke with some of the standard operating procedures of corporate giving.[9] While corporations traditionally view their giving as aligned with and supporting the core business functions, such as sales, marketing, and government relations, the gifts generated by the events of September 11 were made largely free of the usual "give and take" of corporate philanthropy, in which companies demand and get plenty of "return" for their giving.[10] Because of the unique circumstances, few corporations sought to reap self-interested advantage from their citizenship work following the tragedy. In this sense, the disaster brought forth a purer and more disinterested form of corporate giving than is usually seen, one animated by a desire to offer support regardless of the bottom line. There was no clear effort to assess and quantify the impact of these gifts or to demonstrate through measurement that they contributed to the bottom line in some way.

Although foundations and corporations made significant contributions, individual donors played a larger role in the mobilization of the philanthropic response. Individuals gave money, blood, material goods, and volunteer time in the wake of September 11, with a total value of over $1 billion.[11] One notable breakthrough for individual donors was the use of the Internet to convey contributions. Prior to September 11, many viewed Internet fund-raising as an underachiever that had produced only modest results while imposing substantial technical costs. After the attacks, Americans turned to the Internet to channel their compassion and giving at a surprising rate. One possible explanation for this lies in the nature of a crisis and the desire for immediate action that it brings with it. Donors used the Internet to give in record numbers because it represented a fast and efficient way to give, once the decision to give had already been reached. Many donors gave online not because they saw a banner advertisement or a call for money, but because they were looking for a simple way to fulfill a charitable decision that had already been made. Donors used the Internet to give because they knew which organizations they wanted to help and where to reach them quickly.[12] Small individual donors are typically the least likely to insist on accountability systems or evaluations as a condition for their support. After September 11, the small contributions that flowed were not connected to demands for proof of impact, only assurances that the funds reached those in need and were not being consumed by intermediary organizations.

The capacity to give and help must be joined with a capacity to receive. Relief funds needed to be created in the aftermath of the September 11 attacks to allow the philanthropic impulse to be translated into concrete action. These funds included a small group of large and visible charities that quickly provided a channel for foundation, corporate, and individual contributions. The three largest recipients of contributions—the Red Cross Liberty Disaster Relief Fund, the New York Community Trust and the United Way of New York City's September 11th Fund, and the New York City Mayor's Office's Twin Towers Fund—all had one thing in common: they were backed by old and respected organizations that had the public's confidence and trust, making the development of new measurement and accountability systems less urgent. In a period of great uncertainty and trouble, it was necessary for the major recipients of relief funds to be above reproach and have the capacity to translate contributions quickly and efficiently into caring and assistance.[13]

For all the success of the relief efforts in mobilizing support for victims, difficult questions soon emerged about what role private philanthropy should play in disaster and, more important, how private efforts should be organized. Given the size and range of the private philanthropic response to September 11, it was inevitable that a number of issues, controversies, and criticisms would arise in regard to the collection, administration, and disbursement of funds. The main issues broke down into three main categories: the efficiency of the process, the effectiveness of the charitable strategy, and the equity of the results. It is difficult to know whether any or all of these three problems could have been avoided had the giving proceeded more deliberately and been connected to some kind of ongoing evaluation system designed to locate problems needing correction. In retrospect, it is clear that some of the objections to the giving were at least partially connected to the speed and urgency in the disbursement of funds. The learning that occurred all happened well after the fact, once funds were fully disbursed. While some lessons did emerge that might be helpful in future situations in which disasters produce an outpouring of giving, it remains unclear whether some of the mistakes made will be avoided in the future should philanthropy have to work again under intense pressure to move funds quickly. The procedural shortcuts that were taken solved the problem of getting big institutions to act quickly, but at the same time these shortcuts created some real programmatic problems.

Efficiency has at least two main dimensions in the case of disaster relief: speed and cost. On the one hand, donors legitimately want disaster funds to be pushed out the door just as fast as possible so that help quickly gets to those in need. At the same time, funds need to be disbursed at a reasonable cost; most of the charitable resources should be directed at the needs of victims, rather than to administrative overhead. Yet, in the case of the response to September 11, speed was compromised at times, and administrative costs became an awkward issue for several of the relief charities.[14] Complaints about overhead rates were frequent and demands for lower staffing and faster disbursal rates became common. The process for disbursing funds soon became a target of criticism, as those in need sensed a disconnect between the processes being proposed and the nature of the need that was to be met. Interestingly, complaints about overhead were the result not of information surfacing through formal evaluations or assessments, but rather of media accounts of charitable spending. Few donors think of the media as part of their accountability and assessment strategies although in practice the media can be the source of critical information about program performance. After September 11, the media became the principal mechanism for holding charities accountable, although state regulators also got involved.

Speed and cost are surely both critical dimensions on which to evaluate a charitable effort, but effectiveness is important, too. Charities that receive donations must use these funds to fulfill a charitable mission, and in the process they must at times make difficult choices regarding how best to allocate available funds. In the case of this disaster, the vast majority of grantmaking involved cash assistance to the families of victims. Throughout the relief effort, some voices, particularly within the world of large foundations, urged that a broader grantmaking agenda be considered, one that addressed the needs of displaced workers, threats to civil rights at a time of heightened suspicion, and neighborhood and community needs around the sites of the attacks. After September 11 generated a huge outpouring of contributions, the idea of using relief funds to support efforts aimed at a broad range of public needs was appealing because it appeared to fulfill the duty of charities to use their funds responsibly. However, in the pursuit of greater levels of effectiveness, charities had to be careful to adhere to the wishes of the donors and to fulfill their intentions, which often did not involve the search for highly leveraged interventions. Representatives of the philanthropic establishment in New York attempted at times to make the argument that cash assistance alone would not be the most effective use of the resources raised and that the needs of the affected communities were in fact broader. However, these suggestions never gained much traction.[15] While the need to help displaced low-wage workers, to combat possible racial profiling, to help neighborhoods reorganize, and to carry out other indirect services may have been real, donors were focused on something simpler and more concrete: the needs of the victims' families. Few donors seemed to care about the effectiveness of their gifts. For many individual contributors, a crucial part of giving turned out to be the expression of compassion and caring.

Beyond efficiency and effectiveness, the relief charities were subject to considerable second-guessing about the equity of their decisions. Equity concerns focused both on the amount of funds that various groups of victims received from private sources, as well as on the effect this new disaster giving would have on existing nonprofits in New York and Washington. If funders were the chief source of effectiveness concerns, the families of the victims took on the role of publicly articulating equity concerns, starting soon after the attacks. The preponderance of funds for families of uniformed service personnel, especially firefighters, created the appearance that some families might end up being overcompensated for their loss compared to others. In seeking to compensate victims, private efforts were forced to deal with the issue of fairness and equity and to develop a plan that provided assistance without delivering unreasonable amounts of money. This task was made harder when the government decided to enter the field and offer its own compensation packages, a decision that created new, and even more complex, equity concerns. In addition to sorting out equity issues between families, relief funders also had to contend with fairness issues raised by the large universe of nonprofit organizations not involved in the disaster relief effort. These nonprofits worried about being squeezed as funds flowed freely to relief organizations active after September 11. With Americans giving en masse to relief charities amid a deepening economic slowdown, many nonprofit leaders worried that Americans' charitable impulse would run dry.

Although several controversies arose related to the administration and expenditure of billions of dollars of relief funds, the real implications of this chapter in the history of American philanthropy are potentially more profound, yet harder to see immediately. In making choices about the kind of help that would be offered, donors defined a vision of giving in times of need that was distinctly closer to old-fashioned charity aimed at offering direct help without preconditions than to modern, ambitious philanthropy aimed at the root causes of social problems. The return of charity was remarkable in that the moral authority and claims of organized philanthropy have loomed large in recent decades. Detailed strategic planning followed by careful program tracking and performance measurement gave way to more impulsive and emotionally charged mechanisms. When needs were great and when the stakes were high, donors turned back to a centuries-old style of giving in which compassion, not performance, was central.

The aftermath of September 11 has thrown many of the assumptions and ambitions of modern institutional philanthropy into some doubt. At a moment of national crisis and uncertainty, one might have expected that donors would have gone to ever greater lengths to ensure that their funds were used for the most effective purposes imaginable and for the most highly leveraged solutions to the crisis that arose after the attacks. One might also have expected that charities would compete to attract donations by designing innovative strategies, programs, and interventions. But almost nothing of the kind happened. To be sure, a few foundations tried to make the case that the needs of displaced low-wage workers and community members near the sites needed attention, and that the rights of immigrants required safeguarding at a time of great anger. These messages were drowned out by a much louder chorus for something far more simple: aid to the families of victims. The claims of organized philanthropy fell largely on deaf ears and the most basic forms of charity and victim assistance— the giving of cash grants to those in need—took center stage. It was not long before even the largest and most institutionalized donors fell in line in terms of abandoning decades of rhetoric and practice related to grant-making.

Of course, all of this raises the interesting question of why old-fashioned charity rose up from the ashes after the disaster and what this tells us about the claims of scientific philanthropy today. The simplest way to interpret the turn away from "high-impact," "high-engagement," or "high-leverage" giving is to point to the need for certainty that relief funds would meet the needs of victims. Large administrative overhead, complex programs, long-term planning—all may have appeared too uncertain to those who were moved to give. By contrast, cash transfers seemed concrete and they guaranteed that contributions would be of some value to those in need. In this sense, charity's relationship to philanthropy may well be like banking's relationship to venture capitalism. In times of trouble, donors may well seek out a safer but lower rate of return. The risk profile of modern philanthropy may simply have been too great for donors feeling the need to do something concrete.

The response to September 11 demonstrates that there are times when performance data and program design are neither possible nor even desired. Philanthropy sometimes needs to proceed based on the facts available, regardless of whether better giving could potentially result from careful study or planning. If this is indeed the case, the question that remains is whether old-fashioned charity and almsgiving exhibited in the philanthropic response to disaster will make a broader comeback. Probably not, because the number of situations donors will encounter, such as the one after September 11, is likely to be very limited. What is clear is that in a world in which the hubris within philanthropic circles has increased with every passing decade, a small chink in the armor may have appeared. When everything was at stake and when the whole country was watching, high-performance professional philanthropy anchored in strategizing and evaluation beat a hasty retreat and gave way to primitive charity. It was a retreat that was barely noticeable to some, but whose consequences are likely to only become more obvious over time, as we continue to reflect on what was learned about the nature of private assistance in times of great national need.

Finally, when it comes to the intersection of measurement and knowledge, the philanthropy that followed September 11 demonstrated that while evidence of impact is desirable, it cannot always be made a precondition for giving. The quality of giving might have been higher in New York had the donors studied the needs of the victims and the community more carefully. The impact of the billions of dollars delivered might have been greater had better accountability systems been built for ensuring that intermediary organizations were not duplicating each other's work. The broader field might have been able to learn something more profound about how best to respond to this sort of tragedy in the future had an evaluation system been designed to go along with the disbursal system that ultimately delivered funds to victims. In the end, however, the episode also serves as a reminder of the limits of evaluation and knowledge in the world of giving and its irrelevance in some cases when all that is intended is the relief of suffering in times of crisis. While it is possible that future attacks may prompt new outpourings of assistance, it is far from evident—even if knowledge about disaster philanthropy could have been codified after September 11—that such knowledge could be applied in the future. The fog of crisis in philanthropy can be deep and disorienting and it can render the link between knowledge and action tenuous.

Pathways

At its heart, philanthropy is about the strange and difficult union of personal values and public needs. At times, these two forces come together in powerful and transformative ways. In other cases, there is unresolved tension between the two that nags at the donor and community, sometimes receding, at other times remaining strongly felt for years. This tension between private and public can be a potent force for change and innovation when the values of the donor and the needs of the community find alignment. Philanthropy affirms the belief that the private visions and values of donors can inform and enrich public life. For those committed to centralization and standardization, the ways of philanthropy—its chaotic and unorganized nature—will surely frustrate. For those with greater patience and tolerance, philanthropy can be at once a valuable instrument of community change and personal expression. Although the relationship giving forges between giver and recipient is complex and involves both money and power, philanthropy can—at its best—overcome these challenges.

Much of the discussion here has been about the challenge of constructing and carrying out a philanthropic strategy. This turns out to be a difficult task that requires considerable work on the part of the giver over a period of time. While it is tempting to take the word "strategy" and conjure up an abstract and disembodied process of careful reflection, giving involves doing just as much as it involves thinking. Of course, the relative mix of thought and action in philanthropy varies considerably from one donor to the next, and, for some donors, from one gift to the next. Still, those who give ultimately seek to improve the effectiveness of their giving, whether it be defined in instrumental or expressive terms or in some combination of the two. The main argument of this book is that building a sound strategy for giving has to be understood as a critical part of the process of moving toward greater levels of effectiveness. Only by getting better at understanding and implementing a strategy for giving will donors be able to produce greater public and private returns over the years. The development of a strategy for giving must, just like the idea of achieving greater levels of effectiveness, be understood as an evolutionary process, one that unfolds over time as donors build knowledge and confidence.

If strategy building and improved effectiveness do in fact represent two critical goals that major donors have in mind, one might reasonably ask how the two are related in practice (see figure 10.1) Here, some difference of opinion exists. One school might argue that strategy is ultimately prior to effectiveness, in that donors must have a clear conception of what they are doing for it to have any real chance of succeeding. Taken to an extreme, this approach leads to a kind of conceptual philanthropy, one in which planning and consultation can become cumbersome and extended. Within the world

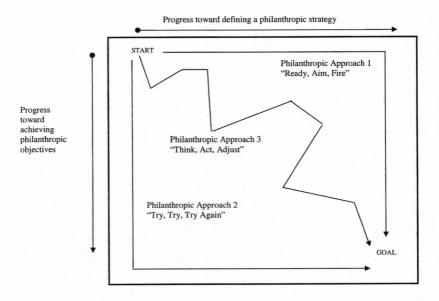

Figure 10.1 **Relationship between philanthropic strategy and philanthropic objectives.**

of foundations, this approach, which can be dubbed "ready, aim, fire" (with a heavy emphasis on the first and second elements), often spends a large amount of time and resources readying the philanthropic checkbook and aiming the philanthropic sights. Bringing in consultants, talking with experts from academe, comparing notes with other foundations working in the same field, and commissioning white papers that set forth the approach to be taken are all common in foundations that believe in the power of reason and planning. And to some extent, this work is valuable in that it can help donors avoid costly and embarrassing mistakes and help ensure that philanthropic funds are introduced only when the terrain has been properly prepared.

The patience of donors can be taxed too heavily by the first approach to making progress in philanthropy. For those with an action orientation, a second approach to making philanthropic progress looms larger and more appealing. It is based on a more inductive approach to giving and holds that most of what is needed to build strategy can only be located in the real world of practice and experience. For these more hardy philanthropic experimenters, the operating mantra is "try, try, try again," which has a heavy emphasis on repetition. This more experimental and experienced-oriented approach to giving is most commonly found in wealthy individual donors who are able to operate without having to seek the approval of a governing board or a professional staff. For the philanthropic principals, learning on the go and making mistakes along the way is the surest way to arrive at a compelling and battle-tested strategy to guide giving.

Between these two extreme positions, a more sensible middle ground exists in which strategy development and progress toward practical objectives unfold interactively. By making some initial strategic choices, pushing ahead with experiments, considering lessons learned, working to define and refine strategy, and then starting the whole process over again, donors can slowly navigate from a starting position where little has been achieved and where strategy is undeveloped to a position where significant outcomes are achieved and where a strategy for giving informs philanthropy. This model of philanthropic learning might be termed "think, act, adjust," although it could just as easily be termed "act, think, adjust." Getting from the start to the end is an admittedly complex and unpredictable process, which can include both encouraging breakthroughs and disheartening setbacks. However, by adopting an iterative approach to relating strategy and practice, donors are most likely to make progress in both areas. Lessons learned can be used to inform planning, and refinements in strategy can help advance progress toward objectives.

There are conditions in which it is either inappropriate or impossible to balance strategy and action, times when philanthropic action simply must be decisive and speedy, driven more by commitment than by reason. Timing in this sense can be critical, with little room for careful strategy formulation. In such cases, donors may need to compromise some short-term effectiveness in the name of responsiveness and focus on learning on the go. In other instances, when long-term community problems are the subject of the philanthropic intervention, a much more deliberative process may well be in order. Two examples from Chicago illustrate this difference.

The Steans Foundation decided to focus its energies on fashioning a comprehensive and sustained intervention in the Lawndale neighborhood on the west side of Chicago, an area with all the problems that can beset a community, including violence, high levels of unemployment and poverty, and weak schools. Rather than rush in and begin developing programs and funding activities, this small family foundation hired an executive director who had credibility in the community, having run popular youth programs for a year, and charged him with the task of setting up a storefront office and listening to what residents thought the real needs of the neighborhood were. Over time, as the foundation became more confident about its ability to assess and respond to the neighborhood's need, it began to fashion a broad program aimed at assisting residents. Because it was a relatively new player in the nonprofit scene, the Steans Foundation began with the first approach described in figure 10.1 and built strategy. Over time, as its confidence and competence increased, it has moved closer to the second model of grantmaking, with more learning through practice.

A very different approach was taken by a group of Chicago donors soon after the state approved a major governance shakeup in the public school system: each school would be governed by its own local school council, elected by the school community. This changed the entire governance and accountability system of the schools. Individual and institutional donors of all sizes knew at once that this was a critical and rare opportunity to make a change in a public school system that for years had been criticized and attacked for failing to educate children. With a relatively short window between the time of the announced reform and the election of the new local school councils, huge amounts of work needed to get done, both in terms of encouraging people to run for election and in getting citizens to the polls to take part in the elections. Rather than construct an elaborate theory around voter education and mobilization, the funders tapped the resources of organizations and systems that were already in place in communities to channel their efforts toward the upcoming school elections. There was no search for the optimal service providers, rather just a quick effort to get funds to known community groups that might take swift action to ensure that a major reform effort was not crippled by lack of awareness or poor voter turnout. In many ways, the approach started with the third model of grantmaking depicted in figure 10.1 and, as time went on and as new waves of elections occurred, it moved closer to the middle model in which strategy building and practice are built through an iterative process that oscillates between the two poles.

In trying to find the right mix of knowledge and experience, it is useful to recognize that a fair amount of the success of the programs supported by donors comes down to the quality of the person who will actually be responsible for the work getting done. A critical part of being a successful and effective donor thus involves spotting and choosing talented and committed people who can both help devise strategy and then implement it effectively. When all else fails in the nonprofit sector, the one remaining constant is that organizations and programs depend on strong leadership and good management. The irony in philanthropy is that much of the system that is in place for making giving decisions focuses on everything but the individual. To secure a grant from a foundation or corporation, a nonprofit must usually write a clever and intriguing letter of inquiry to pique the interest of a program officer, then submit a detailed proposal and budget spelling out what will be done and how, and usually, though not always, submit to a site visit or come in for a meeting with the donor. While there is a personal element in much of individual philanthropy, institutional donors have sublimated this element of the grantmaking process by pushing if off in the process and by placing such a high premium on the contents of proposals. The irony of the procedural systems that most of the large foundations have put in place is that instead of making their grantmaking more insightful and effective, it often simply rewards organizations that have mastered the art of proposal writing and the work of fund-raising more generally. The reason so much emphasis is placed on the written words of grantseekers is because there is a deeply held belief that the ability to render an organization's plans and intentions clearly in written form is a good predictor of the capacity of the organization to manage well and deliver effective programs. This assumption rests on very shaky grounds.

Nonprofit organizations in all fields are filled with talented people. Some come from fields as remote as engineering and environmental science, others enter after years of work in neighborhoods and informal community groups. While their training may be either formal or informal, the ultimate determinants of success in the nonprofit sector often are as related to personality and interpersonal skills as to technical proficiency and skill. To be sure, there are parts of the nonprofit sector where research and knowledge are critical, but there are vast parts of the nonprofit terrain where an ability to understand other people and to know how to make a personal connection is absolutely critical. A substantial part of the work of organizations that focus on the delivery of services involves establishing and maintaining relationships, sometimes with very troubled and disadvantaged populations. It can be difficult and demanding work that requires a strong core set of values and commitments to sustain it. Direct service also demands an eye for operational detail and an ability to set up systems that are innovative, efficient, and durable. Good managers are able to spot problems early and move to make changes in midcourse. These traits of effective nonprofit leaders are not the constant and compulsive focus of donors, however. The grantmaking processes that operate across institutional philanthropy are rarely set up to capture things such as interpersonal skills or value commitment or operational savvy. Rather, a huge amount of weight is placed on the capacity of leaders to produce documents spelling out what they would do if they were given charitable funds. Because success in philanthropy involves progressing along the middle path depicted in figure 10.1, donors benefit greatly when they are able to select and work with the nonprofit leaders who can help navigate this twisting path. In selecting grantees, a key consideration should therefore be the likelihood that the leader of the organization selected will be a productive contributor to the voyage between strategy building and program delivery.

In the end, there is no single solution to the question of how much reason and how much reaction should figure into philanthropy. The mix will depend both on the strategic direction established by the donor and on the problem or issue being tackled. In some cases, such as the crisis after September 11, there is simply no time to engage in careful planning and systems building. The needs are great and the public pressure for action is so intense that philanthropic reaction will naturally triumph over a reasoned rollout of services. Absent the pressures of crisis response, donors are able to inform decisions about what kinds of programs to implement by drawing on evaluation data of similar efforts that have been implemented in other localities. By studying what other donors have learned in their work on similar problems in other situations, donors can avoid repeating philanthropic history and reduce—although probably not eliminate—the trial-and-error nature of much of philanthropy. In some human fields, including early childhood development, the amount of data on probable impact and information on program design available is enormous. In other fields, such as youth violence reduction, the data is spottier and often amounts to a few case studies of successful local initiatives. In still other areas, the data is either poor or difficult to apply. Still, knowing something about what others have learned can be valuable to donors starting out in a field. Making strong and sensible linkages among measurement, knowledge building, and ultimately philanthropic action is a challenge. It requires an appreciation of what good evaluation data looks like, an understanding of the limits of evaluation research when it comes to predicting or even informing the future, a willingness to spend money on knowledge building (particularly when the results may be generalizable), and a realistic understanding of the dialectic between strategy building and strategy execution that is needed in philanthropy to achieve much progress. Donors will make progress toward all these goals by understanding that their giving will inevitably involve the continuous work of strategizing, acting, reacting, measuring, knowing, and adjusting.

Conclusion

One of the challenges in exploring the nature of philanthropic strategy is that giving has so many different forms, ambitions, and ideals. Philanthropy lacks the coherence of a traditional occupation or field because it still operates largely without a settled doctrine or a set of accepted practices. In fact, one of the most interesting features of philanthropy is that it is practiced not only by a homogeneous group of wealthy elites, but by people from all walks of life. Donors come to giving with a huge range of life experiences, which in turn shape their philanthropic objectives. The purposes and values expressed through philanthropy by individual donors, and to a lesser extent by institutional donors, are translated into a patchwork quilt of good work, with plenty of room for disagreement about substance and methods. While in politics some of the core disagreements that parties have over policies and priorities get resolved through regular elections, in philanthropy these differences simply coexist indefinitely. And compared to business, in which a transparent bottom line and a set of clear lines of ownership focus corporate strategy to produce value for shareholders, donors are not bound by any such responsibilities. By way of conclusion, I would like to briefly set forward a few examples of the astounding kaleidoscope of values and visions that animate philanthropy and revisit some of the central claims about strategy that this book has advanced.

One critical element of strategic giving involves the selection of a core value proposition. While there are many different ways to make these personal experiences, donors often start by reflecting on their lives, the turning points they have lived through, and the institutions that have given real meaning to their lives. One example of this is the gift of David Goodhand and Vincent Griski, who began to reconnect with their alma mater, the University of Pennsylvania, through a series of smaller gifts, including programs and a scholarship fund for gay or lesbian students on campus, and then made one of the largest gifts ever in support of a university-based center for gay and lesbian students.[1] The two men had attended the university in the 1980s and began to live together then. One of their memories of their time at the university was the strong support they felt the campus as a whole gave to gay students. After Goodhand retired from Microsoft and Griski left a Wall Street investment house, they decided to give back to their school by promising to underwrite the $2 million renovation of a building that would become a new gay and lesbian student center. The donors chose to get involved with the project by researching student needs and visions for a center, helping with the strategic planning, and working with an architect on the plans for the center. Perhaps the most time-consuming part of their commitment was to help the university raise the $5 million in additional funds that would be needed to endow the center.

Starting with an institution that made a central contribution to one's life is a very common way for donors to begin their philanthropic work. Familiarity breeds a certain serenity and confidence that is useful in getting over the hurdle of making large commitments. Slowly building up to a major gift to a favored institution may be reassuring, but not always necessary. When the commitment of the donor is very strong and the identity and ideals of the institution are so clearly defined in the donor's mind, major gifts can flow very quickly, as they did in the case of Keenan Sahin, who was able to show up at a fund-raising dinner at MIT in 1999 because a business trip was canceled. After dinner, Sahin told MIT's president Charles Vest that he had something to say. Vest introduced him, unsure of Sahin's intentions. Sahin went to the podium and noted that up until a half hour earlier no one, not even himself, knew what it was he was going to say. This founder of a successful billing technology company then announced a $100 million gift to his alma mater, one of the biggest recorded gifts to any educational institution. Sahin explained that he made the decision on the spur of the moment and out of pure gratitude to the school he had attended for undergraduate and graduate degrees. Sahin, raised in Turkey, said that he was persuaded to attend MIT by a call from the dean of graduate studies at MIT, and that choice deeply affected his life.

Sahin named a committee to decide how best to use the funds—after the announcement of the gift and its size. Sahin and the committee eventually decided to give $75 million to MIT's School of Humanities, Arts and Social Sciences, with the balance going into a discretionary strategic fund, to be used by the university president as he sees fit. The actual allocation of funds bolsters the point that Sahin made his gift out of pure gratitude to the school; he attended the Sloan School of Business but agreed to devote his gift to another MIT division that was in greater need. While the size of the gift was noteworthy, the way in which it was made and the purpose to which it was directed are interesting as well. The balance between planning and acting were inverted in this case, as purposes were sorted out after the decision to give was made. Sahin's experiment with following an emotional urge to give thanks and then working out the details later stands in contrast with most of the assumptions and processes of institutional philanthropy, in which careful exploration of needs and program details precedes the decision to give. It is impossible to judge which procedure for giving is wiser, but it is possible to note that philanthropy can and does accommodate both ways of working.

While wealthy donors like Goodhand, Griski, and Sahin can give back to institutions that have helped them, donors lacking education have few to thank but themselves for their success in facing a different challenge. Giving can be less about what has been significant and meaningful and more about what might have been significant and meaningful. Giving to causes that can help others avoid some of the trials and tribulations endured by donors is a different starting point for philanthropy, but one that reflects the fact that not all donors follow the same path. Although it is common to hear of immigrants taking on low-income, menial jobs and working hard for years to help family members, sometimes the quest for a better life leads to entrepreneurship and risk taking. Roberto Ramirez took the stereotype of the Hispanic janitor and turned it on its head. Starting with just $120 from his own pocket, Ramirez founded Tidy International Inc., a custodial service company, which today serves large, impressive facilities in and around Chicago such as the Chicago Symphony Orchestra and the Boeing and Blue Cross Blue Shield headquarters. Ramirez immigrated from Mexico with his family when he was age fourteen, without knowing any English. Shortly thereafter, Ramirez's father, a public official of Mexico, was assassinated and Ramirez dropped out of school to work at various menial jobs to support his widowed mother and his eight siblings. Ramirez got his start in custodial work as a janitor himself, and eventually worked up the ranks to become a supervisor of custodial services at major business complexes. When his desire to learn more about the business side of things from his employer was rebuffed, Ramirez decided to start his own firm and learn how to manage on the fly.

Originally the sole employee of Tidy International, Ramirez has built a custodial and cleaning services company that employs a couple hundred of workers. He now uses his success to help others in the Hispanic community, particularly students and children. Through his foundation, the Jesus-Guadalupe Foundation, Ramirez provides scholarships to young Hispanic students to encourage them to stay in school—something the donor wishes he had done himself. Specifically, the Jesus-Guadalupe Foundation provides modest college scholarships to first-generation Hispanic students in Illinois. To complement these scholarships, Ramirez also provides part-time jobs at his company to young people whom he mentors. While his story of overcoming adversity is admirable, it also helps to underline the fact that giving back to one's "community" can be a powerful motive and that it can be linked to dreams and realizations about what institutions and forms of assistance might have been helpful along life's way, rather than on what help was actually received by the donor. Ramirez insists on the importance of an education he never had and focuses his philanthropy on helping young people find their own roads to success.

Philanthropy is something practiced not only by little-known entrepreneurs but also by celebrities. Some of the biggest names in African American philanthropy include athletes such as basketball stars Michael Jordan and David Robinson, who have transferred celebrity into fundraising and giving efforts. But few philanthropic efforts are carried out by athletes who have served as role models through their athleticism and leadership on courts and fields, and who have also gone on to serve as civic leaders. Alan Page, a National Football League Hall of Fame member who played for the Minnesota Vikings, is currently a supreme court justice in the state of Minnesota and a local philanthropist. Page managed to get through law school while playing in the NFL, and added philanthropy as an avocation after he first realized in full the need for better education efforts as a player: four of the nine defensive linemen on his team could not read their playbook. In 1988, Page set up a scholarship in his name to help minority students attend college and pursue a solid education. In 2003, over 550 students in Minnesota became Page Scholars. In addition to receiving monetary support, Page Scholars are required to tutor and mentor young elementary school kids, extending the impact of the scholarship fund to more people. Page encourages and emphasizes the importance of moving away from admiring and exalting athletes and celebrities as role models. Page urges his scholars and everyone around them to recognize the example given by those who get up every morning and act as responsible citizens.

All five of these diverse donors chose to work in the most popular of all philanthropic fields: education.[2] However, the translation of this common interest into philanthropic action was very different, leading to a gift that advances an agenda close to the hearts of two donors, to one that meets the fundamental needs of an alma mater, to one that simply affirms the power of education and opportunity, to one that connects to personal experience and community needs. These exemplars of philanthropy's breadth could have been chosen to represent the huge substantive variation in the causes selected, since philanthropy is active in fields as diverse as basic research, affordable housing, job training, legal services for the poor, the performing arts, environmental protection, global health, and an endless list of other areas. However, within just the education field, the pluralism of approaches and emphases comes through clearly enough: Sahin's thank-you to his alma mater is very different from Ramirez's commitment to the educational opportunities which he himself missed, which in turn has little to do with Goodhand and Griski's intent or Page's principled efforts. The pluralistic nature of giving is manifest not only in the substantive choices that donors make about what types of programs to support, but it is also manifest in the way in which commitments to common concerns are translated into very different forms of actions.

There are thousands of other examples of donors who have constructed visions of the common good and then moved to render more real their ideals through philanthropy. Across all economic classes, racial divides, and ideological boundaries, donors have given to problems, issues, and institutions that mean something to them.[3] Although it is unlikely that in every case social welfare has been maximized, in aggregate, philanthropy has certainly contributed to the public good. The private visions of donors and the beliefs that these acts of giving represent constitute a chorus of voices directed toward different audiences and delivered in very different keys. The result, however, is not dissonance, but rather a novel chorus that sounds different depending on where one is sitting and how one listens. For progressives who are impatient about generating radical and decisive social change, this process of sorting and separating will test their tolerance for incrementalism. For conservatives, the foolishness and naïveté of some gifts will be unbearable and seem positively wasteful. Philanthropy is not principally about politics in the end, however, and these concerns are somewhat misplaced. Giving is an activity that may have political consequences, but at its heart it is a process of imagining the common good starting from one's own life experiences and values.

The framework presented in chapter 4 and then elaborated in chapters 5 through 9, while neutral on core substantive issues, does point to five questions that donors need to confront as they begin to chart their philanthropic plans. What is valuable to my community and me? What kinds of nonprofit activity will work best? What vehicle can best be used to accomplish my goals? When should my giving take place? What level of engagement and visibility do I want for my giving? When each question is posed independently, there are no universally appropriate answers to any one of them. There are, however, sets of responses that coalesce more or less well together and achieve some consistency. This points to the basic premise that strategic giving should be understood as the alignment of the five core philanthropic dimensions (see figure C.1). Some donors will start their giving with answers to one or more of the five questions. Others will approach the task of building a strategy with an entirely open slate. In either case, constructing a coherent strategy involves checking and rechecking over time— and as experience increases—the alignment of all elements in an effort to find a consistent, mutually supporting model for giving. When answers to all five questions fit well together, the probability of achieving the desired public impact and satisfying the donors' underlying needs is high. Moving toward alignment, I believe, is thus the central task of the strategic donor. Achieving alignment is also a critical step in the move toward the more effective, accountable, and legitimate exercise of philanthropic power.

Filling in this picture with well-chosen and strategically aligned choices demands work at the beginning, middle, and end of the process of giving. As donors do this work, they should also think carefully about how they understand their roles in the broader social context in which they choose to do their giving as well as their own motives and talents. I have suggested the factors that weigh in favor of a particular perspective on giving, one that seeks to connect the public needs of a community with the private values and commitments of donors. While there is certainly much merit in the idea of philanthropy as a purely productive tool for meeting pressing public needs, I have argued that there is a substantial limitation to this perspective. If philanthropy is nothing more than the quiet and agnostic satisfaction of community needs, it really has not defined for itself a position that is much

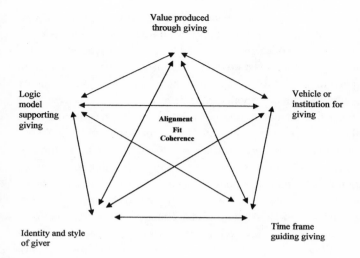

Figure C.1 **The philanthropic prism.**

different from that of government. And given the capacity of government to raise funds through taxation, philanthropy is not likely to be able to out-spend the public sector any time soon nor mandate that critical changes be achieved. As a consequence, philanthropy is unlikely to really achieve its ultimate potential if all it seeks to do is shadow and supplement public provision.

This leads to the second competing perspective on giving, one that I have tried to emphasize, that starts with a different premise entirely. Closely aligned with an expressive and value-centered understanding of philan-thropy, it holds that only when philanthropy is centered on the personal interests and commitments of donors will it fulfill its calling to breathe pluralism and innovation into society. Accordingly, philanthropy is best conceived as a private activity that allows donors to use their funds to ex-plore their own private visions of the public good. Rather than apologize for having interests and values, donors should be encouraged to act on them. Some donors do this by giving to organizations that have played important roles in their lives or in the lives of their family. Others give simply because they identify on a personal level with a particular cause or organization. Not only is giving grounded in values likely to be sustainable over time since it is grounded in lasting human experiences and emotions, but it also stands the best chance of injecting new blood in the field.

The premise that philanthropy is as much about the donors as it is about the public has radical consequences not only for how one goes about giving, but for how one assesses philanthropy and structures public policy to support it. Instead of castigating giving that does not proceed based solely on an analysis of the most urgent human needs, the public may need to be more open to the fact that philanthropy must have a certain autonomy and protection within which donors can operate. To communities in need and nonprofits demanding more funding, this argument will seem a little obscure and even difficult to accept. But it is only necessary to think about the supply of future philanthropic funds to understand why taking seriously the needs and interests of donors is important. Only when donors have the ability to use their philanthropy to do something that is meaningful to them will giving likely flow at high levels. After all, if the choices of donors are subject to endless second-guessing or greater public oversight, the line between private philanthropy and government action will become blurred. It is the donor's ability to direct charitable dollars to causes and organizations that are important to the donor that activates the impulse to give and defines philanthropy's special purpose in a democracy.

The opposition of private values and public purposes that frames too much of our current thinking about philanthropy ultimately rests on a false dichotomy, however. It overlooks the fact that the majority of donors ultimately want to produce both private and public benefits. Success in helping others is often what will give the most satisfaction to donors, since few givers will take any pleasure from giving that fails to achieve its objectives. The political divide that has split philanthropy has made it hard for donors to pursue the most important calling of all: the definition of the points of intersection between their private interests and the public needs. When the donor seeks to do something that is personally satisfying while also creating an important benefit for the local community, the task of strategy formulation can require substantial reflection and research. This task is the very first and most critical one for donors.

In practice, few donors in search of both public and private benefits have achieved the kind of strategic fit they desire. Often only some of the points of the philanthropic prism are clearly defined and well aligned when donors begin to engage in philanthropy. Strategic imbalance can take many forms. On the one hand, some donors have a sense of what cause or value is worth pursuing and some may have a sense of what style of giving best suits them. However, little thought may have been given to the best structure and time frame to guide their giving or to the type of recipient organization that stands the best chance of success. On the other hand, some donors come to philanthropy with a clear sense that they want to establish a foundation that will exist in perpetuity, even though they have little substantive direction. Other donors may have a time frame for their giving, which may be shaped by estate or income tax consideration, and little more. Still others will know that they want to be very engaged in their giving and have identified a field in which to focus, but lack further strategic direction. For all these donors, work on all five dimensions of the prism would add depth and coherence to their philanthropic vision.

The temptation to proceed with giving in the absence of a coherent strategic plan is strong. No matter how badly grants may turn out and no matter how poorly decisions may be made, donors rarely face any criticism from the world of nonprofit organizations. Indeed, there is always a long line of organizations anxious and grateful to help donors dispose of what Andrew Carnegie once termed "surplus wealth." The problem with this dynamic is that it makes it very easy for donors to dive into philanthropy with the hope of eventually coming to a vision and strategy through experimentation. In practice, this rarely occurs. Donors that begin their giving with a confused picture of their philanthropic goals rarely find them in the field. Instead, they are led out of caution to embark on a series of small philanthropic excursions that often lead nowhere. Not knowing what, how, when, and where to give frequently leads to an approach that can be termed "spray and pray," in which money is disbursed widely in small amounts with the hope that somewhere, somehow, something will happen. While the risks that a major philanthropic mistake will be made are diminished by such an approach, the chances of significant success are at the same time quite small. Before embarking on this kind of haphazard form of giving, donors should, according to the framework presented here, devote time to conceptualizing a broader philanthropic strategy that can guide them in their work. The task of the strategic donor is to work on the *entirety* of the philanthropic prism until each point is defined, polished, and in alignment with the others. Only when donors have achieved this complex and challenging level of fit can they claim that their giving has truly become strategic. Only when giving becomes strategic will donors have a higher probability of creating value for the public and for themselves.

Another recurring theme in this analysis of philanthropy is the importance of human values and convictions to the world of philanthropy. I argued at the outset that the core problems of effectiveness, accountability, and legitimacy have rattled around the world of giving for a long time. I also suggested that the growing professionalization of grantmaking, particularly in the larger foundations, has attempted to address these two issues by bringing greater rigor and procedural safeguards to philanthropic decision making and by focusing on the evaluation of grantee organizations. Tightening up philanthropy's front- and back-end processes has allowed some of the larger foundations to claim both increased levels of effectiveness and greater accountability. However, something very important has been neglected in this move. As philanthropic funds have gravitated to private foundations and as donors have over time entrusted their giving to others, a central element in philanthropy has been compromised. The private values, commitments, passions, and perspectives of individual donors are slowly overwhelmed by more agnostic, uncontroversial, and acceptable procedural values of professional staff. This would not be a problem if philanthropy were simply about the efficient provision of human services. But, again, this is not the case. The fundamental rationale for philanthropy is far broader than simply the channeling of private funds to public purposes. Philanthropy is about pluralism, expression, and innovation just as much as it is about redistribution and change. To justify the whole infrastructure around giving and to deliver fully on its potential contribution to society, philanthropy must strive toward and achieve something far bigger and broader than the competent production of useful goods and services. It must allow individuals to connect their private visions of the public good to real public problems and, in the process, to enliven the public sphere.

Implicit in my claims about the importance of private values in philanthropy is a concern about the creeping professionalization of giving. As major individual donors choose in large numbers to turn over their wealth to foundations where professional philanthropic managers will decide how best to give far out into the future, something troublesome is occurring. The expressive, impassioned, and opinionated fingerprints of the donor on philanthropy are slowly washed away by time and replaced with more instrumental and neutral philanthropic identities. While grantmaking professionals may have the best of intentions and strive earnestly to have philanthropic funds achieve their highest values, something is still lost when the delicate balance of public purposes and private values is tipped in the direction of the former to the detriment of the latter. Public policy could redress some of this drift by rewarding donors who act both sooner and more decisively. Not only would a more favorable treatment of lifetime giving support the expressive dimension, it would also lead to a more aggressive and serious attempt to fulfill the claims of philanthropy over charity about getting to the root causes of problems and solving them before they are allowed to grow worse. Arguing for a return of the donor and the power of personal commitment is hardly outlandish. As Paul Ylvisaker, the great teacher and observer of foundations, once noted: "Philanthropy originally was a one-to-one act of charitable giving. It is now practiced almost impersonally—in some cases by large bureaucracies—and by a code of behavior that frowns on becoming emotionally involved with its clientele. Dispassionate analysis is the hallmark of the trade, which is plied not by, but on behalf of, a now-distant donor."[4]

Repositioning philanthropy in terms of its expressive and instrumental content—either through changes in public policy or through shifts in philanthropic norms—would do a lot to remedy this situation and inject life into the field in the future. I have made at least two arguments in this book why it is in the public interest to encourage philanthropy to validate and reaffirm the private values that individuals are able to bring to giving. The first is that these idiosyncratic and unexpected private formulations of both what items on the public agenda deserve greater attention and how they should best be supported are essential to philanthropy differentiating itself from government. Without a large and noticeable value content, giving will begin to look like nothing more than a small-scale supplement to public funding.[5] Not only are there not enough resources in philanthropy to do a very good job at this, it is not clear that this would necessarily be its highest value contribution even if philanthropy could extend government priorities and programs. The second argument for a more donor-centered philanthropy is simpler. While the large private foundations occupy a fair amount of the philanthropic limelight, some of the most interesting and provocative giving is likely to be carried by living donors who—unlike their institutional counterparts—are striving albeit imperfectly to craft a legacy for themselves, repay important debts to institutions, build new models for program delivery, and act on behalf of a public need. Thus, the sheer complexity of motives and intentions that lie behind individual giving is more likely to lead to provocative ideas and visions than the more straightforward search for effectiveness, accountability, and legitimacy that pervades the world of philanthropic institutions. Finding ways, either through shortened time horizons for giving or through alternative giving vehicles, to empower and encourage principals to act philanthropically, rather than defer key decisions to competent but detached philanthropic agents, is a central priority for both preserving the vitality of philanthropy and strengthening public policies that encourage giving.

While the public profile of philanthropy has been rising, particularly as public funds for new discretionary programs have tightened, the role of philanthropy in the broader construct of civil society still needs to be fully specified. This is a complex task that can only be sketched suggestively here by looking to a promising point of entry. A lively debate about the relationship between civil society and democracy has unfolded over the past decade, one in which philanthropy appears to have a potential role. Civil society is usually defined to include mediating institutions[6] such as family, church, and voluntary associations. Its importance has been the subject of extensive theorizing and philosophizing from the time of the Founding Fathers to Hegel to Tocqueville. More recently, however, the discussion has focused on the relationship between social capital—the networks of trust and reciprocity that emerge from associational life—and democratic institutions. One school has argued that strong social capital institutions are critical to a vital democracy. Revisiting some of Tocqueville's claims about the way voluntary action in civil and political associations teaches the skills needed for active citizenship in democratic societies, these studies have rekindled interest in the proposition that democracy depends on the cultivation of civic skills through an active associational life. Against these claims, other arguments have been advanced seeking to restore the place and significance of the state in cultivating the values needed for a strong civil society. Rather than looking to associations for the training needed for democracy, the counterargument emphasizes the significant role government can play in teaching the values and practices needed to support democracy. No matter where one comes out in this debate about the function and significance of civil society, an interesting question emerges about philanthropy's place in this complex equation.[7]

One way to think about philanthropy's role with regard to civil society institutions is to see giving as providing the financial infrastructure needed to convert some of the impulses and ideas percolating in civil society into concrete programs and organizations. Philanthropy enables civil society by providing grants to those parts of the associational landscape that are eligible for tax exemption. Of course, there are large numbers of grassroots associations, formed and operated informally, that survive without major financial inputs from donors. These informal organizations survive through member contributions of labor and material. Churches, synagogues, and mosques are essential elements of civil society, providing individuals with communities of faith and networks of support. Not surprisingly, the majority of annual giving in the United States is from individuals to religious organizations,[8] usually to the local congregation. This small-scale giving supports a major part of civil society and allows Americans to have memberships not only in political communities, but in faith communities. For the more secular parts of civil society, organized philanthropy constitutes a critical source of support. Nonprofit organizations of all sizes and shapes receive significant support from philanthropy, which allows these organizations to deliver a range of services from critical health programs to edifying cultural programs. However, understanding philanthropy as a financial institution supporting civil society is a very narrow way to think about the role of giving in democratic societies.

The very act of giving can and should be understood as a core civil society activity, which contributes both to the formation of social capital and to the functioning of democracy. Philanthropy involves a process that draws individuals out into the public sphere and invites them into new experiences and worlds. While Maimonides would have advised separation, the contact that donors have with recipients—even with all the distortion that transfers of money involve—can create opportunities for new forms of social capital to emerge, especially between individuals and groups that come from very different backgrounds and experiences. Americans have little trouble creating bonds of friendship and cooperation within the boundaries of class, race, and geography. Philanthropy can be an instrument for overcoming these boundaries and exposing donors to new realities and perspectives, particularly when individual donors both choose a high level of engagement and when they work on problems and in places not readily familiar. Thus, while there is a tendency to think of the act of giving as something that supports important work by others, there is a critical element of philanthropy that in and of itself transforms the people who engage in it.

Asking that philanthropy contribute to the strengthening of civil society and the building of social capital between segments of the population that otherwise never overlap is a lot. However, philanthropy represents a very potent instrument for the accomplishment of such concrete purposes as political and social change and greater equity, as well as the less tangible but still essential goals of supporting pluralism, innovation, and expression. Rather than simply accept giving for what it is and what it does, donors should be encouraged to think about their giving strategically, in a structured and systematic way that seeks to cultivate both the art of identifying and communicating the private values that guide and motivate donors and the science of transforming these impulses to help into gifts that satisfy significant public needs.

Philanthropy may not always be directed toward popular causes or groups that embrace broadly held beliefs. Nevertheless, it is the very act of trying to act on behalf of the public interest that has the most significance. In the absence of philanthropy, a critical engine for the accomplishment of public purposes would be removed and expectations of government would surely increase. This might be a desirable outcome if one believes that civil society distracts citizens from looking to the state to define a common national set of values and commitments about public responsibilities. This book contends that philanthropy has a vital role to play as an independent actor in society, acting not simply based on what government defines as public needs, but in its own autonomous way. With some distance from government and with a fair amount of individuality encouraged, the expressive and instrumental dimensions of giving—representing in turn the art and science of philanthropy—can flourish together. In this process, donors can contribute not only to the needs of society as they are collectively defined and understood, but also to those needs that may be largely misunderstood or neglected. If donors can find a distinctive voice to guide their giving, locate a public problem that calls for attention, and construct coherent plans for accomplishing their goals, I believe they will have taken a major step toward meeting the challenge of strategic giving. While the concepts and frameworks presented here are designed to make this work easier, it will likely be a long journey of exploration and discovery. Urging donors on in this journey is what lies at the end of this path. Strategic giving represents the best and most lasting solution to the challenges of effectiveness, accountability, and legitimacy that have long faced private philanthropy.

Notes

Introduction

1. Bremner (1980) provides an account of the early evolution of American giving and caring.

2. While American philanthropy dwarfs that of other countries, philanthropy is spreading in other industrialized countries; see Anheier and Toepler (1999) on the rise of foundation philanthropy abroad.

3. Several organizations actually carry out this data collection work with considerable skill and present annually their findings on the amount, source, and purpose of giving on an annual basis. See American Association of Fund Raising Counsel (2004) for ample data on giving trends.

4. A clear picture of the major trends in giving over the past three decades can be found in Collins (2000), which culls data from many sources to sketch a landscape of giving.

5. Wolff (1999) takes up the issues of how wealth and income levels affect giving, as well as the relative level of societal need, focusing on poverty levels.

6. On the role of religious organizations in the wider nonprofit economy, see Biddle (1992).

7. Geography is a factor in the way donors approach giving; Wolpert (1989) identifies a range of local factors shaping giving.

8. While there is an abundant professional literature on the craft of grantmaking, much of this literature lacks grounding and conceptual depth. Not only is this literature heavily skewed toward institutional funders, it rarely tackles core issues of strategy or presents a coherent argument about the fundamental features of effective giving.

9. For an analysis of how the meaning and significance of charity has shifted over the past century, see Loseke (1997).

10. Gross (2003:47) observes that there has never been a point when charity stopped and gave way to philanthropy, but rather both have long coexisted albeit in tension: "To suggest that personal charity disappeared in the early republic would be a caricature of reality. Throughout the nineteenth century, as today, a great many men and women took responsibility for aiding the indigent and helping the needy ... But a tension arose between the two strains of benevolence—traditional charity and modern philanthropy—that runs through American history to the present."

11. For an overview of the rise of charity and the search for a cure to poverty, see Schwartz (2000) and Himmelfarb (1991). Early attempts to help the poor focused heavily on reforming their character and habits, not just providing relief.

12. Gross (2003:32) makes this point by revisiting John Winthrop's vision in 1630 of "City upon a Hill" graced by benevolence and caring: "In this perspective, charity was not restricted to giving alms to the poor. Having spurned the mercenary sale of indulgences by the Church of Rome, the Puritans revived the larger meaning of caritas or Christian love. It could take many forms and inspire diverse sorts. It could be simply a gift of 'good advice, a kind word, or an exhortation to piety,' offered by anybody to a neighbor in need. A poor man could be just as charitable as a rich one."

13. For the Catholic interpretation of the meaning of charity see Oates (1995:165), which notes the voluntary but necessary function of giving: "Unlike many other religious denominations, the Catholic Church does not exclude from membership those who contribute little or nothing to the support of its corporate good works. Yet it insists that, while religion encompasses more than these works, it is through them that members give public testimony to their faith. Thus charity critically defines the committed Catholic. Those who do not give in accord with their means, while not excluded from the church, are not full participants in its life."

14. The question of whether the obligation to help resides with individuals or government has been debated a great deal during the past century. See Critchlow and Parker (1998).

15. See, for example, Herbert Croly's (1993) early elaboration of progressivism and the critique it contains of traditional forms of charity. Schambra (2004:2) interprets the progressive legacy in philanthropy as follows: "The modern foundations arose at the same time as, indeed reflected and magnified, the progressive movement at the beginning of the 20th century. Progressives believed that industrial peace depended on the transfer of political power away from everyday citizens and chaotic, parochial, benighted local institutions, into the hands of centralized, professionally credentialed experts trained in the new sciences of social control. The first large foundations eagerly bought into the idea that the new social sciences offered an indisputably objective and rational way to order public affairs, and deal with the causes, not just the symptoms, of social disorder."

16. The early evolution of settlement houses, which provided services of all kinds, to poor and immigrant populations in cities, is told in Bremner (1988).

17. This crowding-out concern has been analyzed empirically over the years in many different ways, and it is far from clear that charitable giving leads to lower government spending. In fact, the research has actually suggested that government

spending has a mildly discouraging effect on giving. An overview and reinterpretation of the crowding-out hypothesis can be found in Brooks (2000).

18. Benjamin Franklin's formulation was as follows: "Human felicity is produced not so much by great pieces of good fortune that seldom happen, as by little advantages that occur every day. Thus, if you teach a poor young man to shave himself, and keep his razor in order, you may contribute more to the happiness of his life than in giving him a thousand guineas. The money may be soon spent, the regret only remaining of having foolishly consumed it; but in the other case, he escapes the frequent vexation of waiting for barbers, and of their sometimes dirty fingers, offensive breaths, and dull razors; he shaves when most convenient to him, and enjoys daily the pleasure of its being done with a good instrument." See chapter 8 in Franklin (1996) for more on self-reliance.

19. See Fox (1992) for a reinterpretation of the legacy of Carnegie's gospel of wealth a century later.

20. Karl (1992) provides an analysis of Carnegie's views on giving and social responsibility.

21. Carnegie (1992:12).

22. Carnegie (1992:11).

23. Carnegie's philanthropy focused on a range of fields and topics. He created several institutions in addition to the Carnegie Corporation, including the Carnegie Endowment for the Advancement of Teaching, whose history is told in Lagemann (1983).

24. Rockefeller (1909:113).

25. Rockefeller (1909:110).

26. Rockefeller was explicit in his desire to avoid charity. After an early meeting, one of the founding trustees wrote a memo for the board setting out key principles for the Rockefeller Foundation, the first of which was that "individual charity and relief are excluded" and the last of which was that "as between objects which are of an immediately remedial or alleviatory nature, such as asylums for the orphan, blind, or cripples, and those which go to the root of individual or social ill-being and misery, the latter objects are to be preferred." See Fosdick (1952:22–23).

27. Walker was constantly urging her workers to "rise above the laundry and kitchen and to aspire to a place in the world of trade and commerce." See Bundles (2001:153).

28. Mulhearn (2000:3).

29. Philanthropy by contemporary African American women is examined in Hine (1990).

30. Here I am building on the fourfold framework advanced by Kenneth Prewitt (1999a and 1999b), who suggests that philanthropy contributes social change, redistribution, efficiency, and pluralism. Others, including Paul Ylvisaker, have staked out different claims about the role of foundations and philanthropy. Ylvisaker (1999d: 362–367) defined five core roles: a financial support role (grantmaking, lending, insuring, and investing); a catalytic role (initiating, accelerating, leveraging, collaborating, and convening); a conceptualizing role (analyzing, defining and redefining, focusing, inventing, and testing); a critical role (commenting, approving and disapproving, advocating, gadflying, and serving as social conscience); and a community

building role (bonding or unifying, balancing, and leading). The nonprofit industry through its trade association (Independent Sector 1988) has nominated a long series of functions that justify the tax-exempt status of the sector, including its contributions to pluralism, community, civic participation, human development, preservation, and creativity.

31. On the complexities of working toward community change, see Brown, Chaskin, Hamilton, and Richman (2003).

32. A history of the interaction of private foundations with organized labor is available in Magat (1999).

33. On the role of think tanks in the policy process, see Smith (1991), which documents the way in which these institutions were created and managed to produce and disseminate ideas. For a more critical assessment of the role of conservative foundations in the public policy domain, see Covington (1997).

34. For a clear presentation of the Gramscian critique of philanthropy, see Odendahl (1990) and Fisher (1983), which argue that elite philanthropy reinforces class structures and sustains a kind of cultural imperialism. Roelofs (2003:2) also adopts a Gramscian perspective on foundations and suggests that foundations provide the second level—after the state—through which hegemony is maintained: "A central group of liberal foundations exerts 'hegemonic' power over civil society . . . Hegemony now operates on a global scale, facilitating the globalization of both political and civil society."

35. Frumkin (1992:20–21). For a fuller discussion of the Soviet disdain for philanthropy, see Frumkin (1992).

36. Arnove (1980:1).

37. Ross (1968), quoted in Arnove (1980:1).

38. The relevance of the venture capital model to the work of foundations is described in Letts, Ryan, and Grossman (1999).

39. For one perspective on innovation in philanthropy, see National Commission on Philanthropy and Civic Renewal (1997), which argues that donors can find innovations in their communities and can support organizations that are doing work that government has either ignored or failed to carry out effectively.

40. An account of philanthropy's support of Salk's research can be found in Sealander (1997).

41. The transition from philanthropic initiative to government program is not always a smooth one. Philanthropist Eugene Lang's decision to promise to students at the school he attended as a child to pay for college if they would just stay in school and work hard was spread to 180 "I Have a Dream" Projects—the name Lang gave to his first effort—in twenty-seven states and sixty-four cities, serving well over 13,500 Dreamers. When New York State attempted to imitate the program, it had decidedly mixed results because the passion and commitment of the donor was missing from the pledge.

42. Bornstein (2003:3) has chronicled the work of social entrepreneurs. He finds the range and quality of social innovations is stunning and notes that at the source of all this are individuals: "Important social change frequently begins with a single entrepreneurial author: one obsessive individual who sees a problem and envisions a new solution, who takes the initiative to act on that vision, who gathers resources

and builds organizations to protect and market that vision, who provides the energy and sustained focus to overcome inevitable resistance, and who—decade after decade—keeps improving, strengthening, and broadening that vision until what was once a marginal idea has become a new norm." While the notion of social innovations is appealing, it is not always demonstrably evident that everything that is classified as innovative in the nonprofit sector actually is so. Some of the most successful work often involves adaptation and modification of ideas and practices long in circulation. Still, a fair amount of emphasis is placed on the development of new models for service delivery.

43. Catholic giving has a reputation for focusing on helping those in real need and attempting to promote, even on a small-scale, greater equity and justice. See Brown and McKeon (1997) on the work of Catholic charities in the provision of human services.

44. This point is made best by Kenneth Prewitt (1999a). The importance of pluralism and its connection to civil society has been the subject of much research and theorizing. For an excellent argument about the contribution of voluntary associations to pluralism, see Rosenblum (1998:17), which explains: "[T]he simple existence of a dense array of associations—whether congruent with the public norms of liberal democracy or incongruent, alien and adverse—may contribute little to the moral uses of pluralism . . . [I]t does not suffice for moral development that the social stock of value and practices carried by associations is abundant if the lives of men and women are terminally fixed and situated, if they are unable to exploit freedom of association. The possibility of shifting involvements among associations—the experience of pluralism by men and women personally and individually—is what counts."

45. Conservatives have been attracted to the idea of philanthropic and associational pluralism as a bulwark against the power of the state. See Murray (1988), where Edmund Burke's idea of "little platoons" are revisited in the American context.

46. See Karl and Katz (1981).

47. The values-expressive content of all voluntary, nonprofit, and philanthropic activity is explored in Frumkin (2002), where I make the distinction between the instrumental and expressive dimensions of nonprofit activity and argue that both are central to understanding the functioning of the entire sector.

48. Progressive critiques of philanthropy offered by groups such as the National Center for Responsive Philanthropy have alternatively seen something wasteful or sinister in the ability of donors to enact their values through giving. Pointing to the tax exemption given to donors and to the tax-exempt status of private philanthropic foundations, progressives and watchdog organizations have emphasized the public responsibilities of donors.

49. The linkage between philanthropy and policy and intellectual elites is long-standing and strong. See Karl (1997) for a historical perspective.

50. British writer Ben Whitaker (1974:49) commented about American philanthropy's image enhancing character: "In the U.S., where philanthropy cannot buy titles, the designation of a foundation or a gallery is a ready means of seeking immortality at the same time as passing on increased status to your heirs."

51. A full account of the founding and early development of the foundation bearing Amy Biehl's name can be found in Harper (2000).

52. The federal and state laws pertaining to nonprofit organizations is complex and evolving. The best treatment of the regulation and oversight of nonprofits can be found in Fremont-Smith (2004).

53. Here I am adapting a figure developed in Clotfelter (1985:7).

54. One of the most significant financial trends in the broader nonprofit sector is the rise of earned income in the form of dues, fees, and charges as a percentage of overall nonprofit budgets. While donations still constitute an important source of capital, most nonprofits depend on their clients and customers to pay for services, while looking to donors to provide seed funding for new efforts and initiatives. For graphs showing this trend in recent decades, see Collins (2000).

55. American Association of Fund Raising Counsel (2004:259).

56. American Association of Fund Raising Counsel (2004:259).

57. Shuman (1989:148).

58. On the topic of how to structure donor-recipient relations, see Bolduc, Buchanan, and Huang (2004). This is a relationship that is fraught with tension and about which it is hard to get unbiased information, since few nonprofits are eager to talk critically about the funders that support their work.

59. I am indebted to Christine W. Letts, who originally conceived and organized the Executive Session on the Future of Philanthropy and invited my participation in the process.

Chapter 1 | Philanthropy and the Public Sphere

1. Hunter (1968) provides an early overview of the arguments for the tax deductibility of charitable contributions.

2. The debate over and the eventual passage of the Tax Reform Act of 1969 containing major regulations bearing on foundations prompted broader study and consideration of the role of private philanthropy. Two major research efforts during this period, known as the Peterson and Filer Commissions after their chairmen, were initiated by John D. Rockefeller III. The Peterson Commission was created to head off what some feared would be disastrous congressional intervention into foundations, while the Filer Commission supported what turned out be a critical early wave of research on giving and public policy. For a summary of the work of Filer Commission findings, see Commission on Private Philanthropy and Public Needs (1975). A documentary history of these two commissions can be found in Brilliant (2000).

3. For a discussion of the complex distributional issues embedded in foundation giving, see Margo (1992).

4. A good account of the implications of the tax code for philanthropy can be found in Simon (1986).

5. Not only can philanthropy question government social policy, it can attempt to reshape it. See Smith (2002) on the instruments of change.

6. For an account of this legislative initiative, see Buntin and Letts (1994).

7. A discussion of the Arizona experiment and data on its effect on charitable behavior can be found in De Vita and Twombly (2004:5), where the conclusion is mixed: "Name recognition and brand image seem to have been instrumental in leveraging charitable contributions from potential donors and taxpayers. Smaller and

lesser known groups, which abound in local communities, appear to be at a disadvantage under this policy."

8. Attempts to clarify the rules surrounding lobbying have been numerous and motivated by a desire to free nonprofits up to be more active politically. One publication that lays out the rules clearly for nonprofit managers is Smucker (1999).

9. A fuller discussion of the ways foundations in particular engage the policy process can be found in Ferris and Mintrom (2002), where five general approaches that foundations adopt in engaging the policy-making process are identified: funding activities that can have significant effects on policy; creating stores of knowledge that can affect how others think about policy issues; forging alliances among individuals and organizations that allows them to bring their skills and resources to bear on policy problems; building and maintaining strong relationships with policy makers; and developing and sustaining reputations as credible and reliable policy players.

10. See Ellsworth and Lumarda (2003).

11. The way donors have interacted with recipients around the world has varied greatly over the past century. Rosenberg (2003:242–243) observes that international philanthropy has at times "accented a difference between philanthropist and recipient, rescuer and needy, affluent and dependent; this difference could reinforce American feelings of exceptionalism and superiority. Yet, these philanthropic traditions also often took shape within discourses of the universality of human experience, emphasizing respect for cultural variety. This universalism could suggest less hierarchy, sometimes diminishing the relevance of national borders and sometimes enlarging the space within which philanthropic recipients could themselves shape outcomes. Far from being univocal, in short, philanthropic efforts . . . claimed both special national virtues and a larger universalized vision."

12. Brown, Khagram, Moore, and Frumkin (2000) considers the role of nonprofits in structuring intersector relations.

13. A practical guide to some of the challenges of international grantmaking can be found in Nichols and Mackinnon (2004:10): "International funders cope constantly with the reality that their grantees are far away. Distance affects how grantmakers follow the progress of a project, support grantees solving problems, and handle such mundane issues as currency exchange. Yet even more than distance, cultural difference is a challenge that requires constant attention when working overseas. . . . Careful due diligence, an open mind, and a respectful attitude are all crucial to effective international grantmaking."

14. Curti (1963).

15. Matthews (1997).

16. Arnove (1980).

17. For a discussion of the different meanings of justice in different social and political contexts, see Walzer (1984).

18. A different way to think about this issue is in terms of transnational financial transfers between individuals and their home communities, in which case the amount of money becomes considerable. See Chen (2003:5), which argues that "diaspora philanthropy—based on strong personal, cultural, and community ties—offers unique promise in the realm of philanthropy. Diaspora communities have long evidenced a strong sense of obligation and desire to assist extended families and homeland com-

munities. An estimated $100 billion in annual remittances flow from citizens of the U.S. to their 'home' countries. Increasingly, this informal support is augmented by more structured, professional philanthropic initiatives with broader and personal objectives."

19. Ylvisaker (1999b) provides a balanced perspective on the subject of giving and government.

20. Here I am building on a threefold typology of public-nonprofit relations offered by Young (1999).

21. Kingma (1989) examines the crowd-out question and the literature around it.

Chapter 2 | Central Problems in Philanthropy

1. The idea of philanthropy as a two-way street with strategic dimensions to each is set out well in Ostrander and Schervish (1990), where a threefold typology of grantseeking and a threefold typology of grantmaking approaches are presented.

2. One study surveyed foundations and discovered that the concept of effectiveness was in fact constructed in very different ways by respondents. Ostrower (2004:8) grouped foundations "according to how they rank across for scales that measure different effectiveness components and approaches." The four scales employed were proactive orientation to grantmaking (pursuing foundation-designed programs and offering more than just checks), technical assistance and capacity building (helping nonprofits develop management capacity and offering assistance in addressing governance and fund-raising challenges), policy and advocacy (engaging the political and policy worlds), and internal staff development (building the skill set of foundation workers). There were significant differences among respondents in terms of which of these practices were associated most closely with effectiveness in philanthropy, demonstrating that the very concept of effectiveness is highly contested within institutional philanthropy.

3. A candid account of the bottom-line orientation of corporate donors can be found in Himmelstein (1997).

4. Philanthropy is full of ambiguity and uncertainty, but Karoff (2004:20) advises donors: "In order for philanthropy to be great, to be heroic, we have to believe in ourselves and put away the Silly Putty of insecurity. We have to believe that there are untold numbers of unsung heroes in the very communities that we hope to improve. Accept the ambiguity—we know nothing but we know a great deal, we have very little to work with but we have many resources, we have done nothing but we have done a lot."

5. For discussions of the various forms that philanthropic collaborations can assume, see Buhl (1991). Looking at a series of recent attempts at foundation collaboration, Sharp (2002:5–6) posits that "collaboration is generally thought to produce these ends/values: providing the possibility of scale; expanding potential for knowledge exchange and development; providing safe haven and risk pooling; giving broader purchase and traction; and expanding the leverage potential for foundation dollars." Beyond these presumed advantages, Sharp finds that foundation collaborations also serve as "incubators for new ways of working," including tools for faster and more flexible grantmaking, the construction of new patterns of learning, and the ability to work across program boundaries more effectively.

6. On the link between evaluation and effectiveness, see Bertelsmann Foundation (2000), where grantmakers and experts explore the topic.

7. Burghardt, Rangarajan, Gordon, and Kisker (1992).

8. Zambrowski and Gordon (1993).

9. A large collection of reports and papers were produced in connection with this evaluation. Among them are Burghardt and Gordon (1990), Gordon and Burghardt (1990a,b), Handwerger, Strain, and Thorton (1989), Handwerger and Thorton (1988), Hershey (1988), Hollister (1990), Maynard (1990), and Maxfield (1990).

10. Foundations have relied on staff and outside experts to conduct evaluations. Looking at assessment techniques used in government, philanthropy has over time developed a set of practices and systems to support the search for knowledge about program impact. For a critical history of foundation evaluations, see Hall (2004).

11. Ihejirika (1995).

12. McRoberts (1994).

13. Kiernan (1996).

14. I am indebted to L. David Brown for helping me to distinguish these different conceptions of accountability.

15. It is not uncommon for grant letters to nonprofit organizations to state explicitly that the grant does not create any future obligations for the donor. While performance and reporting are expected of nonprofits, donors structure grants in a way that leaves them unencumbered and their own options open.

16. Much has been written on social change philanthropy and the alternative fund movement. See Ostrander (1995), Jenkins and Halcli (1999), and Jenkins (1998, 1989).

17. The perspective of social change philanthropy is expressed clearly in Collins and Rogers (2000), which contains a workbook for donors seeking to support grassroots efforts at promoting community change.

18. Controversy still exists about whether trustees should be compensated for their work. One view is that trusteeship is a form of public service that should be understood as voluntary and uncompensated. See Ahn, Eisenberg, and Khamvongsa (2003). A more flexible perspective focusing on assessing reasonable payment for trustees is presented in Council on Foundations (2002).

19. For a discussion of the problem of perpetuity, see Nielsen (1996:247), which notes: "A striking characteristic of the vast array of American foundations is that a large majority are created to last 'in perpetuity.' One important factor that has produced this pattern is surely sentimentality. A great many foundations are created by older donors well aware of *memento mori*. The prospect of death and the hope of remembrance hang over the proceedings. The idea of a permanent memorial in the form of a foundation has powerful force in those circumstances."

20. One of the problems with these surveys is that they may have a serious sampling bias because few grantees, even with promises of anonymity, are likely to feel comfortable criticizing their funders. And nonprofits that have been turned down are rarely if ever surveyed, though they too have had "service encounters" with foundations. An example of this kind of survey can be found in Center for Effective Philanthropy (2003).

21. For an early examination of the work of foundations and assessment of their contribution to society, see Weaver (1967).

22. I am drawing on Applbaum (2004), which makes the distinction clearly between the notions of descriptive and normative legitimacy.

23. One common effort is focus on documenting outcomes and impact in an effort to shift the focus from legitimacy to accountability. On the challenges inherent in this move, see Walker and Grossman (1999).

24. For an account of the broad characteristics of professions and their quest to maintain control over expert knowledge, see Abbott (1988).

25. Further discussion of the issue of professionalization in philanthropy can be found in Frumkin (1995, 1998, 1999).

26. On the value dimension in giving, see Karoff (2004), which contains reflections by experienced grantmakers and where the importance of core values is a theme.

Chapter 3 | Donors and Professionals

1. Andrews (1956).

2. Bremner (1988); Andrews (1950).

3. For a history of postrevolutionary charity in New England, see Wright (1992).

4. Many accounts of philanthropy's early support of education exist, including Bremner (1988) and Sealander (1997).

5. Rosenwald (1983) describes the dangers of perpetual foundations.

6. For an account of Rockefeller's early encounters with government and his plans for the Rockefeller Foundation, see Fosdick (1952).

7. On the struggle for a charter for the Rockefeller Foundation and the personality of John D. Rockefeller that made this struggle so difficult, see Collier and Horowitz (1976) and Chernow (1999).

8. Fosdick (1952) provides an insider's account of how John D. Rockefeller slowly built up his foundation after a struggle to get his institution chartered.

9. Rose and Stapleton (1992:548).

10. See Edie (1987) for the longer-term story of the relationship between private foundations and Congress.

11. See Hammack (1998:334–335) on the early evolution of community foundations and their place within the changing philanthropic landscape: "The community foundation spread quickly from its Cleveland origin between 1914 and 1929. Two regions proved most receptive: the Midwest, where community foundations fit effectively into the civic culture, and the Northeast, where nonprofit organizations already played such important roles. Trust companies, which at the time provided valued investment management and advising services to many people who held large estates, took the lead in promoting community foundations everywhere."

12. Loomis (1950) is one of the earliest attempts to track the growth and spread of community foundations.

13. Lagemann (1989:261) points out that the shift of control from donor to trustee shaped the fundamental vision and direction of the Carnegie Corporation: "In 1911, when Andrew Carnegie founded the Carnegie Corporation, he had hoped that the foundation would finance and organize new institutions to increase opportunities for education, self-improvement, and exposure to culture. These institutions would,

in turn, discover 'genius' in the few and develop individual self-discipline and a capacity for cooperative social interaction in the many. From Carnegie's perspective, this is how the Corporation would contribute to governance . . . The trustees who had defined the Corporation, and their successors on the board and staff, had not fully subscribed to Carnegie's views of governance, philanthropy, and purposes. They had hoped that the Corporation could contribute to governance more directly—in the 1920s, by helping to establish new institutes of expert, scientific research; in the 1950s, by refining the knowledge government officials and diplomats could call upon in their negotiations with other countries; and in the 1960s, by informing government action quite directly, through public advocacy."

14. On the general growth and evolution of the nonprofit sector including foundations see Bowen, Nygren, and Turner (1994).

15. Aldrich (1988) explored the cultural and social dimensions of affluence.

16. Lindeman ([1936] 1988:44) argues that the establishment ties of early foundation trustees contributes to the generally careful and conservative approach of foundations to their giving: "Foundations do not represent a 'conspiracy' on the part of the guardians of vested wealth designed to influence culture in one direction. More accurate would be the statement that these vested funds represent a consistently conservative element in our civilization, and that wherever their appropriations are accepted there enters at the same time this subtle influence in the direction of protecting the value system in existence, that is, of conserving the status quo."

17. Lindeman ([1936] 1988) and Andrews (1956).

18. Karl and Katz (1981:266) explores the boundary issues between public and private raised by philanthropy.

19. The account is given in Hall (1992).

20. See Ford Foundation (1949).

21. Magat (1979:18).

22. Magat (1979:28).

23. The early administrative practices of foundations are tracked in Andrews (1956).

24. For two perspectives on the way TRA 1969 shocked foundation leaders and shaped foundation practices, see Andrews (1973) and Cuninggim (1972).

25. Pifer quoted in Cuninggim (1972:211). Alan Pifer (1984) wrote widely about philanthropy and foundations.

26. Wallace (1971:1).

27. Shakely (1980:22).

28. Committee on the Foundation Field (1970:1).

29. O'Connell (1997:35–54) tells the story of how Independent Sector developed.

30. The attendance of annual meetings is reported in *Foundation News* between 1970 and 1979.

31. Shakely (1980:24).

32. Magat (1984:26).

33. Council on Foundations (1974:56).

34. Tweedy (1970:57).

35. Rossant (1970:190).

36. To guide new practices, manuals on communications began to appear urging

foundations to take seriously the work of using press releases, annual reports, and other forms of public information. See Richman (1973).

37. Council on Foundations (1971:101).

38. Tweedy (1970:58).

39. Magat (1984).

40. Council on Foundations (1979:48).

41. McCagg (1970:49).

42. Whiting (1970:173).

43. Whiting (1970:174).

44. Joseph (1982).

45. See Wilensky (1964) on the trend toward stretching the concept of a profession to cover many occupations.

46. Council on Foundations (1973).

47. Council on Foundations (1973:3).

48. Council on Foundations (1980:8).

49. Council on Foundations (1980:8).

50. A conservative critique of the work and approach of the Council on Foundations can be found in Olasky (1993), which locates in the council's work a stifling political correctness and lack of tolerance.

51. Council on Foundations (1990:1). See Olasky (1993) for a discussion of the impact of promulgation of a philanthropic code of conduct.

52. Joseph (1983c:64).

53. Council on Foundations (1977) presents a full reaction to the provisions included in TRA 1969 as part of the Filer Commission work.

54. Labovitz (1973:105).

55. Wallace (1971:4).

56. The limitations of these data are clear. By considering only the most recent position held prior to entrance to the foundation field, the data do not always capture the breadth of experience brought to the field by the new entrants. Another limitation of the dataset is its focus on large foundations. Small foundations may not be fully represented in the sample because they are less likely to be members of the Council on Foundations, the publisher of *Foundation News*, and because they are not in the habit of sending hiring notices to the foundation press. While large foundations do the bulk of all hiring in a small job market, they do not convey a comprehensive picture of the vast array of foundations on the philanthropic scene.

57. Council on Foundations (1994) surveys council members; it is a good source of data on the staffing levels and hiring practices of private foundations that identify with the goals and principles of the council.

58. Dorgan (1995).

59. Armbruster (1974).

60. Freeman and Council on Foundations (1981) is an important book mainly because it presents in one place a compact and coherent vision of what a professionally managed foundation should look like and how it should conduct its work.

61. Bonine (1971:244).

62. Joseph (1983b:48).

63. Joseph (1983a:43).

64. Wallace (1971:1).

65. Representative of the early impulse toward greater evaluation in the post–TRA 1969 era is Bolman (1970).

Chapter 4 | The Idea of Strategic Giving

1. From Porter (1985) to Mintzberg, Ahlstrand, and Lampel (1998) to dozens of alternative formulations, business leaders have a large literature of both technical and popular books to help with the formulation of strategy.

2. One attempt to connect corporate and philanthropic strategy can be found in Porter and Kramer (1999), which develops the idea of "unique positioning" in the philanthropic context.

3. This account is adapted from Rosegrant (2000).

4. A detailed study of donors in New York and their motives for giving can be found in Ostrower (1997).

5. While Diamond received many awards for her giving and was profiled in the media on several occasions, the best account of her philanthropic work can be found in Bates (1995).

6. The issue of perpetuity and donor intent are explored in Wooster (1998a), which tracks cases in which the intent of donors has been thwarted by those left behind to carry out philanthropic work, as well as cases in which limited-life foundations have been used effectively by donors to control their legacy.

7. On selecting and using philanthropic intermediaries wisely, see Szanton (2003).

8. I owe the term "philanthropic prism" to James E. Austin, who suggested it upon seeing this model.

9. There is a vast literature on fund-raising tactics, but less on the underlying issue of how best to appeal to donors. A presentation of the complexities of making sound appeals to major donors can be found in Tobin (1995).

10. Personal religious conviction is a potent starting point for many donors and has long been used by fund-raisers in campaigns. McManus (1990:116) denounces this practice: "Exploitive misuse of biblical words to produce philanthropy and donations to religion is wrong regardless of its success in raising large amounts of money for commendable purposes. And all the more so when this misuse seduces contributors into making good donations for the wrong reasons."

11. The intricacies of nonprofit finances and the multiple sources of nonprofit capital are described in Tuckman (1993:230). After detailing the many ways in which nonprofit organizations can finance their operations from a variety of sources including foundations, individuals, corporations, government agencies, and other entities, Tuckman actually concludes that given all the complexity and uncertainty in the financial environment of the sector, nonprofits are well advised to look within: "All nonprofits have a potential ability to gain access to capital through their ability to budget a positive surplus and to accumulate funds through time. Such surpluses provide both an internal source of funds and evidence of financial strength and fiscal soundness that increase the chance of obtaining external funding."

12. For a concise introduction to the world of foundations, see Smith (1999), which breaks down the historical evolution of foundations into five periods.

13. On finding the right level of quality programmatic support and maximizing their contribution to grantmaking, see Shmavonian (2003:4), which observes that "the difficulties involved in staffing stem from: inadequate understanding of what the program professional jobs entail; an essential combination of personal qualities and professional skills for the work that are typically not found in a single individual; and an emphasis on substantive knowledge and experience in the fields of grantmaking interest to foundation, rather than on the skills and experience needed for the process-oriented work of institution building and field-building, and the administrative demands of a regular schedule of grants."

14. Center on Philanthropy and Public Policy (2000) asks difficult questions about what really has changed in philanthropy in recent years and whether and how the field is capable of learning and innovating.

15. An excellent history of the moral and ethical dimensions of anonymous giving can be found in Smith and Johnson (1990).

16. On the powerful drive to bring families into philanthropy, see Esposito and Foote (2003).

Chapter 5 | Dimensions of Philanthropic Value

1. For the range of purposes in philanthropy, see Schervish (1994), which presents narratives of donors describing their life courses and how these connect to a broad range of social concerns.

2. On the imperative to pursue justice through philanthropy, see Ylvisaker (1999a).

3. Much has been written on the nature of the tax treatment of gifts. For an overview of the main issues, see Clotfelter (1985) and Hochman and Rodgers (1986).

4. Data on religious giving is fairly sound, though variations between reported and actual church attendance have been reported and raise some questions. See Hadaway, Mahler, and Chaves (1993).

5. One study of foundation giving reported a general liberal bias. However, attempts to classify philanthropy as either too liberal or too conservative obscure the far deeper and more complex question of effectiveness. For an attempt to render a judgment about the political leaning of foundations based on their grants, see Nagai, Lerner, and Rothman (1991).

6. Schervish and Havens (2000) seek to focus on the need to encourage donors by giving them the opportunity to identify with causes and make personal connections.

7. On the sources of caring and commitment, see Staub (1995).

8. On the broader topic of the secular and religious reasons people give both time and money, see Wuthnow (1990a:7–8), where the function of dicta is discussed: "All the religious traditions that have sunk roots in American soil embrace teachings about believers' responsibilities to their fellow human beings. The admonition found in both the Hebrew and Christian scriptures to love one's neighbor as oneself is widely known. Other teachings prescribe an ethic of care for fellow believers, for sojourners and resident aliens, and for those with physical and spiritual needs. Many of these prescriptions have been codified in the highly memorable dictums and narratives of religious traditions such as the Golden Rule, the Beatitudes, and the parable of the Good Samaritan." The interpretation of these accounts is as varied as the denominations that draw upon them, leading to strict requirements connected to giving to more open-ended approaches. See also Wuthnow (1990b).

9. For an example of small-scale gifts directed at common purposes, see Mac Donald (2000), which explores the Hundred Neediest Cases charity.

10. There are legal constraints on what nonprofits can do in the process of raising funds. See Hopkins (1990).

11. See Duronio (1997) on the nature of direct mail fund-raising work.

12. The history and recent evolution of the United Way is explored in Brilliant (1990:262), which also tracks the emerging competition for workplace giving: "By the time of the United Way centennial celebration, competition in the workplace had become a fact of organized fund raising, with the existence of over eighty-five alternative funds with their own member agencies and constituency groups . . . The consensus view of organized charity was seriously threatened by the emergence of these competing groups, while the declining percentage that United Way dollars represented of agency budgets weakened the federation idea."

13. For a broad historical account of cultural philanthropy, see McCarthy (1984).

14. The challenge of rendering explicit and lasting one's charitable intent can be significant. For an account of one foundation's efforts, see Stoneman Foundation (2001).

15. What is ironic about this distinction is that the Ford Foundation is often cited as the quintessential runaway foundation, which no longer reflects the beliefs and commitments of its founder, Henry Ford, a tycoon with heartfelt interests in free enterprise and free markets. At the end of his life, the founder's son, Henry Ford II, explained his decision to resign from the board of the foundation: "I had the Ford Foundation in my hand at one time. Then I lost it, and lost it of my own volition. I gave it away on my own. I was young, inexperienced, and stupid. I just muffed it. It got out of control, and it stayed out of control. And now it's gone, of course." See Wooster (1998a:32).

16. In making the case against the wisdom of a large amount of money being focused on one small geographic region, Simon (1987:648) famously argued in the context of the Buck Trust case, where the narrow scope of giving of a large trust was being litigated, that large foundations generally operate nationally and work on large problems: "What emerges is a pattern of philanthropic behavior that is, with the solitary exception of the Buck Trust, remarkably consistent, so much so that we can refer to it here as 'the philanthropic standard.' We may describe the standard this way: Large-scale charitable giving, regardless of the particular objectives it pursues, serves a community that is broadly defined in terms of population size and socioeconomic class. In its infancy, a foundation's charitable program may be narrowly constricted, with severe limits on the size and shape of the beneficiary community. But as the resources grow, the giving program reaches out beyond its parochial origins to address a more populous and diverse slice of humanity. In short charity may begin at home. But large-scale charity does not stay there." Of course, the fundamental and unanswered question arising from Simon's observation is whether it is wise for the field of philanthropy to think in terms of adherence to "a philanthropic standard" or whether the true standard is one of diversity and pluralism where no single standard should ever obtain.

17. On the long history of trusteeship and all the challenges involved in governing ownerless organizations like nonprofits, see Hall (1999).

18. The linkage between faith and the impulse to help is explored in Allahyari

(2000:4), where the concept of "moral selving" is developed to describe "the work of creating a more virtuous, and often more spiritual, person. Moral selving may be understood as one type of deeply emotional self work. It involves a concern for transforming the underlying moral self."

19. The tradition of almsgiving in Catholicism is discussed in McManus (1990).

20. One criticism of the work of mainstream faith-based organizations such as Catholic Charities is that they have slowly become secularized human service agencies. See Anderson (2000) for an argument against convergence and secularization.

21. Geography can focus giving, but it can also be a challenge for those running foundations, especially when board members are dispersed across the country and far away from the target community. See Stone (1999:60) on the way distance places special demands on family foundations: "The key to continuity for geographically dispersed family foundations is the same for all family foundations: finding a mission that embraces the family's core values and that coincides with the needs of society."

22. A forward-looking examination of the challenges of getting nonprofit boards to perform well can be found in Kwoh and Tang (2003).

23. On the quest for greater impact and new philanthropic tools, see Streeter (2001), which considers new developments in venture philanthropy and attempts to track performance more accurately.

24. A management philosophy aimed at preserving and cultivating the expressive quality of charitable work of all kinds has been developed by Mason (1996). The alternative paradigm centers on encouraging the enactment of values and commitments by those who work in nonprofit organizations.

Chapter 6 | Logic Models

1. A useful guide to developing and applying a logic model can be found in W. K. Kellogg Foundation (2001), where the use of this tool is presented in a workbook format designed to lead donors through the process of rendering explicit their beliefs and assumptions about how interventions produce impact.

2. Tempest (2000) tracks the founding and evolution of the New Schools Venture Fund.

3. On the difficulty of moving school reform forward through philanthropy, see McKersie (1999), where the discussion is anchored in concrete experiences of Chicago grantmakers trying to contribute to school improvement. For an account of the difficulties faced in implementing the Annenberg Challenge, see Domanico (2000).

4. I am indebted to Mark H. Moore for suggesting a variant of this fivefold framework.

5. On the foundation field's overall lack of commitment to supporting individual excellence, see Freund (1996:22–23): "The overall purpose of supporting individuals is to serve the common good. That does not mean that foundations can make a piece of the pie available to anyone and everyone who wants it. Fair-handedness should not be the primary concern of foundation programs. The responsibility, Warren Weaver of the Rockefeller Foundation said, 'is to support excellence,' to consider those who are already good and help them become better so that they may be scouts penetrating the frontiers of knowledge, opening new opportunities for the future."

Freund bemoans the pressure put on foundations by nonprofit organizations "representing the infirm, the uneducated, and the economically disadvantaged" to support efforts to address broad social problems and inequities that foundations are ultimately ill-equipped to solve.

6. Donors may want lean and efficient nonprofits, but the data indicate that giving is more driven by mission and commitment than by the underlying operational efficiency of the recipients as measured by overhead rates. Frumkin and Kim (2000) found that fund-raising expenditure was a much better predictor of contributions than low overhead rates. See also Tobin (1994) for more on the distortions these numbers can produce.

7. The Edna McConnell Clark Foundation has sought to focus its grantmaking strategy on "institution building" and the strengthening of nonprofit organizations. Foundation president Michael Bailyn (2002:4) explains: "This foundation now concentrates most of its grantmaking on a single area . . . youth development. But instead of trying to invent better ways of serving youth, or trying to reform the way public bureaucracies work in youth development, we are devoting all of our resources to strengthening strong, high-performance organizations that already have a demonstrably successful approach to the subject . . . There is a place, of course, for foundations that pioneer new ideas and try to influence the performance of big delivery systems. We are not on a mission to convert all of philanthropy to our way of thinking. We are, though, pursuing something that is just as critical to good philanthropy as program innovations and the system-change agendas, and yet is far less common: the practice of finding well-run, productive organizations and helping them grow, manage better, produce more, and demonstrate their results."

8. One of the challenges of funding policy work is that it can be difficult to track and measure impact. For one foundation's experience with policy-focused grantmaking, see Holton (2002).

9. Miller (2003), which tracks the work of conservative donors and the rise of more conservative politics, overstates the case. However, the underlying point is still important: shaping elite opinion can potentially have a far greater impact than slowly building grassroots programs.

10. Some critics of foundations have argued that foundations have not been sufficiently aggressive in either their support of social justice or untested ideas. See Dowie (2001) for a critique of foundation timidity.

11. The letter of gift to a New York foundation in 1930 by the donor makes the point: "Experience seems to show that in an enlightened democracy, private organized philanthropy serves the purposes of human welfare best, not by replacing functions which rightfully should be supported by our communities, but by investigating, testing and demonstrating the value of newer organized idea for sustained undertakings . . . I hope, therefore, that the [Josiah Macy, Jr.] Foundation will take more interest in the architecture of ideas than in the architecture of buildings and laboratories." Quoted in Harrison and Andrews (1946:77).

12. Hirschhorn and Gilmore (2003:6) considers not just how ideas can be promoted by donors, but how ideas themselves influence grantmakers: "Ideas that might be the germs of philanthropic programs emerge from the social and political currents of the time and work together to create an ecology of ideas. The connections

between ideas, and the ways they reinforce and contradict each other, often determine whether a single idea is likely to spread and become a compelling basis for social change."

13. On the interplay of philanthropic experience and creativity, see Brousseau (2003), which suggests that there are five "foundations of creativity" in philanthropy: the presence of a motivating belief and core values; a set of cognitive skills that could be deployed to do the work more effectively; a high level of interpersonal competence that facilitates good working relationships; an ability to cross boundaries and operate in different settings; and a sense of journey and adventure.

14. See Coleman (1990) on the challenge of connecting micro explanations of human behavior to macro social outcomes.

15. David (2000) observes that funders tend to equate "strategic grantmaking" with top-down approaches focusing on ideas and policy, while nonprofits see a focus on the development of leadership at the grassroots as strategic.

16. A walk through the toolkit of grantmakers searching for greater levels of effectiveness can be found in Orosz, Philips, and Knolton (2003). See also Orosz (2000) for a primer for professional grantmakers on process and systems, which moves through building relationships with applicants, reviewing proposals, declining and investigating proposals, conducting site visits, writing the funding document and presenting it to the foundation board, managing funded projects, closing and exiting projects, and increasing the impact of funded projects.

17. While nonprofit organizations desire general operating support, they rarely get it. See Independent Sector (2004).

18. Foundation Center (2003).

19. Arrick (2002) provides practical advice on how competitions and RFPs can be used.

20. Nichols and Mackinnon (2004:16) notes that some of these advantages can be offset by higher transaction costs, especially when regranting intermediaries are employed. Even with these costs, donors often prefer to work through some kind of intermediary organization that can provide staff expertise, linguistic abilities, familiarity with political and cultural contexts, and access to local networks.

21. For examples of joint funding efforts, see Northern California Grantmakers (1985).

22. For a full discussion of the conditions necessary for successful interorganizational collaboration, see Austin (2000), which emphasizes the need for alignment in partnerships along a series of dimensions.

23. On the challenges of putting collaborative funding into practice, see Robinson (2001), which tells of the Rockefeller family's experience.

24. Light and Hubbard (2003:10) defines capacity building as "activities that strengthen an organization so that it can more effectively fulfill its mission. Capacity building focuses on improving the leadership, management, and/or operations of an organization—the skills and systems that enable a nonprofit to define its mission, gather and manage relevant resource and, ultimately, produce the outcomes it seeks." Grants that support capacity building are thus different from project grants that are contingent on the delivery of narrowly defined programs and projects.

25. A discussion of one foundation's experience with capacity-building grantmaking can be found in Campobasso and Davis (2001).

26. The Northwest Area Foundation, in Minnesota, announced in 1997 that it would abandon its traditional categorical grantmaking programs and focus all its giving on a small number of geographical communities rather than spread its funds more broadly. See Stauber (1999) for details on making this significant shift.

27. See Dees (1998 and 2001) for an argument that nonprofits are really part of a social enterprise spectrum ranging from purely philanthropically supported to entirely commercially funded, with many hybrids in the middle. Purely philanthropic organizations appeal to goodwill, are mission driven and focus on creating social value. Purely commercial organizations appeal to self-interest, are market driven, and aim to create economic value. In between are hybrid organizations that have mixed motives, balance mission and market considerations, and seek to simultaneously produce social and economic value. See also Clohesy (2003) which examines the trend toward blurred boundaries between public, business, and nonprofit sectors.

28. Hall (2004:48) reminds us that evaluation can and does have different meanings and different implications depending on the orientation of the funder: "It is a common misconception that foundations are primarily committed to pursuing instrumental ends, to maximizing the efficient use of funds to bring about particular results. Whereas some grantmakers may view their work instrumentally, many others are likely to be dedicated to expressive purposes—propagating values rather than solving problems or changing society . . . Because foundations are so diverse, varying not only in size and scope of ambition but in purpose, it is a mistake to assume that evaluation methods appropriate to instrumentally oriented grantmakers are going to be useful to expressively oriented ones."

29. An economic explanation of the growth of nonprofits is available in James (1986).

30. David (2002:5) notes that sustainability can be a complex goal in philanthropy: "Sometimes we [the California Wellness Foundation] continue to fund something because *we* believe it should be sustained rather than because there's any genuine demand for it, perhaps to validate our initial judgment and subsequent investment of dollars. This is a particular risk of initiative-style grantmaking, where the source of the idea is the foundation itself. It can be difficult for a foundation to acknowledge failure when such efforts prove unsustainable."

31. For an interesting discussion of the role of endowments in higher education, see Hansmann (1990).

32. On the interaction of funders and recipients, see Martenson and Podolny (1999).

33. I owe this conceptualization of scale to Christine W. Letts.

34. Bradach (1998) gives a fine overview of the principles and practices of franchise organizations in the business world. While there are substantial differences between companies and nonprofits, some of the core issues are much the same.

35. Espinoza (1990) looks at the economics of buying franchises and elaborates some decision rules.

36. DeLeon (1990) offers an overview of the obstacles to successful replication along with ideas for making such efforts work.

37. On the many challenges to successful program replication and for a typology of replication strategies, see Replication and Program Services (1994:i), which found that replication "does not typically occur as a result of deliberate public policy, but

more often as a private entrepreneurial effort that is in essence analogous to starting a new business. That is, replication happens because a champion (usually the creator and initial operator of the program prototype) who finds financial backers, develops a plan to market his or her product, and takes it to new localities." Interestingly, this study found that "[m]ore often than not, the program replicated did not have in hand research evidence that proved their effectiveness. Their attractiveness was more often based on a combination of widespread local need for the program to meet a particular problem or need; widespread recognition of the particular program being replicated because of aggressive marketing or media attention; and the champion's ambition, fundraising ability and marketing savvy."

38. See Karl and Katz (1987).

39. Brest (2004) tells how one large foundation goes about its work and thinks about strategy formulation and execution and concludes with a broader observation about the challenges of increasing philanthropic effectiveness and the usefulness of good strategy: "[T]his essay . . . assumes that nonprofit organizations, including funders, would be more effective in achieving their aims if they developed and implemented strategic plans based on robust causal models, and if they used indicators of progress under those plans as the basis for managing their day to day activities. Like any other theory of change, these assumptions must ultimately meet the tests of evaluation. Evaluation may be tricky here, since it requires comparing the outcomes of organizations that are and are not outcome-oriented, and it may be difficult to get outcome data for those that are not. But difficult does not mean impossible, and as more organizations follow a strategic approach it should be possible to collect relevant data. In the meantime, we proceed in the belief that the theory of change is not entirely speculative: Developing and implementing clear and empirically-based strategies to achieve well-defined outcomes has conduced to success in the private and public sector as well."

Chapter 7 | Institutions and Vehicles

1. For a rosy perspective on wealth and family dynamics, see Collier (2001).

2. For a nuanced perspective on the intergenerational transfer of values and the concept of legacy, see Hamilton (2001:1): "It is precisely the ongoing legacy of values, vision, and giving that holds family foundations together (or may tear them apart), propels them creatively into the future, and is the basis of their positive impact on society. Just as donor intent has received important attention over the last fifteen years, it is hoped that the more robust idea of a living legacy will receive much more attention in the next fifteen years. Legacy is not a 'dead hand'; it is, instead, a living, 'helping hand' that is entrusted to and guides succeeding generations of family trustee and foundation staff."

3. See Breitenreicher and Pine (2003).

4. A functional description of the many roles played by foundations can be found in McIlnay (1998:170–173), which compares foundations to judges, editors, citizens, entrepreneurs, and partners: "Foundations are judges because their fundamental task is to determine the merits of grantseekers and the projects they propose, to decide that one applicant shall be funded and another shall not . . . Foundations are editors

because they associate the quality of applicants with the caliber of their writing, linking the ability to describe a project cogently with the capacity to administer it efficiently . . . Foundations are citizens because, like people in a democracy, they have responsibilities to their fellow citizens: grantseekers, other foundations, and associations in philanthropy . . . Foundations are activists because they support people and organizations that seek to formulate public policy or lead movements on behalf of people such as the poor . . . Foundations are entrepreneurs because they are the venture capitalists of philanthropy, able to support people, projects, and organizations unlikely to receive funds from conventional donors such as corporations or government . . . Foundations are partners because they fulfill their mission through the work of other people and organizations, without whom they would have little or no constructive purpose."

5. Williamson's (1981) theory of TCE begins with an explicit commitment to efficiency and holds that efficiency is the main factor in organizational changes.

6. On the evolution of community foundations, see Seeley et al. (1957).

7. Community foundations have been criticized for being too cautious and risk-adverse as a result of their need to constantly market themselves and attract new donors. Rather than fund social change organizations, community foundations tend to favor more mainstream and established institutions. A detailed discussion of this issue can be found in National Committee for Responsive Philanthropy (1989).

8. Emerson (1962).

9. Pfeffer and Salancik (1978).

10. Lumarda (2003).

11. For discussions of the interplay of family philanthropy and community foundations, see Ekstrom (2002) and Foote (2000:61), where the attractiveness of this combination is summed up: "For all their appeal of ease and simplicity in formation, low cost in expense and human labor in management, and tax advantages, donor-advised funds bear highly specific and unique characteristics. They enable families to find the right mix of giving vehicles; to involve themselves to the degree they wish in grantmaking; to use philanthropy as a means for family cohesiveness; and to train the next generation in family traditions of giving."

12. Questions of ultimate control do come up in community foundations pitting donors and foundation managers against each other. Frumkin (1997) looks at two cases where donors left behind funds and instructions for community foundations only to have their philanthropic intents either reinterpreted or contravened. Hammack (1998:331) notes that there are certain features of community foundations that demand trust: "Those who commit unrestricted funds to a community foundation agree to support purposes they cannot know, purposes that are certain to be changed in ways they cannot anticipate by a group of people whose identities and commitments are also certain to change. It was this very arrangement that [Frederick H.] Goff described as an instrument 'for cutting off . . . the dead past from the living present.' "

13. For an exposition of the underlying tax issues related to corporate philanthropy, see Sugin (1997).

14. Corporate giving may depend on the presence of a solid bottom line, but some critics have argued that corporations tend to support organizations that are actually

hostile to capitalism. See DiLorenzo (1990), which attempts to classify grants by corporations according to the underlying ideology of the recipient organizations.

15. Companies can do more than just make gifts. Public-private partnerships can be forged that link companies to communities and local government efforts, as Golberg (1989) suggests.

16. One of the most clear-cut examples of the link between the bottom line and philanthropy is the practice of cause-related marketing, which frequently links company support of a particular cause to product sales, usually with a percentage of sales or profits going to a charity. Adkins (1999) provides a good overview of the practice and some of the issues it raises for companies, nonprofits, and consumers.

17. For an account of the evolution of corporate philanthropy, see Karl (1991).

18. Hannan and Freeman (1977).

19. Astley (1985), Nelson and Winter (1984).

20. Corporations may be limited in how much they can give by the business cycle, but Hood (1996) argues that there are many other ways that they can and do contribute to the common good.

21. The ethical issues related to corporate philanthropy are explored in Gurin (1989), where a set of test questions are proposed to sort out the many motives in corporate philanthropy.

22. On the steady development of the foundation field, see Nelson (1987).

23. See Reed (2004), where MacArthur Foundation nongrant expenditures are reported to have been $26 million on administrative expenses and $52 million on investment expenses.

24. See, for example, Bremner (1988) and Hall (1992).

25. For a general landscape of the field of family foundations, see Lawrence (2002).

26. The Surdna Foundation is one of the larger family-controlled foundations; Stone (2001) considers how tradition is sustained across generations there.

27. A recent survey of family foundations found that the field broke down into three main types of institutional arrangements: the founder- or donor-controlled foundation, the collaborative family-operated foundation, and the family-governed professionally operated foundation. "All the cases were either one of the three or in transition from one to another . . . They are not developmental stages, because a foundation could start in any one, stay in any one, or move back and forth." National Center for Family Philanthropy (2003:11).

28. Esposito (2001b:25) considers the ways values permeate family philanthropy: "Family philanthropy can be both a family value and a vehicle for expressive values. Its vitality begins in shared values and its future may be dependent on the family's ability to inspire and pass on these values. This doesn't preclude conversations— even arguments—about donor legacy, perpetuity, program priorities, board composition, or even the role of personal giving. It provides the context for those conversations. It can also provide the common ground or understanding needed to make quality decisions and ensure satisfying family relationships over many generations."

29. On establishing and maintaining mission focus within family philanthropy, see Pechman (2000).

30. Massing (2000).

31. For a full discussion of many of the most important issues in contemporary Jewish philanthropy, see Tobin (2001:11), which explains: "Most Jews do not want to embrace a system that forces them to choose between building Jewish community in the United States versus social welfare needs in Israel, versus rescuing Jews from the former Soviet Union, or feeding an elderly Jew in Eastern Europe versus sending a Jewish child to a Jewish-sponsored preschool in the United States. Ultimately, asking Jews to choose between communities, between causes, between purposes, creates untenable choices." Also useful in understanding the distinctive issues and concerns of Jewish donors is Tobin and Rimor (1990).

32. Rosenblatt (1992) brings out the dilemmas facing Jewish federations in an era of donor-driven giving and disintermediation.

33. Jack Shakely of the California Community Foundation led an unsuccessful campaign to turn regulators against gift funds. Competitive threats are simply not something common in instutional philanthropy and tend to be resisted.

34. Steuerle (1999).

35. Berry (1999:86) notes that there is some resistance to the ideas of endowments and perpetual philanthropic institutions among Native Americans: "Building endowments requires a long-term effort. For donors, particularly individuals, there is a perceived notion of reserves or permanent funds as elite or part of the 'white man's world.' In Indian country, most wealth is communal or tribal, and perhaps, formal structures or endowments may evolve from these roots."

36. For a fuller exploration of Native American philanthropic issues, see Wells (1998).

37. For background on new forms, see W. K. Kellogg Foundation (2000).

38. On the distinctive issues facing women in philanthropy and the broader non-profit sector, see Odendahl and O'Neill (1994).

39. On the value and viability of maintaining philanthropic vehicles, see Bernholz (2004:140): "By turning our view from philanthropic giving organizations to product combinations, we see the potential for new suites of offerings, the entry points for new purveyors, and the opportunities for new product development. We also see the likelihood that donors of significant wealth will be using more than one product or suite of products."

Chapter 8 | Giving Styles

1. For an account of some of the more colorful figures in the history of philanthropy, see Nielsen (1996).

2. Newman (2002) considers the broad range of motives held by donors and how fund-raisers can think strategically about them.

3. A discussion of motives can be found in Kelly (1997). A different framework, focused on donor identities, can be found in Prince and File (1994). Schervish (1997b: 85–86) observes: "Identify any motive that might inspire concern—from heartfelt empathy to self-promotion, from religious obligation to business networking, from passion to prestige, from political philosophy to tax incentives—and some millionaires (as well as some nonmillionaires) will make it the cornerstone of their giving. The complex part about the charitable motivation of the wealthy is that those who hold

great wealth and consciously direct it to social purposes invariably want to shape rather than merely support a charitable cause. Although everyone who makes a gift wants to make a difference, those who make a big gift want it to make a big difference."

4. In explaining the psychological dynamics behind giving, Schervish (1994:8) uses the concept of hyperagency, which is "the ability to determine the conditions and circumstances of life instead of merely living within them. As agents, most people search out the most suitable place for themselves in a world constructed by others. As hyperagents, the wealthy construct a world that suits their desires and values."

5. Sometimes donors get ahead of the demand curve and create capacity for which there is no sustainable market support once charitable dollars run out. For a tale of overly ambitious funding in the arts, see Kreidler (1996). On the challenge of finding earned income to replace private grants, see Stevens (1996).

6. Batson (1990) sums up a series of experiments conducted over a decade and concludes that people are more likely to assist a person in need when that person appeals to their empathy and compassion.

7. For discussions of the functions and determinants of prosocial behavior, see Eisenberg and Miller (1987) and Clary and Snyder (1991).

8. See Jencks (1990) for a broad consideration of the forms in which altruistic behavior becomes manifest.

9. Fultz, Batson, Fortenbach, McCarthy, and Varney (1986:761) presents the results of two experiments suggesting that "the motivation to help evoked by empathy is not egoistic motivation to avoid negative social evaluation. Instead the observed pattern was what would be expected if empathy evokes altruistic motivation to reduce the victim's need." See also Piliavin and Charng (1990:27) for a review of the social science literature on altruism; the paper argues that there has been a "paradigm shift away from the earlier position that behavior that appears altruistic must, under closer scrutiny, be revealed as reflecting egoistic motives . . . True altruism—acting with the goal of benefiting another—does exist and is part of human nature."

10. Hoffman (1981) argues that there is biological evidence that altruism is part of human nature.

11. Andreoni (1990:473) argues that the pure theory of altruism is ultimately untenable: "When people make donations to privately provided public goods, they may not only gain utility from increasing total supply, but they may also gain utility from the act of giving. However, a simple public goods model ignores this phenomenon . . . On the other hand, the impure altruism model leads to predictions that are intuitive and that are consistent with empirical regularities." For an earlier critique of the limits of pure altruism, see Andreoni (1988). Benson and Catt (1978:90) find impure altruism in the fact that the way donors are asked for money shapes how they view giving and how much they will donate: "Contributions are considerably greater when the recipient's plight is defined as externally—rather than internally—caused and when the solicitor presents a feeling good rather than a social responsibility justification for giving."

12. See Batson (1990:341–344).

13. On the danger of pushing the rational actor model too far and seeing self-interest everywhere, see Sen (1990).

14. Spiegel (1995:635) is an example of the kind of economic analysis that takes charity to be "a strategic selfish activity that increases the welfare of the contributors without altruism."

15. Smith and Johnson (1990) tells the following medieval tale to illustrate the self-serving nature of some donors: "Count Thibaut of Champagne had a well-deserved reputation for being generous. On one occasion he loaded his pack horse with shoes and ointments intending to give them to the poor as he traveled through the countryside. A monk asked him why he was doing this himself rather than relying on his servants to distribute the gifts. Thibaut replied: 'I engender in myself greater love of the poor; I excite among them greater devotion and gratitude so that they will pray for me more frequently and fervently; and I implant a more vivid impression in their hearts.' "

16. Andreoni and Scholz (1998:422) finds that there is a connection between giving and the "social reference space" within which the donor operates, leading to a conclusion that donors do in fact have "interdependent preferences" that shape their philanthropic decisions.

17. See Galaskiewicz and Burt (1991) on the elite networks in Minneapolis and their effect on giving.

18. Schervish (1997a).

19. Schervish (1995).

20. Glazer and Konrad (1996) argue that giving can be understood as a signaling activity that provides donors with a way to announce to others their social positions and situate themselves within groups of people with the same relative wealth.

21. Schervish (1997a) underlines the importance of donors feeling a personal connection to causes and the necessity of philanthropy having personal meaning.

22. Jackson, Bachmeier, Wood, and Craft (1995) reviews many of the previous studies and then presents the results of a survey of eight hundred Indiana residents, finding that religious and associational ties do lead to higher levels of giving.

23. For a fuller exploration of the link between giving and faith, see Hall (1990) and Wood and Hougland (1990).

24. Wuthnow (1990b) provides a variety of perspectives on the interaction of faith, commitment to causes, and giving.

25. Schwartz and Howard (1984).

26. See Hodgkinson (1990) and Hodgkinson, Weitzman, and Kirsch (1990:108–109), which presents the results of a survey indicating that not just belief but participation predicts giving and volunteering: "The proportion of respondents who contributed and volunteered increased by frequency of church attendance . . . Respondents who reported attending religious services once a week were also more likely to give and volunteer both to religion and other charities." Interestingly, religious attendance was found to decrease as income increases, suggesting that "generosity with money and time is not so much determined by income as by level of religious commitment." Clain and Zech (1999) also reports findings that support the claim that churchgoers who contribute more to their church are also more generous when it comes to supporting other charitable organizations.

27. Wood and Hougland (1990).

28. See Cornes and Sandler (1994) and Sugden (1984) on public goods and giving.

29. Wolff (1999) provides a good overview of the issues related to tax and giving.

30. One of the many empirical studies of the impact of taxes on donation is Barrett, McGuirk, and Steinberg (1997), which finds that taxes determine the long-run level and timing of donations. Randolph (1995) considers the timing of charitable giving as income and tax policy change.

31. See Feldstein and Clotfelter (1976) and Boskin and Feldstein (1977), which show that giving is in fact sensitive to tax policy. Clotfelter (1980) suggests that the effect of tax policy on giving may be smaller than previously thought. Clotfelter (1985) provides reviews of more recent literature. Schervish and Havens (2001) explores the different effects of income and wealth on giving.

32. Smith, Kehoe, and Cremer (1995:124) reports findings suggesting that "the decision about whether to give or not give may be influenced in different ways and by a different set of variables than the subsequent decision about how much to contribute."

33. See Tamari (1987) for a full discussion of the Jewish perspective on not just giving, but also ethics and economics.

34. In an ethnography of soup kitchens, Poppendieck (1998) traveled around the country and experienced firsthand the effect of receiving charity at one food pantry: "[I]n so hospitable and undemanding an atmosphere, where an assertion of need is the only requirement, the whole weight of our culture's attitude toward those in need came crashing down upon me. I was being offered charity. Not an earned recompense for earlier contributions, not an entitlement based on our mutual interdependence, but a gift, given in response to my very deficit. For a brief moment, I was the hungry person dependent on the kindness of strangers, and I felt, profoundly, my powerlessness, my inadequacy, and something verging on shame."

35. Confronted with philanthropic appeals, the determinants of a donor's decision to give become a complex mix of financial and personal factors. See Murphy (2000).

36. Letts and Ryan (2003:26) focuses on high-engagement philanthropy, which they define as "a performance-centered strategy where alignment, reliable money and strategy coaching are used together to convert a grant-making relationship into an accountability relationship that uses power to improve performance."

37. On the trend toward disintermediation in philanthropy and higher donor engagement, see Frumkin (2000).

38. Reading and interpreting financial statements requires practice and skill. For an introductory guide, see Stevens (1989).

39. For a landscape of philanthropic support of the arts, see Wyszomirski (1999).

40. Engagement is often constrained by institutional identity. A discussion of the way leaders and boards negotiate roles can be found in Center for Effective Philanthropy (2004). See also McFarlan (1999).

41. See Harbaugh (1998) for an analysis of the strategic implications for fund-raisers of the fact that donors seek prestige and recognition when they make gifts.

42. A key intellectual support of the political movement to "reinvent government" through businesslike practices was Osborne and Gaebler (1992). For another early formulation of this logic, see Williams, Webb, and Phillips (1991:45), which argues: "When government views itself as a funder, it is primarily concerned with distributing money. When it sees itself as an investor, it becomes more focused on what happens after the grant . . . The concept of investment enters as one or more agencies

charged with dealing with a given problem employ funds to target investments to achieve specific benefits. This progression from funding to investing is the starting point for results."

43. For an attempt to apply the concept of return on investment to philanthropy, see Emerson (2000). On the conceptual confusion embedded in the idea of venture philanthropy, see Sievers (1997:44), which notes: "There is no counterpart in the nonprofit world to the for-profit world's single bottom-line variable, return on investment (ROI) . . . But what about the nonprofit world? Its very premise, the 'nondistribution constraint,' eliminates the single element of profit as an ultimate goal. What is in its place? Well, many things: benefits of the enterprise to clients, commitment of the participants or board members, intrinsic values advanced by the organization, positive changes in public policy, improvement of the lives of a particular disadvantaged group or society as a whole . . . in other words, the spectrum of ways in which the nonprofit sector contributes to the material, associative, aesthetic, and moral advancement of society."

44. Fleishman (2004:106) points to at least one major flaw in the investment metaphor: "To my mind, the analogy frequently made between for-profit venture capitalists and social venture capitalists—the foundations and wealthy individuals—has in fact been overdrawn. For-profit venture capitalists assume ahead of time that they will sow many more seeds than will sprout. They go into a mix of ventures only after calculating the risks that each entails, and with this knowledge they are willing to undertake very significant risks. Typically they expect eight or nine out of every ten investments to fail, and one or two to succeed mightily, more than making up for the losses. How many foundations have officers and trustees who would be comfortable with a record of one or two wins out of ten tries?"

45. Some nonprofits chafe at the burdens placed on them by venture philanthropists. See, for example, Carlson (2000) for the recipient perspective on engaged giving.

46. Hooker (1987:131–132) contains an extended confession by a seasoned university grantseeker about the exaggerations and distortions that enter into philanthropic relationships when substantial amounts of money are involved: "It is so easy to see ourselves in a win-lose contest with the institutions of society and with each other. When combined with the grant seeker's belief in the worth of his cause and his conviction that it should therefore be supported by the foundation of choice, the broader context of adversarial relationships promotes truth-stretching in proposals . . . Philanthropy as an institution has an obligation to achieve a level of integrity well above that of society in general. The overriding purpose of the institution of philanthropy is to improve the world in all its aspects, particularly those that pertain to values. This purpose cannot be accomplished well if philanthropic agencies do not themselves exemplify the highest ideals and values."

Chapter 9 | Time Frames for Giving

1. One of the earliest and most valuable studies of the payout question can be found in Steuerle (1977).

2. The payout rate issue in foundation philanthropy has been studied in great

detail. Reports and claims for both slow and fast rates are available. On the cautionary side, see the financial models and analysis in Cambridge Associates (2000), Salamon and Voytek (1989), and Salamon (1991).

3. The payout rate was originally set at 6 percent, then lowered to 5 percent. Recently, Congress has contemplated changes to the rule that allows foundations to count as "qualifying distributions" toward meeting the minimum payout. Instead of allowing both grants and administrative expenses to count as qualifying distributions, bills have been introduced seeking to have only grants qualify. The net effect of such a change were it to be enacted would be to increase the amount of foundation funds that reach nonprofit organizations each year. See U.S. Congress (2003).

4. My discussion in this section draws on prior work with Akash Deep. For a fuller treatment of the payout issue, see Deep and Frumkin (2002).

5. A quick summary of the conflicting arguments and claims about foundation payouts can be found in Harrison (1999).

6. While progressives tend to make the equity argument, it is often supplemented by an argument that higher payouts are feasible without eroding foundation endowments. See Merhling (1999) and National Committee for Responsive Philanthropy (2003).

7. For a discussion of the challenge of philanthropic discounting, see Frumkin and Deep (2000).

8. The clearest case for some kind of discounting in philanthropy can be found in Jansen and Katz (2002).

9. Brealey and Myers (1999).

10. Dasgupta and Heal (1974).

11. See Lind (1995) and Weiss (1989) on intergenerational equity.

12. Rosenberg (1994:164) makes a different but related point, suggesting that the cost of a gift must include the forgone earning power of the financial assets that have already been disbursed: "The elimination of an asset from net worth is not the only cost of giving. Obviously, the removal of compounding earning power from this net cost is a loss, too. Thus, even though a contributed dollar will lead to a tax deduction that lowers its expense below a dollar, the remainder is gone—as are its future earnings."

13. I owe this point to David Scudder, who pointed out that there is no "nonprofit price index" that donors can rely upon in thinking about costs over time.

14. See Lumley (1997) and Munasinghe et al. (1996).

15. Cowen and Parfit (1992) argues against the use of social discount rate.

16. Klausner (2003).

17. A donor's perspective on the issue of perpetuity and the challenge it raises can be found in Peters (2004), which emphasizes the fact that limited-life foundations are liberating and create a sense of urgency, not usually found in foundations that have unlimited time to pursue their missions.

18. Hirsch (1967) has argued that meaning must be unchanging and grounded in the author's intention, while the significance of a text can and does change as history and circumstances themselves change constantly.

19. Laird (1988:973).

20. Laird (1988:974).

21. See Chester (1979, 1989) and Atkinson (1993) for analyses of the uses and abuses of the doctrine of cy pres, as well as for ideas about how it might be reformed.

22. Simon (1987:655).

23. The issue of donor intent is discussed in Wooster (1998b).

24. For a forceful argument about the parallels between interpreting the intent of the Founders and those of donors, see Bork (1993).

25. The issue of donor intent played itself out in a battle for control of the Buck Trust, a charitable bequest left for the benefit of needy residents in Marin County, California. Given the relative wealth of Marin, a court battle ensued when the trustee of the local community foundation charged with administering the trust sought to modify the terms of the trust and distribute funds outside Marin, where the trustee thought the needs were greater. For an account of this legal struggle, see Simon (1987) and Maloney (1987).

26. A full account of the Barnes saga can be found in Anderson (2003).

27. Wooster (1998a:18).

28. Sutton (1987).

29. A detailed account of all aspects of this case can be found in Sidel (2003).

30. Philanthropic support to help former slaves was replaced by support for predominantly black colleges in the South. See Anderson (1997).

31. Quoted in Wells (2001:59).

Chapter 10 | Measuring, Knowing, and Acting

1. See DiMaggio (2001:252) for a frank and accurate assessment of the performance measurement challenges in the broader nonprofit sector: "In order to make any confident statements about the effectiveness of an organization or set of organizations, we need what social scientists call a 'causal model.' Such a model is an account of goals and the factors that lead to their achievement. It details the processes by which objectives are attained and describes the processes in terms of discrete variables. The variables can be measured, and the relationships of the variables to one another and to desired outcomes can be expressed mathematically . . . In fact, we rarely understand the relationship between cause and effect well enough to make confident estimates of the performance of organizations."

2. See Bernholz (2002:19) on the way in which foundations wield influence when working through associations. She cautions, however, that there are limits to this approach: "An association clearly expands on the ability of individual foundations simply by bringing to bear on an issue 'the power of many.' However, the proliferation of foundation associations may cause a backlash effect, as policy makers need to determine which association speaks for which elements within the philanthropic industry."

3. For an account of the Robert Wood Johnson Foundation's journey toward a greater emphasis on performance measurement, see Giudice and Bolduc (2004). The foundation settled on an adaptation of the Balanced Scorecard featuring multiple performance dimensions, including measures of the quality of grantmaking strategy, survey results of grantee perceptions of the foundation, staff satisfaction with their

work, and composite achievement of programmatic targets. One of the difficulties in this attempt to achieve a global assessment of mission effectiveness is that many of the assessments must be based on reports and assessments produced by the foundation's own staff.

4. Annie E. Casey Foundation (1995).

5. See Baker, Costello, Wynn, Merry, and Richman (2001).

6. For the lessons learned at one foundation about evaluation, see Brousseau (2004:14), which cautions against fixating on establishing causality and overlooking less formal ways that donors can and do learn: "What if we were to simply admit that for many foundation grants, assigning causality and identifying outcomes are either impossible or simply not worth the cost? The desire to measure outcomes, and to know precisely how much of an effect results from a grant or grantmaking program, stems from a positive motivation for funders to look critically at the work we fund—and the current emphasis on accountability is continuing to fuel this movement. As well motivated as the quest for outcomes is, it often backs us into a corner that results in disappointment, defensiveness and inability to see other positive effects. This single-minded emphasis on causal attribution assuredly serves to dampen creativity for other methods of understanding, assessing and communication the work accomplished through grants."

7. An argument against complex and ambitious social interventions and in favor of simpler forms of aid can be found in Olasky (1992, 1996).

8. A total of 143 private foundations had, as of February 2002, pledged or donated $185 million to relief and recovery efforts—for an average of just about $1.3 million per foundation. Most gifts were in the range of $10,000 to $200,000. The largest donations, all over $10 million, came from Atlantic Philanthropies, Carnegie Corporation of New York, Ford Foundation, Lilly Endowment, Andrew W. Mellon Foundation, and Starr Foundation. The September 11th Fund, one of the main charities created after the disaster to receive contributions, and the American Red Cross were the main beneficiaries of foundation grants, although a number of small specialized charities also received funding. Some foundations gave to specific types of organizations that fell within the purview of their respective missions. The Robert Wood Johnson Foundation, for example, gave $5.3 million to New York City–area health-care organizations that had been disrupted by the attack, and the Lumina Foundation for Education established a $3 million scholarship fund for children of attack victims.

9. Corporations stepped forward to offer their support following September 11, making gifts both directly and through their corporate foundations. A total of 543 corporations had, as of February 7, pledged or donated $621 million to relief and recovery efforts—for an average of $1.14 million per corporation. In some cases, both the corporate and foundation arms of companies gave money to relief and recovery efforts. Such was the case with Fannie Mae and the Fannie Mae Foundation. Most corporate gifts were in the range of $25,000 to $200,000, but there was a significant number of multimillion dollar gifts. The largest donations included those from Coca-Cola Company ($12 million), Deutsche Bank ($13 million), ExxonMobil ($15.25 million), Pfizer/Pfizer Foundation ($10.5 million), and Verizon Foundation ($13 million) (Renz 2002).

10. The language of "return" is part of the move to replace the term "corporate philanthropy" with "corporate social investing." For a presentation of this approach, see Weeden (1998).

11. According to a survey done two months after the disaster, 66 percent of Americans said they gave money to support attack victims and their families, with an average donation of $134, and a median donation of $50 (Steinberg and Rooney 2005). Nationally, blood donations ran some three to five times higher than usual in the days immediately following the attacks, according to the New York Blood Center. The American Red Cross received close to 1.2 million units of blood between September 11 and October 30, as compared to the 380,000 units the organization estimates it would have received during the same period of time if the attack hadn't occurred. However, the organization learned within just twenty-four hours of the disaster that blood needs were minimal, because most of the victims were killed in the attacks.

12. Despite the overwhelming success of online giving immediately following the attacks, Internet donations dropped off considerably in the following months. Thus, while the Internet was a potent source for channeling the first wave of compassion, its relevance diminished with time as the vast majority of donors eventually sought out more traditional means to give such as by mailing a check or calling a telethon or an organization.

13. Many other organizations channeled funds and services to relief and recovery efforts, including the International Association of Fire Fighters (IAFF), which created the New York Fire Fighters 9–11 Disaster Relief Fund to support the families of firefighters killed in the attacks; the New York Times 9/11 Neediest Fund, established to help the poorest of those directly affected by the attacks; the American Society for the Prevention of Cruelty to Animals (ASPCA) Disaster Relief Fund, which provided rescue assistance, medical treatment, and homes for pets whose owners were killed or missing as a result of the attacks; Catholic Charities USA, which established the Terrorist Attack Relief Fund; the Salvation Army, which set up the National Disaster Fund, Operation Noble Eagle, and Operation Compassion Under Fire to help victims and their families pay for basic needs, such as housing, utilities, food, and transportation; the Robin Hood Relief Fund, a fund of the Robin Hood Foundation in New York City, which raised funds to support low-income victims and their families. Other funds were established to provide scholarships for the children of victims and for a range of additional purposes.

14. With so many relief efforts and funds operating, a different kind of efficiency concern surfaced, one connected to the overall coordination of efforts. To improve the efficiency of the disbursement process overall, some in government believed that it was essential to coordinate and track cash awards and services, so as to avoid duplication of effort, wastefulness, and even potentially fraud. Under pressure from many directions, a coalition of about a dozen charities announced in December the creation of the 9/11 United Services Group. The coalition was created to coordinate relief efforts and oversee a database of records on some 30,000 people affected by the attacks. The group plans included the creation of a case management program to assist applicants for relief aid, a toll-free hotline for affected persons, and an informational Web site. In response to concerns over privacy, the 9/11 United Services Group

took security precautions and allowed only a small handful of people access to the database. With the creation of this centralized database, relief efforts were ultimately able to achieve some level of coordination.

15. As hundreds of millions of dollars poured into the Red Cross, the organization faced a clear dilemma. It could exclusively write checks to victims, or it could attempt to use some of these to advance its broader organizational mission of helping those in need during disasters in the future. In the name of using the funds the most effectively, the Red Cross's initial plan was to set aside some September 11 donations for a general emergency fund and strategic blood reserve. This turned out to be a disastrous decision, at least from a public relations perspective. In the face of mounting criticism, the Red Cross announced on November 11 that it would restrict the scope of its Liberty Fund to immediate disaster relief, financial assistance to families affected by the attacks, and direct support costs. The Red Cross's desire to use the fund effectively ultimately led the organization to suffer a major public relations disaster at a time when the organization should have been cementing its image as the leading private charity in the United States concerned with helping people in distress. Its mistake was simply to underestimate the significance donors attached to their charitable intent and to overestimate the importance of effectiveness at a time of national crisis.

Conclusion

1. For a broader discussion of sexual orientation and philanthropy, see Badgett and Cunningham (1998), which contains a survey of gay, lesbian, bisexual, and transgendered (GLBT) donors. The findings include that GLBT donors give more than the general population, that political and advocacy organizations receive a large proportion of these gifts, that equal support is given to nongay organizations, and that those donors who are open about their orientation give more than those that are not.

2. On routes to effective giving in the field of education, see Finn and Amis (2001).

3. On the intersection of race and philanthropy, see Smith, Shue, Vest, and Villarreal (1999). After surveying giving across a number of groups including Mexicans, Filipinos, and Chinese, these authors conclude that ethnic philanthropy is deeply linked with family and kinship, shaped by religion, avoids mainstream organizations other than churches, and tends to support family and kin outside the U.S. through large numbers of smaller contributions. Carson (1993, 1990) consider the special issues in African American philanthropy. Diaz (1999), Ramos (1999), and Petrovich (1989) focus on giving among Latinos.

4. Quoted in Ylvisaker (1999e:319). See also Ylvisaker (1999a, 1999b, 1999c, 1999d) for a deep understanding of the challenge of effective philanthropy.

5. The importance of personal commitment and individual caring to effective giving is argued in Husock (2000).

6. Neuhaus, Berger, and Novak (1996) pointed to the importance of mediating institutions, which could serve as a bridge between large political institutions and individuals.

7. See Schooler (1995:29–30) on the way donors can create community and engage in "civil philanthropy": "By investing in civil society and strengthening civic communities, foundations have cost-effective opportunities to affect significantly the

ways in which communities operate, meet human needs, and solve problems. Civil philanthropy focuses on the process through which communities work and, when the process (public problem-solving, civic dialogue, civil society) is strengthened as a result of foundations' investments, we can expect increased levels of public and private goods and services available for meeting charitable, philanthropic needs."

8. For a helpful typology of all the many forms of religious organizations, see Jeavons (1998:81), which suggests that "rather than try to capture the religiousness of an organization overall or in the abstract," it is more helpful to focus on "seven basic aspects of an organization where it is important to ask of its 'religiousness.' First, how religious is the organization's self identity? Second, how religious are its participants? Third, how religious are its material resources and their sources? Fourth, how religious are its goals, products or services? Fifth, how religious are its decision-making processes? Sixth, how religious is its definition and distribution of power? Seventh, how religious are the other organizations or organizational fields with which it interacts?"

Bibliography

Abbott, Andrew D. 1998. *The System of Professions: An Essay on the Division of Expert Labor.* Chicago, IL: University of Chicago Press.

Adkins, Sue. 1999. *Cause Related Marketing.* Oxford, UK: Butterworth-Heinemann.

Ahn, Christine, Pablo Eisenberg, and Channapha Khamvongsa. 2003. "Foundation Trustee Fees: Use and Abuse." Center for Public and Nonprofit Leadership, Public Policy Institute, Georgetown University.

Al Sayyid, Mustafa K. 1995. "A Civil Society in Egypt?" Pp. 269–293 in Augustus R. Norton, ed., *Civil Society in the Middle East*, vol. 1. Leiden: E. J. Brill.

Aldrich, Nelson W., Jr. 1988. *Old Money: The Mythology of America's Upper Class.* New York, NY: Vintage.

Allahyari, Rebecca Anne. 2000. *Visions of Charity.* Berkeley, CA: University of California Press.

American Association of Fund Raising Counsel. 2004. *Giving USA.* Glenview, IL: American Association of Fund Raising Counsel.

Anderson, Brian C. 2000. "How Catholic Charities Lost Its Soul." *City Journal* 10 (1): 28–39.

Anderson, James D. 1997. "Philanthropy, the State, and the Development of Historically Black Public Colleges." *Minerva* 35 (3): 295–309.

Anderson, John. 2003. *Art Held Hostage: The Battle over the Barnes Collection.* New York, NY: Norton.

Andreoni, James. 1988. "Privately Provided Public Goods in a Large Economy: The Limits of Altruism." *Journal of Public Economics* 35 (4): 57–73.

———. 1990. "Impure Altruism and Donations to Public Goods: A Theory of Warm-Glow Giving." *Economic Journal* 100 (401): 464–477.

Andreoni, James, and John Karl Scholz. 1998. "An Economic Analysis of Charitable Giving with Interdependent Preferences." *Economic Inquiry* 36 (3): 410–428.

Andrews, F. Emerson. 1950. *Philanthropic Giving*. New York, NY: Russell Sage Foundation.

————. 1956. *Philanthropic Foundations*. New York, NY: Russell Sage Foundation.

————. 1973. *Foundation Watcher*. Lancaster, PA: Franklin and Marshall College.

Anheier, Helmut K., and Stephan Toepler, eds. 1999. *Private Funds, Public Purpose*. New York, NY: Kluwer Academic/Plenum Publishers.

Annie E. Casey Foundation. 1995. *The Path of Most Resistance*. Baltimore, MD: Annie E. Casey Foundation.

Applbaum, Arthur Isak. 2004. "Legitimacy in a Bastard Kingdom." Working paper, Center for Public Leadership, Kennedy School of Government, Harvard University.

Armbruster, Timothy D. 1974. "Foundation Administration Moves into a New Era." *Foundation News* 15 (6).

Arnove, Robert F. 1980. *Philanthropy and Cultural Imperialism*. Bloomington, IN: Indiana University Press.

Arrick, Ellen. 2002. "Using Competitions and RFPs." *GrantCraft*, paper 1. New York, NY: Ford Foundation.

Astley, W. Graham. 1985. "The Two Ecologies." *Administrative Sciences Quarterly* 30: 224–241.

Atkinson, Rob E. 1993. "Reforming Cy Pres Reform." *Hastings Law Journal* 44: 1111–1158.

Austin, James E. 2000. *The Collaboration Challenge*. San Francisco, CA: Jossey-Bass.

Badgett, M. V. Lee, and Nancy Cunningham. 1998. *Creating Communities: Giving and Volunteering by Gay, Lesbian, Bisexual, and Transgender People*. New York, NY: Working Group on Funding Lesbian and Gay Issues.

Bailyn, Michael A. 2002. "A Letter from the President." Pp. 3–14 in *Annual Report of the Edna McConnell Clark Foundation*. New York, NY: Edna McConnell Clark Foundation.

Baker, Stephen, Joan Costello, Joan Wynn, Sheila Merry, and Harold Richman. 2001. "Marking Progress in Community Initiatives." Chapin Hall Center for Children, University of Chicago, March.

Barrett, Kevin Stanton, Anya M. McGuirk, and Richard Steinberg. 1997. "Further Evidence on the Dynamic Impact of Charitable Giving." *National Tax Journal* 50 (2): 321–334.

Bates, Mariette J. 1995. "An American Phenomenon: A Qualitative Study of a Metropolitan Foundation with a Ten Year Life Span." Doctoral dissertation, Union Institute Graduate School.

Batson, C. Daniel. 1990. "How Social an Animal?" *American Psychologist* 45 (3): 336–346.

Benson, Peter L., and Viola L. Catt. 1978. "Soliciting Charity Contributions: The Parlance of Asking for Money." *Journal of Applied Social Psychology* 8 (1): 84–95.

Bergstrom, Ted L. 1986. "On the Private Provision of Public Goods." *Journal of Public Economics* 29 (1): 25–49.

Bernholz, Lucy. 2002. "Critical Junctures: Philanthropic Associations as Policy Actors." Working paper, School of Policy, Planning, and Development, University of Southern California.

————. 2003. "Spending Smarter: Knowledge as a Philanthropic Resource." Pp. 233–264 in Frank L. Ellsworth and Joseph Lumarda, eds., *From Grantmaker to Leader*. New York, NY: Wiley.

————. 2004. *Creating Philanthropic Capital Markets*. New York, NY: Wiley.

Berry, Mindy L. 1999. "Native-American Philanthropy: Expanding Social Participation and Self-Determination." Pp. 31–105 in Council on Foundations, ed., *Cultures of Caring*. Washington, DC: Council on Foundations.

Bertelsmann Foundation. 2000. *Striving for Philanthropic Success: Effectiveness and Evaluation in Foundations*. Gütersloh, Germany: Bertelsmann Foundation Publishers.

Biddle, Jeff E. 1992. "Religious Organizations." Pp. 32–133 in Charles T. Clotfelter, ed., *Who Benefits from the Nonprofit Sector?* Chicago, IL: University of Chicago Press.

Bolduc, Kevin, Phil Buchanan, and Judy Huang. 2004. *Listening to Grantees: What Nonprofits Value in Their Foundation Founders*. Boston, MA: Center for Effective Philanthropy.

Bolman, Frederick. 1970. "The Need to Evaluate a Foundation." *Foundation News* 11 (1): 20–21.

Bonine, Robert. 1971. "One Part Science, One Part Art." *Foundation News* 12 (6): 244–249.

Bork, Robert H. 1993. *Interpreting the Founder's Vision*. Washington, DC: Philanthropy Roundtable.

Bornstein, David. 2003. *How to Change the World: Social Entrepreneurs and the Power of New Ideas*. Oxford: Oxford University Press.

Boskin, Michael, and Martin Feldstein. 1977. "Effects of the Charitable Deduction on Charitable Contributions by Low-Income and Middle-Income Households." *Review of Economics and Statistics* 59: 351–354.

Bowen, William G., Thomas I. Nygren, and Sarah E. Turner. 1994. *The Charitable Nonprofits*. San Francisco, CA: Jossey-Bass.

Bradach, Jeffrey L. 1998. *Franchise Organizations*. Boston, MA: Harvard Business School Press.

Bratton, Michael. 1989. "Beyond the State: Civil Society and Associational Life in Africa." *World Politics* 41 (4): 407–430.

Brealey, Robert, and Stewart Myers. 1999. *Principles of Corporate Finance*. 6th ed. New York, NY: McGraw-Hill.

Breitenreicher, Joe, and Leslie Pine. 2003. "Issues of Foundation Planning." Pp. 203–230 in Frank L. Ellsworth and Joseph Lumarda, eds., *From Grantmaker to Leader*. New York, NY: Wiley.

Bremner, Robert H. 1980. *The Public Good: Philanthropy and Welfare in the Civil War Era*. New York, NY: Knopf.

————. 1988. *American Philanthropy*. Chicago, IL: University of Chicago Press.

Brest, Paul. 2004. "Update on the Hewlett Foundation's Approach to Philanthropy." Unpublished manuscript. William and Flora Hewlett Foundation.

Brilliant, Eleanor L. 1990. *The United Way: Dilemmas of Organized Charity*. New York: Columbia University Press.

————. 2000. *Private Charity and Public Inquiry*. Bloomington, IN: Indiana University Press.

Brody, Evelyn. 1997. "Charitable Endowments and the Democratization of Dynasty." *Arizona Law Review* 39 (3): 873–948.

———. 1998a. "The Limits of Charity Fiduciary Law." *Maryland Law Review* 57 (4): 1415–1500.

———. 1998b. "Of Sovereignty and Subsidy: Conceptualizing the Charity Tax Exemption." *Journal of Corporation Law* 23 (4): 585–629.

Brooks, Arthur C. 2000. "Public Subsidies and Private Giving." *Journal of Policy Analysis and Management* 19 (3): 451–464.

Brousseau, Ruth Tebbets. 2003. "Experienced Grantmakers at Work: When Creativity Comes into Play." In Patricia Patrizi, Kay Sherwood, and Abby Spector, eds., *Practice Matters: The Improving Philanthropy Project*, Working Paper Series. New York, NY: Foundation Center.

———. 2004. *Reflections on Evaluating Our Grants.* Woodland Hills, CA: California Wellness Foundation.

Brown, Dorothy M., and Elizabeth McKeon. 1997. *The Poor Belong to Us: Catholic Charities and American Welfare.* Cambridge, MA: Harvard University Press.

Brown, Eleanor. 1999. "Patterns and Purposes of Philanthropic Giving." Pp. 212–230 in Charles T. Clotfelter and Thomas Ehrlich, eds., *Philanthropy and the Nonprofit Sector in a Changing America.* Bloomington, IN: Indiana University Press.

Brown, L. David, Sanjeev Khagram, Mark H. Moore, and Peter Frumkin. 2000. "Globalization, NGOs, and Multisectoral Relations." Pp. 271–296 in Joseph S. Nye and John D. Donahue, eds., *Governance in a Globalizing World.* Washington, DC: Brookings Press.

Brown, Prudence, Robert J. Chaskin, Ralph Hamilton, and Harold Richman. 2003. "Toward Greater Effectiveness in Community Change: Challenges and Responses for Philanthropy." In Patricia Patrizi, Kay Sherwood, and Abby Spector, eds., *Practice Matters: The Improving Philanthropy Project*, Working Paper Series. New York, NY: Foundation Center.

Buhl, Alice C. 1991. *Patterns of Cooperation among Grantmakers.* Washington, DC: Council on Foundations.

Bundles, A'Lelia. 2001. *On Her Own Ground: The Life and Times of Madam C.J. Walker.* New York: Scribner.

Buntin, John, and Christine W. Letts. 1994. "Tax Incentives for Charitable Giving." Case 1357.0, Kennedy School of Government, Harvard University.

Burghardt, John, and Anne Gordon. 1990. *More Jobs and Higher Pay: How an Integrated Program Compares with Traditional Programs.* New York: Rockefeller Foundation.

Burghardt, John, Anu Rangarajan, Anne Gordon, and Ellen Kisker. 1992. *Evaluation of the Female Single Parent Demonstration: Summary Report.* Princeton, NJ: Mathematica Policy Research.

Burke, Colin B., and Peter Dobkin Hall. 2002. "Historical Statistics of the United States Chapter on Voluntary, Nonprofit, and Religious Entities and Activities: Underlying Concepts, Concerns, and Opportunities." Working paper 14, Hauser Center for Nonprofit Organizations, Harvard University.

Cambridge Associates, Inc. 2000. *Sustainable Payout for Foundations.* Grand Haven, MI: Council of Michigan Foundations.

Campobasso, Laura, and Dan Davis. 2001. *Reflections on Capacity Building.* Woodland Hills, CA: California Wellness Foundation.

Carlson, Neil. 2000. "But Is It Smart Money? Nonprofits Question the Value of Venture Philanthropy: Responsive Philanthropy." *NCRP Quarterly,* spring.

Carnegie, Andrew. 1992. "The Gospel of Wealth." Reprinted at pp. 1–31 in Dwight F. Burlingame, ed., *The Responsibilities of Wealth.* Bloomington, IN: Indiana University Press.

Carson, Emmett D. 1990. "Patterns of Giving in Black Churches." Pp. 232–252 in Robert Wuthnow, Virginia Hodgkinson, et al., eds., *Faith and Philanthropy in America.* San Francisco, CA: Jossey-Bass Publishers.

————. 1993. *A Hand Up: Black Philanthropy and Self-Help in America.* Washington, DC: Joint Center for Political and Economic Studies.

————. 2003. "A Foundation's Journey into Public Policy Engagement." Pp. 157–174 in Frank L. Ellsworth and Joseph Lumarda, eds., *From Grantmaker to Leader.* New York, NY: Wiley.

Center for Effective Philanthropy. 2003. *Grantee Perception Report (Sample).* Cambridge, MA: Center for Effective Philanthropy.

————. 2004. *Foundation Governance: The CEO Viewpoint.* Cambridge, MA: Center for Effective Philanthropy.

Center on Philanthropy and Public Policy. 2000. *What's New about the New Philanthropy?* Los Angeles, CA: University of Southern California.

Chaves, Mark. 1998. "The Religious Ethic and the Spirit of Nonprofit Entrepreneurship." Pp. 47–68 in Walter W. Powell and Elisabeth Clemens, eds., *Private Action and the Public Good.* New Haven, CT: Yale University Press.

————. 1999. "Religious Congregations, Welfare, and 'Charitable Choice.'" American Sociological Review 64 (6): 836–846.

Chen, Lincoln C. 2003. *Diaspora Philanthropy: Perspectives on India and China.* Cambridge, MA: Global Equity Initiative, Harvard University.

Chernow, Ronald. 1999. *Titan: The Life of John D. Rockefeller.* New York, NY: Vintage.

Chester, Ronald. 1979. "Cy Pres: A Promise Unfulfilled." *Indiana Law Journal* 54 (407): 41–70.

————. 1989. "Cy Pres or Gift Over?: The Search for Coherence in Judicial Reform of Failed Charitable Trusts." *Suffolk University Law Review* 23: 41–70.

Clain, Suzanne Heller, and Charles E. Zech. 1999. "A Household Production Analysis of Religious and Charitable Activity." *American Journal of Economics and Sociology* 58 (4): 923–946.

Clary, E. Gil, and Mark Snyder. 1991. "A Functional Analysis of Altruism and Prosocial Behavior." Pp. 119–148 in Margaret S. Clark, ed., *Prosocial Behavior.* Newbury Park, CA: Sage.

Clohesy, Stephanie. 2003. *Blurred Boundaries and Muddled Motives: A World of Shifting Responsibilities.* Battle Creek, MI: W. K. Kellogg Foundation.

Clotfelter, Charles T. 1980. "Tax Incentives and Charitable Giving: Evidence from a Panel of Taxpayers." *Journal of Public Economics* 13: 319–340.

————. 1985. *Federal Tax Policy and Charitable Giving.* Chicago, IL: University of Chicago Press.

Cohen, Jean L., and Andrew Arato. 1992. *Civil Society and Political Theory.* Cambridge, MA: MIT Press.

Coleman, James S. 1990. *Foundations of Social Theory.* Cambridge, MA: Harvard University Press.

Collier, Charles W. 2001. *Wealth in Families.* Cambridge, MA: Harvard University Development Office.

Collier, Peter, and David Horowitz. 1976. *The Rockefellers.* New York, NY: Dutton.

Collins, Chuck, and Pam Rogers, with Joan P. Garner. 2000. *Robin Hood Was Right: A Guide to Giving Your Money for Social Change.* New York, NY: Norton.

Collins, Michael. 2000. "Philanthropy Industry Notes." Case CR15-98-1446.0, Kennedy School of Government, Harvard University.

Colwell, Mary. 1993. *Private Foundations and Public Policy: The Political Role of Philanthropy.* New York, NY: Garland Publishing.

Commission on Private Philanthropy and Public Needs. 1975. *Giving in America.* Washington, DC: Commission on Private Philanthropy and Public Needs.

Committee on the Foundation Field. 1970. "Report of the Committee on the Foundation Field." Manuscript on file at the Foundation Center.

Cornes, Robert, and Todd Sandler. 1994. "The Comparative Static Properties of the Impure Public Good Model." *Journal of Public Economics* 54 (3): 403–421.

Council on Foundations. 1971. "Five Practices: The Field Foundation" *Foundation News* 12 (3): 101.

———. 1973. *Some General Principles and Guidelines for Grantmaking Foundations.* Washington, DC: Council on Foundations.

———. 1974. "On Communications." *Foundation News* 11 (3): 56.

———. 1975. "Some Thoughts on Employment." *Foundation News* 16 (5): 48.

———. 1977. "Private Foundations and the 1969 Tax Reform Act." Pp. 1557–1599 in *Research Papers*, sponsored by the Commission on Private Philanthropy and Public Needs. Washington, DC: U.S. Department of the Treasury.

———. 1979. "Reducing Confusion: A Checklist for 1979." *Foundation News* 20 (1): 48.

———. 1980. "Recommended Principles and Practices for Effective Grantmaking." *Foundation News* 21 (5): 8–10.

———. 1990. *Principles and Practices for Effective Grantmaking.* Washington, DC: Council on Foundations.

———. 1994. *Foundation Management Report.* Washington, DC: Council on Foundations.

———. 2001. *Foundation Management Series*, vol. 1, *Finances, Portfolio Composition, Investment Management, and Administrative Expenses in Private Foundations.* Washington, DC: Council on Foundations.

———. 2002. *Determining Reasonable Compensation for Foundation Directors and Trustees: A Guidance Memorandum from the Board of Directors of the Council on Foundations.* Policy memo, December 6. Washington, DC: Council on Foundations.

Covington, Sally. 1997. *Moving a Public Policy Agenda: The Strategic Philanthropy of Conservative Foundations.* Washington, DC: National Committee for Responsive Philanthropy.

Cowen, Tyler, and Derek Parfit. 1992. "Against the Social Discount Rate." Pp. 144–

161 in Peter Laslett and James Fishkin, eds., *Philosophy, Politics, and Society*, series 6, *Justice between Age Groups and Generations*. New Haven, CT: Yale University Press.

Critchlow, Donald T., and Charles H. Parker, eds. 1998. *With Us Always: A History of Private Charity and Public Welfare*. Lanham, MD: Rowman and Littlefield.

Croly, Herbert. [1909] 1993. *The Promise of American Life*. New Brunswick, NJ: Transaction.

Cuninggim, Merrimon. 1972. *Private Money and Public Service: The Role of Foundations in American Society*. New York, NY: McGraw-Hill.

Curti, Merle. 1957. "The History of American Philanthropy as a Field of Research." *American Historical Review* 62 (2): 352–363.

———. 1963. *American Philanthropy Abroad*. New Brunswick, NJ: Rutgers University Press.

Dasgupta, P., and G. Heal. 1974. "The Optimal Depletion of Exhaustible Resources." *Review of Economic Studies* 41 (6): 3–28.

David, Tom. 2000. *Reflections on Strategic Grantmaking*. Woodland Hills, CA: California Wellness Foundation.

———. 2002. *Reflections on Sustainability*. Woodland Hills, CA: California Wellness Foundation.

Deep, Akash, and Peter Frumkin. 2002. "The Foundation Payout Puzzle." Working paper 9, Hauser Center for Nonprofit Organizations, Harvard University.

Dees, J. Gregory. 1998. "Enterprising Nonprofits." *Harvard Business Review* 76 (1): 54–67.

———. 2001. "Social Entrepreneurship." Pp. 1–18 in J. Gregory Dees, Jed Emerson, and Peter Economy, eds., *Enterprising Nonprofits*. New York: Wiley.

DeLeon, Richard H. 1990. *Replication: A Strategy to Improve the Delivery of Education and Job Training Programs*. Philadelphia, PA: Public/Private Ventures.

De Vita, Carol J., and Eric Twombly. 2004. "Charitable Tax Credits." Policy brief, July 1. Urban Institute, Washington, DC.

Diaz, William A. 1999. "Philanthropy and the Case of the Latino Communities in America." Pp. 248–274 in Charles T. Clotfelter and Thomas Ehrlich, eds., *Philanthropy and the Nonprofit Sector in a Changing America*. Bloomington, IN: Indiana University Press.

Dietel, Bill, Tory Dietel Hopps, and Jonathan Hopps. 2003. "Impact of the New Economy and Foundations." Pp. 81–118 in Frank L. Ellsworth and Joseph Lumarda, eds., *From Grantmaker to Leader*. New York: Wiley.

DiLorenzo, Thomas J. 1990. *Patterns of Corporate Philanthropy*. Washington, DC: Capital Research Center.

DiMaggio, Paul. 2001. "Measuring the Impact of the Nonprofit Sector on Society Is Probably Impossible but Possibly Useful: A Sociological Perspective." Pp. 249–272 in Patrice Flynn and Virginia A. Hodgkinson, eds., *Measuring the Impact of the Nonprofit Sector*. New York, NY: Kluwer Academic.

Domanico, Raymond. 2000. *Can Philanthropy Fix Our Schools?* Washington, DC: Thomas B. Fordham Foundation.

Dorgan, Charity Anne. 1995. *Statistical Handbook of Working America*. New York: ITP.

Dowie, Mark. 2001. *American Foundations: An Investigative History*. Cambridge, MA: MIT Press.

Duronio, Margaret A. 1997. "The Fund Raising Profession." Pp. 37–57 in Dwight F. Burlingame, ed., *Critical Issues in Fund Raising*. New York, NY: Wiley.

Edie, John A. 1987. "Congress and Foundations: Historical Summary." In Teresa Odendahl, ed., *America's Wealthy and the Future of Foundations*. New York, NY: Foundation Center.

Edwards, Michael. 2004. *Civil Society*. Cambridge, UK: Polity Press.

Egger, Robert. 2002. *Begging for Change*. New York, NY: Harper Collins.

Eisenberg, Nancy, and Paul A. Miller. 1987. "The Relationship of Empathy to Prosocial Behaviors." *Psychological Bulletin* 101 (1): 91–119.

Ekstrom, Helmer. 2002. *The Practice of Family Philanthropy in Community Foundations*. Washington, DC: National Center for Family Philanthropy.

Ellsworth, Frank L., and Joseph Lumarda, eds. 2003. *From Grantmaker to Leader*. New York, NY: Wiley.

Emerson, Jed. 2000. "The Nature of Returns: A Social Capital Markets Inquiry into Elements of Investment and the Blended Value Proposition." *Social Enterprise* paper series no. 17.

Emerson, Richard. 1962. "Power-Dependence Relations." *American Sociological Review* 89 (2): 31–41.

Espinoza, Geraldo J. 1990. "Note on Buying a Franchise." Unpublished paper, Harvard Business School.

Esposito, Virginia M., ed. 2001a. *Faith and Philanthropy: Grace, Gratitude, and Generosity*. Washington, DC: National Center for Family Philanthropy.

————. 2001b. "Family Values, Family Philanthropy." Pp. 18–25 in Charles H. Hamilton, ed., *Living the Legacy: The Values of Family Philanthropy across Generations*. Washington, DC: National Center for Family Philanthropy.

Esposito, Virginia M., and Joseph Foote. 2003. "Family Philanthropy in Twenty-First Century America." Pp. 3–40 in Frank L. Ellsworth and Joseph Lumarda, eds., *From Grantmaker to Leader*. New York, NY: Wiley.

Feingold, Mordechai. 1987. "Philanthropy, Pomp, and Patronage." *Daedalus* 116 (1): 155–178.

Feldstein, Martin, and Charles T. Clotfelter. 1976. "Tax Incentives and Charitable Contributions in the United States." *Journal of Public Economics* 5 (1–2): 1–26.

Ferris, James M., and Michael Mintrom. 2002. "Foundations and Public Policymaking: A Conceptual Framework." Working paper, School of Policy, Planning, and Development, University of Southern California.

Finn, Chester E., Jr., and Kelly Amis. 2001. *Making It Count: A Guide to High Impact Philanthropy*. Washington, DC: Thomas B. Fordham Foundation.

Fisher, Donald. 1983. "The Role of Philanthropic Foundations in the Reproduction and Production of Hegemony." *Sociology* 17: 206–233.

Fleishman, Joel L. 2004. "Simply Doing Good or Doing Good Well." Pp. 101–128 in H. Peter Karoff, ed., *Just Money: A Critique of Contemporary American Philanthropy*. Boston, MA: TPI Editions.

Foote, Joseph. 2000. *Family Philanthropy and Donor-Advised Funds*. Washington, DC: National Center for Family Philanthropy.

Ford Foundation. 1949. *Report of the Study for the Ford Foundation on Policy and Program*. Detroit, MI: Ford Foundation.

Fosdick, Raymond. 1952. *The Story of the Rockefeller Foundation*. New York, NY: Harper.

Foundation Center. 2003. *The PRI Directory*. New York, NY: Foundation Center.

Fox, Kenneth. 1992. "A Businessman's Creed: A Centennial Perspective on Carnegie's 'Gospel of Wealth.'" Pp. 94–117 in Dwight F. Burlingame, ed., *The Responsibilities of Wealth*. Bloomington, IN: Indiana University Press.

Frank, Robert T. 1999. *Luxury Fever*. Princeton, NJ: Princeton University Press.

Franklin, Benjamin. 1996. *Autobiography*. New York: Dover.

Freeman, David F., and the Council on Foundations. 1981. *The Handbook on Private Foundations*. Washington, DC: Seven Locks.

Fremont-Smith, Marion. 2004. *Governing Nonprofit Organizations*. Cambridge, MA: Harvard University Press.

Freund, Gerald. 1996. *Narcissism and Philanthropy: Ideas and Talent Denied*. New York, NY: Viking.

Friedman, Thomas L. 2000. *The Lexus and the Olive Tree*. New York, NY: Anchor Books.

Frumkin, Peter. 1992. "Philanthropy in a Cold Climate." *The Freeman* 42 (2): 18–24.

———. 1995. "Strangled Freedom." *American Scholar* 64 (4): 590–597.

———. 1997. "Fidelity in Philanthropy: Two Challenges to Community Foundations." *Nonprofit-Management & Leadership* 8 (1): 65–76.

———. 1998. "The Long Recoil from Regulation: Private Philanthropic Foundations and the Tax Reform Act of 1969." *American Review of Public Administration* 28 (3): 266–286.

———. 1999. "Private Foundations as Public Institutions: Regulation, Professionalization, and the Redefinition of Organized Philanthropy." Pp. 69–98 in Ellen Condliffe Lagemann, ed., *Philanthropic Foundations: New Scholarship, New Possibilities*. Bloomington, IN: Indiana University Press.

———. 2000. "The Face of the New Philanthropy." *The Responsive Community* 13 (3): 41–48.

———. 2002. *On Being Nonprofit*. Cambridge, MA: Harvard University Press.

Frumkin, Peter, and Akash Deep. 2000. "Systematic Philanthropy." Working paper, Hauser Center for Nonprofit Organizations, Harvard University.

Frumkin, Peter, and Mark T. Kim. 2000. "Strategic Positioning and the Financing of Nonprofit Organizations." *Public Administration Review* 61 (3): 266–275.

Fukuyama, Francis. 1992. *The End of History and The Last Man*. New York, NY: Free Press.

Fulton, Katherine, and Andrew Blau. 2003. "Trends in 21st Century Philanthropy." Working paper, Global Business Network.

Fultz, Jim, C. Daniel Batson, Victoria A. Fortenbach, Patricia M. McCarthy, and Laurel L. Varney. 1986. "Social Evaluation and the Empathy-Altruism Hypothesis." *Journal of Personality and Social Psychology* 50 (4): 761–769.

Galaskiewicz, Joseph, and Ronald S. Burt. 1991. "Interorganizational Contagion in Corporate Philanthropy." *Administrative Sciences Quarterly* 36: 88–105.

Gary, Tracy, and Melissa Kohner. 2002. *Inspired Philanthropy*. San Francisco, CA: Jossey-Bass.

Gaudiani, Claire. 2003. *The Greater Good*. New York, NY: Times Books.

Giudice, Phil, and Kevin Bolduc. 2004. *Assessing Performance at the Robert Wood Johnson Foundation: A Case Study*. Boston: Center for Effective Philanthropy.

Glazer, Amihai, and Kai Konrad. 1996. "A Signaling Explanation for Charity." *American Economic Review* 86 (4): 1019–1028.

Golberg, Peter. 1989. "Corporate Social Responsibility and Public-Private Partnerships." Pp. 341–352 in Virginia Hodgkinson, Richard Lyman, and associates, eds., *The Future of the Nonprofit Sector*. San Francisco, CA: Jossey-Bass.

Gordon, Anne, and John Burghardt. 1990a. *The Minority Female Single Parent Demonstration: Local Context and Target Population*. New York, NY: Rockefeller Foundation.

————. 1990b. *The Minority Female Single Parent Demonstration: Short-Term Economic Impacts*. New York, NY: Rockefeller Foundation.

Grace, Kay Sprinkel, and Alan L. Wendroff. 2001. *High Impact Philanthropy*. New York, NY: Wiley.

Grantmakers for Education. 2003. *Maximizing Impact: Lessons Learned in Education Philanthropy for Changing Public Policy, Replicating Success, and Sustaining Programs*. Portland, OR: Grantmakers for Education.

Gross, Robert A. 2003. "Giving in America: From Charity to Philanthropy." Pp. 29–48 in Lawrence J. Friedman and Mark D. McGarvie, eds., *Charity, Philanthropy, and Civility in American History*. Cambridge, UK: Cambridge University Press.

Gurin, Maurice G. 1989. "Phony Philanthropy?" *Foundation News*, May–June, 32–35.

Hadaway, C. Kirk, Penny Long Mahler, and Mark Chaves. 1993. "What the Polls Don't Show: A Closer Look at U.S. Church Attendance." *American Sociological Review* 58 (6): 741–752.

Hall, John A., ed. 1995. *Civil Society: Theory, History, Comparison*. Cambridge, MA: Blackwell.

Hall, Peter Dobkin. 1990. "The History of Religious Philanthropy in America." Pp. 38–62 in Robert Wuthnow, Virginia Hodgkinson, et al., eds., *Faith and Philanthropy in America*. San Francisco, CA: Jossey-Bass Publishers.

————. 1992. *Inventing the Nonprofit Sector*. Baltimore, MD: Johns Hopkins University Press.

————. 1997. "Philanthropy, Public Welfare, and the Politics of Knowledge: Reflections on Giving Better, Giving Smarter." Unpublished manuscript.

————. 1999. "Resolving the Dilemmas of Democratic Governance: The Historical Development of Trusteeship in America, 1636–1996." Pp. 3–42 in Ellen Condliffe Lagemann, ed., *Philanthropic Foundations: New Scholarship, New Possibilities*. Bloomington, IN: Indiana University Press.

————. 2004. "A Historical Perspective on Evaluation in Foundations." Pp. 27–50 in Marc T. Braverman, Norman A. Constantine, and Jana Kay Slater, eds., *Foundations and Evaluations*. San Francisco, CA: Jossey-Bass Publishers.

Hamilton, Charles H. 2001. "Legacy: The Helping Hand of Family Philanthropy." Pp. 1–11 in Charles H. Hamilton, ed., *Living the Legacy: The Values of a Family's*

Philanthropy across Generations. Washington, DC: National Center for Family Philanthropy.

Hammack, David C. 1989. "Community Foundations: The Delicate Question of Purpose." Pp. 23–50 in Richard Magat, ed., *An Agile Servant: Community Leadership by Community Foundations*. New York, NY: Foundation Center.

————, ed. 1998. *The Making of the Nonprofit Sector in the United States*. Bloomington, IN: Indiana University Press.

Handwerger, Sharon, Margaret Strain, and Craig Thorton. 1989. *The Minority Female Single Parent Demonstration: Child-Care Referral Options*. New York, NY: Rockefeller Foundation.

Handwerger, Sharon, and Craig Thorton. 1988. *The Minority Female Single Parent Demonstration: Program Costs*. New York, NY: Rockefeller Foundation.

Hannan, Michael T., and John Freeman. 1977. "The Population Ecology of Organizations." *American Journal of Sociology* 82: 929–964.

Hansmann, Henry A. 1990. "Why Do Universities Have Endowments?" *Journal of Legal Studies* 19 (1): 3–42.

Harbaugh, William T. 1998. "What Do Donations Buy? A Model of Philanthropy Based on Prestige and Glow." *Journal of Public Economics* 67 (2): 269–284.

Harper, Everett. 2000. "The Amy Biehl Foundation Trust." Case SI-01, Graduate School of Business, Stanford University.

Harrison, C. R. 1999. "It's How You Slice It." *Foundation News and Commentary*. November–December, 32–36.

Harrison, Shelby M., and F. Emerson Andrews. 1946. *American Foundations for Social Welfare*. New York: Russell Sage Foundation.

Henderson, Bruce E., ed. 1992. *Philanthropy in the Americas: New Directions and Partnerships*. New Brunswick, NJ: Transaction Publishers.

Hershey, Alan. 1988. *The Minority Female Single Parent Demonstration: Program Operations*. New York, NY: Rockefeller Foundation.

Hess, Gary R. 2003. "Waging the Cold War in the Third World: The Foundations and the Challenges of Development." Pp. 319–339 in Lawrence J. Friedman and Mark D. McGarvie, eds., *Charity, Philanthropy, and Civility in American History*. Cambridge, UK: Cambridge University Press.

Himmelfarb, Gertrude. 1991. *Poverty and Compassion*, New York, NY: Random House.

Himmelstein, Jerome L. 1997. *Looking Good and Doing Good: Corporate Philanthropy and Corporate Power*. Bloomington, IN: Indiana University Press.

Hine, Darlene Clark. 1990. " 'We Who Specialize in the Wholly Impossible': The Philanthropic Work of Black Women." Pp. 70–93 in Kathleen D. McCarthy, ed., *Lady Bountiful Revisited*. New Brunswick, NJ: Rutgers University Press.

Hirsch, E. D. 1967. *Validity in Interpretation*. New Haven, CT: Yale University Press.

Hirschhorn, Larry, and Thomas North Gilmore. 2003. "Ideas in Philanthropic Field Building: Where They Come From and How They Are Translated into Actions." In Patricia Patrizi, Kay Sherwood, and Abby Spector, eds., *Practice Matters: The Improving Philanthropy Project*, Working Paper Series. New York, NY: Foundation Center.

Hochman, Harold M., and James D. Rodgers. 1986. "The Optimal Tax Treatment of Charitable Contributions." Pp. 224–245 in Susan Rose-Ackerman, ed., *The Economics of Nonprofit Institutions*. New York, NY: Oxford University Press.

Hodgkinson, Virginia A. 1990. "The Future of Individual Giving and Volunteering: The Inseparable Link between Religious Community and Individual Generosity." Pp. 284–312 in Robert Wuthnow, Virginia Hodgkinson, et al., eds., *Faith and Philanthropy in America*. San Francisco, CA: Jossey-Bass Publishers.

Hodgkinson, Virginia A., Murray S. Weitzman, and Arthur D. Kirsch. 1990. "From Commitment to Action: How Religious Involvement Affects Giving and Volunteering." Pp. 93–114 in Robert Wuthnow, Virginia Hodgkinson, et al., eds., *Faith and Philanthropy in America*. San Francisco, CA: Jossey-Bass Publishers.

Hoffman, Martin L. 1981. "Is Altruism Part of Human Nature?" *Journal of Personality and Social Psychology* 40 (1): 121–137.

Hollister, Robin G., Jr. 1990. *New Evidence of Effective Training Strategies*. New York, NY: Rockefeller Foundation.

Holton, Ruth. 2002. *Reflections on Policy Grantmaking*. Woodland Hills, CA: California Wellness Foundation.

Hood, John M. 1996. *The Heroic Enterprise*. New York, NY: Free Press.

Hooker, Michael. 1987. "Moral Values and Private Philanthropy." *Social Philosophy and Policy* 4 (2): 128–141.

Hopkins, Bruce R. 1990. "Legal Issues in Fund Raising and Philanthropy." Pp. 204–221 in Jon Van Til et al., *Critical Issues in American Philanthropy: Strengthening Theory and Practice*. San Francisco, CA: Jossey-Bass Publishers.

Hughes, Robert. 2003. "Philanthropies Working Together: Myths and Realities." In Patricia Patrizi, Kay Sherwood, and Abby Spector, eds., *Practice Matters: The Improving Philanthropy Project*, Working Paper Series. New York, NY: Foundation Center.

Hunter, Willard T. 1968. *The Tax Climate for Philanthropy*. Washington, DC: American College of Public Relations Associations.

Husock, Howard. 2000. "How the Agency Saved My Father." Pp. 41–68 in Myron Magnet, ed. *What Makes Charity Work?* Chicago, IL: Ivan R. Dee.

Ihejirika, Maudlyne. 1995. "Seven Stars in Oprah's Pilot: Charity Plan Gives Families a Chance." *Chicago Sun-Times*, September 15.

Independent Sector. 1988. *Why Tax Exemption? The Public Service Role of America's Independent Sector.* Washington, DC: Independent Sector.

———. 2004. *Guidelines for the Funding of Nonprofit Organizations*. Washington, DC: Independent Sector.

Jackson, Elton F., Mark D. Bachmeier, James R. Wood, and Alizabeth A. Craft. 1995. "Volunteering and Charitable Giving: Do Religious and Associational Ties Promote Helping Behavior?" *Nonprofit and Voluntary Sector Quarterly* 24 (1): 59–78.

James, Estelle. 1986. "How Nonprofits Grow: A Model." Pp. 185–195 in Susan Rose-Ackerman, ed., *The Economics of Nonprofit Institutions: Studies in Structure and Policy*. New York, NY: Oxford University Press.

Jansen, Paul J., and David M. Katz. 2002. "For Nonprofits, Time Is Money." *McKensie Quarterly* (1): 124–133.

Jeavons, Thomas. 1998. "Identifying Characteristics of 'Religious' Organizations."

Pp. 79–95 in N. J. Demerath III et al., eds., *Sacred Companies: Organizational Aspects of Religion and Religious Aspects of Organizations*. New York, NY: Oxford University Press.

Jencks, Christopher. 1990. "Varieties of Altruism." Pp. 54–70 in Jane Mansbridge, ed., *Beyond Self-Interest*. Chicago, IL: University of Chicago Press.

Jenkins, J. Craig. 1989. "Social Movement Philanthropy and American Democracy." Pp. 292–314 in Richard Magat, ed., *Philanthropic Giving: Studies in Varieties and Goals*. New York, NY: Oxford University Press.

———. 1998. "Channeling Social Protest: Foundation Patronage of Contemporary Social Movements." Pp. 206–216 in Walter W. Powell and Elisabeth Clemens, eds., *Private Action and the Public Good*. New Haven, CT: Yale University Press.

Jenkins, J. Craig, and Abigail L. Halcli. 1999. "Grassrooting the System? The Development and Impact of Social Movement Philanthropy, 1953–1990." Pp. 229–256 in Ellen Condliffe Lagemann, ed., *Philanthropic Foundations: New Scholarship, New Possibilities*. Bloomington, IN: Indiana University Press.

Joseph, James A. 1982. "The Donee as a Philanthropic Stakeholder." *Foundation News* 23 (6): 1.

———. 1983a. "1969–1983: From Abuses to Access—A Different Spotlight." *Foundation News* 24 (4): 43.

———. 1983b. "Professional Development: New Questions for a New Era." *Foundation News* 24 (5): 48.

———. 1983c. "Why the Concern with Principles?" *Foundation News* 24 (6): 64.

Kamrava, Mehran. 2001. "The Civil Society Discourse in Iran." *British Journal of Middle Eastern Studies* 28 (2): 165–185.

Karl, Barry D. 1991. "The Evolution of Corporate Grantmaking in America." Pp. 20–33 in James Shannon, ed., *The Corporate Contributions Handbook*. San Francisco, CA: Jossey-Bass Publishers.

———. 1992. "Andrew Carnegie and His Gospel of Philanthropy: A Study in Ethics of Responsibility." Pp. 32–50 in Dwight F. Burlingame, ed., *The Responsibilities of Wealth*. Bloomington, IN: Indiana University Press.

———. 1997. "Philanthropy and the Maintenance of Democratic Elites." *Minerva* 35 (3): 207–220.

Karl, Barry D., and Stanley N. Katz. 1981. "The American Philanthropic Foundation and the Public Sphere 1890–1930." *Minerva* 19 (2): 236–270.

———. 1987. "Foundations and Ruling Class Elites." *Daedalus* 116 (1): 1–40.

Karoff, H. Peter. 2004. "Saturday Morning." Pp. 3–22 in H. Peter Karoff, ed., *Just Money: A Critique of Contemporary American Philanthropy*. Boston, MA: TPI Editions.

Keane, John. 1998. *Civil Society*. Palo Alto, CA: Stanford University Press.

Kelly, Kathleen S. 1997. "From Motivation to Mutual Understanding." Pp. 139–162 in Dwight F. Burlingame, ed., *Critical Issues in Fund Raising*. New York, NY: Wiley.

Keohane, Robert O., and Joseph S. Nye. 2001. *Power and Interdependence*. New York, NY: Longman.

Khagram, Sanjeev, James Riker, and Kathryn Sikkink, eds. 2002. *Restructuring World Politics: Transnational Social Movements, Networks, and Norms*. Minneapolis, MN: University of Minnesota Press.

Kiernan, Louise. 1996. "Oprah's Poverty Program Stalls: Despite High Hopes, Only 5 Families Graduate in 2 Years." *Chicago Tribune*, August 27.

Kiger, Joseph. 1954. *Operating Principles of the Larger Foundations*. New York, NY: Russell Sage Foundation.

Kingma, Bruce R. 1989. "An Accurate Measurement of the Crowd-Out Effect, Income Effect, and Price Effect for Charitable Contributions." *Journal of Political Economy* 97 (5): 1197–1207.

Klausner, Michael. 2003. "When Time Isn't Money." *Stanford Social Innovation Review*. 1 (1): 50–59.

Krass, Peter. 2002. *Carnegie*. New York: Wiley.

Kreidler, John. 1996. "Leverage Lost: The Nonprofit Arts in the Post-Ford Era." *Journal of Arts Management, Law, and Society* 26 (2): 79–100.

Kwoh, Stephanie, and Bonnie Tang. 2003. "The Foundation Board of the Twenty-First Century." Pp. 177–202 in Frank L. Ellsworth and Joseph Lumarda, eds., *From Grantmaker to Leader*. New York, NY: Wiley.

Labovitz, John R. 1973. "1969 Tax Reform Reconsidered." Pp. 101–131 in Fritz Heinman, ed., *The Future of Foundations*. Englewood Cliffs, NJ: Prentice Hall.

Lagemann, Ellen Condliffe. 1983. *Private Power for the Public Good*. Middletown, CT: Wesleyan University Press.

————. 1989. *The Politics of Knowledge: The Carnegie Corporation, Philanthropy, and Public Policy*. Chicago, IL: University of Chicago Press.

————, ed. 1999. *Philanthropic Foundations: New Scholarship, New Possibilities*. Bloomington, IN: Indiana University Press.

Laird, Vanessa. 1988. "Phantom Selves: The Search for a General Charitable Intent in the Application of the Cy Pres Doctrine." *Stanford Law Review* 40: 973–987.

Lawrence, Steven. 2002. *Family Foundations: A Profile of Founders and Trends*. New York, NY: Foundation Center.

Lenkowsky, Leslie. 1999. "Reinventing Philanthropy." Pp. 122–138 in Charles T. Clotfelter and Thomas Ehrlich, eds., *Philanthropy and the Nonprofit Sector in a Changing America*. Bloomington, IN: Indiana University Press.

Letts, Christine W., and William P. Ryan. 2003. "Filling the Performance Gap: High-Engagement Philanthropy—What Grantees Say about Power, Performance, and Money." *Stanford Social Innovation Review* 1.1 (Spring 2003): 26–33.

Letts, Christine W., William P. Ryan, and Allen Grossman. 1999. "Virtuous Capital: What Foundations Can Learn from Venture Capitalists." *Harvard Business Review* 75 (2): 36–44.

Light, Paul C., and Elizabeth Hubbard. 2003. "The Capacity Building Challenge: A Research Perspective." In Patricia Patrizi, Kay Sherwood, and Abby Spector, eds., *Practice Matters: The Improving Philanthropy Project*, Working Paper Series. New York, NY: Foundation Center.

Lind, Robert C. 1995. "Intergenerational Equity, Discounting, and the Role of Cost-Benefit Analysis in Evaluating Global Climate Policy." *Energy Policy* 23 (4/5): 379–389.

Lindberg, Marc, and J. Patrick Dobel, 1999. "The Challenges of Globalization for Northern International Relief and Development NGOs." *Nonprofit and Voluntary Sector Quarterly* 28 (4): 4–24.

Lindeman, Eduard C. [1936] 1988. *Wealth and Culture: A Study of One Hundred Foundations and Community Trusts and Their Operations during the Decade 1921–1930.* New Brunswick, NJ: Transaction Publishers.

Lindsey, Lawrence B. 1989. "Charitable Giving Options That Do Not Affect Government Revenue." Pp. 285–298 in Virginia Hodgkinson, Richard Lyman, et al., eds., *The Future of the Nonprofit Sector.* San Francisco, CA: Jossey-Bass Publishers.

Loomis, Frank D. 1950. *Community Trusts of America 1914–1950.* Chicago, IL: National Committee on Foundations and Trust for Community Welfare.

Loseke, Donileen R. 1997. " 'The Whole Spirit of Modern Charity': The Construction of the Idea of Charity, 1912–1992." *Social Problems* 44 (4): 425–444.

Lumarda, Joseph. 2003. "Philanthropy, Self-Fulfillment, and the Leadership of Community Foundations." Pp. 41–79 in Frank L. Ellsworth and Joseph Lumarda, eds., *From Grantmaker to Leader.* New York, NY: Wiley.

Lumley, S. 1997. "The Environment and the Ethics of Discounting: An Empirical Analysis." *Ecological Economics* 20 (1): 71–82.

Mac Donald, Heather. 2000. "Behind the Hundred Neediest Cases." Pp. 124–144 in Myron Magnet, ed., *What Makes Charity Work?* Chicago, IL: Ivan R. Dee.

Magat, Richard. 1979. *The Ford Foundation at Work: Philanthropic Choices, Methods, and Styles.* New York, NY: Plenum Press.

————. 1984. "Out of the Shadows," *Foundation News* 25 (4): 24–33.

————. 1999. *Unlikely Partners: Philanthropic Foundations and the Labor* Movement. Ithaca, NY: Cornell University Press.

Maloney, Douglas J. 1987. "The Aftermath." *University of San Francisco Law Review* 21: 681–690.

Margo, Robert A. 1992. "Foundations." Pp. 207–234 in Charles T. Clotfelter, ed., *Who Benefits from the Nonprofit Sector?* Chicago, IL: University of Chicago Press.

Martenson, Edward A., and Joel Podolny. 1999. "Strategic Issues for the Arts: The Impact of Foundations on the Strategic Outlook of Arts Organizations." *National Arts Stabilization Journal* 2 (3): 35–37.

Martin, Mike W. 1994. *Virtuous Giving: Philanthropy, Voluntary Service, and Caring.* Bloomington, IN: Indiana University Press.

Mason, David E. 1996. *Leading and Managing the Expressive Dimension: Harnessing the Hidden Power Source of the Nonprofit Sector.* San Francisco, CA: Jossey-Bass Publishers.

Massing, Michael. 2000. "Should Jews Be Parochial?" *American Prospect* 11 (23): 30.

Matthews, Jessica. 1997. "Power Shift." *Foreign Affairs* 76 (1): 50–61.

Maxfield, Myles, Jr. 1990. *Planning Employment Services for the Disadvantaged.* New York, NY: Rockefeller Foundation.

Maynard, Rebecca. 1990. *Child Care Challenges for Low-Income Families.* New York, NY: Rockefeller Foundation.

McCagg, Louis B. 1970. "A New Dimension for Foundations." *Foundation News* 11 (2): 49–50.

McCarthy, Kathleen D. 1984. "American Cultural Philanthropy: Past, Present, and Future." *Annals of the American Academy of Political and Social Science* 471: 13–26.

————. 1987. "From Cold War to Cultural Development: The International Cultural Activities of the Ford Foundation, 1950–1980." *Daedalus* 116 (1): 93–118.

McFarlan, F. Warren. 1999. "Working on Nonprofit Boards: Don't Assume the Shoe Fits." *Harvard Business Review* 77 (6): 65–80.

McIlnay, Dennis P. 1998. *How Foundations Work*. San Francisco, CA: Jossey-Bass Publishers.

McKersie, William. 1999. "Local Philanthropy Matters: Pressing Issues for Research and Practice." Pp. 329–358 in Ellen Condliffe Lagemann, ed., *Philanthropic Foundations: New Scholarship, New Possibilities*. Bloomington, IN: Indiana University Press.

McManus, William E. 1990. "Stewardship and Almsgiving in the Roman Catholic Tradition." Pp. 115–133 in Robert Wuthnow, Virginia A. Hodgkinson, et al., eds., *Faith and Philanthropy in America*. San Francisco: Jossey-Bass Publishers.

McRoberts, Flynn. 1994. "Winfrey's Offer Stirs Avalanche: 30,000 Want to Board Raft Out of C.H.A. Life." *Chicago Tribune*, September 18.

Meck, Margaret M., and Kathryn Sikkink. 1998. *Activists without Borders*. Ithaca, NY: Cornell University Press.

Merhling, P. 1999. *Spending Policies for Foundations: The Case for Increased Grants Payout*. San Diego, CA: National Network of Grantmakers.

Miller, John J. 2003. *How Two Foundations Reshaped America*. Washington, DC: Philanthropy Roundtable.

Mintzberg, Henry, Bruce Ahlstrand, and Joseph Lampel. 1998. *Strategy Safari*. New York, NY: Free Press.

Mulhearn, Christine. 2000. "Women in Philanthropy: Madam C. J. Walker." Case CR14–00-1568.0, Kennedy School of Government, Harvard University.

Munasinghe, M., et al. 1996. "Applicability of Techniques of Cost-Benefit Analysis to Climate Change." Pp. 145–178 in James P. Bruce, Hoesung Lee, and Erik F. Haites, eds., *New Climate Change 1995: Economic and Social Dimensions of Climate Change*. New York, NY: Cambridge University Press.

Murphy, T. B. 2000. "Financial and Psychological Determinants of Donor's Capacity to Give." Paper presented at the 13th Annual Symposium of the Indiana University Center on Philanthropy, Indianapolis, August 24.

Murray, Charles. 1988. *In Pursuit of Happiness and Good Government*. New York, NY: Simon and Schuster.

Nagai, Althea K., Robert Lerner, and Stanley Rothman. 1991. *The Culture of Philanthropy: Foundations and Public Policy*. Washington, DC: Capital Research Center.

National Center for Family Philanthropy. 2003. *Generations of Giving: Leadership and Continuity in Family Philanthropy*. Washington, DC: National Center for Family Philanthropy.

National Commission on Philanthropy and Civic Renewal. 1997. *Giving Better, Giving Smarter*. Washington, DC: National Commission on Philanthropy and Civic Renewal.

National Committee for Responsive Philanthropy. 1989. *Community Foundations: At the Margins of Change*. Washington, DC: National Committee for Responsive Philanthropy.

———. 1994. *Community Foundations and the Disenfranchised*. Washington, DC: National Committee for Responsive Philanthropy.

———. 2003. *A Billion Here, A Billion There*. Washington, DC: National Committee for Responsive Philanthropy.

Nelson, Ralph L. 1987. "An Economic History of Large Foundations." In Teresa Odendahl, ed., *America's Wealthy and the Future of Foundations*. New York, NY: Foundation Center.

Nelson, Richard, and Sidney Winter. 1984. *An Evolutionary Theory of Economic Change*. New York, NY: Harper and Row.

Neuhaus, Richard John, Peter L. Berger, and Michael Novak, eds. 1996. *To Empower People: From State to Civil Society*. Washington, DC: AEI Press.

Newman, Diana S. 2002. *Opening Doors: Pathways to Diverse Donors*. San Francisco, CA: Jossey-Bass.

Nichols, Rebecca, and Anne Mackinnon. 2004. "International Grantmaking: Funding with a Global View." GrantCraft, paper 10. New York, NY: Ford Foundation.

Nielsen, Wlademar A. 1985. *The Golden Donors: A New Anatomy of the Great Foundations*. New York, NY: E. P. Dutton.

————. 1996. *Inside American Philanthropy: The Dramas of Donorship*. Norman, OK: University of Oklahoma Press.

Nittoli, Janice. 2003. "Acts of Commission: Lessons from an Informal Study." In Patricia Patrizi, Kay Sherwood, and Abby Spector, eds., *Practice Matters: The Improving Philanthropy Project*, Working Paper Series. New York, NY: Foundation Center.

Northern California Grantmakers. 1985. *Perspectives on Collaborative Funding*. San Francisco, CA: Northern California Grantmakers.

Oates, Mary J. 1995. *The Catholic Philanthropic Tradition in America*. Bloomington, IN: Indiana University Press.

Obler, Jefferey. 1981. "Private Giving in the Welfare State." *British Journal of Political Science* 11 (1): 17–48.

O'Connell, Brian, ed. 1983. *America's Voluntary Spirit*. New York, NY: Foundation Center.

————. 1987. *Philanthropy in Action*. New York, NY: Foundation Center.

————. 1988. "Private Philanthropy and the Preservation of a Free and Democratic Society." Pp. 27–38 in Robert Payton, Michael Novak, Brian O'Connell, and Peter Dobkin Hall, eds., *Philanthropy: Four Views*. New Brunswick, NJ: Transaction.

————. 1997. *Powered by Coalition*. San Francisco, CA: Jossey-Bass Publishers.

Odendahl, Teresa, ed. 1987. *America's Wealthy and the Future of Foundations*. New York, NY: Foundation Center.

————. 1990. *Charity Begins at Home: Generosity and Self-Interest among the Philanthropic Elite*. New York, NY: Basic Books.

Odendahl, Teresa, and Michael O'Neill, eds. 1994. *Women and Power in the Nonprofit Sector*. San Francisco, CA: Jossey-Bass Publishers.

Okten, Cagla, and Burton A. Weisbrod. 2000. "Determinants of Donations in Private Nonprofit Markets." *Journal of Public Economics* 75 (2): 255–272.

Olasky, Marvin. 1992. *The Tragedy of American Compassion*. Washington, DC: Regnery.

————. 1993. *Philanthropy Correct: The Story of the Council on Foundations*. Washington, DC: Capital Research Center.

————. 1996. *Renewing American Compassion*. Washington, DC: Regnery.

Orosz, Joel J. 2000. *The Insider's Guide to Grantmaking*. San Francisco, CA: Jossey-Bass Publishers.

Orosz, Joel J., Cynthia C. Philips, and Lisa Wyatt Knolton. 2003. "Agile Philanthropy: Understanding Foundation Effectiveness." Working paper, Grand Valley State University.

O'Rourke, Kevin, and Jeffrey Williamson. 1999. *Globalization and History*. Cambridge, MA: MIT Press.

Osborne, David, and Ted Gaebler. 1992. *Reinventing Government*. Boston: Addison Wesley.

Ostrander, Susan A. 1989. "The Problem of Poverty and Why Philanthropy Neglects It." Pp. 219–236 in Virginia A. Hodgkinson, Richard Lyman, and associates, eds., *The Future of the Nonprofit Sector*. San Francisco, CA: Jossey-Bass Publishers.

————. 1995. *Money for Change*. Philadelphia, PA: Temple University Press.

Ostrander, Susan A., and Paul G. Schervish. 1990. "Giving and Getting: Philanthropy as a Social Relation." Pp. 67–98 in John Van Til et al., *Critical Issues in American Philanthropy*. San Francisco, CA: Jossey-Bass Publishers.

Ostrower, Francie. 1989. "Donor Control and Perpetual Trusts: Does Anything Last Forever?" Pp. 279–291 in Richard Magat, ed., *Philanthropic Giving: Studies in Varieties and Goals*. New York, NY: Oxford University Press.

————. 1997. *Why the Wealthy Give*. Princeton, NJ: Princeton University Press.

————. 2004. *Attitudes and Practices Concerning Effective Philanthropy: Executive Summary*. Washington, DC: Urban Institute.

Payton, Robert L. 1989. "Helping the Underserved Abroad: The Case of Famine Relief." Pp. 248–258 in Virginia Hodgkinson, Richard Lyman, and associates, eds., *The Future of the Nonprofit Sector*. San Francisco, CA: Jossey-Bass Publishers.

Pechman, Virginia. 2000. *Grantmaking with a Purpose: Mission and Guidelines*. Washington, DC: National Center for Family Philanthropy.

Peters, Daniel S. 2004. "Foundation Perpetuity: Forever is a Long, Long Time." Speech delivered at the annual meeting of the Council on Foundations, April 27, Toronto, Canada.

Petrovich, Janice. 1989. "The Future of Hispanics and Philanthropy." Pp. 237–247 in Virginia Hodgkinson, Richard Lyman, and associates, eds., *The Future of the Nonprofit Sector*. San Francisco, CA: Jossey-Bass Publishers.

Pfeffer, Jeffrey, and Gerald Salancik. 1978. *The External Control of Organizations: A Resource Dependence Perspective*. New York, NY: Harper and Row.

Pifer, Alan. 1984. *Philanthropy in an Age of Transition: The Essays of Alan Pifer*. New York, NY: Foundation Center.

Piliavin, Jane Allyn, and Hong-Wen Charng. 1990. "Altruism: A Review of Recent Theory and Research." *Annual Review of Sociology* 16: 27–65.

Poppendieck, Janet. 1998. *Sweet Charity: Emergency Food and the End of Entitlement*. New York, NY: Viking.

Porter, Michael E. 1985. *Competitive Advantage*. New York, NY: Free Press.

Porter, Michael E., and Mark Kramer. 1999. "Philanthropy's New Agenda: Creating Value." *Harvard Business Review* 77 (6): 121–130.

Prewitt, Kenneth. 1999a. "Foundations as Mirrors of Public Culture." *American Behavioral Scientist* 42 (6): 977–986.

————. 1999b. "The Importance of Foundations in an Open Society." Pp. 17–29 in Bertelsmann Foundation, ed., *The Future of Foundations in an Open Society*. Gütersloh, Germany: Bertelsmann Foundation.

Prince, Russ Alan, and Karen Maru File. 1994. *The Seven Faces of Philanthropy*. San Francisco, CA: Jossey-Bass.

Radley, Alan, and Marie Kennedy. 1995. "Charitable Giving by Individuals: A Study of Attitudes and Practice." *Human Relations* 48 (6): 685–709.

Rafferty, Renata J. 1999. *Don't Just Give It Away: How to Make the Most of Your Charitable Giving*. Worcester, MA: Chandler House Press.

Ramos, Henry J. 1999. "Latino Philanthropy: Expanding U.S. Models of Giving and Civic Participation." Pp. 147–187 in Council on Foundations, ed., *Cultures of Caring*. Washington, DC: Council on Foundations.

Randolph, William C. 1995. "Dynamic Income, Progressive Taxes, and the Timing of Charitable Contributions." *Journal of Political Economy* 103 (4): 709–738.

Reed, Cheryl L. 2004. "Foundations Do World of Good—But High Costs Draw Attention." *Chicago Sun-Times*, July 11, p. 16.

Reis, Thomas K., and Stephanie J. Clohesy. 1999. *Unleashing New Resources and Entrepreneurship for the Common Good*. Battle Creek, MI: W. K. Kellogg Foundation.

Renz, Loren. 1974. "On Communications." *Foundation News* 15 (3): 56.

———. 2002. *Giving in the Aftermath of 9/11: Foundations and Corporations Respond*. New York, NY: Foundation Center.

Renz, Loren, et al. 2000. *International Grantmaking II: An Update on U.S. Foundation Trends*. New York, NY: Foundation Center in Cooperation with the Council on Foundations.

Replication and Program Services, Inc. 1994. *Building from Strength: Replication as a Strategy for Expanding Social Programs That Work*. Philadelphia, PA: Replication and Program Services.

Richman, Saul. 1973. *Public Information Handbook for Foundations*. New York, NY: Council on Foundations.

Robinson, Kim. 2001. *Collaborative Grantmaking: Lessons Learned from the Rockefeller Family's Experiences*. Washington, DC: National Center for Family Philanthropy.

Rockefeller, J. D. 1909. *Random Reminiscences of Men and Events*. New York, NY: Doubleday.

Rodrik, Dani. 1997. "Sense and Nonsense in the Globalization Debate." *Foreign Policy* 107 (summer): 19–37.

Roelofs, Joan. 2003. *Foundations and Public Policy*. Albany, NY: SUNY Press.

Rose, Kenneth W., and Darwin H. Stapleton. 1992. "Toward a 'Universal Heritage': Education and the Development of Rockefeller Philanthropy, 1884–1913." *Teachers College Record* 93 (3): 536–555.

Rosegrant, Susan. 2000. "Give and Take: Philanthropy and the Central Park Children's Zoo." Case C15-00-1555.0, Kennedy School of Government, Harvard University.

Rosenberg, Claude, Jr. 1994. *Wealthy and Wise: How You and America Can Get the Most out of Your Giving*. Boston, MA: Little, Brown and Company.

Rosenberg, Emily S. 2003. "Missions to the World: Philanthropy Abroad." Pp. 241–257 in Lawrence J. Friedman and Mark D. McGarvie, eds., *Charity, Philanthropy, and Civility in American History*. Cambridge, UK: Cambridge University Press.

Rosenblatt, Gary. 1992. "Can Federations Survive?" *Jewish Journal* 35: 16–22.

Rosenblum, Nancy. 1998. *Membership and Morals*. Princeton: Princeton University Press.

Rosenwald, Julius. 1983. "Principles of Public Giving." Pp. 119–128 in Brian O'Connell, ed., *America's Voluntary Spirit*. New York, NY: Foundation Center.

Ross, Aileen D. 1968. "Philanthropy." In David Sills, ed., *International Encyclopedia of the Social Sciences*, 12:78. New York: MacMillan.

Rossant, M. J. 1970. "Where Do We Stand Now?" *Foundation News* 11 (5): 190–191.

Salamon, L. M. 1991. *Foundation Investment and Payout Performance: An Update*. New York, NY: Council on Foundations.

———. 1994. "The Rise of the Nonprofit Sector." *Foreign Affairs* 73 (4): 109–122.

Salamon, L. M., and K. Voytek. 1989. *Managing Foundation Assets: An Analysis of Foundation Investment and Payout Procedures and Performance*. New York, NY: Foundation Center.

Schambra, William. 2004. "What Is Conservative Philanthropy?" Speech delivered at Kennedy School of Government, Harvard University, March 17.

Schervish, Paul G. 1990. "Wealth and the Spiritual Secret of Money." Pp. 63–90 in Robert Wuthnow, Virginia Hodgkinson, et al., eds., *Faith and Philanthropy in America*. San Francisco, CA: Jossey-Bass Publishers.

———. 1994. *Gospels of Wealth*. Westport, CT: Praeger.

———. 1995. "Gentle as Doves and Wise as Serpents: The Philosophy of Care and Sociology of Transmission." Pp. 1–16 in Paul G. Schervish et al., eds., *Care and Community in Modern Society*. San Francisco, CA: Jossey-Bass.

———. 1997a. "Inclination, Obligation, and Association." Pp. 110–138 in Dwight F. Burlingame, ed., *Critical Issues in Fund Raising*. New York, NY: Wiley.

———. 1997b. "Major Donors, Major Motives: The People and Purposes Behind Major Gifts." Pp. 85–122 in Dwight F. Burlingame and James M. Hodge, eds., *New Directions for Philanthropic Fundraising*. San Francisco, CA: Jossey-Bass.

Schervish, Paul G., and John Havens. 2000. "The New Physics of Philanthropy: The Supply-Side Vectors of Charitable Giving." Working paper, Social Welfare Research Institute, Boston College.

———. 2001. "Wealth and the Commonwealth: New Findings on Wealth and Philanthropy." *Nonprofit and Voluntary Sector Quarterly* 30 (1): 5–25.

Schooler, Dean. 1995. *Philanthropy's Commitment to Creating Civil Communities*. Bloomington, IN: Indiana University Center on Philanthropy.

Schwartz, Joel. 2000. *Fighting Poverty with Virtue*. Bloomington, IN: Indiana University Press.

Schwartz, John J. 1994. *Modern American Philanthropy*. New York, NY: Wiley.

Schwartz, S. H., and J. Howard. 1984. "Internalized Values as Motivators of Altruism." Pp. 229–255 in Ervin Staub, et al., eds., *Development and Maintenance of Prosocial Behavior*. New York, NY: Plenum.

Sealander, Judith. 1997. *Private Wealth and Public Life*. Baltimore, MD: Johns Hopkins University Press.

Seeley, John R., et al. 1957. *Community Chest*. Toronto: University of Toronto Press.

Sen, Amartya K. 1990. "Rational Fools: A Critique of the Behavioral Foundations of Economic Theory." Pp. 25–43 in Jane Mansbridge, ed., *Beyond Self-Interest*. Chicago, IL: University of Chicago Press.

Shakely, Jack. 1980. "Tom Troyer Appraises the Tax Reform Act of 1969." *Foundation News* 21 (3): 19–24.

Sharp, Marcia. 2002. "Foundation Collaborations: Incubators for Change?" Working paper, University of Southern California, School of Policy, Planning, and Development.

Shmavonian, Nadya K. 2003. "Foundation Strategies for Attracting and Managing Talent." In Patricia Patrizi, Kay Sherwood, and Abby Spector, eds., *Practice Matters: The Improving Philanthropy Project*, Working Paper Series. New York, NY: Foundation Center.

Shuman, Michael H. 1989. "A Grantee Bill of Rights." *Foundation News*, March–April, 147–150.

Sidel, Mark. 2003. "Law Philanthropy and Social Class: Variance Power and the Battle for American Giving." *University of California Davis Law Review* 36: 1145.

Sievers, Bruce. 1997. "If Pigs Had Wings." *Foundation News and Commentary*. November–December, 44–46.

Silver, Ira. 2000. "The Ecology of Philanthropic Agenda Setting: Foundations, Community Organizations, and the Negotiation of Urban Poverty Reform." Paper presented at the annual meeting of the American Sociological Association.

Simon, John G. 1986. "Charity and Dynasty Under the Federal Tax System." Pp. 246–264 in Susan Rose-Ackerman, ed., *The Economics of Nonprofit Institutions*. New York, NY: Oxford University Press.

————. 1987. "American Philanthropy and the Buck Trust." *University of San Francisco Law Review* 21 (4): 641–679.

Slaughter, Ann Marie. 1997. "The Real New World." *Foreign Affairs* 76 (5): 183–197.

Smith, Bradford, Sylvia Shue, Jennifer Lisa Vest, and Joseph Villarreal. 1999. *Philanthropies in Communities of Color*. Bloomington, IN: Indiana University Press.

Smith, James Allen. 1991. *The Idea Brokers*. New York: Free Press.

————. 1999. "The Evolving Role of American Foundations." Pp. 34–51 in Charles T. Clotfelter and Thomas Ehrlich, eds., *Philanthropy and the Nonprofit Sector in a Changing America*. Bloomington, IN: Indiana University Press.

————. 2002. "Foundations and Public Policy Making: A Historical Perspective." Working paper, School of Policy, Planning, and Development, University of Southern California.

Smith, James Allen, and Anthony P. Johnson. 1990. "The Invisible Hand of Charity: Anonymity in Theory and Practice." Unpublished manuscript.

Smith, Vincent H., Michael R. Kehoe, and Mary E. Cremer. 1995. "The Private Provision of Public Goods: Altruism and Voluntary Giving." *Journal of Public Economics* 58 (1): 107–126.

Smucker, Bob. 1999. *The Nonprofit Lobbying Guide*. Washington, DC: Independent Sector.

Spiegel, Menahem. 1995. "Charity without Altruism." *Economic Inquiry* 33 (4): 625–639.

Staub, Ervin. 1978. *Positive Social Behaviour and Morality*. Vol.1: *Social and Personal Influences*. New York, NY: Academic Press.

————. 1995. "How People Learn to Care." Pp. 51–67 in Paul Schervish et al., eds., *Care and Community in Modern Society*. San Francisco, CA: Jossey-Bass.

Staub, Ervin, et al., eds. 1984. *Development and Maintenance of Prosocial Behavior: International Perspectives on Positive Morality.* New York, NY: Plenum.

Stauber, Karl. 1999. *Does Community Matter? The Role of Community in Addressing Poverty.* St. Paul, MN: Northwest Area Foundation.

Steckel, Richard, Robin Simmons, Jeffrey Simmons, and Norman Tanen. 1999. *Making Money While Making a Difference.* Homewood, IL: High Tide Press.

Steinberg, Kathryn S., and Patrick M. Rooney. 2005. "America Gives: A Survey of Americans' Generosity after September 11." *Nonprofit and Voluntary Sector Quarterly* 34 (1): 110–135.

Steuerle, C. Eugene. 1977. "Pay-out Requirements for Foundations." Pp. 1663–1678 in *Research Papers*, sponsored by the Commission on Private Philanthropy and Public Needs. Washington, DC: Department of the Treasury.

———. 1999. "Will Donor-Advised Funds Revolutionize Philanthropy?" *Charting Civil Society* 5. Washington, DC: Urban Institute.

Stevens, Louise. 1996. "The Earnings Shift: The New Bottom Line Paradigm for the Arts Industry in a Market-Driven Era." *Journal of Arts Management, Law, and Society* 26 (2): 101–113.

Stevens, Susan Kenny. 1989. *Analyzing Financial Statements: Council on Foundations Institute for New Staff.* St. Paul, MN: Stevens Group.

Stone, Deanne. 1999. *Grantmaking with a Compass: The Challenge of Geography.* Washington, DC: National Center for Family Philanthropy.

———. 2001. *Sustaining Tradition: The Andrus Family Philanthropy Program.* Washington, DC: National Center for Family Philanthropy.

Stoneman Foundation. 2001. *A Foundation Establishes a Statement of Legacy.* Washington, DC: National Center for Family Philanthropy.

Streeter, Ryan. 2001. *Transforming Charity.* Indianapolis, IN: Hudson Institute.

Sugden, R. 1984. "Reciprocity: The Supply of Public Goods through Voluntary Contributions." *Economic Journal* 94 (376): 772–787.

Sugin, Linda. 1997. "Theories of the Corporation and the Tax Exempt Treatment of Corporate Philanthropy." *New York Law Review* 41 (3/4): 835–879.

Sutton, Francis X. 1987. "The Ford Foundation: The Early Years." *Daedalus* 116 (1): 41–92.

Szanton, Peter L. 2003. "Toward the More Effective Use of Intermediaries." In Patricia Patrizi, Kay Sherwood, and Abby Spector, eds., *Practice Matters: The Improving Philanthropy Project*, Working Paper Series. New York, NY: Foundation Center.

Tamari, Meir. 1987. *With All Your Possessions: Jewish Ethics and Economic Life.* New York, NY: Free Press.

Tandon, Rajesh, and Kumi Naidoo. 1999. "The Promise of Civil Society." Pp. 1–16 in Rajesh Tandon and Kumi Naidoo, eds., *Civil Society at the Millennium*. Bloomfield, CT: Kumarian Press.

Tempest, Nicole. 2000. "New Schools Venture Fund." Case 9–301-038. Boston, MA: Harvard Business School Publishing.

Tobin, Gary A. 1994. "Effects of Administrative Cost Perceptions in Major Gift Decisions." Pp. 95–113 in James M. Greenfield, ed., *Financial Practices for Effective Fund Raising.* San Francisco, CA: Jossey-Bass Publishers.

———. 1995. "Between the Lines: Intricacies of Major Donor Communication."

Pp. 61–77 in Dianne A. Brehmer, ed., *Communicating Effectively with Major Donors: New Directions for Philanthropic Fundraising*. San Francisco, CA: Jossey-Bass Publishers.

————. 2001. *The Transition of Communal Values and Behavior in Jewish Philanthropy*. San Francisco, CA: Institute for Jewish and Community Research.

Tobin, Gary A., and Mordechai Rimor. 1990. "Jewish Giving to Jewish and Non-Jewish Philanthropy." Pp. 134–164 in Robert Wuthnow, Virginia A. Hodgkinson, et al., eds., *Faith and Philanthropy in America*. San Francisco, CA: Jossey-Bass Publishers.

Tocqueville, Alexis de. 1997. *Memoir on Pauperism*. Chicago, IL: Ivan R. Dee.

Tokar, Brian. 1997. *Earth for Sale: Reclaiming Ecology in the Age of Corporate Greenwash*. Boston, MA: South End Press.

Tuckman, Howard. 1993. "How and Why Nonprofit Organizations Obtain Capital." Pp. 203–232 in David C. Hammack, ed., *Nonprofit Organizations in a Market Economy*. San Francisco, CA: Jossey-Bass Publishers.

Tweedy, Mary J. 1970. "How Can Foundations Be Strengthened?" *Foundation News* 11 (2): 56–58.

U.S. Congress, House of Representatives. 2003. *H.R. 7: To Amend the Internal Revenue Code of 1986 to Provide Incentives for Charitable Contributions by Individual and Businesses, and for other Purposes*. Report #108–270, Part I. 108th Cong., 1st sess., September 16.

Van Til, Jon, et al. 1990. *Critical Issues in American Philanthropy*. San Francisco, CA: Jossey-Bass Publishers.

W. K. Kellogg Foundation. 2000. *E-Philanthropy, Volunteerism, and Social Changemaking*. Battle Creek, MI: W. K. Kellogg Foundation.

————. 2001. *Logic Model Development Guide*. Battle Creek, MI: W. K. Kellogg Foundation.

Walker, Gary, and Jean Grossman. 1999. "Philanthropy and Outcomes: Dilemmas in the Quest for Accountability." Pp. 449–460 in Charles T. Clotfelter and Thomas Ehrlich, eds., *Philanthropy and the Nonprofit Sector in a Changing America*. Bloomington, IN: Indiana University Press.

Wallace, Martha R. 1971. "The Foundation Meets the Fund Raiser." *Foundation News* 12 (1): 1–5.

Walton, Ann D., and F. Emerson Andrews. 1960. *The Foundation Directory: Edition 1*. New York, NY: Foundation Library Center by Russell Sage Foundation.

Walzer, Michael. 1984. *Spheres of Justice*. New York, NY: Basic Books.

————. 1991. "The Idea of Civil Society." *Dissent* 49 (spring): 293–304.

Weaver, Warren. 1967. *U.S. Philanthropic Foundations: Their History, Structure, Management, and Record*. New York, NY: Harper and Row Publishers.

Weeden, Curt. 1998. *Corporate Social Investing*. San Francisco, CA: Berrett-Koehler Publishers.

Weiss, E. B. 1989. *In Fairness to Future Generations*. Dobbs Ferry, NY: Transnational Publishers.

Wells, Ronald Austin. 1998. *The Honor of Giving: Philanthropy in Native America*. Bloomington, IN: Indiana University Center on Philanthropy.

————. 2001. "Donor Legacy: What Is It That History Teaches?" Pp. 52–65 in

Charles H. Hamilton, ed., *Living the Legacy: The Values of a Family's Philanthropy across Generations*. Washington, DC: National Center for Family Philanthropy.

Whitaker, Ben. 1974. *The Philanthropoids: Foundations and Society*. New York, NY: Morrow.

Whiting, Basil. 1970. "Is There a New Grantor-Grantee Relationship?" *Foundation News* 11 (4).

Wilensky, Harold L. 1964. "The Professionalization of Everyone." *American Journal of Sociology* 70 (2): 137–158.

Williams, Harold S., Arthur Y. Webb, and William J. Phillips. 1991. *Outcome Funding: A New Approach to Targeted Grantmaking*. Rensselaerville, NY: Rensselaerville Institute.

Williamson, Oliver E. 1981. "Economics of Organizations." *American Journal of Sociology* 87: 548–577.

Wolff, Edward. 1999. "The Economy and Philanthropy." Pp. 73–98 in Charles T. Clotfelter and Thomas Ehrlich, eds., *Philanthropy and the Nonprofit Sector in a Changing America*. Bloomington, IN: Indiana University Press.

Wolpert, Julian. 1989. "Key Indicators of Generosity in Communities." Pp. 377–402 in Virginia Hodgkinson, Richard Lyman, and associates, eds., *The Future of the Nonprofit Sector*. San Francisco, CA: Jossey-Bass Publishers.

Wood, J., and J. Hougland. 1990. "The Role of Religion in Philanthropy." In Jon Van Til et al., *Critical Issues in American Philanthropy*. San Francisco, CA: Jossey-Bass.

Wooster, Martin Morse. 1998a. *The Great Philanthropists and the Problem of Donor Intent*. Washington, DC: Capital Research Center.

———. 1998b. *Should Foundations Live Forever?: The Question of Perpetuity*. Washington, DC: Capital Research Center.

Wright, Conrad Edick. 1992. *The Transformation of Charity in Postrevolutionary New England*. Boston, MA: Northeastern University Press.

Wuthnow, Robert. 1990a. "Religion and the Voluntary Spirit in the United States: Mapping the Terrain." Pp. 3–21 in Robert Wuthnow, Virginia A. Hodgkinson, et al., eds., *Faith and Philanthropy in America*. San Francisco, CA: Jossey-Bass Publishers.

———. 1990b. "Improving Our Understanding of Religion and Giving: Key Issues for Research." Pp. 271–283 in Robert Wuthnow, Virginia A. Hodgkinson, et al., eds., *Faith and Philanthropy in America*. San Francisco, CA: Jossey-Bass Publishers.

———. 1991. *Acts of Compassion: Caring for Others and Helping Ourselves*. Princeton, NJ: Princeton University Press.

———. 1997. *The Crisis in the Churches: Spiritual Malaise, Fiscal Woe*. New York, NY: Oxford University Press.

Wyszomirski, Margaret J. 1999. "Philanthropy and Culture: Patterns, Context and Change." Pp. 461–480 in Charles T. Clotfelter and Thomas Ehrlich, eds., *Philanthropy and the Nonprofit Sector in a Changing America*. Bloomington, IN: Indiana University Press.

Ylvisaker, Paul. 1999a. "Social Justice and the Role of Philanthropy." Pp. 293–305 in

Virginia Esposito, ed., *Conscience and Community: The Legacy of Paul Ylvisaker*. New York, NY: Peter Lang.

————. 1999b. "The Relationship between Private Philanthropy and Government." Pp. 306–317 in Virginia Esposito, ed., *Conscience and Community: The Legacy of Paul Ylvisaker*. New York, NY: Peter Lang.

————. 1999c. "The Spirit of Philanthropy and the Soul of Those Who Manage It." Pp. 340–347 in Virginia Esposito, ed., *Conscience and Community: The Legacy of Paul Ylvisaker*. New York, NY: Peter Lang.

————. 1999d. "Small Can Be Effective." Pp. 359–369 in Virginia Esposito, ed., *Conscience and Community:-The Legacy of Paul Ylvisaker*. New York, NY: Peter Lang.

————. 1999e. "Ethics and Philanthropy." Pp. 318–328 in Virginia Esposito, ed., *Conscience and Community: The Legacy of Paul Ylvisaker*. New York, NY: Peter Lang.

Young, Dennis. 1999. "Complementary, Supplementary, or Adversarial?" Pp. 31–67 in Elizabeth T. Boris and C. Eugene Steuerle, eds., *Government and Nonprofits*. Washington, DC: Urban Institute.

Young, Oran R. 1997. *Global Governance*. Cambridge, MA: MIT Press.

Zambrowski, Amy, and Anne Gordon. 1993. *Evaluation of the Female Single Parent Demonstration: Fifth-Year Impacts at CET*. Princeton, NJ: Mathematica Policy Research.

Index

politics (*continued*)
282, 402-3n42; change implemented
through, 179, 184-85; donor's intent
and, 322-24; performance measurement and, 334-35; philanthropy
as enhancing career in, 20; public
needs and, 149, 150-51; social
change impacted by, 189-90; in
values dimension, 154, 390n5. *See
also* government; lobbying
poor and poverty: approach to alleviating, 36-37; contours of rural, 299,
300; critique of relief for, 13-14;
direct assistance for, 9; early basis
for relief of, 378n11; payout rate
decision and, 301-2; performance
measurement and, 343-45, 348;
post-9/11 assistance for, 407n13. *See
also* public needs; social problems
Poppendieck, Janet, 402n34
population ecology approach, 229-32,
236
Porter, Michael E., 389n2
power asymmetry: accountability issues
and, 56, 72-73, 77; criticism of, 5;
between donors and nonprofits, 265;
legitimacy and, 56-57; performance
measurement and, 347-48; questions about, 289-90; social service
reform initiative and, 346; in venture
philanthropy, 288
Prewitt, Kenneth, 379-80n30
principal-agent relationship, 312-15
private foundations: description of,
220, 232-33; equity and payout
rate issues in, 301, 303-4; family
foundations compared with, 239;
institutional theories on, 233-36,
237-38; mission of, 250-51; as
percentage of all foundations, 238;
self-liquidating provisions for, 326-
28; venture philanthropy in, 282-83
proceduralism, 123-24
process and procedural issues: accountability and, 80-81, 82-83; evaluation
of, 337; instrumentalism linked to,

162-65; legitimacy drawn from, 85,
87; personal element needed in,
360-62
professionalization: absent in charity,
6; administrative costs and, 114-15;
affirmative action and, 112; agenda
setting and, 290-91; context of,
90-92; effects of, 121-24; funding
practices and, 119-21; impetus for,
102, 104-5; instrumentalism and,
162-65; legitimacy issues and, 87-
89; measuring effectiveness and,
62; mixed results of, 89, 371-73; in
private foundations, 233-36; shortcomings of, 123-24, 126-27, 128
professional staff: accountability issues
and, 77-78; code of ethics for, 110-
14; duties of, 314-15; evaluations
by, 338-39, 385n10; expertise of,
115-17, 198; training programs for,
117-19
profile. *See* acclaim and recognition;
anonymity; giving styles
program-related investments (PRIs),
193
programs: collaborative type of, 199-
200; commercial type of, 200-201;
community vs. area-focused type
of, 198; effectiveness of, 57-61;
evaluations of, 201, 333-42, 385n10;
expansion of, 205-6; leadership and
management of, 360-62; leverage
theories and, 197-98, 201-3; overall
strategy vs., 215, 396n39; pilot
and new initiative type of, 198-99;
private funding for public, 200;
replication of, 207-9, 395-96n37
progressivism, 6, 77, 190, 378n15
prosocial value orientation, 256
psychology. *See* giving styles
public needs: contours of, over time,
295-300, 343-45; definitions of,
149-52; discounting idea and,
307-8; discourse on, 18, 35, 102,
127, 291-92; free market and,
33-36; payout rate decision and,